Praise for Coin Street Chroni~~cles~~

"Once you've opened this book, you won't ~~be able to put it down until tea-~~time! It draws you into a world you've never known so that you believe in it, love it, and don't want to leave—though it has disappeared."

> —**Elizabeth Socolow**, author, *Between Silence and Praise*,
> and *Laughing at Gravity: Conversations with Isaac
> Newton*, which won the Barnard Poetry Prize

"Gwen Southgate's writing brings into clear focus a world that is often blurred by viewing it through the lenses of sentimentality and nostalgia. Sharply drawn characters and incidents enliven scenes of a city childhood and interludes of evacuation that showed a keenly observant child very different people and surroundings."

> —**Elizabeth Danson**, author, *The Luxury of Obstacles*

"I greatly enjoyed Gwen Southgate's book. Southgate has managed to combine humour and pathos, along with a vivid, detailed account of a city and its history and some of its families. I think Coin Street Chronicles will become a classic."

> —**Dr. Terri Apter**, Senior Tutor at Newnham College,
> Cambridge University, and a Fellow in psychology. Author of
> many books on relationships: mothers, daughters and sisters.

"I found the early chapters a bit slow … but the later chapters faster and much more gripping."

> —**Freeman Dyson**, Professor Emeritus of the Institute for Advanced
> Study, Princeton. Mathematical Physicist, winner of many awards, author
> of many books, and a regular reviewer in *The New York Review of Books*

Coin Street Chronicles

Memoirs of an Evacuee from London's Old South Bank

GWEN SOUTHGATE

iUniverse, Inc.
Bloomington

Coin Street Chronicles
Memoirs of an Evacuee from London's Old South Bank

iUniverse Star
an iUniverse, Inc. imprint

iUniverse books may be ordered through booksellers or by contacting:

iUniverse
1663 Liberty Drive
Bloomington, IN 47403
www.iuniverse.com
1-800-Authors (1-800-288-4677)

ISBN: 978-1-936236-81-7 (sc)
ISBN: 978-1-936236-82-4 (e)

Library of Congress Control Number: 2011916165

Printed in the United States of America

iUniverse rev. date: 11/1/2011

To the family—past, present and future

Contents

From Pillar to Post

Acknowledgments

So many people have given support and help in the writing of this book: my children, sisters and brothers, relatives and friends on both sides of the Atlantic. It is impossible to mention all of you by name, but to everybody who provided feedback as to what worked—or didn't work—I want to say a big, heartfelt, "Thank You."

Very special thanks go to Elizabeth Socolov and Elizabeth Danson, writers and poets both, who have given generously of their time, energy, and expertise, and patiently encouraged and guided me. They helped to "shape" the final product, as did Anne Zeman and my husband's brother, Michael, who both critiqued the entire manuscript and made invaluable suggestions. For the painstaking pursuit of punctuation problems, Jean Bahr nobly rose to this unglamorous challenge and helped to keep my nose to the grindstone. And to my local group of stalwart supporters, led by the indefatigable Helen Goddard and Anthea Spencer, a huge debt of gratitude is due for all their enthusiasm, encouragement, and feedback

Last, but by no means least, how can I adequately thank my long-suffering husband, who has given unstinting support to this endeavor. He has ironed out innumerable computer crises, kept my feet on the ground with his trenchant critical reviews, and in self-defense, taken over the laundry and other essential household tasks. For all of which, "Thank You, David!"

Preface

It was a casual kitchen conversation with my son, then about nine or ten, which sowed the seed from which this chronicle grew. An incident from my childhood had figured in that conversation, and afterwards, he stared at me as if I were a stranger and said, "I never knew any of that about you!" And I realized, for the first time, that my children knew me only as I was then: a mother of four, living a comfortable, privileged existence in Princeton, New Jersey, enjoying an active social life with like-minded and well-educated souls.

Of course, our children did know that their father and I had left England and settled in the United States, which was why they rarely got to see their grandparents, aunts, uncles and cousins. But as far as I was concerned, it was as if they knew me only from the neck up. So much of what had made me who I was by the time they knew me, had somehow never been talked of. Unlike my own mother, I had not sat my children on the kitchen table and washed them from head to toe every night, telling them stories of my childhood as a way to make this process more palatable. With two-and-a-half baths in the house, why ever would I? Midst all the mod cons something had been lost. I vowed to myself that, one day, when I had more time to myself, I would put pen to paper and leave my children with at least a skeletal outline of where I had come from. The seed lay dormant for a very long time. Almost a quarter of a century. Not until the children were grown with families of their own and I had retired after more than twenty years as a High School teacher, did I put pen to paper.

And, as my story unfolded, so did another: my mother's story. This came about of its own accord, and made me very happy when I realized what was happening. For at my mother's funeral, some years before I embarked on this enterprise, I had experienced outrage unlike any I'd had ever known when I heard her described as "just an ordinary woman who lived an ordinary life." That was how my brother had chosen to portray her. Having just arrived from the other side of the Atlantic, the first I knew of this was when I heard the minister intone those words in a bare, somewhat unreal, little crematorium chapel. I wanted to leap up on my seat to set the record straight, to disabuse the small gathering in the chapel of this monstrous notion, to declare at the top of my lungs: "*No*! She was *not* ordinary! Her life may look like that from the outside, but no ordinary woman would have struggled as she did, against extra-ordinary odds and at such cost to herself, to make sure that we, her children, got every scrap of education that we could benefit from! *She was no ordinary woman!*" I didn't stand up and yell, of course. I simply couldn't disrupt my mother's funeral; and that's why I was so happy to discover that her story had managed to tell itself.

I also came to realize that yet another untold story had unfolded, also of its own accord: the story of a place, and a time, and a way of life, all of which have virtually vanished. As a result, although this chronicle can be read as a personal memoir that ends at the point where my life became something that my children would recognize as "normal," it is also a portrait of Britain and of those among her people that I knew during eighteen eventful years in the 1930s and 1940s.

Gwen Southgate

Introduction

I grew up in a drab yet oddly colorful neighborhood of London during the 1930s and 1940s. *Coin Street Chronicles* tells the story of those years and ends as I, finally, escape from the limiting nature of that working class world and head off to university. But my personal story is just part of a much broader tapestry, one which portrays the sweep of life in Britain at that time as seen through the eyes of one for whom it was the backdrop of childhood. Having known this world from a worm's eye view so to speak, puts me in a unique position to narrate its story, because, as far as I know, none of my fellow worms tunneled far enough out of it to sit down and write about their experiences.

The setting of Part I is mainly on the south bank of the Thames, not far from Waterloo Station, an area that is now one of London's cultural showpieces and known as The South Bank. However, in *Coin Street Chronicles,* before the capitalization of its name, the south bank is a crowded, grimy, busily industrial area. It is also home to many hardworking, warm-hearted Londoners, and it is they who bring it to life and provide its Cockney-like character, even as they struggle with the Depression of the 1930s, the privations of the war, and the Blitz of the 1940s. Their stories, and that of a particularly generous family that comes to my family's rescue after my father's death, weave their way through the fabric of this memoir.

Evacuated from the city at the age of ten, my horizons suddenly expand in Part II, as the scene shifts, first to Dorset, then Surrey, then South Wales. I spend the six years of World War II living with six different families in these widely separated areas, with many abrupt transitions and good-byes—some sad, some glad—and much settling into new settings that run the gamut from a remote farm to a mining town. Midst all these changes, I wrestle with the customary demons of adolescence plus the problems of wartime: in particular with the Blitz that threatens everyone I know in the Coin Street area. Indeed my family has two close shaves—much too close for comfort—and when I go home during school holidays I too get a taste of air raids.

After the war, I become a quasi-evacuee for another two years, fleeing from a difficult, violence-prone stepfather. Eventually, eight years of living away from my family and adapting, chameleon-like, to the personalities associated with every new "home," leads to the disturbing question: "Who am I, really?" And this question remains in the air as I leave home to start yet another new life, as a college student. I exult in my near-miraculous escape from the culture of poverty, an escape due in large part to the determination of my feisty mother; yet I am appalled by the wide gulf that I see opening up between me and those that I love who are still mired in it.

PART I

Rough an’ Ready

Chapter 1

Coin Street

"I LET THIS ROOM ta two, not ta three," snapped old Ma Tanner.

Thus, according to my mother, did the outside world acknowledge my entry into it. For I was the unwelcome third occupant of Mrs. Tanner's second floor front room on Coin Street, in a grimy corner of London on the south bank of the Thames. In that one room, their home for four years, my parents had slept, cooked and eaten meals, washed dishes and clothes and themselves, and had sat by the fire in the evenings. And now, in that room on a cold morning in January 1929, I had just been born.

"Yew was all of two hours old when ol' Ma Tanner knocked on the door," the story continued. "The crafty old so-and-so ... she knew yer father wasn't 'ome. 'E didn't wanna leave me, but the midwife wanted 'im out'a the way, so I told 'im ta go t'work. We couldn't afford ta lose the money, in any case. Ma Tanner, she must've waited till she saw the midwife leave before comin' up. Jus' stood there in the doorway, she did, far enough in ta nose around an' check that you 'adn't already messed up 'er precious room, I s'pose.

"Fer the last coupl'a months we'd bin expectin' the ol' gal ta say somethin', becos' it was plain as the nose on yer face that I was in the fam'ly way. At last ... after four years! Till then I s'pose she must've reckoned she was safe an' we wasn't gonna 'ave no kiddies. But not a dickybird [word] from 'er till the day yew was born. Mind yew, there'd bin plenty of 'ard looks an' loud sniffs ev'ry time I went down ta empty the slop bucket or use the lav. I'd bin ready fer 'er, too. She'd 'ave got an earful, I c'n tell ya! Yer father used ta git all nervous an' often said, 'Now May, don't yew go an' upset the ol' lady.' But like I told 'im, we'd bin good tenants. Paid our rent ev'ry week ... on the dot, too, even though we'd bin through some 'ard times ... it was about time the ol' gal 'ad somethin' ta moan about!"

On the day of my birth, however, old Ma Tanner had chosen her moment

1

well. My mother was tired and uncharacteristically speechless, at least long enough for Mrs. Tanner to have her little say and then retreat to her own quarters on the ground floor. At any other time, a direct confrontation would indeed have unleashed an earful. But after that initial outburst about the additional occupant of her "second floor front," Mrs. Tanner never again came out in the open, never actually told my parents to leave; instead, she waged an unrelenting battle of nerves, aimed at making things more and more uncomfortable for them. A big bone of contention was the baby carriage, a large dark blue affair that we still possessed seven years later when my mother first related this story to me. Old Ma Tanner took exception to it being parked in the common hallway, even for a few moments.

"The minute we got in, she'd pop out of 'er room an' jus' stand there, starin', with 'er arms folded on 'er chest, while I bumped that bloomin' pram up the stairs into our room," Mum continued, still indignant at the memory. "Of course, I 'ad ta take yew up first, ta put yew down somewhere safe. An' that got 'arder as yew got bigger, specially once yew started runnin' around. 'Cos we was there till yew was just over two."

As part of the battle of nerves, Old Ma Tanner stopped my mother using the clothesline in the back yard—just when the need for this was most acute. Thereafter, all the laundry generated by two adults and a small child was dried in front of the fire, and my parents' one-roomed home was permanently draped with wet washing.

"I got me own back on 'er though, the day we moved. I was goin' downstairs ta empty the very last slop bucket an' I tripped … accident'ly-on-purpose-like! I emptied that bucket all right! From top ta bottom o' those bloomin' stairs it went, all over the new carpet she'd put down when she 'eard we was leavin'. I made sure it was a good ripe bucketful, too, with plenty o' tealeaves an' fish scraps an' p'tater peelins, an' yew should'a seen the ol' gal's face! Yer Dad an' me, we often 'ave a good laugh over that bucket o' slops, an' 'e always says, 'It certainly don't pay t'get on the wrong side o' *yew*, May!'"

◆　　◆　　◆

On the day I first heard this story, my mother and I were making our way back from The Cut, a bustling, colorful street market close to Waterloo Station. We did most of our shopping there, not from the stores that lined both sides of the street—they were too expensive—but from the "barrer boys". Along each curb their hand-pushed barrows were piled high with fruit, vegetables, fish, saucepans, clothing, bolts of fabric and even dead-eyed rabbits and chickens—very dead, but not skinned or plucked. The barrow boys were cheeky Cockneys, yelling come-and-buy messages that proclaimed the superior quality and value-for-money of their goods in a raucous stream-of consciousness flow that continued even while serving a customer. These verbal torrents were interrupted only by an exchange of banter with favorite regular customers or an argument with a shopper who dared voice doubts about the quality of the merchandise. Unlike today's supermarkets, customers "dahn The Cut" didn't get to handpick the produce, and woe betide the unwary shopper who didn't keep a sharp watch to make sure no over-ripe plums or damaged potatoes found their way into her shopping bag. Occasionally a barrow was "manned" by a tough-looking, brawny woman wearing a man's cap who was sneakier than her male counterpart when it came to slipping in a bruised apple or a sprouting onion. These women drove harder bargains, too.

My favorites were the fish barrows. I loved the vinegary smell of ready-to-eat winkles, cockles, and mussels and was entranced by the colors and intricately whorled shells of the big whelks. But best of all were the live eels that squirmed, shiny, lithe, and black, in a deep tray just below my eye-level. When the fishmonger's big red hand plunged into that heaving, tangled mass and selected a few wriggling eels, I shuddered: I knew what came next and watched with horrified fascination as the eels were decapitated by a few swift blows of his sharp knife. Jellied eels were considered a great delicacy, but I couldn't bear the thought of putting one of those black creatures in my mouth and biting into it. I steadfastly refused to "try one … jus' a taste. C'mon. One li'l bite! Ya don't know wha'cha missin', ya silly 'fing!" I preferred to remain happily ignorant about jellied eels.

On this particular day, we had gone down The Cut for the usual big Saturday shop—the day Dad got his week's wages—and my mother was heavily laden with two large shopping bags, while I "helped" by carrying a small one. Playing a role in the shopping, instead of just tagging along, was a recent promotion in recognition of the fact that I was now seven years old. It made me feel grown up and had encouraged me to ask a question that I'd been mulling over for some time. For my mother did not, in general, welcome questions; more often than not, she slid around them or gave a curt rebuff. But on this occasion she'd surprised me with that long story about Ol' Ma Tanner, which had come tumbling out in response to my asking: "Mummy, why don'cha go an' see Louie no more?"

Louie was a really good friend of our family, and Mum often used to go and have a cup of tea with her; but after Louie and Harry got married, these visits had stopped. However, Louie continued to come and see us. So I was puzzled. I'd begun to wonder whether this lop-sided arrangement was an accepted part of the grown-up world; a world that I was becoming dimly aware of; a world that seemed mysterious and peculiarly arbitrary. Grown-ups seemed to just *know* about things. Like what was allowed, and what wasn't. Where to go for things. How to get there. Which bus to take. Or whether to go by train. And how much it would cost. A really mind-boggling puzzle to me, at age seven, was the housing arrangements of the world. I looked around the crowded neighborhood and wondered who decided which family should live in which house? On which street? In which part of the city? I recently got a sharp reminder of those half-forgotten perplexities when my five-year-old grandson asked his mother, "Mummy, how will I know how to get to work?" I knew exactly how he felt: that had been one of my concerns at his age.

On the question of visiting Louie and Harry, I was prepared to accept that there was a prohibition on visiting newly-weds if that was indeed part of adult-world rules. But I needed to know. I needed to understand how *my* visits to Louie and Harry fit into the scheme of things, because, since they got married, my weekend visits to their neat, newly furnished little flat on the top floor of Mrs. Tanner's house had come to be the highlight of my week. The moment their door closed behind me, I became an instant "only child," in delicious contrast to our house where I was the eldest of three, with two rambunctious brothers so close in age that they were, effectively, twins. Very close-knit twins. I was rarely included in their games, and neither did I welcome them into mine. Most of the time we simply co-existed in two different worlds—theirs, all rough and tumble, and mine, all dolls and solitary fantasy.

The wonderful thing about Louie and Harry's flat was its quiet orderliness: I could do all my favorite things without being pestered, jigsaw puzzles had no missing pieces, and no one jogged the table or spilled the pieces on the floor. There was even a special table where they could be safely left in mid-puzzle. And I could play interminable games of make-believe with the marvelous collection of old buttons that Louie kept in an oval biscuit tin that had a picture of a pretty, bonneted, crinolined lady on the lid. What a relief it was not to be disturbed by two bouncy boys as I carefully arranged my button-people in neat rows, two to a desk, in the classroom of which I was the teacher. Each button-child had a personality, and, as in a real school, some were good, but some were naughty and had to be "dealt with." I happily whiled away countless hours with this school and its sometimes-problematical students.

Then there was Harry's collection of games: they included a figure-of-eight race track round which we raced wind-up cars, and a pond on which two swans "swam" on real water. These elegant long-necked birds were propelled by a piece of something white that you inserted under their tails, and the reaction of this with the water provided the propulsion, Harry said. But white stuff or no, to me it was magical, and—though I didn't like the smell of the white stuff—I loved to watch the swans gliding silently across that little lake. No doubt, a steady diet of this peaceful lifestyle would have found me missing my own chaotic, shabby home. But in small doses, that top-floor flat was a precious haven, and I was anxious for re-assurance that my escape hole was not going to vanish, like Mum's visits to Louie had.

"Well," Mum laughed, as she wound up her 'ol' Ma Tanner' story, "so ya c'n see why I can't go an' see Louie now ... not in *that* 'ouse ... not after that bucket o' slops! Ol' Ma Tanner might spit in me eye! Or I might spit in 'er's! An' I wouldn't like ta get Louie off on the wrong foot with the ol' gal. Yew could've knocked me down with a feather when Louie told me where they was goin' ta live after they was married ... in ol' Ma Tanner's top floor flat, of all places! Right over the room you was born in."

I was still uneasy. My mother's explanation of why she never visited number nine Coin Street had not resolved the question of *my* visits. Was I still an unwelcome intruder to Mrs. Tanner, a lady of whom I was terrified even before I learned about that first, unremembered encounter? She was a short, fierce, shoulders-back, head-high-in-the-air, unsmiling, and unbending old woman. On the occasions when she *did* actually bend, there was an audible creak that, I now know, came from her corset. Buskies, as they were known to their wearers—ladies on the wrong side of middle age—were all-purpose, one-piece garments that held in place buttocks, waist, bosoms, and anything else that needed holding in place. However, at the age of seven, I knew nothing of these suits of armor and was most intrigued by Mrs. Tanner's occasional sound effects. Her sparse, pepper-and-salt hair, very thin on top, was pulled tightly back in a small bun that bristled with hairpins, and, particularly intriguing, was a long curling hair that protruded from one nostril and moved gently back and forth as she breathed. I knew better than to stare at this quivering whisker, but I found it impossible to take my eyes off it and longed to ask if it tickled. Fortunately, Mrs. Tanner's beady brown eyes hadn't noticed my lapse of manners, and she'd never actually said *anything* to me, either welcoming or unwelcoming. Was this a good sign? Or a bad one?

"But 'ow about me?" I asked, anxiously.

"The ol' gal don't seem to 'ave cottoned on ta 'oo yew are," Mum chuckled. "I'd love t'see 'er face when the penny *does* drop!"

This was not a sentiment I shared. I had no desire to see Mrs. Tanner's face when she discovered that the grown version of that additional occupant of her "second floor front" was now a regular visitor to her top floor flat. I resolved to be especially quiet and unobtrusive on my visits and, thereafter, crept up and down the stairs that my mother had struggled with on a daily basis; and down which she had emptied the bucket of slops. They were steep, narrow stairs, and, even at age seven, I could see what a tricky, tiring business it must have been to lug that heavy old pram up or down, and around the sharp bend near the top, before and after every excursion. My mother's need for revenge

5

became more understandable each time I climbed those stairs—with bated breath, for fear that Old Ma Tanner would make the connection with that unwelcome addition of seven years ago and promptly banish me from her top floor flat, my new-found refuge.

Having once told the story of how Old Ma Tanner greeted my arrival into this world, Mum often retold it, adding bits and pieces along the way, gradually painting a fuller picture of that part of my parents' lives. One of my favorite additions was her account of the day she officially registered my existence when I was about a month old. Mrs. Tanner's attitude toward her tenants' enlarged family had shown no change for the better, so my mother decided to kill two birds with one stone. After registering my birth at the Registry Office, she'd pop into the police station next door, "jus' ta find out whether we could be thrown out by the ol' dear." On the day she chose, there happened to be snow on the ground and wheeling the pram was out of the question, so she wrapped me up warmly and took the bus.

Names had been picked well ahead of time, so as soon as my gender was known, I was Gwynneth Yvonne. Gwynneth was Dad's choice, a name chosen in the middle of World War I by Dad's best mate for *his* daughter. As this Welshman lay dying in the mud of a Flanders trench, he begged Dad to get a message to his wife who was expecting their first child: if the baby was a girl, he wanted her to be called Gwynneth. My father, when home on leave, did go to Wales, did get the message to the wife in time, but the baby turned out to be a boy. So in memory of his pal, Dad resolved to use the name Gwynneth if he should ever have a daughter of his own. At the time, this did not seem likely, because my father was already over thirty and regarded as a confirmed bachelor by those who knew him well; nevertheless, thirteen years later, he kept the promise he'd made to himself in memory of his long-dead friend.

The second name, Yvonne, was then added, but as my mother sat on the bus heading for the Registry Office, "I got ta thinkin'," she said. "Yer father chose Gwynneth, an' Yvonne was what Auntie Ada an' Uncle Bill wanted—they was ta be yer godparents, so it was on'y right they should 'ave a say. But what about *me?* I 'adn't got a bloomin' word in edgeways! An' I was the one what 'ad this baby! So I added Eileen. In front, too … I wasn't gonna jus' tack it on at the end. Yer father was furious when 'e found out. But there wasn't nothin' 'e could do about it, so 'e just 'ad ta lump it."

Which was how I acquired a lengthy, exotic string of names (exotic for Waterloo, at any rate) that I have often cursed when struggling with inadequately sized boxes on official forms. I think I understand my father's anger at the addition of Eileen: he was a man who'd left school at thirteen but, in his untutored way, seems to have loved language and had a real feel for it. In their meager one-roomed home on Coin Street, he often read aloud to my mother in the evenings, while she knitted or mended. Usually, she told me, the choice was Dickens, of which Dad had a complete set, won in a crossword puzzle competition—further evidence of his talent for words and language.

Dickens was probably the only choice, for I seriously doubt that their library was extensive. Apart from the occasional newspaper, that set of Dickens was the only reading material I remember seeing in our house until I was eight or nine and was given *Grimms' Fairy Tales* and a big fat *Golden Bumper Fun Book*—or some such name. I still have *The Pickwick Papers* from Dad's red-backed set: it is badly printed on poor paper that is now yellow and brittle (but it is about eighty years old, come to think of it, so maybe it wasn't poor quality paper, after all). By the time I was seven, Dad was reading Dickens to *me*. This was a special treat and my most favorite thing to do on a winter evening; he selected so carefully, so well, shielding me from the long discursive passages that would have been boring to me at that age. They certainly were disappointingly beyond me when I tried to read *Oliver Twist* and *David Copperfield* by myself, after he died.

My Dad may have been unique among his fellow Waterloo residents in that, if he had a bit of spare cash, he loved to go to a Shakespeare play at The Old Vic, which was just a few streets away on Waterloo Road. This, too, seems to confirm his good "ear" for language and explains why he was so cross about the extra name my mother added. He probably liked the sound of Gwynneth Yvonne Redfern, which flows pleasantly, even in the flat tones of Waterloo, and that flow is definitely broken by the addition of Eileen, in front. My mother's little act of defiance was so typical. Feisty? Definitely … ! Subtle? Not exactly …

The police station was next on my mother's agenda that day. There she recounted her story: Ma Tanner's "welcoming" remark, the pram problem, the loss of clothes-line privileges, and the mounting mutterings about "that baby cryin'." I'm sure she painted a colorful picture, and her choice of policeman was fortunate, for she happened upon a sympathetic ear belonging to a big, burly fellow who was a sucker for babies. Before she even started on her tale of woe, he'd carried me all over the police station, showing me off as proudly as if I were his own. Then he stood behind the high, polished counter, rocking me gently in his arms, Mum said, while she went through her litany and wound it up by asking whether Mrs. Tanner could "throw us out on ta the street"—snow-covered, remember; my mother had chosen her day well, too. The response was emphatic:

"Look 'ere, duck," said the burly policeman. (Mum, who hailed from Sussex, not London, always mimicked his thick working class London accent). "Yew jus' tell that ol' dear she 'as anuvver fink comin'. Makin' yew come dahn 'ere fru all this bloomin' snow. Wiv' this 'ere baby, an' all. Yew don't owe no rent an' never 'ave done … righ'? Seems ta me, yew ain't never given the ol' gal an ounce o' trouble, 'xcep' fer this li'l darlin' cryin' a bit. We can't do nuffink abaht the pram an' the washin'-line, but—Gor blimey!—she can't frow yew out' jus' 'cos ya gotta baby …

"If she gives yew any more trouble, me luv, yew tell 'er t'come an' see *me*. Or jus' le' me know—an' I'll pay *er* a visit. She'll git a piece o' me mind, awl right' … somefink she won't fergit in an 'urry, yew c'n be'cha boots! She don't know when she's well awf, I'll tell 'er … wiv' good tenants like yew an' yer 'ubby. She gits 'er rent on time … an' yew don't come rollin' 'ome blind drunk a' closin' time. S'trewf'! She sh'd be countin' 'er blessins' 'stead o' belly-achin'!"

Reassured that they couldn't be thrown out, as long as they paid the rent and didn't roll in drunk when the pubs closed, my mother waged what might be called border skirmishes with Old Ma Tanner for another two years, until a Council house [municipal housing] came through for us.

We'd been on the waiting list since I was born, but the list was long, and many others had even more desperate need, though Mum had advanced our cause by landing herself in hospital with what she described as "white leg." My sister and I looked this up, years later, to find out if the medical profession knows of this colorful condition. And it does. White leg, we read, is known medically as thrombosis and is frequently precipitated by a botched, self-induced abortion—as in our mother's case, she told me when I was old enough to be told such things. At the time, doctors and nurses remonstrated with her, trying to get her to promise not to repeat this dangerous foolishness. Her response was to shrug and ask what *they* would do if *they* had to deal with Old Ma Tanner when she found out there were to be *four* occupants of her "second floor front." The end result was a flurry of urgent letters from the doctors to the Housing Authority, which probably cut our waiting time for a Council house by a year or so.

Another beneficial by-product of my mother's desperate act was that a family across the street took care of me while she was in hospital: a family that was to figure hugely in our future. For many years I knew them as the Odds-n-Arrises, until I learned about the letter *h* and discovered that their names were spelled H-o-d-d and H-a-r-r-i-s. Even then, it was not clear whether the *h* was meant to be silent in Hodd, and, to this day, I'm not sure. But this is an academic point: in Waterloo, an aitch at the beginning of a word might as well not be there! There were four Hodds: Ernie the patriarch; Big Rose his second wife; Louie, his only child by his first wife, who died of TB when Louie was a baby; and Violet, the product of his union with Big Rose. Then there were two Harrises, Georgie and Little Rosie, Big Rose's children by *her* first marriage. I never heard tell what happened to that husband, but Little

Rosie was born in 1918, so he may have been one of the last victims claimed by The Great War—as World War I was always called.

I was introduced to the 'Odds-n-'Arris' clan through Little Rosie when I was a few weeks old, and she asked if she could wheel me up and down the street in my pram. "Wheeling a pram" was a time-honored rite of passage for girls who'd reached the age of ten or eleven, an important marker, their first tentative step into the world of grown-ups. The adult world gave an equally tentative acceptance: the first approval for pram pushing was given oh, so provisionally and hesitantly. I vividly recall reaching this momentous divide, remember feeling that I might burst with pride as I carefully pushed my first pram-and-baby back and forth. I was dying for the sleeping occupant to wake and need me to do something—*But, please God, don't let 'im cry*—and nervously aware of grown-up eyes following my every move, on the watch for the slightest hint of irresponsibility. Ten years earlier, when I was the pushee, my mother was only too glad to give Rosie a trial run, so to speak, so that Dad could have his tea in peace; tea-time was the signal for my daily crying jag, apparently. And Rosie was such a satisfactory pram-pusher that her privileges were soon extended, and she was allowed, first to cross the road with me, then to take me into the Hodds' house occasionally.

I became a regular visitor to that house, and, while Mum was in hospital with her white leg, the Hodds insisted that I live with them. I was about eighteen months old, and from later acquaintance with this generous, boisterous family, I am sure I was thoroughly fussed over and played with and generally spoiled rotten during my stay with them. It was quite a lengthy stay, long enough for me to acquire some language, and according to my mother, when she eventually came out of hospital, "yew was calling Big Rose 'Mum,' like everyone else in that 'ouse, an' wouldn't call me nothin' but 'Lady.' Fer weeks yew jus' refused ta call 'er Aunt Rose, an' I was get'in' quite upset with still bein' Lady. But in the end, yew come up with 'Aunt-mum,' fer Big Rose, an' that give us all a good laugh." And this name suited Big Rose so well and became so widely accepted that, to the end of her very long life, she was Aunt-mum to everyone: the butcher, the baker, the coal-man, the insurance man, the rent collector, the milkman, and even to her own children!

She was a remarkable lady: large, in keeping with the name, Big Rose, that she'd gone by before I re-named her, and had a heart that was big and generous to match. I never met anyone else who could talk, smoke, and cough—all at the same time, non-stop. She was a chain smoker and always had a cigarette firmly in place, wiggling furiously up and down, with the ash falling freely as she talked. And coughed. It was hard to believe that her "fag" wasn't *stuck to* her bottom lip ... else it must *surely* fall out of her mouth. Her chain smoking was a highly perfected, streamlined operation: a fresh-lighted cigarette was already in place before the tiny stub of the old one was removed, just a fraction of a second before it burned her lips!

With her "nineteen ta the dozen" high-speed delivery, Aunt-mum could "talk the 'ind leg awf a donkey," my mother said, and it was mighty difficult to escape, because she so rarely paused. She did, I suppose, occasionally take a breath, but it was hard to catch her in the act. When you were in a hurry, she was a menace, and Mum would often say, "Quick! Let's go the other way," if we spotted her in the distance; and we'd veer swiftly down a side street to avoid a lengthy entrapment. During the war, even the wail of an air raid siren didn't give Aunt-mum pause once she'd launched into one of her monologues, but it did provide her listeners a plausible reason for saying "Well, we gotta go. Must git dahn the shelter 'fore Jerry gits 'ere!"

In keeping with most of the Waterloo population, Aunt-mum's culinary skills were decidedly run of the mill; she was in the business of dispensing love, not fancy food. However, there were two notable exceptions, and both were centered on bread. She produced the world's very best bread-and-butter, using her own unique technique. First, she spread the butter on, thickly, *before* cutting off the slice of bread. Then, fag in mouth, talking and coughing, she hugged the already-buttered loaf close to her chest, and sliced it towards herself with a long thin-bladed knife, cutting a slice so thin that only the pre-applied buttery layer held it together. A truly gourmet dish, especially when cut from a crusty bakery loaf still warm from the oven. And never a trace of cigarette ash was ever found on this delicacy.

She also made good use of day-old bread—never used for bread and butter in those days when bread contained no preservatives—and this formed the basis of her other culinary triumph: bread pudding, as only she could make it. The stale bread was kept in a large bowl until there was enough for a pudding, and then it was broken into pieces, soaked in water, and the excess water squeezed out by hand—a disgustingly mushy procedure, that I loved to help with. After mixing in eggs, sugar, sultanas and spices, this mess was baked until the top was crisp and crusty, and the result was heavy, moist, immensely satisfying, and *indescribably* delicious. It was the closest thing to cake that ever appeared on the Hodds' table apart from the rich fruitcake of Christmas Day. But who needed an ordinary run-of-the-mill cake, when you could have Aunt-mum's bread pudding?

Wartime rationing, with its butter allowance of two ounces per person per week, forced changes in her bread-and-butter, as the butter layer got thinner, and the bread slice got thicker; but, after the war, when butter eventually became plentiful again, her specialty was restored to its former glory. However, no wartime shortages put a dent in Aunt-mum's chain-smoking. She was never seen without a cigarette in her mouth, and her cough became so bad and so persistent that everyone expected her to keel over at an early age. But she confounded the prophets by living to a ripe old age, well into her eighties, a much loved, always-generous old lady, smoking, talking, and coughing, to the very end. And still known to everybody as Aunt-mum.

Chapter 2

Elbow Room

TWO ROOMS DOWN AND two rooms up. Or was it three? What I do remember clearly is that all the rooms in our Dagenham house seemed small, even to me, and I was only six when we left that sprawling, municipal housing estate about eleven miles north-east of London. But how palatial their long-awaited council house must have seemed to my mother and father after living in one room for six years—with a young child and an uncooperative landlady for the last two. So much elbowroom they now had! And such unaccustomed privacy: no more sharing the lavatory with the other tenants in the Coin Street house; no more lugging the pram up stairs under Old Ma Tanner's watchful eye; no more complaints about the noise of "that baby." There was now a garden, too, for Mum to hang out washing, for Dad to discover an unexpectedly green thumb, and for me to play in.

Our family quickly expanded to fill the newfound elbowroom with the addition of two brothers before I was three. "Three under three!" Mum used to say, and, though true only for a month, what a hectic month it must have been. The boys were as different as it is possible for two boys to be. Bertie, the older one, started life as an underweight, scrawny, little thing that, physically, may have occupied very little space, but, in other respects, took up essentially the whole house and most of the twenty-four hours in each day. For he needed hourly feeds and slept little in between. "'E certainly did 'is share o' screamin'," said Mum. "An' we 'ad ta give 'im a lotta water between feeds. Ta wash out the poison that got in 'is blood when 'e was born. So 'e tiddled a lot an' used ta get so wet I 'ad ta strip 'im. Several times a day, sometimes. It seemed like I was always at the sink doin' washin'." All this washing was done by hand and hung up to dry—indoors, if it was raining—so it was just as well that we were no longer residents of Mrs. Tanner's second floor front room.

Derek, on the other hand, was a whopping ten-pounder at birth, as sturdy as Bertie was frail, and, for a while, they weighed almost the same, but Derek soon overtook his older brother in that department. Ensconced at opposite ends of the commodious pram that had been such a trial in Coin Street, they were always assumed to be twins, albeit twins of amazingly different appearance. Bertie was thin, blue-eyed, and pale-skinned, with wisps of curly blond hair; solidly built Derek had huge, brown eyes, a swarthy complexion, and a mop of dead-straight black hair.

Derek's birth had been a difficult three-day marathon, an ordeal that took my mother by surprise. She always maintained that the Salvation Army nurse was to blame for this protracted labor: "Silly devil of a nurse … give me a sleepin' draught, she did, an' it sent the baby ta sleep 'stead o' me! In the end, they 'ad ta drag Derek out. Tore all my insides, they did. Jus' ta save 'im. Black an' blue 'e was, an' 'ad ta be walloped 'ard ta get 'im ta cry." Hindsight makes me wonder if the difficult delivery was related to the self-induced abortion that led to my mother's white leg. But perhaps it was simply Derek's size. I was told these gory details when Mum, presumably, thought I was old enough to hear about such matters—but long before I knew the "facts of life." Indeed, as far as my mother was concerned, I am still ignorant of that body of knowledge. She certainly never breathed a word about it.

Bertie continued to be delicate and couldn't digest solid food until he was almost three. In addition, every six months, as regular as clockwork, he'd be covered from head to toe with boils, big, painful boils that took several weeks to clear up. "Workin' all that poison out of 'is li'l body, they are," Mum would declare as she bathed, lanced, and covered the boils with bandages, while Bertie kicked and screamed, prolonging the agony. The bandages were all re-used—boiled, washed, ironed, and rolled—so these boil episodes added a lot of extra work for our already-busy mother. And, to make matters worse, Bertie was a whiny, clingy, little thing, a "Mummy's boy" who didn't like her to be out of his sight and bawled his head off if she were. "I dunno!" she often said, in exasperation. "No peace fer the wicked, they say. I can't even go t'the bloomin' lav without 'im!"

◆　　◆　　◆

The first clear memory that I can call my own, as distinct from stories I was told, is set in Dagenham. I am about four, and we are standing in line to get a diphtheria injection. The line is very long. It stretches the entire length of one long road, snakes around the corner, and continues along the next road. The day is cold and dreary, but no one is complaining. Memories of the countless funeral processions in the last diphtheria epidemic are too recent and too vivid for there to be much talk about anything else. Many in that line lost one or more family members and are anxious to take advantage of the newly available immunization against this highly infectious, dread disease. In our extended family we suffered only one death, that of a cousin, but a family across the street was almost wiped out. They had been a boisterous family of eight, and only two, a child and a grandparent, had survived. Their former rowdiness had been a problem, and I wasn't allowed to play with the little girl from "*that* house," but all was forgotten and forgiven as people gave pennies they could ill afford to help pay for those six funerals.

My tonsils had been the cause of many scares and many cultured "swabs" to find out if I had diphtheria, and all those false alarms led to early removal of the troublesome tonsils. "Out they come, the day yew was two," said Mum. "We'd 'ad enough o'that lark, an' so 'ad the doctors!" But the tonsillectomy was premature. A tiny stump of tonsil grew afterwards, so I continued to get tonsillitis, but less often and less severely. And, once inoculation lessened the fear of diphtheria, it was no longer a big deal: just a few days in a bed made by pushing two armchairs together in front of the fire, with crayons and a new coloring book. To this day, the smell of wax crayons evokes that scene: the improvised bed, the warm fire, and the miserable discomfort of swollen tonsils.

The move to Dagenham gave my father a few square yards of soil to play with, and he became a passionate gardener. Eventually, he acquired two allotments as well, and, from then on, we never lacked for vegetables. Allotments, rows and rows of rectangular plots carved out of a nearby field, were a gift from the government: every unemployed man was entitled to one, to help eke out the dole money. Dad gladly accepted the offer of a second allotment by a fellow dole recipient who lacked the energy to do all that digging and weeding. It was a rare win-win situation, because the other fellow was happy to be free of the allotment and glad of the occasional bag of potatoes or carrots Dad gave him in gratitude for what he saw as a favor to himself. How did my father find the time and energy for all that gardening? He was in his late forties, no longer a young man, and not in robust health. Furthermore, every day he cycled into London in search of work on an old sit-up-and-beg gear-less bike, along a road that was cobbled most of the way, and was probably the dreariest eleven miles that England had to offer. I did this trip on a bike, once, when I was in college, and was shocked to discover what a wearisome ride it was—even for a healthy young person. It must have seemed an interminable journey to my Dad, day after day, week in week out, in all weathers.

And, when lucky enough to find a job, he then put in eight hours of heavy work; he carried hods of bricks, pushed wheelbarrows around, or dug holes (with a shovel, not a backhoe)—any manual job that did not require going up a ladder. For an old leg wound from WW I precluded him from climbing ladders and reaping the benefits of a lengthy, low-paid apprenticeship, which had qualified him as a master craftsman, skilled in the making of decorative moldings for ceilings and columns. In the nineteen-thirties, precious few buildings were being built, and my father's daily round of building sites was often to no avail. He then had no choice but to turn around his old clunker of a bike to head back home, and, Mum often said, "When 'e couldn't find work I think 'e would've gone mad without 'is garden an' allotments. 'E could never understand 'ow some of the men jus' sat around doin' nothin', day after day, when they could at least 'ave bin growin' somethin' to put on the table fer their kiddies."

It is the garden of that house, Nine Warrington Road that I remember most clearly. It was long and thin, had a fence on each side, and backed on to a tall, dark brown, wooden building. A narrow concrete path ran down the middle, and, close to the house, were two patches of grass separated by low hedges from Dad's neat rows of cabbages and carrots. We were supposed to play on the grassy bits, but the long path through the vegetable patch was irresistible when riding my Fairy Cycle—a first-size two-wheeler, inherited from Viley Hodd. It was difficult to maneuver, though, for a beginner, and, until I was old enough to venture out onto the sidewalk, frequent tumbles into the cabbages were met with considerable disapproval.

Our house had a stucco-pebble-dash finish that frustrated my early attempts to master the art of playing ball-against-the-wall, because the ball bounced off that knobbly surface in unpredictable directions. I envied my friend next door, Jeannie Cheek, the smooth-finished walls of her house. (This was a small, but not unimportant attempt by the London County Council to vary the otherwise uniform appearance of hundreds of identical houses on this new Estate, built to re-house people from London slums.) But Jeannie's smooth wall was off bounds for ball bouncing most of the time, because Mrs. Cheek's elderly father couldn't stand the repetitive tap-tap-tap of the balls on the wall next to his favorite armchair. He would shuffle out in ragged felt slippers, the sleeves of his collar-less shirt rolled up, exposing his hairy, heavily tattooed arms, and flap a folded newspaper, yelling, "Stop that infernal racke', ya li'l blighters!"

I found those tattoos, hidden under a forest of gleaming, curving hairs, simply amazing. They made all the yelling and newspaper-flapping worthwhile, but, for Jeannie, they were a familiar sight, and she was not anxious to provoke an evening of "Gramps bein' cross." And so, Grumpy Gramps, as she called him when out of earshot, caused our acquisition of ball-catching skills to be put on hold until we were big enough to go to the far end of the road and play ball against the wall of the church hall.

I was consumed with curiosity about Gramps' tattoos, but Jeannie's only explanation was that "'e used t'be a sailor." This wasn't a very satisfactory answer, but it was the one I got from Mum, too. So it had to suffice. But I puzzled a lot over this connection. What was it about a boat that required you to have blue pictures painted on your arms? "It ain't paint, silly! It don't never wash awf," Jeannie informed me scornfully, "'cos it was done wiv' needles." *Needles?* This startling piece of information raised the possibility that a tattoo was like our recent diphtheria inoculation. Maybe it protected sailors from terrible diseases at sea. The disease hypothesis was strengthened when I met my first real soldier and discovered that soldiers also had tattoos—no doubt to protect *them* from equally terrible diseases in foreign parts. It was many years before I learned that tattoos are ornamental and entirely optional. But that merely deepened the mystery. And to this day I really don't get it: what *is* the attraction of tattoos? Not the pictures themselves, surely. Most are hideous, and the process sounds quite painful. So what is it that drives people to get tattooed? How many get to hate the thing after the initial novelty wears off? Or, trickier yet, when the name of the sweetheart to whom it is dedicated is no longer appropriate?

Memories of the inside of our Dagenham house are vague; which is odd, since I must have spent much more time indoors than out. I can visualize only two of the rooms. The front room was not used often, but on rainy days we were allowed to play in there to get us out from under Mum's feet in the kitchen, and we devised a number of "front room games"—games that weren't possible in the cramped and busy kitchen. The one that stands out most vividly involved the kitchen chairs, which we dragged into the front room and put in a line, on their backs, to form a train. The chairs had round seats and curved backs, and, as we sat on the backs, grasping the seat like a steering wheel and rocking from side to side, we could simulate a satisfyingly exciting ride. These versatile playthings could be boats, cars, and wild animals … whatever we fancied. Sometimes we had races, but this was an ill-advised variant, since it involved scuffing them across the floor to the detriment of chairs *and* floor. Mum's sharp ears soon picked *that* up, and in she would burst, very cross. Back to the kitchen went the chairs and the three of us. And the front room would be off bounds for a while.

Another front room game was Rent Collector, a game that I always played by myself; the boys simply couldn't whip up any enthusiasm for it. The sideboard [buffet] played a major role in Rent Collector, because its drawers and cupboards had little handles that hung down like doorknockers. Armed with pencil and paper, and with some buttons in an old handbag slung around my neck, I pretended to be the rent-lady knocking on each "door" to collect the rent. I engaged in imaginary conversations with each tenant, gave change with the buttons, and solemnly made notations as to whether the occupant had, or had not, paid that week's rent. In imitation of the real rent-lady, paid-up tenants got genial inquiries as to their collective health, while the delinquents received terse cautionary remarks. My delight in all this was such that I often welcomed a rainy day.

The kitchen is the other room that I remember clearly; perhaps because its dominant feature was the bathtub, a very long, deep bathtub: long enough for adults to stretch out to their full length. When not in use as a bath, its top was covered with a board; this allowed it to double as a work surface—a definite back-breaker for your average housewife, since it was only about two feet high, but perfect for me. I spent many happy hours at this child-size kitchen counter "helping" my mother, especially when she made pastry and gave me bits of spare dough. An empty vinegar bottle sufficed as our rolling pin, and I was endlessly fascinated by the impression left on the dough by the letters and pattern embossed on the bottle. Dad was always the lucky recipient of the finished product; it was a bit grubby from much rolling and re-rolling, not to mention being dropped on the floor a few times, but he always managed to convince me that he had eaten, and enjoyed, this delicacy.

For its primary purpose the bathtub had serious shortcomings. First, its location—in the kitchen, of all places—and second, one tap was a phony, because no plumbing was provided for hot water. That had to be heated on the gas stove, which was both time-consuming and hazardous with small children under foot. But at least the bath had a drain and was easy to empty. This was a huge improvement for most Estate residents who had come from houses with galvanized iron tubs that hung on outside walls when not in use, and these were filled *and* emptied by hand. Emptying was a two-person operation: the tub was carried to the sink, tipped up and slanted sideways to clear the ceiling, and in low-ceilinged kitchens it was almost impossible to empty out the last inch or so of water. No wonder "takin' a barf" had been a once-a-week ritual, at best, unless you had a chimney sweep or a coalman or a dustman in the family and had to struggle with the tin tub on a daily basis.

However, even with the luxury of a built-in bath, for most Estate residents the ritual of a weekly bath persisted, because it was still not an easy operation. The heavy countertop had to be cleared, lifted off, and stored somewhere; and it was quite a performance to heat water on the stove for those full-size bathtubs, not to mention the cost. Especially for families on the dole, as so many were in the thirties. We three were really in trouble if we played too energetically in the bath and accidentally pulled out the plug, letting some precious hot water drain away prematurely.

Rumor had it that some people on the Estate, especially those on "the rough side," used their bathtubs to store coal, but opinions varied as to why.

The most damning view was that it was a matter of sheer ignorance, that "those people" had no idea what a bathtub was for; but if Mum's sister was anything to go by, there was no validity to this coal-in-the-bathtub rumor. Auntie Lilly lived on the rough side, and there was no coal in her bathtub. A most fastidious lady, was Auntie Lilly; her family certainly knew what a bathtub was for and made good and proper use of this welcome addition to their lives.

Chapter 3

A Memorable Birthday

MEMORIES FROM BEFORE THE age of five are fragmentary and dreamlike, fuzzy and vague—yet peculiarly vivid. In one, there is a long straight road ... I am walking along it with Dad ... to Romford Market, I think ... wearing white gloves ... must be Sunday. Each front garden has a low wall with pillars ... and a heavy chain of blunt spikes is slung between the pillars ... I set each chain swinging as we pass ... looking back, the chains are still swinging as far as the eye can see ... each out of step with its neighbors ... but in step with another somewhere along the road. The chains have soiled my gloves ... Dad scolds me ... the two of us guiltily try to clean them up so Mum won't know. I am sitting in a dentist chair ... coming round from "gas " ... I see a never-ending line of dentists, getting smaller and smaller and smaller (mirrors on the walls?) ... walking home, puzzling over this strange image ... with a hankie at my mouth to staunch the bleeding. A frantic search for a boot ... one of Dad's good Sunday boots ... last seen in Bertie's hand ... finding the boot, weeks later, among the cabbages ... sodden and ruined ... much crossness about the ruined boot ... yet everyone is laughing. Clothes, put to dry on the fireguard ... flickering flames ... shivering outside with no coat. ... Clanging fire engine and rushing firemen ... water everywhere ... and tea leaves, because Mum had grabbed the slop bucket and thrown the slops over the flames ... "Prob'ly saved the 'ole house from goin' up, Missis," said the fireman ... giving her a pat on the behind.

My fifth birthday is the only one that stands out clearly from the mists of early childhood. It was memorable for actually being celebrated with a party—my first and last birthday party, but I had no way of knowing that at the time—and my mother had dreamed up something very special. There had been no card or present, just a quiet "Happy Birthday!" when I woke up, but I hadn't been expecting anything more so wasn't disappointed. The first surprise came after breakfast when Mum said, "Ya know, Gwen, I bin thinking. This afternoon while the boys are 'avin' their kip [nap], yew could 'ave a li'l birthday party. If yew'd like to, that is?" *If I'd like to?* I'd never encountered the word "rhetorical," but knew intuitively that my mother expected no answer to this question. She had just made me the happiest girl in Dagenham, and I could hardly wait for the boys to go to bed after dinner [lunch].

The party itself was surprise enough, but as I was sitting on the kitchen table in time-honored fashion, being washed from head to toe for this momentous occasion, my mother pulled another surprise from her sleeve. "Oh dear! Wha'cha gonna wear?" she said. "It rained yest'adee so yer other frock's still wet. Ya'll just 'ave ta put this grubby one back on agin. Wait a minute, though ... p'raps I c'n find somethin' else. Stay there ... I'll jus' go an' see." She disappeared upstairs, leaving me on the table, legs dangling, wondering why all the fuss. What was wrong with a grubby dress?

When she came down, any thought of making do with the dress I'd just taken off vanished: for she was holding the most gorgeous frock I had ever seen—the one that, for weeks, we'd both gazed at longingly in a shop window when we went shopping. It had held pride of place right in the center of the window, and we'd stopped to admire it almost every day. Pink and sleeveless, with a simple round-necked bodice and a tiny bow on each shoulder, its glory lay in row after row of gentle frills that rippled down to the hemline of the skirt. I was speechless to see it in my mother's hands and couldn't believe that it really was for me.

I was also bewildered. On so many occasions as we stood gazing at this apparition, Mum had said, "Much as I'd love t'see yew in it, Gwen, yer Dad's out o' work. We jus' don't 'ave the money." But, somehow, she had found the money for this dream of a dress. It seemed like magic. The magic turned out to lie in her deft fingers, her trusty sewing machine, and her sharp imagination. A completely self-taught seamstress, my clever mother had made a copy of the dress, *just from looking at it.* During our window-gazing sessions she'd carefully taken note of every detail and, after we children were in bed, had transformed a scrap of pink taffeta, scrounged from somewhere, into a perfect replica.

The birthday party consisted of Jeannie Cheek coming to tea, and each of us consuming a cup cake with white icing. There were no candles, no gift-wrapped present, no party games; but none of these was missed, since we had no idea that they were the traditional trappings of birthday parties. My first encounter with gift-wrap was the embarrassing absence of it on the gifts I gave to my husband's family the first Christmas I spent with them—they kindly pretended not to notice, while I longed for a convenient hole to swallow me up. But at age five, I was blissfully unaware of such niceties; indeed, I was thrilled out of my tiny mind just to have a friend in to tea, and iced cupcakes were another unlooked-for splendid treat.

On that afternoon, the afternoon of my fifth birthday, wearing that glorious pink frock and eating a cupcake with my friend Jeannie, I felt like a princess and knew, for the first time, what it meant to "be on cloud nine." I never loved a dress as I loved that one, with the tiny bows on the shoulders and the cascade of frills. It was my pride and joy, and I often insisted on wearing it on days that were really too cold for a thin, sleeveless taffeta affair. Inevitably, however, came the day when I was forced to admit that it was too small for me, but I refused to part with that dress. No way was I going to consent to "'andin' it down fer some other girl tew enjoy," as Mum wanted. The frock, in all its pink glory, stayed in the wardrobe and, for many years, was the garment of choice to wrap a doll in for pretend parties.

Mum had made the dress to help make up for the fact that I couldn't start school immediately after my birthday, because I'd hurt my hand and had to wait until after Easter when the next term started. I'd been eagerly anticipating the start of school, because Dad had made good use of the spare time forced upon him by frequent unemployment and taught me to read and do simple sums, so I just couldn't wait to get to school for more of this good stuff. The pickings in our house were slim: the only reading material—other than Dad's Dickens, which was way over my head—was the occasional discarded newspaper, found on a bus or a park seat. I used to watch for Dad to come home, hoping he'd be carrying a paper tucked under his arm, anticipating the excitement of sitting on his lap, trying to decipher the words.

The accident that injured my hand happened one day when I was playing in the snow up by the church hall, and a boy slammed the metal gate, neatly lopping off the tip of one of my fingers. Funny stuff, memory: one would expect to remember such a traumatic event; but I have no more than a hazy recollection of running home, worried about getting blood on my winter coat. However, I must have been screaming, because my mother and Mrs. Cheek came rushing out to meet me. A quick look told Mum the story. Leaving the boys and me with Mrs. Cheek, she raced up to the church hall, following the trail of blood, and hunted around in the snow until she found the missing fingertip. "I 'oped t'stick it back on an' save 'er finger," she told Dad that evening.

I have mercifully blanked out on the subsequent visit to the hospital. How we got there, I can't imagine. We had no car. Nor did anyone we knew. A taxi was out of the question. The nearest telephone was probably miles away, and in any case, telephones were not a part of our world. I seriously doubt whether anyone in Dagenham knew how to use one. We probably went to the hospital by bus, the fingertip carefully wrapped in a clean hanky in Mum's pocket.

The hospital doctor commended my mother for her quick thinking, but shook his head. "I'm very sorry. There's no hope of re-attaching the fingertip. It was too late by the time you got here," he said. In fact, there was a strong possibility that the risk of infection from the rusty old gate—in those pre-antibiotic days—might require amputation below the first joint, but he was reluctant to do this, "'Cos yew was a girl an' might play the pianer one day," Mum always said. Why the problem of a stubby finger should be gender-specific, I never understood; and, as for playing the piano, we stood little chance of ever owning a piano, let alone paying for lessons. After much discussion among the doctors, and Mum's assurance that she'd somehow get me to the hospital every day for the finger to be checked for infection, it was decided not to amputate. And so began daily trips to the hospital. Mrs. Cheek took me on the back of her bike, while Mum kept an eye on Jeannie and her little brother. I was furious at missing the chance to play with Jeannie every day—*in my own house*. This was unheard of. Nobody was ever invited into someone else's home to play.

Instead, off we went every morning, Mrs. Cheek and I, with me mounted precariously on the back of her squeaky old bike, on the little carrier rack to which she usually strapped her shopping. It was miserably cold. My legs, bare above silly knee-high gaiters, suffered the most, because I had to hold them out at an angle so my feet wouldn't catch in the back wheel. I held on to Mrs. Cheek's abundant form as best I could, with arms too short for the task—and one of them in a sling. My face was squished against her rear end, and the rough tweed of her coat rubbed my cheek sore as *her* cheeks moved to and fro to the rhythm of her stoic pedaling. It can't have been a joy ride for Mrs. Cheek either, but that good lady uncomplainingly made the trip with me every day until the risk of infection was over; after which, once a week sufficed.

A big surprise was in store for us one day, soon after we'd progressed to weekly checks. As we changed the dressing at home one night, Dad noticed a tiny bit of nail growing from the stump—contrary to all expectations. On our next hospital visit, I vividly remember sitting on the lap of the doctor who'd been so anxious not to amputate, telling him that I had a surprise for him, and then watching the delight spread over his face when he saw that little sliver of nail. For that nice young doctor was as thrilled as we were.

However, I was beside myself with frustration about not going to school; so many things were impossible with only one hand, since the usable hand was the wrong one. With practice, I developed some facility with my left hand, but it was slower and clumsier, and, as the injured finger became less painful, I often slipped my right hand out of the sling, but was constantly on the alert to slide it back if I heard someone coming. I learned, however, not to pull this trick for writing or drawing. Mum and Dad could always tell ... somehow.

Chapter 4

A Chancy Business

IT WAS LOVE AT first sight. The moment I set eyes on that sweet face and little rosebud of a mouth, the peaches-and-cream complexion and blue eyes fringed with thick lashes, I was swept off my feet. The blue was the blue of cornflowers, and fine, black rays radiated from each jet-black pupil. A hat covered her hair, but slender, arching eyebrows suggested that it was not blond. However with that captivating face, hair color was of no importance. No hair at all would have been just fine, by me. Indeed, that turned out to be the case: her hair was just painted-on raised whorls, but I thought her the prettiest doll I'd ever seen. And I wanted her—oh, so badly—more than I had ever wanted anything in all my five years.

The head of my much-loved Margaret Rose had shattered a few weeks earlier, when she fell off the seat of my school desk. It was on a Friday afternoon, the day on which, if we'd been good all week, we were allowed to bring a toy back to school after dinner, as a special end-of-the-week treat. Poor Margaret Rose. Jimmy Barton had pushed me along the seat, making me, in turn, push her; and before I could grab her, she'd pitched off the seat. Her head hit the floor with a loud crack and was smashed to smithereens, apart from her eyeballs, which lay there, intact, the only remaining recognizable feature of Margaret Rose. Trying not to cry, because the boys would laugh at me, I watched in horror as Miss Johnson swept the shards—and those ghastly eyeballs—into the wastepaper basket. Beautiful, willowy, well-dressed Miss Johnson: her shiny chestnut-brown hair had a neat fringe and was shingled at the back, and she was everything that the mums and aunties of my acquaintance were not. But not even the elegant, adored Miss Johnson could soften the blow of Margaret Rose's broken head.

I carried the headless torso home, hidden under my cardigan so that what was left of Margaret Rose should not be an object of ridicule. "Can she be mended? Please? *Please?*" I begged. We took her to the Doll Hospital, but the cost of a new head was way beyond our budget. And part of me was relieved. With a new face, she wouldn't have been the same. What I really wanted was my old Margaret Rose with her two chipped-off fingers and an eyelid that got stuck halfway until you helped it with a gentle nudge. Like most of my toys, she was a hand-me down from Viley Hodd who, in common with hundreds of little girls in England in the 1930s, had named her after one of the two little princesses who would take up residence in Buckingham Palace a few years later when their Uncle Edward abdicated to marry his true love, Mrs. Simpson. My shabby Margaret Rose had long since lost any resemblance to her famous namesake, but I had loved her. And now I missed her, terribly.

As I said, after one glance at this new doll I was enchanted: visions of dressing and undressing her, giving her baths and cradling her in my arms before putting her to bed danced through my head. Oddly enough, she entered my life in the classroom where Margaret Rose had met her demise. Miss Johnson held her up for the class to see: a small doll, about sixteen inches long; dressed in a hand-knitted outfit that consisted of a Kelly green hat and coat, both edged with white angora; a white lacy dress; and underneath, as Miss Johnson demonstrated, a white vest and knickers (snicker, snicker, from the boys). This elegantly clad creature was to be raffled, along with another toy suitable for a boy. Miss Johnson explained how a raffle worked and said there would be two winners, one girl and one boy. The tickets cost thr'pence [three pennies] and the raffle would be drawn in two weeks. *For three pennies there was a chance that this gorgeous doll could be mine?* I raced home to break this incredible news to my mother, but she didn't see it in the same light.

"Thr'pence? Fer a raffle ticket? Don't be s'daft! Jus' where d'ya think I c'n find thr'pence t'throw away like tha'? Jus' fer a *doll*? Even if ya win, that is."

"But she's *so* pret'y, Mummy. An' she's got all these clothes ... even a vest an' a pair o' knickers ... wiv' real elastic. An' 'er clothes all come off ... Please, Mummy, please ... "

My pleas were in vain. Dad was more sympathetic and took up my cause, but Mum was adamant, and they argued about it until there was only one day left before the raffle draw. I was beside myself with anxiety and kept imagining some other girl walking away with the coveted doll—which I had named Audrey, as if she were already mine.

Finally, Dad said to Mum, "Well, if yew won't give 'er the thr'pence, then I will."

"An' jus' where would yew put yer 'ands on thr'pence, I'd like t'know?" she retorted. Dad had to admit that he hadn't a penny to call his own at that particular moment, but added, "I'll give it back t'ya on Monday, when we get the dole. She c'n 'ave my next week's spendin' money."

"That means no crossword," said Mum. (The weekly dole was twenty-nine shillings and thr'pence, and Dad got to keep the three pennies, which he always spent on the same thing: two stamps to send off entries in the crossword puzzle competitions of two Sunday newspapers, the *News of The World* and *The People*, I think.)

"I know, I know … But that's a waste o' money, any'ow … I don't ever win."

"Wadd'ya mean? Ya never win? Yew've won several times!" Mum was very proud of Dad's prizes and loved to boast about them to anyone who would listen.

"Not first prize, though, an' that's the on'y one what counts. It's money we need! Not a basket o' fruit, like last time—when I come in third!"

"Well … we certainly could do with the money. But a basket o' fruit's bet'er than a kick in the teeth. Ain't it? An' 'ow about those books, when ya come in second? Yew've always got yer bloomin' nose stuck in one o' them!"

"The Dickens? … Yeah … but money's what we really want. An' chances are I won't win *that* next week. So I might as well give the kiddy a chance ta win 'erself this doll."

My mother finally accepted this argument, but it soon transpired that not even Dad's sacrifice of a chance at the big prize was going to get me a raffle ticket. There wasn't enough money in the house *today*, the last day to buy a ticket.

"Look," Mum said, emptying her handbag onto the kitchen table and counting out the coins. She separated them into piles, one pile for each day. "There's just enough fer bread 'n milk an' a bit o' meat fer Sunday dinner. Veg we've got, but I can't go down the garden an' pick bread an' meat like they was Brussels Sprouts. We just ain't got three pennies ta spare. Not till the dole money comes on Monday … an' that'll be too late fer this bloomin' raffle."

"There's gotta be another thr'pence *somewhere* in this 'ouse," Dad protested.

"Yew find it then, mate," Mum shot back.

We searched, Dad and I, in every nook and cranny, looking for the odd penny or ha'penny [halfpenny]. We turned out every pocket, scoured every corner of every drawer, emptied out every little jar and pot. And we did, eventually, unearth a total of one penny, four ha'pennies and one farthing! The spare farthing went into Mum's purse, and the next morning, I went off to school, triumphant, with thr'pence for a raffle ticket.

"Now yew mind yew don't lose that money," said Mum, as I left the house. Because of the hole in my coat pocket, we had carefully knotted the coins in the corner of a hankie, and I was cautioned not to take them out of the hankie until I was in the classroom, ready to buy the ticket. A needless admonition! I was terrified of losing any of those coins and anxiously patted my pocket all the way to school. Going home with the raffle ticket was even worse. Miss Johnson helped me knot the ticket in the hankie, but now there was no reassuring bulk to pat every few minutes. I could feel the corner of the hankie, but could the raffle ticket somehow slip out of its knotted corner and fall through the hole in my pocket? I longed to look and see, but didn't dare. However the raffle ticket and I did make it home, where I handed it over to Mum.

Then came the agonizing wait for the raffle to be drawn. The bottom fell out of my stomach every time I entertained the idea that some other girl might, even yet, walk away with my precious Audrey. And Dad and I would then have to face Mum's wrath. I could hear it already: "Thr'pence! Jus' thrown away! All fer nothin'. Nothin' but a useless scrap o' paper. All over a stupid doll! I could've got a pair o' socks fer one o' the boys with that money." Her unanswerable tirade would go on for days. The suspense of not knowing was unbearable, but, finally, came the day of the raffle drawing. I could barely breathe as I watched Miss Johnson pull the winning tickets and waited for her to unfold them and announce the numbers.

"The winning girl is Number 363, and the winning boy … "

I was no longer listening. 363? *That was my number!* My stomach lurched, and for a moment I feared the ultimate disgrace: throwing up over my desk, or over Jimmy Barton. But that danger passed, and I raced home, crying out as I burst into the house, "I won! I won! I've won Audrey!"

But when Mum went to get the ticket from the little pot on the mantelpiece, the "safe" place for small things she didn't want to lose—hooks-and-eyes and buttons and shoe buckles, until she had time to sew them on whatever they had fallen off—the winning ticket was not there! Or anywhere else. Ours was not an orderly household by any stretch of the imagination, but how could the ticket have got lost in *one day?* I wept and wailed and stamped my feet, and we turned that small house upside down, but the raffle ticket was nowhere to be found. At this point, my mother relented and joined the cause; after all, we had invested three good pennies in it, and the prize was in sight, so after dinner, she bundled the two boys into the pram and came back to school with me.

"She's right," Mum assured Miss Johnson. "That *is* the number of 'er ticket. I saw it meself. An' then I put it somewhere safe. But blessed if I know where!"

Kind Miss Johnson, who had swept up the remains of Margaret Rose and probably guessed how much I wanted this new doll, generously gave us till the next morning to see if we could find the missing ticket. "But," she explained gently, preparing me for the worst, "if it hasn't shown up by then, I'll have to draw another winner for the doll."

Finally that evening, after another frantic search, we found the ticket—where we'd expected it to be in the first place—in one of the little blue frosted-glass pots that stood on either end of the mantelpiece. It had got pushed flat against the inside of the pot and, in our frenzy, we had missed it. And so, the next day I became the ecstatic owner of Audrey, and I think Miss Johnson was almost as pleased as I was. So was Dad. He knew how much I wanted that doll, and was, I think, more than compensated for the loss of his weekly fling on the crossword puzzles. Moreover, he was probably as relieved as I was at being off the hook about "wasting thr'pence."

I loved Audrey with such passion; loved her to pieces, in fact. Her rosebud mouth had a tiny opening through which I fed vast quantities of water with a miniature baby bottle. This was long before Betsy-Wetsy dolls, and Mum kept saying that she didn't think this was a good idea. And she was right: when I undressed Audrey for the hundred-and-umpteenth time to give her a bath, she fell apart! Her head, her arms, her legs—they all just fell off. She was not designed to deal with a steady diet of water, and the elastic that held all her parts together had rotted. Once again I stared in dismay at the shattered remains of a beloved doll, but this time there was no question of a visit to the Doll Hospital; the rest of Audrey was beyond repair, too. The inside of her body cavity was not a pretty sight.

But what a wonderful year we'd had! She'd been so special. For one thing, she was the first doll I'd chosen a name for. Margaret Rose was an already-named hand-me-down, and I never had the heart to call her something different; it seemed bad enough that she was being discarded and given away, poor thing. But why I chose the name Audrey is lost in the mists of time, apart from a vague memory of liking the way it looked when written.

During our year together Audrey went everywhere with me, except when I rode my bike or went to school. I was often tempted to put her in my bike basket, " 'Cos she don't like bein' left by 'erself." Mum would point out, with varying degrees of patience, that Audrey might get broken if I took a tumble off the bike, so I never did risk a bike ride with her. Instead, I'd tuck her up cozily in the cardboard box that was her bed, and she slept while I rode my bike; though I kept popping in, just to see that she was all right. The cardboard box, decorated with a couple of ribbons, was Audrey's daytime bed, but at night she slept with me; just as she shared my chair at mealtimes and my bath on bath night. In addition, I gave her a bath every day in the dishwashing bowl or washed her from head to toe with a damp face cloth. But I never took Audrey to school with me. The memory of Margaret Rose was too vivid: I could still hear the sound of her poor head hitting the ground and was not about to risk a similar fate for Audrey.

I mourned the loss of Audrey for a long time. But, perhaps because of the chancy way in which I acquired her, the good times we had together had always contained an element of something beyond what one could reasonably expect. There had been the feeling that my year with Audrey could so easily have never happened: the raffle might not have been held; my father might not have been willing to give up his spending money; there might not have been enough money lying around in odd corners; we might not have noticed the hole in my pocket; and Miss Johnson could so easily have pulled 364 instead of 363. *And* we might not have found the "lost" raffle ticket in time! So, my grief at Audrey's demise mingled oddly with gratitude: gratitude to fate, to God, to whatever it was that determined things like winning numbers. At the age of six, I had no clearly formulated ideas on such weighty matters. But I *did* know the important role that Dad had played in my wonderful year with Audrey, and he was the chief recipient of my childish gratitude.

Soon after the demise of Audrey my father won another crossword prize. It was for third place again, not first as he always hoped, and Mum predictably said, "Oh well, a baskit o' fruit's bet'er than a kick in the teeth!" But this time a letter came, announcing that the third prize was a ride in a motor car, and would my father let them know what date would best suit him.

"*A ride in a motor car?*" Dad exclaimed, in disbelief. "Wha' kind of a prize is tha'? Fer a man like me what's out o' work most o' the time? An' with three kiddies ta feed an' clothe!"

His outrage—and Mum's, of course—got even bigger when the newspaper proprietors turned down his request for us children to go along for the ride with him; and grew till it knew no bounds when they refused to let even *one* of us go. The letters went back and forth, trying to settle this matter, and when the final denial arrived, Dad was so disgusted that he tore all the letters into small pieces and vowed never to do another crossword competition. And he never did. Which was a great shame. For years he'd looked forward to that weekly challenge; it had been one of the few highlights in his life.

Chapter 5

Back to Coin Street

NOT LONG AFTER I was six we moved, first to a place called Morden for a short time, and then back to London—to Coin Street, no less. There it was easier for Dad to get to work, if he had a job, or to look for one, if he hadn't. London was where the jobs were. Not that many building sites were hiring in the thirties, but now he could get there early, and it was the early birds that got taken on for the day.

After four years of relative comfort in sunny new council houses with indoor plumbing and nice gardens, it was back to an old house with a dungeon of a basement, an outdoor toilet, no bathtub, and a twelve-foot square high-walled patch of mud for a garden. Ours was the corner house, where Coin Street met Upper Ground. *Upper Ground?* A lower-lying spot would be hard to find—one block from the Thames and only a few feet above the high tide mark. Our kitchen-cum-living room basement had never fully recovered from the record-breaking flood of 1928; the walls were so damp that they felt clammy, and we could sometimes "draw" pictures on them with our fingers! It was a dark room, too. A tall warehouse across the road blocked any trace of sunlight from sneaking through its one small window, which was set just below street level and looked out on a sunken area—known locally as an "airy."

There was one of these areas, about twelve feet by four, with stone steps up to the street and surrounded by iron railings, in front of most houses. It gave access to a coal cellar that could be filled through a manhole in the sidewalk, saving the inconvenience—to coalman *and* housewife—of trekking sacks of coal through the house. But airies had their downside: they collected litter and always smelled, because passing dogs seemed compelled to leave their "mark" on the tall spiked railings, and most of the marking agent went between the railings. Dogs were not the only culprits. After dark, many a local citizen, wending his well-loaded way home from the pub, relieved a bursting bladder between the railings of a convenient airy.

For children too, airies were a menace. Their railings were far enough apart to let balls through, and rarely a day passed without some child knocking nervously on a front door to ask, "C'n I 'ave me ball back, please … it's dahn yer airy." If there was a still-functioning gate in the railings, the usual response was a gruff, "Go dahn an' git it then … Jus' be sharp abahdi'." But many gates had been permanently sealed, and the request then met with a less friendly reception. Few householders welcomed the prospect of going down to retrieve a ball from the unappetizing mess in the airy—but neither did they want kids traipsing through the house to get it.

This part of street life featured in a popular ball-bouncing game called " One, Two, Three O'Lairy," in which you patted a ball to keep it bouncing, and swung your leg over the ball after each line of a singsong chant:

> One, two, 'free O'L-a-i-r-y
> My ball's dahn the a-i-r-y
> Please won'cha give it ta M-a-r-y
> All on a Sundee m-o-r-n-in'.

The winner was the girl (no boy would be caught dead playing this "girl" game) who could repeat this ritual for the longest time, non-stop, and the competition was fierce. There were innumerable versions: clapping at the same time, swinging the leg over twice, first one leg then the other, variations that were limited only by imagination and ambition.

One of our new neighbors was a family called Fippin, whose youngest child had a harelip and cleft palate. Poor little Donnie. It was hard to understand what he said; but Derek and Bertie seemed not to notice, and the three boys, all about the same age, played together a lot. The remarkable thing about the Fippins was that they had adopted Donnie in full knowledge of his cleft palate. Mrs. Fippin's own baby was born in the same hospital and on the same day as Donnie, but lived for only an hour or so; and when Donnie's young mother wanted nothing to do with her baby—wouldn't look at Donnie or put him to the breast—Mrs. Fippin simply reached out for the poor little scrap, saying, "'Ere, I'll take 'im." The young mother handed her baby over readily enough, and before anyone could intervene, Mrs. Fippin had put him to her own breast. The nurses tried to take the baby away from her, afraid he might have difficulty swallowing and choke if not fed carefully. But he was sucking contentedly, and Mrs.Fippin waved them away.

Then and there, Donnie's fate was decided. And Mrs. Fippin had found a way to assuage her grief. Fortunately for everyone concerned, the birth mother—young, unmarried, and overwhelmed by the whole situation, said Mrs. Fippin—agreed to an adoption, and Mr. Fippin raised no objections to rearing this difficult baby.

Donnie turned out to be a lovely sweet-natured child, although he had a myriad of serious problems that did indeed include swallowing; but the Fippins, somehow, always learned how to deal with every challenge. At the time we knew them, they were starting to worry about medical bills for the operations that would be needed to correct Donnie's palate, and neighbors were already planning a "whip round" to help them out when the time came. But Mum told me she didn't think that would make much of a dent in the mountain of debt the Fippins were facing.

When my mother once marveled at the Fippins' willingness to take on a child like Donnie, Mrs. Fippin simply shrugged: "W-e-l-l … me an' Jim, we look at it this way. It's on'y by the grace o' God that it wasn't us wha' give birf' to a baby like Donnie. An' if it *'ad* bin us, yew'd've expected us ta love 'im an' take care of 'im, nah would'ncha?" Lucky Donnie, to have found two people with such big hearts.

It took a while to accustom ourselves to the busy corner on which we now lived. There were lorries from warehouses and factories and the Eldorado Refrigerator plant; long flatbed Bowater lorries stacked high with gigantic rolls of paper; and vans buzzing to and from the sprawling Star building, their tires squealing at every turn. These little red vans were always in a frenzied rush to get the latest edition of *The Star* to newsagents, and to newsboys as they stood on street corners crying, "Read Awl Abahdit!"

On almost every score, other than work for Dad, our return to Waterloo was a giant step backwards. But there was, for me, one huge bonus: we were now only a few houses from the Hodds, so I got to see them more often. The down side was that I no longer got to stay for several days, and I had loved those extended visits. Louie and Harry used to come and fetch me and take me back, and a couple of times I made the trip on Harry's newly acquired motor bike. That was pretty exciting—a bit too exciting one rainy night, when we slid into the back of a truck as we entered a big tunnel under the river, Blackwell Tunnel, I believe. The traffic had been crawling, so we weren't badly hurt, but after that I was not allowed on the motor bike. Secretly, I was relieved: the truck incident had been unnerving, but out of loyalty to Harry and fear of hurting his feelings, I would have had a hard time saying no to him. However, the motor bike disappeared from the scene soon thereafter—at Louie's insistence, and to Harry's disgust, I suspect.

Another bonus from living on Coin Street again was that I benefited more regularly from Viley's discarded toys. With older brothers and sisters, she had an abundant supply of playthings, by Waterloo standards, and could afford to jettison them with fair regularity; *and* space was at a premium in the Hodds' small house. I began to acquire quite a collection of jigsaw puzzles and board games, some with a few pieces missing, but that rarely diminished the fun I had with them. However, no dolls came my way, so there was still a large hole left by Audrey's demise; a hole that became, suddenly, a lot deeper when Viley gave me her doll's pram. It was a small tin pram with many dents, but these were trifling defects, since I had longed for a pram for as long as I could remember. But there was, alas, no doll to put in it until I chanced upon something much more satisfactory, *and* found a use for Audrey's cute little green and white outfit. I had not only kept her clothes, but went through the motions of buttoning and unbuttoning them every once in a while, just for old times' sake.

The change in my fortunes came about because of the mice with which our old row house was overrun. Big, bold, wily mice they were; the boldest would climb on the table when we were eating—and we were not exactly a quiet group—while the wiliest were experts at extracting cheese from mousetraps at no risk to life or limb. Finding an empty trap in the morning enraged my mother. She hated to be outwitted by anyone or anything, but especially by these little four-legged creatures. Added to which, there was the waste of a good piece of cheese: "I got bet'er things t'do with me money than feed those li'l blighters!" she'd rant.

The kitchen was not the only habitat for these cheeky rodents. At night, up in the bedrooms, where Mum was reluctant to set traps for fear one of the boys would get his fingers caught, it was scary to hear them scampering around, squeaking and scratching. I was afraid to close my eyes in case one climbed on to my bed, and afraid to keep them open for fear of what I might see. One night, my worst fears were realized: I woke with a start, eyeball to eyeball with a mouse sitting on its haunches next to my head. I don't know which of us was the more terrified. To my sleepy unfocussed eyes, the mouse looked about the size of a cat, and I can't imagine how big I must have looked to the mouse. Paralyzed with fright, the pair of us, we stared at one another for what seemed an eternity, but the mouse was the first to recover its senses. It turned tail and scampered away, which freed me up to run screaming to Mum and Dad. And I spent the rest of the night in their bed, snuggled safely between them.

Fortunately, we soon acquired a cat, though perhaps it would be more accurate to say that the cat acquired us. He just turned up one day, a skinny, jet-black, alley cat, with a torn ear and a crooked tail, both presumably indicative of a turbulent past. He was given houseroom reluctantly at first, for fear of the cost of feeding him, but it soon transpired that he was a talented mouser and cost-effective compared with baiting traps every night. Even after ridding the house of its squeaking hordes, he existed comfortably on a few table scraps—probably supplemented with a diet of fresh mice from elsewhere, for in that area of warehouses, there were plenty more mice around. When news of his talent spread, he often spent the night on loan to some other household, and rumor had it that he was a good ratter, too. But the only time we witnessed him in action against a rat, he did not emerge as the winner; though he put up a good fight.

We three were ecstatic at having a cat. Our first pet! He was a wonderfully family-friendly animal, despite his killer instinct with the rodent population, and tolerated constant cuddling by me, and being pulled about and chased by the boys. In common with hundreds of black cat owners in England, and with singular lack of imagination, we named him Nigger or Niggy for short. None of us had ever seen a black person, so we were innocent of any racial overtones. I think. I hope. My first encounter with a "colored person" was a couple of years after Niggy's arrival, when I saw white folks with blackened faces in a nigger minstrel show at a Music Hall. This led me to assume that the "ole black Mammy" in a Shirley Temple movie was likewise a white woman with black shoe polish on her face and arms, an assumption that was strengthened by the shininess of her face.

The acquisition of Niggy put an end to the mice *and* to my doll-less condition: for he became Audrey's replacement—a real live doll! His aversion to being bathed was a big disappointment—my first attempt left me so badly scratched that it was the last—and he couldn't be relied upon to be there whenever I wanted him; but when he *was* around, we had such a good time. Speaking for myself, that is. Niggy, of course, never voiced an opinion, but he offered remarkably little resistance, other than his spirited refusal to being immersed in water, so I can only suppose that he was not desperately unhappy in his role as an Audrey-substitute.

Her neat outfit was exactly the right size for him, and once the first garment was in place, he usually stopped struggling, seemingly resigned to his fate. Audrey's clothes, being hand-knitted, were nice and stretchy and, apart from the little white knickers, easy to put on a wriggling cat. Niggy's legs were too long, and he was pretty uncooperative about this garment, so I used to tie a nappy on him, instead. To accommodate his ears, I cut holes in the bonnet, because Mum told me it was cruel to squoosh them. "Cats 'ave very sensitive ears, y' know," she said, authoritatively.

With black paws sticking way out of the sleeves (his arms were longer than Audrey's), and black ears poking out of holes in the bonnet, Niggy let me lay him in the doll's pram and cover him with a blanket. There he would take a nap quite contentedly, and he even got used to being pushed around in the pram while he dozed. One day I went out to play and forgot that he was sleeping in the pram. Mum found him running round and round, still fully clad with the bonnet askew over one eye and frantically trying to get the nappy off so that he could do his business in the usual manner. "The poor thing, that was cruel, t'leave 'im like that," she scolded, when I came home. "Don't yew ever do that agin, me lady, or I'll take them clothes away an' burn 'em."

If Mum was in a good mood, I could scrounge some milk, which I put in an old baby bottle and fed to Niggy—but only on his terms. At first, the milk ended up smeared over his chin, but, once he started cleaning his face and got the taste of it, he happily licked the nipple as I squeezed. It was a far cry from "taking the bottle" as Audrey had, but I was happy to settle for Niggy's technique. At least the milk wouldn't rot *his* insides and make him fall apart.

Attired in Audrey's outfit, Niggy was not as pretty as she had been, but he aroused much more comment when I pushed him around the streets of Waterloo in that tin pram. Old ladies, all prepared to admire my dolly, would peer into the pram, clucking "An' 'ow's yer baby t'day, luv?" and then jump back with a startled, "Oh, me Gawd!" at the sight of Niggy's jet-black, whiskered face surrounded by an angora-trimmed bonnet. Just such an encounter prompted Mrs. Carter, the old lady next door, to give me a doll that had belonged to her daughter, now grown and married, with children of her own. Mrs. Carter probably assumed, quite rightly, that I didn't have a doll and was forced to make do with a cat; but she couldn't know that I was more than happy with this arrangement.

The "new" doll had a porcelain face with delicate, finely chiseled features. It was an exquisite face, but long and thin and grown-up looking, not a nice round baby-face like Audrey's. Her clothes too, of yellowed white satin, were grown-up clothes, an outfit that an elegant young lady might have worn at the turn of the century; but we were stuck with them, because this doll was too tall and slender to wear Audrey's comfy wardrobe. Mrs.Carter couldn't remember the doll's name, so, for the second time in my doll-owning career, I got to pick a name. Because this doll seemed so old-fashioned, I chose for her the most old-fashioned name I could think of: Nellie, the name of the oldest woman I knew, eccentric Old Nell Panswick.

Old Nell, The Pigeon Lady, lived around the corner on Stamford Street, and was both loved and feared by all the neighborhood children. Almost spherical in shape, she moved with great difficulty, shuffling about in an ancient pair of tattered felt bedroom slippers, yelling obscenities at any kid that dared to look at her. She emerged from her house only to feed the pigeons, and the moment she appeared, the birds flocked to her by the dozen, landed on her arms, her shoulders, her head, enveloping her in a cooing, shimmering, mass. Old Nell caressed them, cooing gently in return—an instant transformation from the scary, obscenity-yelling old woman of a few moments earlier.

I'd never seen a doll with articulated arms and legs like Nellie's. They looked ugly, but could be covered up by her long coat, and it was fun to bend her at the knees and sit her on a chair with her feet dangling. The coat boasted a large cape, bordered with lace that—like her stuffed body—had been crudely mended, many times. I heartily disliked Nellie's stuffed body with its badly sewn up "wounds," because I couldn't immerse it in water to give her a bath, and it looked *so gruesome*. In addition, Nellie's head had a circular patch on top from which hair sprouted, while the rest was smooth and hairless, and there was a distinct seam where the two parts joined. It looked like a boiled egg that has had its top sliced neatly off and then replaced, just as neatly. (A trick at which Georgie Harris was an expert.) Nellie's hair reinforced this impression. It went straight up, before falling down to her shoulders—as if someone had held her up by the hair, scalped her by swiftly slicing off the top of her head, and then sewn the scalp back on without troubling to flatten the hair down.

I couldn't bear to look at Nellie's circular "scar," but it was impossible to cover it, because it came too far down her otherwise quite beautiful forehead. When she was new, bangs probably hid that seam, and thick hair masked the baldness of her "back and sides." But by the time I made her acquaintance, any trace of bangs had disappeared, and her hair was too sparse to mask anything. With all those scars and hair loss, Nellie had the frail look of someone recovering from a serious illness, and I was never at ease with this faded beauty.

A couple of other dolls eventually entered my life, but none ever took Audrey's place in my heart, and Niggy remained my "baby" of choice for a long time. Until, poor thing, he succumbed to injuries sustained in the battle with a rat that we watched him lose, just outside our back door. We nursed him carefully, but the wounds got infected and, poor Niggy, he lasted only a few days, this being long before antibiotics. In any case, in our world even people didn't see a doctor unless the situation was dire, so it was extremely rare for a pet to get taken to a vet. We all missed Niggy terribly. But I probably felt his loss the most; for me, he had been so much more than just a cat.

Chapter 6

For Better and for Worse

IN LONDON MY FATHER found work more often, and we were better off financially. But there were so many good things that we'd given up, not the least of which were the friends we'd left behind. I desperately missed Jeannie Cheek and didn't find a friend like her for a very long time.

The air in London was dreadful: thousands of chimneys spewed out sulfurous smoke, making it almost unbreathable much of the time, and occasionally culminating in a thick yellow fog. These "pea-soupers" were sometimes so dense that you could see nothing beyond your outstretched hand; airy railings then became useful navigational aids—though you arrived at your destination looking as if you'd taken up chimney-sweeping. After a few months of breathing this stuff, Dad and I developed bronchitis. His was yearlong and chronic, and I can't imagine how he put in day after day of heavy manual labor after his sleepless, cough-racked nights.

The air was especially bad in winter, because so many coal fires were lit in so many houses, and so many kitchens had a massive coal-burning range that was kept going all day to keep the house warm. Fortunately—as regards air quality, though not the comfort of the occupants—bedroom fireplaces, each with a chimney down which cold winds blew unwelcome drafts, were used only in serious illness. Most illnesses warranted an extra blanket or a brick, hot from the oven and wrapped in an old towel, to keep your toes warm. Only for a real stay-in-bed illness was a bedroom fire lit; lit with great reluctance, because it entailed carrying coals up the stairs, and ashes down: a messy business in either direction. Furthermore, it was difficult to persuade those seldom-used chimneys to "draw" well, and billowing smoke didn't add to an invalid's comfort or well being. Neither did it improve tempers.

Consequently, amongst the sea of chimney pots familiar to anyone travelling by rail into London, it was rare for smoke to issue forth from more than one chimney per house. Sooner or later, those rarely used chimneys developed cracks that let rain in, and led to non-stop running battles with landlords over damp walls. I used to feel sorry for our rent-lady when she came each Monday, because in addition to the rent, she always got an earful from my mother about the damp wall in the top bedroom. Landlords were probably tempted to close off bedroom chimneys once they started to leak, but few did, perhaps because the tenant would then have no means of heating those rooms other than a smelly and dangerous kerosene heater.

The return to Waterloo meant adjusting to a new school. It was a huge adjustment. For starters, the school was not new in the sense that my Dagenham school had been new. It was housed in an old three-story Victorian building with forbidding soot-blackened brick walls and great flights of stone steps. There were three playgrounds: Infants, Junior Boys, and Junior Girls, all devoid of playground equipment and separated from one another, and from the street, by yet more grimy high walls. However, as ugly and depressing as all those walls were to look at, they were perfect for the ball-against-the-wall games so popular with the girls: no windows to break, and no irate householders, like Jeannie's Grumpy Gramps, to yell or flap newspapers.

I started in the Hatfield Street Infants School, which was tucked away in a corner, separated as much as possible from the "big kids." But to get to the Infants entrance, you had to pass through the end of the Girls playground, and that was scary. Those girls were a wild lot, so big and rough and loud. Worse yet, I was scared of my new teacher, Miss Mitchell. She too was grim and forbidding, but at least she wasn't grimy. Quite the opposite: aggressively well scrubbed and squeaky clean, with cheeks that shone like polished apples, she must have used a strong carbolic soap, because she even *smelled* clean. No doubt Miss Mitchell was regarded as a pillar of her community, but to the children in her classroom she was a frumpy old lady with a face like a camel and about the same temperament.

The camel resemblance was recognized dramatically one Saturday morning at the Bake'ouse—the Baker Theater—where Saturday-morning-films-for-kids were shown. The place was full of Hatfield Street pupils, and when a camel appeared on screen, a voice guffawed in the darkness, "'Ey! Look ... ol' Ma Mitchell!" The likeness was quite remarkable, and a ripple of recognition swept through the place. Then pandemonium broke out, with every child who had suffered under Miss Mitchell whooping and hollering with delight. From then on, she was known as "Ol' Camel Face," and, in an odd way, it made many of us feel a bit more affection for her. Perhaps she seemed more human, now that we could laugh at her and about her; maybe we even felt a trace of sympathy for the owner of such an unfortunate face.

In addition to her lack of natural endowments, old Camel Face was a lousy teacher. Thanks to my father, I started school with a good head start, able to read, write and count, and every teacher in Dagenham had recognized this. They had let me sit off in a corner, and work at my own level and pace, when appropriate. But not Miss Mitchell. In her classroom, everybody worked in lock step. Reading Time was particularly excruciating: she started in one corner of the room and worked round it relentlessly, seat by seat, row by row, every student reading one sentence aloud. They were not exactly star readers, and I was bored stiff, listening every day to them stumbling through a simple reading book.

To while away the time, I invented a game in which I read the page vertically instead of horizontally. The first column of words was easy, but finding the second, third, then fourth or fifth words got increasingly harder, as the "columns" got wigglier and wigglier. Sometimes the words formed a silly sentence and gave me a quiet little giggle, but this game landed me in hot water when I became so engrossed that I lost track of who was reading what sentence—and, suddenly, it was my turn. Help! What line are we on? Old Camel Face took a dim view of this. "Gwen Redfern! You are the most exasperating child it has ever been my misfortune to encounter. You *never* know the place! What *am* I to do with you?"

Miss Mitchell's vocabulary was the only thing I liked about her: exasperating, misfortune, and encounter were not exactly run-of-the-mill words for Waterloo. But it never occurred to Miss Mitchell that all she had to "do" with me was give me a more challenging book and let me read by myself. For my near-daily offense of not knowing the place, she "kept me in" for five minutes of playtime; this actually suited me just fine, because I dreaded playtime, with all those rough kids running around screaming and yelling. Playtime in that Infants' playground gave me my first taste of feeling a misfit; a total misfit, I realized, because I didn't even *want* to fit in here. Hatfield Street School was a far cry from the newly built school in Dagenham, which was light and airy and more child-sized, had swings in the playground, and attracted a lot of Miss Johnsons and very few Miss Mitchells.

It took only a few weeks of old Camel Face to squelch my love affair with school—a cruel change, one that I couldn't have imagined. The excitement of going to school had been a central feature of my life. I had complained bitterly because there was no school on weekends, and Monday mornings were eagerly awaited. School holidays had been even more incomprehensible and unwelcome, but now I looked forward to both, like the rest of the Hatfield Street School population.

After a miserable term with Miss Mitchell I "went up" into the next class and had a teacher whose name I forget, but I remember working on my own a lot of the time. Then, somewhat ahead of my age group, I went up to the

Junior School. Went up, literally: up the long flight of broad stone steps to the second floor of the main building, where the classrooms for the eight-and-nine-year-olds were; the ten-and-eleven-year-olds climbed yet another flight of steps to reach their quarters. With this promotion I had the good fortune to be in Mr. Slarks' class, wonderful, jolly, caring, Mr. Slarks. And my love affair with school was re-kindled.

Mr. Slarks generated more laughter per hour than the rest of the teachers put together. Probably more learning per hour, too, if only because every student adored him and was eager to please. Mr. Slarks was delighted whenever any of his charges learned something; but if it was one who'd been having difficulty, he beamed and clapped and jumped up and down like an overgrown child, despite his ample proportions and bald pate. Then he'd find a way for the whole class to celebrate the kid's achievement:

"Well … I think that calls for a joke, don't you?"

"Yeah! Yeah! Tell us a joke, Mr. Slarks! Tell us one!" we'd yell back. And he'd launch into one of his inexhaustible stock of that valuable commodity. His classroom was not the quietest in the school, but it probably had the best discipline—yet, alone among the teachers, I never saw him cane a child. He sometimes got angry and talked about caning and hauled the young offender out to the front of the class; but the standing joke of that classroom was the elusiveness of Mr. Slarks' cane, which he called Charlie. It was always getting "lost," even when in plain view, and Mr. Slarks would loudly lament its loss, begging the class to help in the search for Charlie. This led to a few minutes of mayhem, with Mr. Slarks clowning around in a bizarre game of Hunt-the-Cane, asking how "warm" or "cold" he was, pretending to misunderstand our lustily-yelled instructions. Meantime, the girl or boy who was supposed to be at the wrong end of Charlie, was standing in front of the class, scared at first, but finally laughing and yelling along with the rest of us.

When the cane had been "found," Mr. Slarks stood and looked at it in feigned bewilderment, pretending that he couldn't remember why he had been looking for it in the first place. If some unkind soul reminded him of the miscreant still standing in front of the class, Mr. Slarks developed a serious hearing problem and cupped his hands behind his ears, "Eh? What's that? It's no good … you have to speak up! Louder!" After letting us yell long enough to have expended a useful amount of energy, he'd turn away shrugging his shoulders, put Charlie in a corner where he would stay until needed—and found, again, to be "lost." Then he barked at the culprit who had started all this, "What are you doing, standing there? Get back in your seat. Or I'll have to find Charlie and apply him to that bottom of yours!" The kid scuttled back gratefully, the original tension dissolved, and Mr. Slarks had added yet another adoring pupil to his collection. Even the worst behaved kids, and Hatfield Street School had its share, responded to this remarkable non-punitive discipline.

It took me a while to adjust to the big-ness of everything in the Junior School. Climbing the broad flights of stone steps up to the second floor was intimidating, all the doors were large and heavy and difficult to open, and the corridors—dark and dingy, all bottle green and brownish-tan—seemed immensely long. High ceilings and tall windows made the classrooms nice and bright, but the bottom of those windows was above head level for most of us: too high for anything but a patch of sky to be seen, unless you lucked out and got a back-row seat. For the desks were on shallow steps, each row higher than the one in front, and from the back-row you did get a glimpse of the outside world: Brill's Bakery across the street and the tops of passing traffic—not particularly exciting, but better than nothing. Maybe it was the intent, expressed by the original School Building Committee and executed obediently by the architect, that Hatfield Street students should be spared the distraction of looking out the window. If so, Nature sometimes defeated that intent, providing distractions for the easily distractible: puffy clouds scudding across the sky, or raindrops trickling down windowpanes, inviting silent bets as to which would get to the bottom first, or merge with another raindrop before the end of the race.

In keeping with everything else, the desks were big, big but simple. Each had a wooden seat, wide enough to accommodate the rear ends of two students, and a sloped top with a shelf underneath. There were empty round holes at the front corners of each desktop, for Hatfield Street School had, perhaps wisely, decided against the use of ink-filled inkwells. When I moved on to a school where pencil was not accepted for anything other than rough notes, I found myself ill prepared to deal with pen-and-ink, but at age seven, I was blissfully unaware of this impending trial-by-ink.

The school year was divided into three terms, and at the start of each term there was a general shuffling of bodies. Some students were promoted up to the next class, and some came into the class from the one below. Thus every term started with big questions: Which class will I be in? Who'll be my teacher? Who'll be my desk-mate? The last of these questions was as important as the first two. The teacher made seat assignments and rarely re-arranged them; friends were never seated together, so you could only hope that your desk-mate would, at least, leave you alone. Sometimes you got a constant tease: someone who pinched you, kicked your ankles, poked you under cover of the desktop with a carefully sharpened pencil, passed notes using you as a conduit, or—worst of all—deliberately and silently farted.

Silent blowing off was a much-envied, much-practiced, skill, especially among the boys, and a desk-mate who had mastered this art was the hardest to deal with. Your immediate neighbors would start to snort and giggle, hold their noses, and look accusingly in your direction—and there was no way you could complain to the teacher. Apart from the embarrassment of saying "blowin' awf" in public, to a teacher, it was impossible to prove who was responsible; though the culprit sometimes gave the game away with an ill-concealed smirk. The only strategy was to suffer in silence and hope that, once the novelty wore off, your desk-mate would desist. But that was a faint, rarely realized hope.

The Junior Girls playground was a nightmare. At least in the Infants playground the teachers on duty kept a reasonably watchful eye on the rough children. But here, teachers seemed to assume that we were big enough to look after ourselves and left us to our own devices, settling themselves firmly on the wooden seat that lined one wall in the small covered area where we all huddled if it rained. The difference between our family and the rest of Waterloo—things like clean, ironed clothes, and carefully brushed hair—had, by now, become more glaring, and I was constantly taunted with cries of "Miss 'Oity-Toity," "stuck-up," and "Ol' Toffee Nose." However, in the eyes of the Junior girls, my most unforgivable sin was that I liked school and didn't talk back to the teachers, so the most frequent insults hurled at me were the ones I minded the least: "goody-goody" and "book worm." I was deliberately excluded from any group games, which hurt more than all the taunting, and I spent most of the time leaning against the wall, yearning to be invited into a game—yet hoping to be left alone.

There was no escape. The only solution was to spend as little time as possible in the playground, so I dawdled to school each morning and aimed to get there no earlier than five minutes before 9 o'clock. I hung around outside the playground wall, listening for the whistle, and then made a dash to get through the gate before it clanged shut, so I could take my place in line with the rest of my class. Sometimes I misjudged and had to bear the disgrace of being counted among the latecomers on the wrong side of the playground gate, but this was a risk worth taking: anything was better than one unnecessary minute in that playground.

The same ritual was repeated at two o'clock, after the mid-day dinner break, but there was no way I could avoid the fifteen-minute playtimes, one in the morning, one in the afternoon. I would gladly have done a whole page of extra sums instead of going out for playtime; that was, indeed, my happy fate on days when I hadn't made it to the playground gate in time, but I couldn't pull that trick every day. More than two lates resulted in a note home, and I was not eager to face my mother's wrath for being late to school. She always made sure that I left home in good time, and I didn't want to tell her what was happening with the other girls. I knew only too well how she would berate me for being such a pushover. "Yew get on my nerves," she'd say. "It's time yew learned 'ow ta stand up fer yerself, m'lady. No-one else c'n do that for ya."

Then she'd launch into an oft-told story: "When I was yore age, some of the kids at school started t'call me "Muckraker" and "Shit-arse," 'cos I went round the streets shovelin' up 'orse droppins' ta sell ta people fer their gardens. But nobody ever called me names a second time. Yew c'n bet'cha boots on that! I went fer 'em, 'ammer an' tongs, an' they ended up laughin' out the other side of their mouths. Even when they was bigger than me. They didn't come back fer a second 'elpin', I c'n tell ya! Mind yew, I used ta cop it from me mother, if I come 'ome with me frock torn or a but'on missin'. But I didn't care. It was worth it. I wasn't gonna let anyone make a door-mat of *me*."

I'm sure she didn't. But I was not made of the same feisty material; I just bumbled along rather miserably, doing my best to avoid trouble. Derek, however, was made of sterner stuff. "Cut from the same cloth as me, that one is," Mum would say, approvingly. "No one's gonna walk all over 'im!" And because the two boys were so close and did everything together, by extension, no one made a doormat of Bertie either, even though he had none of Derek's spunk. When Derek went to battle for Bertie—against parents, teachers, other kids, the world at large—he did so regardless of the consequences for himself, and without heed for the fact that sometimes Bertie was the one at fault. And there often were consequences for Derek. He was the one in trouble, when he came home with a bloody nose or missing buttons or a torn shirt (just like Mum, as a girl), but he never laid the blame on Bertie, where it often belonged.

It was amazing how rarely those two boys squabbled. However, in retrospect, perhaps not *that* amazing, because Derek, essentially, always gave in; he couldn't bear to see Bertie cry. Just occasionally Bertie's whining got to him, and he'd say crossly, "Oh, shuddup! Yew get on wiv' my nerves!" but that was the closest to a quarrel that I remember.

When the boys started school, Derek acted dumb so as not to leave Bertie behind, an act that succeeded and ensured that they were always in the same class. Teachers often suspected that Derek could do better, but he steadfastly refused to out-perform Bertie. Not till they got separated years later, did he start to realize his potential. In the school playground, with their clean clothes and well-kept hair, they must have been subject to many of the taunts that tormented me, but Derek's willingness to take on the world stood them in good stead, and made them less rewarding as targets. It also helped that neither of them was fond of school, and could never be called a "goody goody" or a "book worm."

I now had to walk the boys to school every day, under strict instructions not to let go of their hands until they had been safely handed over to a teacher in the Infants playground. No longer able to avoid the Girls playground by skulking around outside the gate, I was in despair until, one day, their teacher asked if I would like to help set up the folding cots on which the five-year-olds took a rest in mid-afternoon. From that day on, before afternoon school I puttered around in the Infants' classroom, setting up the cots, placing on each a brightly colored blanket and making myself generally useful. I loved the colors and soft feel of the blankets, which were so much prettier and softer than the plain scratchy ones we had at home, and, for those few minutes, I was perhaps the happiest girl in Waterloo. Then my duties were extended to cleaning blackboards, banging the dust out of erasers, and setting out paper and crayons. This beat playing school with old buttons!

Eventually I was invited to help before school in the mornings as well, so my before-school playground misery became a thing of the past, and I was in seventh heaven. Playtime breaks got rather worse, though, because now a new taunt followed me around: "Teacher's Pet! T-e-a-ch-e-r's Pe-et!" But I regarded it as a fair trade and was happier than I had been since our return to Waterloo.

Chapter 7

51 Commercial Road

By the time Niggy died, we'd moved again; but not far this time, just a bit further along Upper Ground to where it became Commercial Road. Maybe this section should have been called Lower Ground, because it was even lower than Upper Ground! The basement of our "new" house had been declared unfit for habitation and sealed off, along with the airy and coal cellar, soon after the 1928 flood. The semi-basement kitchen at the back was still usable and not as damp as our old living room had been. But it was plagued with black beetles, lovers of dark, damp places. Ugh! ... How they crunched underfoot if you trod on them.

The loss of the coal cellar led to lots of grumbling: the coalman complained about carrying sacks of coal through the house, and my mother about the coal dust trekked in by his heavy boots. Another feature of this house was that it had no electricity—a major step backward for us—and I remember much swearing and cussing about the temperamental behavior and fragility of gas mantles in light fixtures. I liked the gentle popping and flickering, and the softness of gaslight; but, having recently attained height enough to reach light switches, I found it aggravating to have to wait for a grown-up to "light the gas" for me.

We shared this house with a blind old man we called Grampa Benson, and in part payment of rent, Mum helped him with daily tasks that were difficult for him. The money that she earned with this "job" was the major reason for our move, but for us three there was the added benefit of acquiring a surrogate grandfather. We'd never known any of our grandparents, who'd either died or made themselves scarce before we were born, and we loved Grampa Benson. Especially me: I sat for hours in his room upstairs on the second floor, listening to yarns of army life. In cold weather it was very cozy, because Mum kept his fire going all day, and Grampa Benson often told her how grateful he was for that. "So ya should be," was, invariably, her ungracious response, "with all the coal an' ashes I cart up an' down those bloomin' stairs, ev'ry time yew want a fire!" This was as close as she ever got to letting the old man know that she appreciated the fact that he said thank you. But it really did please her, and she regularly held him up as a role model to us if we were a bit slow to say thank you.

Grampa Benson's room was crowded with shabby, overstuffed solid old furniture, and every square inch of wall was taken up by large gold-framed paintings. They all depicted chaotic and heroic battle scenes, with red-coated soldiers on charging horses, many falling in battle midst lots of dust and smoke. He had fought in the Boer War as a lowly infantryman and solemnly vouched for the accuracy of the paintings, though he was now completely blind and could no longer see them—and I, just as solemnly, believed him.

Grampa Benson was a really nice old man: he joked around a lot and chuckled into his straggly beard, always cheerful, in spite of the limited range of activities now available to him. I never saw him leave that small room, and he couldn't even have a radio in this house devoid of electricity, because battery operated ones were way too expensive for more than occasional listening. We had one for a short time, but had to give it up because of the expense. And I don't know which I missed more: listening to the radio, or going to the "electric" shop with Dad to take the dead battery back and pick up a "new" one. The batteries were big glass affairs, rather like a small car battery with a carrying handle, too heavy (and too fragile) for a child to carry, so I wasn't there to help Dad, just to keep him company and enjoy *his* company. On the trip home with the fresh battery, I remember relishing the anticipation of listening to the radio again—I could almost *taste* the pleasure to come—after a week or so of waiting for there to be enough money for a freshly charged battery.

Grampa Benson's sense of humor sometimes got a bit out of hand and landed him in trouble with our mother, as on the occasion when he called out, "May! May! Come 'ere! Come quick!

"Whas'sa mat'er? What 'appened?" Mum cried, as she came huffing and puffing through the door, after dashing up two flights of stairs

"Oh, me Gawd, May! Thank 'Eavens you come! ... I put me 'ead in the gas oven—an' fergot ta turn the bloomin' gas on!" Grampa Benson chuckled, and Mum was so mad with him that he got nothing but cold food for a few days.

However, Grampa Benson was not the only practical joker in the house. Bertie and Derek played countless tricks on him, and after the gas oven false alarm, Mum had no sympathy: "Serves 'im right, the silly ol' bugger! Gives 'im a taste of 'is own med'cine." However, she drew the line when it came to the boys switching around his salt and pepper pots. Grampa Benson was dependent on everything being in its right place, and, after he rendered several meals inedible with excessive pepper, Mum told the boys to stop that lark. A joke was a joke, but wasting good food was not on.

Mice were no longer a major problem in this house; instead, we were plagued by flies—flies by the million. They came from dustcarts that lined up along the road, waiting to empty their loads of household rubbish on to barges for disposal somewhere in the lower reaches of the Thames. Grim though it sounds, it was actually a rather colorful scene, and not too horribly smelly. The horse-drawn wooden dustcarts were bright yellow and decorated with hand-painted red flowers, and the carthorses, each with a name and lovingly cared for by its driver, were magnificent beasts, with their great hoofs, powerful haunches, and velvety noses. Though we all recoiled from their slobbery mouths. The drivers were a very jolly lot, and a rich source of Knock-Knock jokes and cigarette cards, so we amassed vast collections of these valuable commodities. Elaborate games were devised for the cards, but the greatest pleasure came from doing swaps— film stars for cars (or *vice versa*)—and poring over all those pictures and vital statistics. Girls also collected the transparent cellophane wrapping from the cigarette packs, and folded and re-folded it several times to form thin strips that could be linked together in zigzag fashion to make an ornamental belt. It looked a bit like mother-of-pearl and was quite a fashion statement, especially if the family button box yielded a fancy buckle.

But the flies were a terrible problem, especially in warm weather. Day or night, there was no escaping the constant buzzing or the tickle of a fly landing on you. Sticky flypapers were useless: within minutes of hanging one up, it was completely covered with furiously buzzing flies, kicking like mad, trying to unstick themselves. Our resourceful mother paid us a penny for a 2-lb. jam jar full of corpses, which kept us out of mischief—till the novelty of fly-catching palled—and we did work out to be cheaper than flypapers; but, like them, we barely made a dent in the fly population.

The sealed off airies along Commercial Road had been paved over, and the railings had been removed. This created an unusually wide pavement [sidewalk] that was a perfect playground for the games that were such an important part of the street scene. In addition to games involving balls, cigarette cards, and skipping rope to elaborate rhyming chants, there were many yearlong favorites: hopscotch, leapfrog, Ick-Ack-Ock [Scissors-Stone-Paper], Queenie, Statues, Giant Steps, and a frowned-upon-because-dangerous boys' game that involved the piling up of bodies braced against a wall.

Other games had definite seasons that lasted a few weeks, during which time that particular game dominated the scene. When the hoop season began, there was not a child on the street who didn't scrounge around and find, somehow, from somewhere, a hoop, however battered. Then, as mysteriously as they had appeared, the hoops vanished, their place taken by whips-and-tops, then yo-yos, then marbles, and so it went, until we were back to the hoops again. I suppose the shopkeepers from whom we bought these toys—when we were lucky and got a shiny new one, didn't have to dust off last year's scratched model—had something to do with their seasonal availability. But to us it seemed part of the natural scheme of things: like Christmas in the winter and Easter in the spring.

Soon after all this fun became available, quite literally on our doorstep, I began to put on weight, and my social life took a decided turn for the worse. It quickly became apparent how cruelly fat kids were ridiculed and excluded from those all-important games. I was frequently followed by jeering groups, chanting, "Ol' F-a-t'-y A-r-b-u-n-k-l-e!" and my way of dealing with this was to run indoors, but Mum always sent me right back out to face my tormentors. "Ya gotta learn ta stand up fer yerself," she'd say. Thin-skinned and shy, I never did; and my street life became ever more painful as I put on ever more weight.

The worst incident occurred one day during the whip-an'-top season, when I was walking past Hazel Henderson's house on my way to school. Hazel came out, whip in hand, shouting, "Go away, yew ... get away from my 'ouse. Nobody wants t'play wiv *yew*, Fat'y," and suddenly slashed me across the face with one sharp swipe of her whip. Pretty little Hazel Henderson of all people ... the only child in the neighborhood who looked as if butter wouldn't melt in her mouth. The knot at the end of the whip's leather thong made it a brutal weapon, but no more brutal than her words. I don't know which hurt more. Particularly since what she said was true: I *was* fat and I *was* friendless; *no*body wanted to play with me. I ran home crying, nursing my hurt face and my hurt feelings.

Our mother had little sympathy for self-inflicted cuts and bruises, but an injury from the outside world was a different story. As I saw that day, hell had no fury greater than our mother did when on the warpath avenging an attack on one of us. The angry red welt on my face *did* evoke a sympathetic response from her—but only after she'd satisfied herself that I "'adn't started it." And the sympathy was short-lived. She rapidly went into fighting-revenge mode and dragged me, still crying, back to the scene of the crime. Hazel had gone to school by that time, so Mrs. Henderson was the sole recipient of one of my mother's earfuls, and in fairness to Hazel's mother, she *was* shocked by the ugly stripe running across my face. Nevertheless, in self defense, she protested, "It can't 'ave bin my 'Azel!"

Mum would have none of that. She had armed herself with my whip and threatened to use it if Hazel so much as looked at me the wrong way. "I'll be watchin' … ya' c'n bet'cha life on that. An' ya'd bet'er tell that precious 'Azel of yourn ta keep 'er 'ands to 'erself. The spiteful li'l cat. Or I'll give 'er a taste of 'er own med'cine, shaw as God made li'l apples!" she stormed, brandishing my whip to make sure that her intent was clear. "An' yew too," she added, for Mrs. Henderson's benefit, "if anything like this ever 'appens agin!" Mrs. Henderson retreated indoors. Then Mum mopped the tears on my face with the corner of her pinafore and sent me off to school, exhorting me to " 'urry up, now. Or yew'll be late."

My mother was as good as her word. She kept watch, four times a day, day after day, as I passed the Henderson house on my way to and from school. Once, Hazel happened to come out of her front door and turn towards me—and in a flash, there was Mum, whip in hand, ready to strike. Hazel fled, screaming, into the safety of her house; and Mrs. Henderson must have decided that discretion was the better part of valor, for she did not appear to argue her daughter's innocence with my whip-wielding mother.

Hazel Henderson never troubled me again as I passed her house; but neither did she become a friend, and that was a sad disappointment. For at the time of the whip incident, the Hendersons were new arrivals on the street and seemed more like our families than most, so I had hoped that Hazel and I might be friends. Hazel and her brothers, like us, appeared every morning in clean clothes—shabby, but carefully washed and ironed, just like ours. And they, too, were always in bed by eight, even on the long light summer evenings that are the delight of living in northern latitudes: a well-deserved compensation for the early darkness of winter afternoons. On the street, early-to-bed kids were considered "no fun," because, if included in a game, they often had to leave in the middle. Only under extenuating circumstances—an acute shortage of players, or if they had a much-needed ball or skipping rope—were they invited to play. Many Waterloo youngsters had no set bedtime; some spent the evenings outside a pub, or were left to their own devices till their parents came home at closing time, around ten o'clock. The lingering light and the voices of kids still having fun made it difficult for us early-to-bedders to fall asleep, but arguing, "we can't fall asleep till it's dark, anyway. So we might as well stay out an' play wiv' the uvvers," always fell on deaf ears. However, that never stopped us trying!

There were other strikes against children like us: things such as going to school regularly—especially if you actually enjoyed it—and never going out with unbrushed hair. The scorn of the street for neatly combed hair was tough to take, day in, day out, but we three had learned the hard way that if we slipped out of the house without having our hair brushed, Mum's wrath was even worse. This was probably true for the Henderson children, too.

It was around this time that hair became a big problem for me, a burden that I bore unwillingly, because it seemed so unnecessary. My difficulty was the hairstyle that Mum insisted on. In my opinion, which she completely ignored, of course, it was so embarrassing and so unbecoming. I longed to do my hair like other girls, with a ribbon or a headband, to let it grow long, or, best of all, to part it in the middle with bangs. But my mother was determined to "train" my hair, so that it would "keep its curl"—a pretty far-fetched dream, I thought. At best, my boring brown tresses could be coaxed into a slight Marcel-like wave that ran parallel to the part in my hair; but even this was achieved only by dint of careful shaping when it was wet, followed by a permanent holding action with an enormous hair slide.

I never saw any other child with this hairstyle or that kind of giant hair slide, and I hated both with a passion. Especially the slides. They were about five inches long and bounced in a ridiculous, embarrassing way whenever I hopped or skipped or jumped. I "lost" them, as often as I could without rousing Mum's suspicions. But, no matter how precarious our finances, a replacement always appeared, and my protests were unavailing. "Yew'll be glad when yer older an' don't 'ave t'get perms. Jus' think o' the money yew'll save!" was the invariable response. And oddly enough, my mother was right. In my teens, what I'd seen as singularly unpromising hair began to curl, and I *have* been spared a lot of expense, and *have* been glad. Whether this was the result of her training regime is anyone's guess, but my mother regarded it as a major triumph.

Hazel Henderson had moved into the neighborhood just as my hair-slide misery was beginning, and her gleaming, shoulder-length chestnut ringlets were a source of considerable envy and awe to me. I'd never seen such hair except in pictures of princesses in the storybooks that my first teacher, Miss Johnson, had given me to read; I had longed to be friends with this wondrous creature, so I was doubly saddened by the whip incident. Saddened by the meanness of it and by the inescapable fact that Hazel obviously shared the common antipathy to fatness and would never be my friend.

Chapter 8

The Old Blue Pram

IN ONE OF MY earliest memories, I am trotting along on a cold wintry day, struggling to keep up with my mother's brisk stride and holding on to the handle of the pram that had been such a bone of contention with Old Ma Tanner. The handle curves up like a silver snake, and it feels cold even through my mittens. A sharp wind stings my bare, chapped thighs, and I feel envious of Derek and Bertie, tucked snugly into the pram's cavernous depths.

Chapped thighs were a winter-long source of misery, despite daily dollops of Vaseline; they made it excruciatingly painful to get into a hot bath, so it was, perhaps, just as well that baths were not a daily occurrence. In principle, my legs were protected from the elements by leather gaiters, but these singularly inadequate articles of clothing stopped at the knee. Each gaiter was fastened with a row of closely spaced, teddy-bear-eye buttons—perhaps a dozen—using a special implement like a rug-making tool to hook a tiny leather loop over each little button. It was an elaborate time-consuming operation for such ineffective leg protectors. Why anyone bothered with them is an enduring mystery, except that they must have looked elegant, judging by Mum's triumphant, "There!" as she sat back on her heels after wrestling with all those buttons and eyed me proudly. "Quite the li'l toff ain'cha? Tuppence t'talk t'yew, I s'pose!"

Soon after I started school, gaiters mercifully disappeared from the scene, and not until I read *When We Were Very Young* to my own children, did I come across them again in illustrations of the poem *James James Morrison Morrison Weatherby George Dupree*. I then realized that they must have been an upper middle class status symbol, but how did I come to be the possessor of such classy and, no doubt, expensive garments? Possibly they were hand-me-downs from the Marshes—Mr. Marsh was a bank manager—a family that kept in touch with Mum for many years after she left their employ. In her first job, at age thirteen, she was a live-in housemaid-nursemaid for the Marshes' three girls and also helped out in their small sweet shop.

"Very good ta me, they was," she often told us. "An' Mrs. Marsh always reckoned I should'da bin a nurse. I would've liked to, an' all, but them days, yew 'ad ta buy a uniform before yew could start. I 'adn't got that kind o' money. When Mrs. Marsh 'eard that, she said, in 'er posh lah-di-dah voice, 'Don't you let that stop you, Mabel, my d-e-ah!' That's what they always called me, Mabel. An' she offered ta buy the uniform fer me, but I couldn't let 'er do that. I didn't want ta start off owin' nothin', not even ta the Marshes." As I got older, I came to think it a pity that Mum hadn't jumped at that good lady's offer. She would have made an excellent nurse and would have loved the work. Indeed, much of her life was spent taking care of people, one way or another. Unpaid, of course. How different her life might have been, with a marketable skill like nursing under her belt.

We three loved to hear Mum imitate Mrs. Marsh's "posh" accent—a very good imitation, I discovered, when I met the lady. She took Mum and me out to tea, one day, when she was in London with her middle daughter Betty, "just buying a few clothes for her." Out to tea? In a *restaurant*? At age seven, I didn't know about restaurants; the only eating places I knew, the steam-filled Sausage 'N Mash shops, where working men ate dinner, were a bit on the rough side, perhaps, for the Marshes.

Tea with Mrs. Marsh and her daughter was certainly a memorable, but not entirely successful, occasion. I was ill at ease throughout, overwhelmed by the grandeur of the restaurant (a Lyon's Corner House, maybe, though I remember waitresses in black dresses with frilly, white aprons and headdresses). Tea in our house was a very simple meal: a big plate of bread and butter in the middle of the table—nothing but the best butter, though. None of that cheap new-fangled margarine stuff, Mum always said—and we didn't bother with niceties like individual plates. We ate directly off the oilcloth that covered the table and shared a communal knife, stuck in the jam pot that was handed around for anyone who asked for it. So, even a Lyon's Corner House would have been fancy, by my standards!

A major source of embarrassment that day was the well-manicured state of the Marshes' hands. They put our ugly paws to shame; I hid mine, with their bitten-to-the-quick nails, under the table as much as I could, and kept wishing that Mum would do the same. Her work-roughened hands had traces of grime ingrained in the cracks and under the nails, so they never looked entirely clean. Except on Mondays: then, after the big wash when they'd been immersed in water all day, they were white and soft and wrinkled. Dress was another issue with the Marshes. Their clothes were posher than any I'd ever seen, and I was flabbergasted by the huge number of packages containing "a few clothes for Betty"—the reason for their trip into London that day. Betty didn't look to be in need of much in the way of clothing. Everything she had on looked brand new! But it was their way of talking that caused me the greatest discomfort: acutely aware of our rough speech, I said as little as possible, so as not to embarrass them; they had to have noticed the contrast.

As we were walking home afterwards, Mum asked, "Well, whatever 'appened ta yew? The cat gotcha tongue?" and all I could say was, "I dunno." If she really didn't know, there was no way I could explain. What with one thing and another, I didn't enjoy that tea with the Marshes; it was a relief to go back to handing round the knife-in-the-jam-pot at teatime the following day.

On the day that I first heard about my newborn brush with Old Ma Tanner, we still had the big old blue pram, though it was no longer used to wheel babies around. Bertie and Derek were now about four, and the pram had long since been relegated to occasional use. It was trundled out if there was a heavy load to be carried, and we used it to wheel our floppy Guy through damp, gray November streets before Guy Fawkes Night, crying, "A penny fer the Guy! Please Mister … a penny fer the Guy!" Many men were out of work, so we rarely collected more than a couple of pennies, enough to buy a pack of sparklers, if we were lucky. But we always tried, and always hoped. I loved making the Guy, stuffing rags into some old clothes and drawing a face on the wobbly head, but I hated burning him on the bonfire and was relieved when we didn't have a bonfire. But the two boys always felt cheated if they didn't see the Guy go up in flames.

After the pram lost its wheels, it became a great rocker and probably the most exciting toy we ever had. Derek and Bertie used to sit, one at each end, shrieking, "'Igher! *'Igher!*" while I "pumped" as hard as I could on the handle of the wildly rocking pram. Even better, it could be made to spin at the same time—though I now shudder to think about that—and, adding to the excitement, the backyard sloped slightly, so the spinning-rocking pram would, unpredictably, start to slide downhill as well. I had to jump smartly to get out of its path, while the boys hung on tight and ducked down to protect their heads. Occasionally one of them got his fingers caught between the pram and the wall, but after the grazed knuckles had been washed, dabbed with iodine and bandaged, an accident like this evoked nothing more than, "Stop makin' a fuss. Serves yer right fer playin' sa rough." Unmitigated sympathy was a rare commodity; we were expected to take life's lumps and bumps without tears, particularly if they'd been brought on by our own foolishness.

Eventually (perhaps with some help from our parents), the old pram lost its handle, and after that, it was hard to get a good grip to set it rocking. It was now less exciting, but what it lost in excitement, it gained in versatility. Right side up, on its side, upside down, it became a train, a truck, a boat, a cave, a house, whatever the moment demanded. Best of all was when rain collected in it—if we discovered this before Mum had a chance to empty the water out. Sitting in that old pram, paddling our feet, sailing bits of wood, making mud pies … what wonderful, wet, messy, fun!

Our back garden, small and boxed in on all sides by tall grimy brick walls, was a far cry from the English garden that most people picture when they hear those two words. Even our green-fingered father never succeeded in persuading anything to grow in that sour, rubbish-filled soil. Digging produced artifacts of all kinds: old bottles, bits of bikes, saucepans, rusted tin baths, bed springs … It was like an archaeological dig, except that the finds had negative value, because they had to be disposed of; if they were too big for the dustbin, all Dad could do was to bury them again. Finally, he gave up on the idea of growing anything in this inhospitable spot, so it remained as a dirt patch, and this was perfectly O.K. with us three. On a fine day (by definition: a day when it was not actually raining), it was a great place to play—after Mum had checked for rats, afraid we might accidentally corner one lurking under something. It had happened, once, to me, and once was more than enough. A cornered rat is not a pretty sight. However, when we three got going, there was really no danger: we created such a racket that no self-respecting rat would venture within a mile of us.

With no vegetable patch to worry about, we were free to dig holes, create hills, make tricycle tracks to our hearts' content, and it was perfect for mud pies. But woe betide us if we didn't keep clear of the washing. And there was always washing on the line. A tall forked prop held the line up and kept most of the washing well out of our reach; but big things, like sheets, came down low, and we had to be careful not to touch them. Moreover, the prop itself presented a major hazard. An encounter with a wheel, or a foot, or a ball, could send it crashing to the ground, and bits of washing then trailed in the dirt. "Nah ya've gone an' done it!" the guiltless would say, smugly, to the unfortunate culprit. "Yew won't 'arf cop it!"

This conjured up the fearsome "coppa stick," which was a wooden rod about two-foot long and an inch in diameter. It always sat, in full view, propped up against the wall next to the copper—a large metal tub under which a fire could be lit to heat water. (Coppers, one of the few conveniences of which those old houses could boast, were built into a corner of the kitchen, next to the sink.) The copper stick was used to stir the washing and keep it moving, much like vanes in today's washing machines, and also to transfer heavy wads of water-soaked sheets or clothing from the copper to the sink for rinsing. Over time, all this immersion in hot soapy water had eroded and bleached the business end, leaving it ragged and shaggy, like the trunk of a shagbark tree. That end looked as if it had been softened somewhat, but it was just as hard as the non-business end and made a formidable disciplinary threat.

Our copper stick had never actually been applied to a bottom: if we were misbehaving, it was sufficient for Mum to lean it against her chair or lay it across her lap. Usually, in the event of a clothes prop accident, we all three "copped it" and were sent to play indoors or out on the street, while Mum dealt crossly with the muddied washing. Even without such accidents, our mud-play resulted in extra-dirty clothes and generated plenty of washing—all done by hand in a house with only one cold-water tap—so she had good reason to be cross when we added even more by our carelessness.

The old blue pram finally went out in a blaze of glory. It was chopped up one Guy Fawkes' Night and used to fuel a glorious bonfire, the best we ever had. I did manage to salvage the two pale blue ceramic swallows that had decorated the sides of the pram. I'd always loved those swooping birds and treasured these keepsakes for several years. (I wonder what became of them?)

◆   ◆   ◆

ADDENDUM

Many years later, I unexpectedly got to re-live the delights of a pram-as-rocker, as I watched a bunch of three-year-olds having the time of their lives in a pram that was remarkably like the old blue pram. On the day of our daughter's third birthday party, we'd taken the wheels off a pram and set it on the lawn as a rocker, and, without question, it was the hit of the party. The delight on the faces of those three-year olds as they sat, one at each end of the pram, their squeals of delight and requests for the pumper to make it go, "Higher! *Higher!*" transported me back to the muddy patch of garden in Waterloo, with Bertie and Derek ensconced at either end of our old blue pram. It felt as if the clock had been turned back some twenty years. Except that, even the three-year-olds of the world in which I now lived, knew about the letter *h*.

Chapter 9

The Royals

ONE WINTRY SATURDAY I spent the day with the Hodds, as I so often did. We'd gone down The Cut for the big weekend food shop, and then everybody gravitated to the kitchen, the only warm room in the house. On an indoor Saturday like this, the smokers puffed their way through a huge number of cigarettes, and piles of "fag ends" accumulated in the hearth and had to be swept up and added to the fire at regular intervals—a task that Viley and I fought over, for some obscure reason. Some played darts or cards or "did the pools," and the rest huddled around the fire, reading, knitting, or idly chatting. Uncle Ernie, as usual, monopolized the Sports Page; Rosie leafed through a pile of old film magazines to make sure she'd read every word and gazed admiringly at every film star before the magazines were thrown out; and Viley and I immersed ourselves in some new comics, undisturbed by the whoops and hollers of the dart players, or the non-stop clickety-clack of knitting needles.

Louie and Kitty (Georgie's sweetheart) were always knitting. An endless stream of pullovers, jumpers [sweaters], cardigans, gloves and scarves flowed from their busy, purposeful fingers, and whenever a new ball of wool was needed, Viley and I were expected to help with this production effort. Our job was to hold a skein of wool stretched between our hands, while the would-be-knitter wound the wool into a ball. Swinging your hands gently from side to side made the wool move freely off the skein and sped up the process, but you had to be careful not to get carried away by this; disastrous consequences ensued if the winder's rhythm didn't match that of the skein-holder. Attention also had to be paid to keeping the skein taut or it slipped off your hands and got in a tangle, so this was a tedious arm-aching job, especially if there were snarls to be sorted out. But it was useless to protest. The most pitiful of whines, "Me arms are achin', *so* bad ... " were ignored or, perversely, evoked the dreaded response, "While yer 'ere le's do anuvva one."

At tea time there had been a lot of talk about the death of King George V, who had died a few days earlier, and a sharp division had developed. Some were going the next day to view the dead monarch as he lay in state, "at Westminster ... it's beau'iful, they say," murmured Louie. Georgie and Harry argued, "Everyone ough'a go. It's part of 'ist'ry, after all," which persuaded Rosie and her sweetheart, Perce, to join them. But Aunt-Mum and Uncle Ernie announced that, historic or no, their old bones weren't up to standing in the cold on a wintry afternoon—not when they could be sitting snugly by the fire. Lazy, comfort-loving Kitty agreed, in her adenoidal, whiny voice that Viley and I couldn't stand, that it was "a daft thing ta do."

Kitty was so aptly named. With her slanty green eyes, turn-up nose and short upper lip, she looked, and behaved, just like a cat. She loved to curl up and doze, as close to the fire as she could get, and it was almost a surprise to find that she had no whiskers and didn't purr. But she did have claws and didn't hesitate to use them, if crossed. On this occasion, she came close to hissing, cat-like, at Georgie, until he gave up pleading with her to go with him to see the king.

Then came the question of Viley. She was reluctant at first, but finally allowed herself to be included in the party, because it beat the prospect of an otherwise dreary afternoon, she told me later. Sunday afternoons were always a bore unless we could play outside. After their big Sunday dinner, all the grown-ups put their heads down on folded arms and "took a kip" at the table. Except for Uncle Ernie. He took himself off to his bedroom and slept in comfort, sensible fellow. Viley and I were always hard put to find ways of amusing ourselves that wouldn't disturb all those kippers, as we called them.

I sat wondering whether I wanted to go, too. Part of me did want to see a king, even a dead one; another part just wanted to see a real dead person, in a coffin; and yet another part was keen to see the inside of Westminster Abbey. From walks with Dad, I was familiar with, and impressed by, the outside of the Abbey and had often wondered about the inside. But my mother was always provoked by the mere mention of "the Royals," outraged by what she saw as their luxurious, idle lives. "An' all paid fer by the likes of us!" she'd splutter indignantly, because, since our return to the Coin Street area, the rotten old housing that we lived in was Crown property, and she had to fight tooth and nail to get anything fixed. I knew she'd be furious at the idea of me paying any kind of homage to a member of the royal family, dead or alive. So I said nothing, until Louie suddenly declared, "Gwen should go too. She'd like ta go—wouldn'cha, Gwen? 'Specially if Viley's goin'."

She had done it again: put me in a situation where it was hard to say no, yet equally hard to say yes. Who to please? Louie? Or my mother? I shrugged and murmured, "I dunno," but Louie's mind was made up. "O' course ya do. I'll talk to yer Mum an' Dad, when I take ya back t'night."

And there the matter had rested until we arrived back at my house that evening, and Louie announced, "We're goin' t'see the ol' king t'morra." She was sitting down, but kept her coat on to signal that she wasn't staying long and, by further inference, was not prepared for a lengthy discussion on this, or any other issue.

"Oh, yew are, are ya … " was Mum's absent-minded response, as she took my coat and hung it on the back of a chair to dry in front of the fire. "Well … good luck t'ya. I 'ope yew enjoy standin' in the cold all afternoon. I never wanted ta see 'im when 'e was alive, an' I'm sure I don't want ta stand in line ta see 'im now 'e's dead."

"An' Gwen wants t'come wiv' us," added Louie.

"*She what?*" Louie now had Mum's full attention. Her anti-royalist blood was aroused, and she glared fiercely at me.

"Yeah," said Louie, quite unfazed. "After all, it's part of 'istory, May. So o' course she wants t'come an' see the king layin' in state. Don'cha Gwen?"

I was trapped, once again, between these two strong-willed women. Louie was good at putting me on the spot like this. She'd persuade me to go along with something she'd already set her heart on and then use my agreement, however reluctantly given, to reinforce her case. Of course, sometimes I had agreed only too readily, but at other times, like now, I hadn't even committed myself. But for Louie it was enough that I hadn't disagreed; she blithely translated this double negative as an implied positive. It was hard to deny Louie something to which she'd made up her mind. She was a powerful sulker, and those who crossed her paid a heavy price, a long-drawn-out price. She could keep up a sulk for weeks and rarely lost.

My Dad then entered the fray: "Louie's right, May. After all, kings don't die every day, do they? It might never 'appen agin in our lifetime … As a mat'er of fact, I'd like ta go meself." My heart leapt at the prospect of Dad joining us. There was nothing I'd like better than to go inside the Abbey with him. "But," he went on, "as ya know, I ain't bin feelin' too good lately." It was disappointing to have my newborn hope dashed so quickly, but I wasn't surprised; Dad had been having a rough time with his bronchitis.

As expected, the mere thought of the Royal Family got Mum spitting mad. "Well, I c'n tell ya this … *she ain't goin'*! I won't 'ave 'er kowtowin' ta the bloody royals. What good 'ave they ever done fer the likes of us? Ready ta take the rent money they are, right on the dot, ev'ry Monday mornin'. But not s'quick ta fix the bloomin' roof when it leaks—"

"May, I keep tellin' ya," said Louie, taking advantage of this pause for breath. "It ain't the King what owns this lot. It all belongs ta the Duchy o' Cornwall—"

"Duchy o' Cornwall? Duchy o' My Arse!" Mum broke in, scornfully. "It don't make no diff'rence—Duchy o' This, or Duchy o' That! They're all tarred with the same brush, all part o' the same fam'ly, ain't they? An' not one of 'em cares a brass farthin' fer the likes of us ... the ones what 'ave ta live in their rot'en old 'ouses. Fer weeks I bin pesterin' the rent lady abaht the damp in that top bedroom ... where my kiddies 'ave ta sleep ev'ry night ... But the bloody royals ain't done nothin' abaht *that*, 'ave they?"

Even Louie knew better than to argue when Mum had got herself worked up like this, and she got up to leave, saying, "Well ... we'll come round t'morra afternoon. Just in case ya change yer mind." But she couldn't resist adding, "Don't ferget, May, it *is* an 'istoric fing, an' after all, the king did die on Gwen's birfday—"

"Oh no 'e didn't!" Mum shot back. "It was the day before. Jus' before midnight it was, when 'e died!"

But Louie was already walking away, pretty confident that I'd be ready to go with them to view the late King George V when she called for me the following afternoon. And I was. I don't know why, or how; when I went to bed that evening, Mum was still adamantly against the idea. Dad must have, somehow, persuaded her otherwise.

It was indeed a long line and a long wait; and the cold, gray January afternoon matched the subdued mood of the people in that line, shuffling slowly along, gradually getting closer to their dead king. Darkness set in around four o'clock, and it started to rain, but in an odd way, this brightened things up, because the light from street lamps and passing traffic was reflected from the wet roads. We huddled under umbrellas, but the dampness soon seeped through the soles of our shoes, and we stamped our feet in a vain attempt to keep them warm. But very few people left the line.

We eventually reached the shelter of the Abbey, and the wait, for me at least, had been well worth it. I was awestruck by the beauty of the building and by the reverent quietness, broken only by the sound of shuffling feet and the occasional cough. There were tall candles in beautiful candlesticks and a pervasive aroma of hot wax; a smell I'd always liked. The king himself was a disappointment. He looked quite ordinary—no crown, just a rather tired looking old man—but I had seen all the things on my wish list: a king, a real dead person in a coffin, and the inside of the Abbey, so I was happy. Cold, but happy. (I recently learned that it might have been Westminster Hall, not the Abbey. But it was my first exposure to an interior of such grandeur, and I was duly impressed.)

The walk home warmed us up a bit, but I couldn't wait to take off my sopping wet shoes. And then it felt really good to sit in front of the fire drinking hot cocoa, thawing out my freezing feet. While Mum fussed about my shoes and coat, grumbling that they wouldn't be dry in time for school the next morning, I told Dad what I had seen. He was amused by my disappointment and pleased when I told him, after Mum left the room, that I was glad I'd gone to see the king and the Abbey—crown or no crown.

During the next few months there was a lot of talk about the royal family, as the Duke of Windsor struggled to choose between the throne and Mrs. Simpson. Most people in Waterloo were all for the Duke marrying the woman he loved *and* staying on as king. The fact that she was a divorcee raised few eyebrows, and the objections of the rest of the royal family marked them as "ol' stuffed shirts." Most people really liked the Duke of Windsor and admired his eventual decision to renounce the throne in favor of his true love, although they were sad to lose him as their king. Not so sad, however, that they didn't have a good time celebrating the coronation of the new king, his brother, a little later. Every street had a party, with long food-laden tables set up along the road (devoid of dustcarts, that day), and everyone got a Coronation mug emblazoned with pictures of the new king and queen and the two little princesses. On principle, my mother refused to accept her mug, but she let us three keep ours.

My only other brush with the Royals came later that year, when Princess Elizabeth came to Waterloo to award prizes in a garden contest. A garden contest in Waterloo? Someone's idea of bad joke, surely? But it wasn't a joke to those proud gardeners who, inspired by the contest, had tilled their unpromising patches of mud, many for the first time. Harry was one of them. He and Louie had recently moved to Aquinas Street, and, as occupants of a ground floor flat, had access to the garden at the back. It was a typical small area, about twenty feet square, surrounded by a high brick wall, and was nothing but packed dirt when Harry started digging. A complete novice, he turned out to have a talent for gardening and quickly transformed that unpromising patch, creating flowerbeds on three sides and a pocket-handkerchief of a lawn in the middle. His color scheme and layout—rows of red geraniums, white alyssum, and blue lobelia—was too regimented for my taste, but I never dared tell him this. However, the judges liked it, and Harry was awarded second prize, to his, and Louie's, immense pride and satisfaction.

For some reason, I was chosen to present a bouquet to Princess Elizabeth when she gave out the awards, and was carefully schooled in what to do: walk s-l-o-w-l-y, the bouquet across my outstretched hands, curtsy, give her the bouquet, curtsy again, and then walk s-l-o-w-l-y away *backwards*. Under no circumstances, I was solemnly told, turn your back on the princess.

Apparently, one just did not do that to a royal personage—even though she was a mere slip of a girl, not much older than I was.

I practiced this routine carefully, but no one prepared me for the fact that the ceremony took place on a raised platform. This made me feel very exposed, and I was already self-conscious and nervous, convinced I would drop the bouquet or fall flat on my face. However, all went well until I started walking backwards after presenting the bouquet—and realized that I didn't know where the edge of the platform was. Panic-stricken, I abandoned the protocol, turned my back on Her Royal Highness and made a dash for the steps, back down to *terra firma*.

I flung myself into Louie's arms, thoroughly humiliated, because everyone was laughing at my pell-mell flight across the stage. But I wondered what the consequences of my transgression might be. What did they do to people who broke that solemn rule? I knew that traitors used to be thrown in the Tower of London, but didn't think that was still done. And my offense hardly warranted such an extreme measure, surely. After all, people had laughed about it. And my mother was tickled pink that I had broken The Rule, had actually turned my back on a royal personage—so she clearly wasn't anticipating some dire punishment for me. When nothing happened, no one came to clap me in irons, my fears subsided. But I felt thoroughly confused: why all that fuss if it didn't really matter?

I never again got closer to a member of the royal family, dead or alive, than an image on a screen. Maybe *that* was the Royals' punishment for having broken The Rule ... no more bouquet presentations to princesses.

Chapter 10

Sunday Morning at the Hodds'

Sunday morning in Waterloo. Quiet streets with no clattering of horses' hooves, or rumbling of iron-rimmed cart wheels over cobblestones where these still exist; no roar of huge Bowater lorries, engines straining to get their enormous loads moving—those massive rolls the width of the lorry and stacked like a display of toilet paper for giants. Quiet streets, but busy kitchens. In every basement, all is hustle and bustle; the big meal of the week is under way; and it has to be ready by one o'clock, when the man of the house reappears after slaking his thirst "dahn the local."

I often slept over with Viley on Saturday nights, so I became part of the Hodds' particular brand of Sunday morning craziness. It always started with sizzling noises and wonderful smells wafting up from the kitchen, where a traditional English breakfast was being cooked: a great fry-up of eggs, bacon, sausages and fried bread (always), with fried leftover potatoes (sometimes). On weekday mornings, as they chomped on the usual breakfast of bread-and-butter-and-jam with a cup of tea, everyone looked forward to this Sunday morning treat. It was judged to be well worth the huge pile of greasy plates to be washed afterwards—especially by the men-folk, who played no part in either cooking or clean up.

When everyone had eaten their fill, the men sat around the fire, smoking and reading the paper, while the ladies of the household cleared the table, washed the dishes, and then went upstairs to tackle the beds. For this was the day on which every bed was stripped, feather mattresses and pillows plumped, and sheets changed. Last week's top sheet became the coming week's bottom sheet, this being long before the days of fitted sheets, and each bed got a clean, carefully ironed, delicious-smelling, top sheet. All this sheet changing was in preparation for Monday's Washing Day; a ritual that was adhered to as religiously as Sunday church going might be in small towns and villages. Failure to attend church was the norm here and caused no comment.

I did not know anyone who went to church or Sunday school, but woe betides the woman whose washing wasn't hanging on the line by mid-day Monday. "Wassa mat'er wiv' *'er?*" The question ricocheted from neighbor to neighbor. How did she expect to get through her weekly routine? To get her washing dry in time for Tuesday's ironing? So she could do the bedrooms on Wednesday? The rest of the house on Thursday? The kitchen floor and the big shop on Friday? Only sluts failed to keep this routine. And once acquired, that label was hard to shed.

Viley and I invented a game centered on all the feathers that flew during the Sunday plumping of mattresses and pillows. We kept feathers in the air by blowing them up as high as we could, to give ourselves time to catch them before they hit the floor, and we ran around like mad things, puffing and snatching, squealing and shrieking, the goal being to catch the most feathers. I used my catch to make miniature pillows for a family of tiny celluloid dolls by stuffing the captured feathers into the toe of a discarded stocking and tying the open end with a ribbon or a bit of string. To my mother's annoyance, the knot invariably came undone, and feathers leaked out, so, in self defense, she taught me how to sew; after which, it was not feathers that provoked her wrath, but the sewing needles that I left lying around.

The last upstairs-Sunday-morning-chore in the Hodd household was mopping the bedroom floors to clear them of feathers and dust; dust that, in a corner of the world with many coal fires and much heavy traffic, had accumulated since Wednesday's bedroom-cleaning onslaught. Not until the last mop had been shaken out of the last window, could the really serious business of the day be tackled: cooking Sunday dinner.

The coal-burning range was kept well stoked to get the oven ready for the joint and roast potatoes—Yorkshire pudding, too, if beef was on the menu. On warm days, the kitchen became unbearably hot, even with its one large window wide open; but in Britain's chilly northern climate this was the exception rather than the rule. More often the problem was one of crowding, the kitchen being the only heated room in the house, and a typical Sunday morning in the Hodds' kitchen was not unlike rush hour in Grand Central Station.

In particular the big shallow sink, with its one cold tap, was in great demand. Everyone needed to "'ave a wash"; the men had to shave; and Louie and Rosie were both courting and anxious to wash their precious silk stockings after a Saturday night out with their "fellas." Lots of hot water was the order of the day, and kettle after kettle went on the rings of the old multi-purpose range. Adding to this Sunday morning sink-frenzy, there were potatoes to peel and vegetables to prepare. In fine weather an outside faucet relieved the pressure, and I have very pleasant memories of sitting out there in the sun with Viley, peeling potatoes, shucking peas, and exchanging Knock-Knock jokes. But most of the time, there was fierce competition for the kitchen sink, and tempers got frayed. On one particularly memorable Sunday morning, Rosie wanted to wash her hair:

"Wash yer 'air? *On a Sundee mornin'?* Don't be s'daft!" said Aunt-Mum.

"Oh, *please!* I gotta a wash it," pleaded Rosie. "Me'n Perce'r goin' out t'night."

"Ya should'a fought about that when yew 'ad yer barf on Frid'y night. Why did'ncha wash it then?"

"I was too tired."

"Too *tired?* A young fing like yew? I'm the one wha' should'a bin tired … luggin' the barf in … then 'eatin' up all tha' wa'er. Well, yew've only go' yerself t'blame, me lady. The sink's too busy nah, so ya'll just 'ave t'lump it. So will Perce … I 'spect 'e'll still love ya. Even if ya *do* 'ave greasy 'air!"

Rosie was petite, but her feistiness was legendary. She was not one to give up easily. "It was real late be the time I got my barf. I was last, remember? An' there wasn't much 'ot wa'er when Georgie'd finished … ya know wha' a pig 'e is! Anyway," she added, "it was so late tha' if I *'ad* washed me 'air, it would've bin wet when I went ta bed … "

Rosie had played a trump card. Going to bed with wet hair was regarded as highly undesirable, if not outright dangerous. So Aunt-Mum relented and let Rosie wash her hair. This delayed the vegetable preparations, and Louie and Viley were still chopping cabbage when Uncle Ernie appeared, wanting to wash and shave before going to the pub. They had reached a point of no return with the cabbage, so he had to wait until the sink was clear. Never a patient man, he was in a touchy mood this particular morning and got crosser and crosser as the minutes ticked by.

I loved Uncle Ernie's great belly laugh, and the way he picked me up when we met on the street and twirled me around till I was dizzy. But I was more than a little afraid of this tall, gaunt man with his beak of a nose, stony-gray eyes, and large, bony hands. He had a harsh voice too, and often raised it in anger for he had a decidedly short fuse; when he got "riled up," I was terrified by all the storming and ranting and banging of fists on the table. His anger was short-lived and never, ever, directed at me, though. *That*, I didn't understand. And I often wondered whether Viley was the unfortunate recipient of my share of Uncle Ernie's wrath.

My guilt on this score peaked one night when Viley and I sat by the fire, hogging the two little fireside seats that doubled as coal bins, contentedly reading our way through a pile of old comics and chewing gum. Uncle Ernie hated gum chewing, but we thought he was down the pub for the evening—until he walked through the door, catching us both in mid-chew. He was livid. "'Ow many times do I 'ave ta tell yew? *I won't 'ave that stuff in this 'ouse!* Are ya deaf? Or daft?" he yelled at Viley. She started to cry and threw her gum into the fire, but it stuck on one of the hot bars and the sizzling infuriated Uncle Ernie even more.

"Ach ... ya stoopid li'l bitch! Yew'd bet'er clean that mess awf in the mornin', or I'll skin yew alive. Jus' get out of me sight, now, before I tan yer 'ide!" He started to reach for his belt, but Viley dodged past him and ran upstairs, leaving me, gum in hand, wondering what this angry man would say and do to me. But he said nothing: acted like I wasn't there; and I couldn't stand the unfairness any longer. I burst into tears, threw *my* gum into the fire—where it also stuck sizzling on a hot bar—and dashed upstairs to Viley's bedroom, where we commiserated with one another for the rest of the evening.

The next day when Uncle Ernie related this story, he seemed to find it a huge joke, but I didn't see what was funny. However, that did mark the end of my gum-chewing days; gum simply never tasted the same again. As for the pink wads of bubble gum—that makes bubbles big enough to smear over your face if they pop—I never had the courage to chew that stuff after a boy told me that it would wrap around your heart and kill you if you swallowed it.

On this particular Sunday morning, I could see the thunderclouds gathering as Uncle Ernie waited his turn at the sink. Hoping to escape unnoticed, I crept under the kitchen table, where I was hidden by a tablecloth so large that its fringed border touched the ground, forming a cave into which I could disappear and be cut off from the world, apart from glimpses of passing feet. It was one of my favorite places to be, and I spent hours under that table, playing with Aunt-Mum's box of buttons. But Viley was too big for the luxury of retreating under the table with a seven-year-old, so she was trapped at the sink. As she chopped away at a mountain of cabbage, she became the focus of her father's irritation; and, not being a skilled cabbage-chopper, her ineptness eventually made Uncle Ernie boil over. "Fer Christ's sake, 'urry up, can'cha! I don't wanna stand 'ere all bloody mornin', watchin' yew mess about there," he thundered.

In her effort to hurry, poor Viley cut her finger. She tried to ignore the cut, with disastrous results: for soon there was blood all over the chopped cabbage. The chopping had to cease while her finger was bandaged, and every piece of cabbage had to be re-washed and re-drained. By this time Uncle Ernie was beside himself: "Yer more soddin' noosance than yer worf. Why don'cha just git yerself out of the way! Go fer a walk ... or somethin' ... an' take that one wiv' ya!" I could *feel* his callused finger pointing at me ... he *had* seen me scuttle under the table. Very little escaped that eagle eye.

Viley and I were only too happy to escape from the scene of battle, and we hastily got ready to go out, grumbling a bit about having to fuss with Sunday coats and Sunday shoes instead of slipping into comfy work-a-day stuff. But we knew that nothing less was acceptable for a Sunday morning. We were almost ready when Viley discovered that one of her garters was missing. She was afraid to go without it, fearful that, if she returned with one sock drooping around her ankle, Uncle Ernie would be angry at her "fer lookin' like a bloomin' ragamuffin." After an unavailing search of the bedroom, she said anxiously, "I fink it mus' be in the kitchin. 'Cos I was still gettin' dressed when Louie arst me ta come an' 'elp. We'll 'ave ta go an' look fer it there."

To our dismay, Uncle Ernie was still shaving, peering into the little hinged circular mirror that hung on the wall as he cut great swathes through the lather on his face with a cutthroat razor. I hung back in the doorway while Viley crept in and started looking around, but Uncle Ernie spotted her in the mirror and turned around to yell, "Yew li'l blighters! Ain'cha gone *yet?*"—And cut his chin. We didn't wait for further developments. Still garter-less, Viley grabbed my hand, and we fled.

Relieved to be out of the house, we decided to go across Blackfriars Bridge, along the embankment, then back across Westminster Bridge—a walk that I loved. Approaching Blackfriars, on the south bank of the river, we went past a great mix of warehouses and factories, the tallest of which was the OXO tower. This was my favorite among these otherwise nondescript buildings, because, near its pointed top, the letters O, X, O were boldly displayed in red lights, day and night. On this Sunday morning, the business buildings were silent, but from many pubs spilled bursts of raucous laughter and loud singing accompanied by pianos and accordions. A few pubs were quiet and peaceful, however; in these, if a door swung open, we caught a glimpse of old men smoking pipes and playing cribbage, and we could hear the occasional "thunk" of a dart hitting a dartboard against the murmur of voices and the chinking of glasses.

The moment we turned to cross Blackfriars Bridge, we entered a new world: one that was wide and open and no longer hemmed in by buildings. The sky above and the swirling, brown river below gave a sense of being suspended in space—until a double decker bus rumbled by and spoiled the illusion. And then, at the far side of the bridge, where we turned along the Embankment, yet another world greeted us.

We now had the river on our left and, on our right, a wide road and lots of big important-looking buildings; but they were set back a long way, so there was still a feeling of space, compared with the crowded south bank. Also, in sharp contrast with the London that we knew on a daily basis, this road was tree-lined on both sides. On our side, the south bank, there was not a tree, anywhere—even in the pocket-handkerchief of an asphalt park where we played on the swings and seesaws.

Here on the north bank, the people were different, too. They dressed differently, talked differently, even walked differently. Some were regular toffs: the men had sharp creases in their trousers, wore gloves, and took off their hats and bowed their heads slightly to elegantly dressed women; the women also wore gloves and expensive-looking hats, and clicked along with confident strides in shiny high-heeled shoes. Their clothes, without exception, looked brand new, and Viley murmured, "All so posh!" hurriedly pulling up her drooping garterless sock. And we were glad, after all, to be wearing our Sunday best.

There were also a number of poor old tramps dressed in rags, many layers of rags, who shuffled along carrying bulging bags or pushing battered prams that housed all their worldly possessions. Some sat dozing, or lay stretched out asleep in the seat-lined stone bays that jutted out every hundred yards or so from the embankment and overlooked the river. Viley and I loved to climb onto those stone seats and walk around the bays, staring down at the water; we could pretend that we were on a boat, or in a castle tower acting as lookouts for the approaching enemy, or perchance, a prince on a white horse. But we gave a wide berth to any bay with a resident tramp; in part because we felt as superior to the tramps as, we supposed, the toffs felt to us; but mainly because these dirty, unkempt, hunched-over creatures struck a deep chord of fear in us.

Even the quiet ones scared us, the ones who muttered to themselves and kept their eyes on the ground, seeking to avoid all possibility of contact with the rest of the human race. This, of course, had the desired result: the rest of the human race, like Viley and me, went out of its way to avoid contact. The wild-eyed tramps, the ones that gesticulated frantically as they declaimed about salvation and Judgment Day and the Wrath of the Lord, they were truly terrifying. Rather than walk past one of these scary creatures, we crossed the road, or even turned back on ourselves. I often tried to find out where these poor souls went at night and in cold rainy weather, but never got an answer that made sense. I was told that they curled up in a doorway or under a bridge, wrapped in newspapers or in a cardboard box if they were lucky. That didn't seem probable to me. I wasn't prepared to believe that the rest of the world would simply shrug their shoulders and let this happen.

The Embankment's wide sidewalk was also home to lots of pavement artists. I had no artistic talent myself, and was captivated by these garish pictures: brilliant sunsets, luxuriant flowers, storm-tossed boats, portraits of famous people, and sentimental pictures of dogs and babies. I would have given my right arm (or maybe the left) to be able to draw like this ... and so swiftly! They started with a clean pavement every day, so every one of these pictures had been drawn that very morning. I found this awesome and couldn't bear to think that these masterpieces were doomed to be obliterated at the end of the day. By whom? I wondered. Street cleaners? The police? Or did pavement artists erase their own pictures every night, before they left for home? Where *was* home for them? Did extraordinary people like them live in ordinary houses? Did they have children? Were there children who could say if asked, "My Dad's a pavement artist"? I never did get answers to these questions.

Neither did I get my wish that some of the artists would come to our side of the river. In a few places, the sidewalk was wide enough, but when I mentioned this to my Dad one day, he said, pointing to the sixpences, shillings—even half-crowns—that passers-by had thrown into the artist's up-turned cap on the pavement, "Jus' look at all that silver. On our side, there'd be nothin' but farthin's, ha'pennies an' per'aps a few pennies." And I realized that he was right; it would never happen.

The best part of this walk was the approach to Westminster Bridge, with Big Ben looming bigger and bigger. There was always the hope of being right underneath when it boomed out the hour—so close that the sound seemed to be inside your head. As I lay in bed, I could always hear the chimes of Big Ben, sometimes loud, other times faint, depending on the wind, I was told. It never ceased to amaze me that the sound could travel such a long way—a distance that it took me an hour to walk! On this particular Sunday, we were too early for Big Ben's most spectacular performance, the striking of twelve, and we couldn't wait around, or we'd be late for dinner.

As we crossed Westminster Bridge, there was a strong gusty wind that played havoc with hair and plucked a lot of hats from a lot of heads. The sight of spiffy grown-ups chasing their hats and clutching what had been well-coifed hair-dos set us both giggling, especially when the wind whisked a hat away again, just as its owner reached down to grab it. Then we noticed how comical *we* looked—our hair streaming out behind if we faced into the wind and out in front if we faced the other way—and pointed at one other, shrieking with laughter. When we found that we couldn't walk straight, because the wind was buffeting us around, the giggling got out of control. "Ev'ryone must fink we've spent the mornin' in the pub," Viley spluttered, and we laughed till tears ran down our cheeks. We ended up walking sideways, leaning back into the wind, but it was so gusty that we were in constant danger of falling backward or pitching forward. By this time, we were weak with laughter, which didn't help our endeavors to keep upright. Our mirth proved to be infectious, and a number of fellow strugglers-with-the-wind stopped and laughed with us—which, of course, made us laugh harder. Afterwards, neither of us could say just why we found all this so terribly funny but, for a long time, any mention of it was liable to set us giggling helplessly.

Once off the bridge, the wind was from behind and helped to hurry us home along York Road. For we were in danger of being late for dinner, an unpardonable offense in Uncle Ernie's eyes—Aunt-Mum's, too, after all the effort she'd put into its production. When we opened the door, that incomparable mix of Sunday dinner smells—roast lamb, mint sauce, apple pie and custard—greeted us. Judging by the sounds from the kitchen, dinner was not yet served up, so we scuttled upstairs to tidy our hair before hurrying down to take our places at the table. It was already set, we saw, guiltily; that was supposed to be *our* job. We were just in time. Viley's drooping garter-less sock was out of sight under the table only moments before Uncle Ernie came in.

Aunt-Mum always invited the sweethearts of her offspring for Sunday dinner, so there was quite a crowd round that big oval table. To every-one's relief, Uncle Ernie had got over the morning's fiasco and was in a good mood, despite the little piece of blood-soaked tissue still stuck on his chin. He even commented on our rosy wind-blown cheeks and asked if we'd had a good walk. We simply nodded and smiled. Silence seemed safer than speech, which had the potential to start us giggling all over again.

The meal was progressing happily when Uncle Ernie suddenly pushed his chair back and bellowed, *"Wha' the H-e-l-l ... "* In his hand was a cabbage-laden fork, poised in mid-air, and he was staring at it in pop-eyed disbelief. We all stared, too. *And saw Viley's missing garter, dangling from his fork!* So it *had* been in the kitchen ... in the chopped cabbage.

Uncle Ernie's face turned brick red, and before he exploded, I bolted from the kitchen. I hid under Louie's bed, a big double bed that she shared with Viley, in the room that they both shared with Rosie. The bed was pushed against the wall in a corner, so you could scramble to the farthest corner, and it made a marvelous hidey-hole, second only to the "cave" under the kitchen table. Poor Viley, she had to stay and face her father's fury. I could hear the ranting and raving and lay there on my tummy, biting my nails and feeling guilty—once again—that I'd escaped Uncle Ernie's wrath and Viley hadn't. At last she came running upstairs, flung herself on the bed, sobbing, and I lay on the bed with my arm across her heaving back, weeping with her.

After we'd calmed down, she told me that Rosie made things worse by snickering at the sight of the dangling garter, and then Georgie burst out laughing. Soon everybody was laughing except for Uncle Ernie—and Viley, who didn't dare. In a misguided attempt to back up the laughers, Aunt-

Mum further aggravated the situation: "Aw, come on Ernie! Can'cha see the funny side? A bloomin' *garter* in yer cabbage! Ya should'a seen yaw face!" she guffawed. At least, Viley said, by this time her father was furious with everybody, not just with her.

Viley and I never got to finish our Sunday dinner. We stayed in the bedroom while Uncle Ernie snored through his Sunday afternoon kip in the room next door, and Louie smuggled up some pudding and a pile of old comics to keep us out of mischief. We'd already read the comics at least once, but that didn't matter—it being a curious feature of comics that second, even third, readings were almost as pleasurable as the first—so the afternoon was not so bad after all. As Sunday afternoons went.

The Tale of the Garter-in-the-Cabbage became one of the Hodds' oft-told favorites, and, eventually, even Uncle Ernie was able to laugh about it. But, thereafter, Viley was always careful to have both garters in place before helping in the kitchen.

Chapter 11

Another Memorable Birthday

THE NEXT MEMORABLE BIRTHDAY was my eighth; but, unlike the fifth, it was memorable for reasons other than being celebrated. Birthdays still rarely got more than a passing acknowledgment, so I hadn't been expecting much. Especially since my father had been ill in bed for the last week or so. But it was a big surprise when Mum wouldn't let me go in to see Dad before breakfast, as I always did when he was ill. My hand was already on the knob of their bedroom door when she stopped me and said I couldn't go in.

"P'raps later?" I said.

But the answer was firm: "No. 'E jus' can't see ya t'day." I stood there in disbelief. She couldn't mean it. Couldn't see me today? On my birthday! That hurt, no matter how ill Dad might be. I wandered back downstairs and resolved to try again, later. And try I did. But the door was locked. *Locked*? I'd never encountered a locked door before—not even the front door. "Whatever for? We ain't got nothin' worth pinchin'," Mum always said, and I wasn't aware that we even *possessed* keys for inside doors. I couldn't ask Mum about it, or she'd know that I'd tried again to get in and see Dad. She seemed more than usually busy and pre-occupied, and I spent a long dreary day, consumed with growing resentment at both my parents.

Next morning, I tried their bedroom door again, but it was still locked, and Mum found me there, rattling the doorknob. That was when she broke the news. My father had died, early the day before. She hadn't told me yesterday, because she hadn't wanted to spoil my birthday. I don't remember my mother putting her arms around me, or trying to comfort me in any way. And chances are that she didn't do either. That just wasn't her style. All I remember is feeling stunned and speechless, as we stood there in the dark corner outside the locked bedroom. Then came sounds of a ruckus, and Mum went downstairs to see what Bertie and Derek were up to, leaving me there alone.

I don't know how long I stood in the dark, by that locked door, numb and dry-eyed, before I dragged myself upstairs. I couldn't face Grampa Benson's habitual cheeriness, so I crept past his open door, relieved that he didn't call out and invite me in. I'm sure his sharp hearing told him that I was there, but he undoubtedly knew the situation and wisely recognized that I would want to be alone for a while. But just in case, I climbed as quietly as I could up the next flight of stairs to the top bedroom that I shared with the two boys.

It was the only room in the house with two windows, so it was the brightest and most cheerful, and I had always liked it for that reason; but on this occasion, I was grateful that the sun wasn't shining. I found even the grayness of January too bright and longed for the shadows I had just left, in that corner outside my parents' bedroom, the room where my dead father lay. But there were no curtains to draw, and all I could do to escape the unwelcome brightness was to lie facedown on the bed, with my head under the pillow.

As I lay in this self-imposed darkness I slowly realized that, in my stunned state, I hadn't even asked Mum if Dad *was* still in their bedroom. The locked door probably meant that he was. I desperately needed to know what that door was keeping me from—or keeping from me. Was Dad still in the bed, the bed in which he and Mum had always slept? Did he die in that bed? In that familiar, comfy brass bed? The bed, in which he'd so often lain and let me bounce on his chest, showing off my counting skills: one bounce for each count. A memory suddenly surfaced, of being terribly disappointed one morning when he'd declined to let me demonstrate that I could count up to one thousand. Not even *his* patience had stretched that far. Though it might have, I now thought, had he known that I then firmly believed that 1000 followed 299. More and more memories bubbled up, and each one made me want to weep. Yet I don't remember crying. Either then, or later that day. Not until the day of the funeral did the tears come, and I suppose I must have seemed a heartless little wretch, a "Daddy's Girl," who couldn't squeeze out a tear for him. Yet, here I am, decades later, still mourning his loss.

It is hard to remember exactly what I felt as I lay there, hiding from the light, other than a general sense that my world had been diminished, that a great, gray emptiness yawned. The only emotion that stands out clearly is anger, anger that grew relentlessly. At first, it was anger at Mum, for telling me what she just had. Then it was anger at Dad, for not being there yesterday, and today ... and tomorrow. It gradually sank in that he would never be there, for any of the tomorrows ... and I grew even angrier with Mum for not waking me to say goodbye to him. As I remembered how angry I'd been at Dad when told, "'E jus' can't see ya t'day," the anger with my mother turned to fury. How could she have let that happen? If *only* she had told me yesterday. How could I live with the fact that my last feeling for my father—when I thought he was still alive—had been anger? It was more than I could bear to think about; I actually *hated* my mother for her part in this.

Yet, poor woman, she'd acted for what she saw as the best. I see that now. What I didn't understand at the time is that parents suffer not only their own losses, but their children's, too. All this flashed through my mind, years later, when I was forced to watch our daughters struggling to come to terms with serious problems in their first-borns: one, with a baby having seizures, the other, with a three-year-old autistic. For us as grandparents, the grief was threefold: for ourselves, for those two grandchildren, and for our daughters. We had no way to alleviate their suffering, could do little more than stand by, watching helplessly; only then, did I begin to appreciate what my mother went through on that January day, the day that left her, husband-less, to deal with her all her grief alone.

It must have been a terrible, terrible, day for her: suddenly a widow, at age thirty-seven, with three young children, the oldest eight years old that very day. Just thinking about what the future might hold for the four of us must have been terrifying. And she had to break the news of their father's death to those three children, had to tell one that it had happened on her birthday. My mother had more than her share of grief that day; yet, in her typically undemonstrative way, she displayed none in front of us children. And as I lay on the bed at the top of the house, my head under a pillow, engulfed by my own misery, I was totally unaware of *her* suffering. What was growing in me was not sympathy but rage, rage directed at her. I have since come to see that it was no wonder that anger was the emotion to surface on that bleak, January day. It was, after all, the only emotion we were allowed to display freely in our little family—in common with most Waterloo families, I would hazard a guess. Other emotions were firmly discouraged, were to be suppressed and not shown in public. Like my mother's grief that day.

It took several months to grasp the full implications of my fatherless state: no more evenings on Dad's lap, reading a newspaper to him, or him reading to me and introducing me to the delights of the written word; no more Sunday morning walks with him in St. James's Park or through the quiet, echoing streets of the City of London.

Those City streets, so busy on weekdays, were calm on Sunday mornings, empty of all but a few leisurely strollers like ourselves and head-bobbing pigeons that strutted around, cooing contentedly; even the marble-clad, important-looking buildings seemed to enjoy that day of rest. Never again would my father point out the ones that he had helped build—a mere humble laborer, carrying bricks and shoveling dirt, but I'd loved to hear him talk about his part in all this. It made me feel connected to a world built for important people and important transactions, a world so much larger and grander than the mean streets of Waterloo

Then came the crushing realization that no longer was Dad there for me to bounce questions off. I was in the habit of saving them up for him, because other adults were either too busy or couldn't be bothered to address my childish puzzlement, such as: What is under the road we're walking on? Why does the Thames keep rising and falling? What is wind? Why does the moon keep changing shape?

Suddenly I recalled with a pang walking down a hill one windy night, Mum holding one hand and Dad the other, and noticing a full moon scudding across the sky. Why wasn't it just sitting still, like it usually did, I asked, and Dad explained, in his patient way, that it only looked like the moon was moving—really it was the clouds, being blown across the sky in front of it. I stood still, like he suggested, and looked at the moon carefully to convince myself that he was right. But as soon as I started walking, the moon once more seemed like it was racing across the night sky—until I stood still again.

It was devastating to think that there would be no more occasions like that, no Dad to take questions seriously and answer them to the best of his ability, no grown-up who wouldn't either laugh at me, or—what was even more annoying—at the question itself.

As these realizations washed over me, one by one, in the months after my father died, I felt an overwhelming sense of loss; and it grew, inexorably, along with anger at my unsuspecting mother. As the years passed, each time she added another "sin," real or imagined, for me to be furious about, that anger went up another notch. I neither showed it, nor was I able to talk about it with her; and this troubled me greatly. But in retrospect, I'm glad that she never did know just how angry I felt—or for how long. And I am thankful that she lived to a ripe old age, long enough for the anger to finally subside and for us to be friends.

Chapter 12

A Shifting Landscape

THE FUNERAL TOOK PLACE a week or so later. During that time Dad lay in his coffin in the front room, and the door was kept locked—so there was a key for this room, too—opened only for visiting friends and relatives, who'd come to pay their respects. Not until the morning of the funeral were we three children allowed to go in, and then only for a short time.

It didn't look like our familiar front room. The furniture had been pushed aside, and the coffin was in the middle, on some kind of a trestle. Derek and Bertie weren't tall enough, so they had to be lifted up to see Dad, and as I stood there, waiting my turn, I couldn't help thinking back to King George. Little had I imagined then, as I gazed on a king who died the day before my seventh birthday, that one year later, I'd be looking into another coffin, at my father, who had died on my next birthday.

When Mum told us that we could go in, just to say goodbye to Dad, I'd imagined that I would give him a goodbye kiss. But, confronted with his white, waxen face and firmly closed eyes, I hesitated, and it was a relief to find that, in any case, I wasn't tall enough to bend over and reach his face for a kiss. I had somehow expected his eyes to be open; that was the way I always pictured him in my mind, and it was a blow not to see those soft, brown eyes for what I had known would be the last time. The finality of those closed lids brought home to me, as nothing else had up to that point, that he really was gone. And I had the exact same reaction, fifty years later, when I gazed at my mother in *her* coffin, though I *was* tall enough to plant a kiss on her—oh, so cold—forehead. But, again, it was the tightly shut eyes that brought recognition of the final reality of death.

I couldn't walk away from my Dad, just like that, so I asked timidly, "C'n I touch 'im?" When Mum said, "O' course yew can," I touched my fingertips to his forehead, and its coolness remains a vivid, vivid, memory. Like the closed eyes, that chilly skin was a stark reminder that the Dad I'd known was no more. But I now felt that I had, in some manner, said goodbye to him, and, after a long, last look at his pale, immobile face, I left the room, slowly and reluctantly, yet anxious to leave behind the sweetish smell of unembalmed death.

Shortly after, the sealed coffin, with a few wreaths of flowers on top, was carried out to the waiting hearse, and Mum and a few relatives climbed into an old-fashioned, big-wheeled, shiny black carriage, pulled by splendid black horses. A small crowd had gathered, as always, to watch a funeral. We three children stood at the curb, too, for it had been decided that we would not be going to the cemetery. The boys were quite put out by this and felt cheated of a horse-and-carriage ride, but I was secretly relieved that I wouldn't have to see the coffin lowered into a hole in the ground and covered over with dirt. The little procession was about to leave when something startled one of the horses, making it rear up, jolting the carriage backwards, and I had to quickly jump clear of its big wheel. (Memories of that moment flooded back, eerily, when I saw an identical incident in a Bergman movie.) It was a nasty surprise, but it delayed the departure for the cemetery only a minute or two, and then we three went back indoors after watching the carriages till they disappeared from view around the corner.

The sickly-sweet odor of death lingered for a while, but even when the last trace had gone, I never felt the same about the front room. It had been my favorite place in the house, partly because it contained our only comfy, stuffed furniture—a recently acquired gray and lavender chesterfield with a matching armchair. They were old and shabby, and the nap was rather scratchy for bare legs but endlessly fascinating, because, like a cat's fur, it changed from smooth and shiny to rough and dull, depending which way it was stroked. I had loved curling up next to Dad on that roomy old sofa, stroking the nap first one way then the other, while he read to me in front of a fire, with the gas-light gently burbling and popping in the background.

Another attraction in that room was an ancient wind-up gramophone, for which we had acquired a few records from somewhere, classics such as "Down by the ol' Bull an' Bush" and "My Ol' Man Said Foller the Van". The tunes were barely decipherable through the hissing and clicking as the needle struggled to make its way along the scratched grooves, but we three never tired of listening to them, again, and again, and again. Until, inevitably, came the cry, "That's enough o' that!" and the gramophone lid was firmly closed. I never felt the same about my parents' bedroom, either: the room in which Dad died; the room in which I used to snuggle up with them in the old brass bed on Sunday mornings, reciting verses or multiplication tables. I had no desire to spend time in a room that stirred up such a mix of memories.

But our lives somehow went on. There'd been no money for black outfits, so, for the first year, we wore black bands sewn on our coat sleeves as a sign that we were "in morning" (which is how I heard it—and puzzled mightily that one could be in "morning" for a whole year). Mum had a black dress, and so did I, unfortunately. Louie was adamant about buying it for me, along with a pair of black patent leather shoes, insisting, over Mum's protests, "It's not right, May, fer 'er ta go tew 'er own far'ver's fun'ral in anyfink bu' black."

I'd always longed for black patent leather shoes, but I loathed the black frock. It was very plain, essentially a cylinder gathered in around the neck, "like a bloomin' sack o' pota'as," said Mum, when out of earshot of Louie. I agreed. It made overweight me look even fatter, and it was very itchy. "A loverly bit o' wool," Louie kept saying, as she rubbed a fold of the material between her fingers, and we felt obliged to politely murmur agreement. I had hoped that once the funeral was over, I would never wear the frock again, but Louie had other ideas. To make it less funereal, she added a frilly white collar, thus transforming it, she thought, into a perfect, everyday frock for school. She meant that in the sense of *every* day, I discovered. In deference to Louie, I wore that wretched frock until the weather got warm enough that even she conceded that wool "*was* a bit 'eavy."

The first day back to school after the funeral was a nightmare, a real live, non-dreaming-type nightmare. As I entered the classroom, a sea of pointing fingers and a great hoot of laughter greeted me: "Hey! Look! Dog Toby!" That stupid, frilly collar did indeed make me look like a circus dog, and the class fell about with laughter. I stood, crimson with humiliation, holding a note to excuse my absence for the funeral, and longed for a hole to open up and swallow me. *If only the carriage wheel had crushed me … I could have been lowered into the ground alongside Dad …* These thoughts raced unbidden through my head, and I found to my horror that I was weeping; the absolute last thing I wanted to do in front of the class.

But the jeering class had not reckoned with Mr. Slarks. In a thunderous voice, he silenced them, then sat me in the front row, so I didn't have to walk past rows of grinning kids to get to my usual seat, and gave me his handkerchief to wipe my eyes. He administered a tongue-lashing, the like of which none of us had ever heard. Never had we seen jovial Mr. Slarks *really* angry. No child in that room would soon forget it, and such was his hold over the affection and respect of his students, that none of them so much as snickered at me after that, not even on the playground. And not even though I had to wear that stupid frock every day, for weeks and weeks.

If I'd told Mum what happened that day, perhaps she would have persuaded Louie to let me off the hook about the frock, but I never told a soul. Too embarrassed? Humiliated? Ashamed? Too worried about Louie's hurt feelings, should she learn that her gift was not a resounding success? All of the above. But, most important of all, school and home were supposed to be separate worlds: school problems weren't taken home, and home difficulties were left behind, as you entered the schoolyard gate. That was, in part, why the Dog Toby incident was so painful. Family stuff had spilled into the classroom, and I wasn't about to let classroom stuff go in the other direction.

At home, we gradually settled into a new routine. With our father gone, Mum was the rock to which we three clung, but she was struggling to keep us afloat on a widow's pension and whatever rent Old Grampa Benson could squeeze out of his army pension. She never let on about these financial worries; all we heard was how grateful she was for that widow's pension, and how different things were in her parents' time when "it would've bin the work'ouse fer all of us." But the comforting little pension of eighteen shillings a week, much less than the dole money when Dad had been out of work, wasn't enough, and we had to go on Relief [Welfare]. Before long Uncle Bert, Mum's younger brother, came to lodge with us, and his room-and-board money helped, but not enough to actually get us off Relief. That had to wait till Mum found a cleaning job in a fish shop—possible now that Uncle Bert could watch us while she was gone, since she was back before he left for work.

Unfortunately, this improvement in our finances was short-lived: Mum's hand got infected—a fish-bone got jammed under her thumbnail—so, back on Relief we went until the hand healed, and she could look for another job. Though, with three school age children, her options were rather limited. Early-morning shop-cleaning jobs were snapped up within minutes of the posting of a Help Wanted sign in a shop window; and school-hour jobs, like housecleaning, were rare; few households within a bus ride of Waterloo had that kind of money. Even when working, Mum didn't earn much. Then, as now, cleaning jobs paid poorly and provided no fringe benefits: no sick days, no holidays, nothing other than a handful of cash at the end of each day. But she was never happier than when she could bring home that pitiful handful and get us off Relief.

The infected thumb gave us our one and only glimpse of our mother in tears. Every day she had to go to the hospital for her hand to be examined and cleaned—healing was slow in those pre-antibiotic days—and one rainy Saturday morning, she decided not to drag the three of us along with her. Uncle Bert was at work, so I was left in charge of the boys, with a long list of dos and don'ts and Grampa Benson as back up. The boys promised solemnly to do as I told them, but several things made the situation slip out of control: Mum was gone longer than expected; the rain stopped, and the boys went out to play in the garden; and I decided to wash the floor.

I'd never washed a floor before, but Mum's hand had prevented her from doing it, and I knew she was fretting about it being dirty, so this seemed a good opportunity to start. Feeling quite heroic, I got down on my knees and scrubbed and rinsed, like I'd seen Mum scrub and rinse on countless occasions, but it soon became apparent that this was not as simple as I thought. I couldn't wring out the cloth adequately—having recently sprained both wrists while learning how to roller skate—and the floor ended up clean but *very* wet. There were actual puddles in low spots, where the linoleum was a bit bumpy. This might not have mattered, but the boys kept trekking mud in from the garden, and soon my lovely washed floor was a sea of mud.

I was yelling at the boys to either stay out or stay in, one or the other, so that I could start again and try to get rid of the mud, when Mum walked in. She took in the devastation at a glance and started screaming at me for making such a mess, until the enormity of the mop-up operation, coupled with the pain of her throbbing thumb, overwhelmed her. She sank down into a chair, put her head down on her arms, and burst into tears.

The room was suddenly quiet, apart from her sobs, and we all stared at the spectacle of our mother crying. Then, already upset that my attempt to help had gone so wrong, and now this ... this frightening sight ... I started crying, and that set the boys off. Before long, the realization that we were all in tears brought Mum's crying jag to a stop, and she pulled herself together. She sent the boys upstairs to play in Grampa Benson's room, taught me how to wring more water out of a wet cloth, and, between us, we finished the job that I had started with such high hopes. We all recovered our equilibrium, of course, but that experience left its mark. The three of us had been really scared to witness our feisty, face-up-to-anything mother break down like that.

It wasn't long after that incident that we came home from school one day to find Uncle Bert in the kitchen, instead of Mum. This was very unusual. She was always there, but Uncle Bert explained that she'd gone after a job and would be back soon. Bertie, still a Mummy's boy, didn't like this and started to whine, "I want my Mummy ... I w-a-a-nt m-y M-u-m-m-y!" This was par for the course for Derek and me: Bertie often cried and grizzled if Mum was out of his sight, but Uncle Bert wasn't used to it, and after a few minutes, he could stand it no longer. "Stop that noise! Stop it, yew 'ear me ... ya li'l cry-baby!"

This simply made Bertie cry louder, "M-u-m-m-y! M-u-m-m-y! *I-I W-a-n-t M-y M--u--m--m---y!*" Uncle Bert's response was to grab the wailing child by the shoulders and shake him, yelling, "*Shuddup! Jus' shuddup, can'cha?*" When this didn't work, he shook again, harder. Bertie's cries got louder and louder, and Uncle Bert got angrier and angrier, until, crouching down with his scowling, red face right in front of Bertie's, he screamed, "*Shuddup!* Ya miserable li'l Mummy's boy! *Jus' shuddup!*"

Then, after a pause for breath, he added, "Anyway … she *aincha* Mummy! She's just yer *Auntie* … An' I ain't yer Uncle … *I'm yer far'ver!*"

Bertie's crying stopped abruptly, and there was silence, apart from the ticking of our one-legged, lop-sided alarm clock on the mantelpiece. Then Uncle Bert stood up, let go of Bertie and leaned in the open doorway, with his hand on the lift-latch of the door. A tall man, tall and thin, he was usually taciturn and not very friendly, but as he stood looming over us that day, I felt quite frightened of him and longed to hear Mum's footsteps coming down the stairs.

The three of us were in shock. We simply stared at him in silence, until Bertie started whimpering quietly. But soon came a quavering wail: "Mummy! M-u-m-m-y! … *I w-a-n-t m-y M-u-m-m-y!*" Instead of comforting the poor child—his own child, he'd just said—Uncle Bert bellowed, "I jus' told ya. *She ain't yer Mummy!*" Then he turned on his heels, stomped upstairs to his room, and slammed the door, hard.

We did our best to comfort Bertie, but he was still sobbing when Mum came home. Derek and I were in tears, too, by that time, but Mum quickly reassured us that she was still *our* mother, that Uncle Bert was not *our* father. However, there were no such reassurances for Bertie. It was true, she said, as gently as she could, holding him tightly on her lap; she wasn't his Mummy, and Uncle Bert *was* his Daddy; but, of course, she'd still take care of him, as if she *were* his Mummy; just like she always had.

I don't know which was worse: Uncle Bert's angry proclamation of fatherhood or Mum's reluctant confirmation of it. But poor Bertie. I can't imagine how he felt. He was only five years old, a little boy still. He'd recently lost the man he'd always known as Daddy, and now in the last half-hour, had lost his Mummy too. He'd spent much of his five years clinging to that Mummy, always unhappy when she was out of his sight. All he had now was an angry, cruel, new father—a man who had been a virtual stranger until he came to live with us after Dad died. For Uncle Bert had rarely come to see us in Dagenham, and neither had we seen much of him after we returned to London. On his infrequent visits, he'd always been Uncle Bert to the three of us and had never paid much attention to Bertie, his own son. I remember feeling stunned that a father could be so hidden, and for so long. For as long as I could remember.

Now that "the cat was out o' the bag", Mum told me how it had come about that Bertie lived with us: "Bertie's mother, Grampa Benson's on'y daugh'er, Mary—an' a beau'iful girl she was—well, she died soon after Bertie was born. Blood poisonin' it was, an' as soon as we 'eard, Lilly and me, we went up ta London ta see the poor li'l thing … An' what a scrawny scrap 'e was! Screamin' 'is 'ead off too … ya couldn't believe such a li'l thing could make s'much noise! An' kep' it up day an' night, 'e did, accordin' ta the nurses. The doctors, they told us 'e 'ad the blood poisonin' too … got it through Mary's milk … an' they didn't expect 'im ta live more than a few days." (It seems more likely that the infection was transmitted through Auntie Mary's bloodstream, but in the story, as told, the milk was the villain.)

After one look at this pathetic scrap of humanity, the two sisters decided that they couldn't leave him to spend what was left of his short life screaming, unattended, in a hospital ward. But … who could look after him? Auntie Lilly had four children and a difficult husband, and, while my mother had only one child, a toddler, she was three months pregnant with her second. Nobody else in the Wheatland clan, or in Grampa Benson's family, seems to have been considered as a surrogate parent, and it was finally agreed that Mum was in a better position than Lilly to take the baby. At least to begin with. Decisions about his long-term future would be put on hold, until they knew whether he had a future. The hospital staff was outraged. Such a sick baby needed to be in hospital, they contended, but Mum and Lilly argued, "Even if 'e dies a bit sooner, at least 'e'll get some love an' a bit o' cuddlin' while 'e *is* alive."

"After all," Mum always declared, "the on'y thing the 'ospital could do was feed 'im lots o' water, ta flush the poison out of 'is body. An' we c'd do that at 'ome, just as well. So Uncle Bert an' Lilly an' me, we all signed the forms, an' took Bertie out o' the 'ospital. In spite of what the doctors an' nurses said.

"On the Green Line bus, 'e screamed Bloody Murder all the way ta Dagenham. As we got off the bus, the conductor said, 'Thank Gawd! Now I'll be able ta 'ear meself fink. I'm jus' glad 'e ain't mine … Good luck t'yer, mates, is all I c'n say.' When we got indoors an' changed Bertie's nappy, we saw why the poor li'l scrap was screamin'. 'Is bot'om was red raw! I 'ad ta leave 'im without a nappy fer a few days so it could 'eal up. An' did we ever get sprayed, 'im bein' a boy an' all!"

After a couple of shaky weeks, contrary to all expectations, Bertie began to thrive. By the time he was four months old, his survival was no longer in doubt. "I was 'arf a mind ta take 'im back to the 'ospital an' say, 'See! Yew was all wrong!'" Mum chuckled. But she was, by then, well into her pregnancy and more than a little busy with this still demanding baby. So she never did, never got to savor her moment of triumph, except in private, day by day, as Bertie grew stronger.

Once it was clear that this frail baby was going to make it, Auntie Lilly wanted to help out by having Bertie spend six months with her and Uncle John, then six months with us. But my father wouldn't hear of it. "Yew can't do that ta the poor li'l devil—the boy needs a proper 'ome!" he protested. "If we 'ave 'im at all, we take 'im an' we keep 'im."

"Yer Dad knew on'y too well what it was ta be without a proper 'ome,"

Mum said. "When 'e was about seven, 'is own mother died after 'avin' twins, an' 'is father took one look at 'is dead wife, the newborn babies, an' the six other kids—an' did a bunk! A real rotter 'e was, ol' Bill Redfern. Never stayed around long after gettin' poor ol' Sarah in the fam'ly way, an' jus' showed up—cool as a cucumber—after each of the babies was born. Then, before ya could say 'Bob's yer uncle,' there'd be another one on the way … an' off 'e'd go agin!

"Anyway, 'e skedaddled after Sarah died, an' no one ever saw 'ide nor 'air of 'im agin. So all the kids was put in orphanages. All but the twins—what only lived a few days—an' Bill, the oldest boy. 'Cos 'e was thirteen, old enough t'go out ta work an' take care of 'imself. Catholic orphanages the others was in. Lizzie an' Annie was together in one fer Girls, an' yer Dad an' 'is older brother, Jack, in one fer Boys. But li'l Charlie, 'e went to a place fer toddlers, an' they didn't see 'im agin till 'e was old enough ta join yer Dad and Jack."

My father didn't get to see either of his sisters until after Lizzie, the older girl, left the Girls' orphanage at age thirteen and went out to work. It took her a while to find out where the boys were and save up for the fare to visit them. But after that she kept in touch with all of them and helped them out, one by one, as soon as they reached thirteen and were sent out into the world to take care of themselves. My mother had a very soft spot for Aunt Lizzie: "A good ol' soul she is! As rough an' ready as they come, but she was what kept that fam'ly from driftin' apart."

Derek and Bertie were often thought to be twins, but even those who knew that one was "adopted," always assumed that it was dark-eyed, dark-haired Derek, because Bertie looked like me—blue-eyed and blond. My parents treated them with spectacular disregard for the fact that one was not their own child, though Auntie Ada used to scold Mum, accusing her of spending too much time on Bertie, at Derek's expense. "When they was both toddlers, Derek used ta fall asleep on the floor," Auntie Ada often told me, still indignant at the memory. "Be'ind the bloomin' door ya'd find 'im, fast asleep, wiv 'is bum stuck up in the air. All becos' that muvver o' yourn was too busy wiv Bertie. Always made a fuss about goin' t'sleep, that one did. I used t'say to 'er, 'It's not fair, May. Derek needs yew as much as Bertie does. An' 'e is yer own flesh an' blood, after all. Yew'll be sorry fer this one of these days, yew mark my words.'" But Mum didn't see it that way. For her, Bertie was the needy child, and she doled out her attentions accordingly.

As far as I was concerned, I simply had two brothers who happened to be almost the same age. I had no idea that a six-month age difference was highly improbable. When the boys had started school, just before Dad died, I became aware that Bertie's last name was Wheatland, but this did not strike me as worthy of note. Quite a few families had more than one name, the 'Odds-an-'Arris clan being a familiar example. But after Uncle Bert's revelation the name difference had greater significance, and I started to wonder how many mixed-name families had similar stories tucked away.

My parents never formally adopted Bertie. They had a casual we'll-take-care-of-him arrangement with his father, who—when he had work—contributed two shillings a week for Bertie's keep. To put this princely sum in perspective, unemployment money was about seven shillings a week per person, and a widow's weekly pension paid five shillings for the first child and three for every subsequent one. Which means that Uncle Bert was stingier than the government when it came to providing for his only child ...

Bertie's mother was very young when she died. And Mum was right; she had indeed been lovely, as I discovered from a photo that Uncle Bert kept next to the alarm clock by his bed. That black-and-white photo drew me like a magnet draws a nail. I used to sneak into his room whenever I could, just to sit there, gazing at poor dead Auntie Mary. Her pale face was startlingly beautiful: long and thin, with high cheekbones and framed by a thick, tumbling mass of jet-black hair. The photographer had captured a pensive dreamy expression in her dark eyes, and it was a haunting image.

I yearned for such a face in place of the round, rosy-cheeked version that Nature had allotted me and practiced in front of the mirror, trying to reproduce the hint of an enigmatic smile on Auntie Mary's lips—a smile that I recognized, with a start, when I first saw the Mona Lisa painting. But it was hopeless: I just didn't have the makings of a romantic beauty like poor Auntie Mary, dead at such an early age. Her beauty somehow made her death more poignant. Although that idea troubled me and made me wonder, if I should die young, would I be mourned less because I was not beautiful? That didn't seem fair. Yet I could not shake the feeling that something special had been lost the day that lovely creature ceased to be.

The revelation of Bertie's real father, coming so soon after the death of my own, was deeply troubling. And not only because of the brutal manner in which it had been revealed. The fact that Dad, who'd seemed such a permanent part of our world, could disappear so suddenly, and Bertie's father could emerge so abruptly from the shadows where he had been lurking in the guise of an uncle, threw the whole institution of fatherhood into doubt. And it wasn't only fathers. Grandfathers, too, had emerged unexpectedly. Grampa Benson was the father of our dead Auntie Mary, so Bertie had actually gained a grandfather midst all this re-shuffling. However, lovable as Grampa Benson was, I doubt that this was adequate compensation for Bertie's other losses. Derek and I, too, had learned about two of our grandparents, our Dad's parents, only to have them vanish from the scene in the space of a sentence or two. Such gigantic shifts in our small world. In a matter of weeks.

Chapter 13

The Hodds to the Rescue

EVEN WHEN MUM HAD a job, money was tight. And it would have been tighter had the Hodds not come to the rescue by taking over all my clothing needs, even the boring stuff like socks and nighties. Such generosity! And I was given exactly the same as Viley—as if we were sisters—identical spring outfits at Easter and identical winter coats, with pretty velvet collars and cuffs and cute matching berets. The coats were made to measure by a seamstress, somewhere in Walworth, I think. I just remember long bus rides on dark, rainy evenings, then standing and turning round slowly to be measured and fitted. They were made "on the big side," because this year's Sunday coat was destined to become next year's school coat, so our beautifully tailored coats started out too big and had to be hemmed up. They fitted best just when they were relegated to school use; by which time the hems had to be let down, leaving an ineradicable line where the old bottom edge had been.

The Hodd family also gave our mother bits of fabric left over from various sewing projects; she cleverly converted these into clothes and rarely had to buy anything shop-made. She even taught herself how to make buttonholes and flies, when the boys got too big for elastic-waisted trousers—a feat of which she was justifiably proud. All this help from the Hodds allowed her to concentrate her resources on other essentials, and we were all undoubtedly better clad and better fed than we otherwise would have been.

At Christmas time, too, they told Mum to concentrate on the boys; they'd take care of me. So I began to get toys—new toys—in abundance. The boys did, too, because Mum felt that she had to give them equal treatment, as best she could. In the toy department, we three had never had it so good. Many of my presents were beautifully hand-made: gorgeous doll clothes from the ladies of the Hodd household, and a fabulous dollhouse designed and constructed by the men folk. It had a balcony and a front door that actually opened and had a real knocker and the number 8, my age, painted on it. Mum grumbled about the size of the dollhouse—it *was* big—but it gave me countless hours of pleasure, arranging and re-arranging the furniture, taking care of the tiny dolls who lived in it, and making curtains for the windows—real glass, they were. The walls were all papered, and the furniture was so beautiful that I wept when I first opened up that dollhouse.

It was my all-time favorite plaything, until the following Christmas when the Harry-George-Percy team surprised me with another special handmade gift: a sweet shop, with GWEN's STORE written across the front. Its shelves were laden with small jars of miniature sweets—real sweets—acid drops, jelly babies, humbugs, heart-shaped chalky-crunchy things, and fruit drops of several flavors. The pear drops were my favorites, because the flavor wafted up into your nose as the sweet dissolved in your mouth; fortunately for me, both boys hated them.

The shop also had a working electric light and a tiny balance pan for weighing out the sweets, which I did in miserly fashion, I fear. Derek and Bertie constantly pestered me to open up the shop and sell them some sweets—using buttons as currency—and they were always cross because I was so tightfisted. Indeed, my stinginess was such that almost a year later when war broke out and we were evacuated out of London, more than half the jars remained unopened, including all the scented, chalky-crunchy hearts that none of us liked.

I now could never decide which was my favorite toy: the shop or the dollhouse. But what a delicious dilemma, and how rich my play-life had become, thanks to the Hodds. They also began to play a much larger role in my life by taking me to places to which I would otherwise never have gone: Music Halls, pantomimes, The Ring—a boxing venue in nearby Blackfriars— and Petticoat Lane, one of London's most ancient and colorful street markets. It was "dahn The Lane" that a Pearly King and Queen often appeared, riding in a decorated horse-drawn cart in white outfits covered with gleaming pearl buttons and waving regally to the crowd, despite the decidedly work-a-day white cloth caps on their heads. "Why no crowns?" I always wanted to know, but no one could give me an answer.

Much as I loved going places with the Hodds, some of the treats, like bawdy Music Hall jokes, went right over my head and simply sent me to sleep. And it was a while before I cottoned on to all the gender switches in pantomimes, that uniquely English entertainment, in which an elegant young woman wearing high heels plays the leading man and some well-known male comedian plays an old woman. I found the boxing venue the least pleasurable of all these excursions, since I did not enjoy watching young men and boys knock one another silly, but didn't like to say so, in case anyone's feelings got hurt. Understandably, it was assumed that I had enjoyed the spectacle and the excitement, so I was taken there quite often, and, with each visit, I got deeper into this trap—one entirely of my own making. I came to bitterly regret not voicing my discomfort with boxing the very first time.

More than all the toys and all the excursions, however, what I loved most about the Hodd family was being, in effect, their toy, their plaything. They teased and romped with me endlessly, and I happily lapped up every moment of it. With six young adults around, counting the three sweethearts, there was always someone to pay attention to me; though Kitty, in her cat-like way, could not be relied upon to respond, except on her own terms.

Their only shortcoming as a family, was in the question-answering department. The ladies never made the slightest attempt at an answer, and, to my chagrin, I often found out later that the men-folk had fed me misinformation. As a joke? I was never sure. Georgie, for instance, told me with a perfectly straight face that the North Pole is very cold and the South Pole very hot; in my limited experience of the world at the time, this made perfect sense. I'd heard that the north of Scotland was cold, and the South coast, where Aunt Em lived, was warm and sunny. It was quite a while before I sorted this out. After repeated "leg-pulling" of this kind, I came to distrust *all* their information, and, thus, it was years before I could be convinced that pearls came from inside oysters. A likely story, I said to myself!

Once a year the Hodds went on a "beano" with their pub-pals from the Rose & Crown. Viley and I always walked down to see them pile onto the bus that would take them to the seaside for the day, somewhere like Margate or Southend. Money for this excursion had been put into a "kitty" throughout the year, and since there were several pub stops en route, a lot of beer would be guzzled, a lot of songs sung, and a good, rowdy time would be had by all.

But beanos were strictly for grown-ups, and, as a sort of consolation prize, a "scramble" was arranged for the kids who were being left behind. A hat was passed around, and just before the bus departed, the contents of the hat were hurled high in the air for the kids to scramble for—to pick up as much of the money as they could. The pickings were good for aggressive scramblers, since the donors, with a beer or two under their belts before the passing of the hat, were usually in a generous mood. But I was not good at scrambling. My parents weren't "regulars" at a pub—indeed, neither of them drank at all—and Mum frowned upon beanos as "jus' an excuse ta get drunk." Consequently, I had come to scrambling rather late in life and just tagged along with Viley, staying on the fringe of the mass of scramblers, picking up any stray coins that happened to roll my way. Despite Mum's disapproval, I enjoyed the festivity surrounding beanos; scrambles had an unforgettable atmosphere all their own, a mix of chagrin at being left behind and exultation at the coins jingling in one's pockets—and I sometimes wished that our family *was* part of the pub crowd.

As I got older, I was included when the Hodds had a Knees Up. These were noisy parties with lots to eat and drink: a huge ham, cheese, pickled onions, celery, loaves of crusty bread, a keg of beer for the grown-ups, and fizzy lemonade and potato crisps [chips] for the young ones. There was also much laughing and joking, and singing to the accompaniment of a piano or an accordion or a mouth organ—whatever talent was available. Louie was in great demand on these occasions, because she played the piano, very well indeed, even though she was self-taught and played entirely by ear. After hearing a song only once or twice on the radio, she could sit down and play it straight through. Viley and I were in awe of this remarkable talent, and we often tried to play a song on the Hodds' beat-up sturdy piano, but gave up in disgust when we discovered how unsatisfactory were our efforts to do what came so effortlessly to Louie.

At frequent intervals in the course of a Knees Up, everyone joined in a circle and danced, singing:

> Knees up Muvva Brahn,
> Yer drawers'r 'angin' dahn
> Under the table yew mus' go,
> E-I-E-I-E-I-O!
> If I catch yew bendin'
> I'll saw yer leg right off,
> *S-o-o ... knees up, knees up, don't ge' the breeze up!*
> *Knees up Muvva Brahn!*

The singing was raucous, and dancing is perhaps not quite the right word: the general idea was to bounce up and down, one leg at a time, lifting your knees as high as you could. It was huge fun, especially for kids, for whom it was probably the only dance in their repertoire. When a roomful really got going with "Knees-Up Mother Brown," the floorboards bounced up and down alarmingly, but the Hodds' old kitchen floor always stood the test.

I asked Mum once why we never had a Knees-Up. She gave me a withering look and started on a rant about "all those drunks ... don'cha think we've got somethin' bet'er ta do with our money." As far as I could see, not many people got really drunk at a Knees-Up. Those that did simply disappeared to be sick and then went home, or sat quietly in a corner in the hopes of recovering enough to re-join the festivities. I sometimes wished that my mother were not quite such a sober-sides: she seemed to miss out on a lot of fun in comparison with the Hodds.

I did have the grace to feel conscience-stricken occasionally, because Derek and Bertie weren't part of the picture with the Hodd family, but found that I was powerless to do much about it. Several times I tried. If the Hodds were planning to take me to some place, like a park, that didn't involve any expense, I'd ask Mum if she thought they'd mind me asking if the boys could come too. But her answer was always, "No, don't do that. Don't yew worry about it. I'll make sure the boys 'ave a good time, too." So I gave up asking. Though, in my heart of hearts, I never saw much evidence that Derek and Bertie had anything like as good a time with Mum as I had with the Hodds.

Chapter 14

Topped an' Tailed

EVERY NIGHT FOR AS long as I can remember, we three had been "topped an' tailed" before going to bed. We were taken in turn, youngest first, plonked on the kitchen table stripped to our underclothes, and washed thoroughly, from head to toe—though, occasionally, if we hadn't played outside that day, we got a cursory "lick an' a promise." Tailed was rather a misnomer, because the region beneath the underpants was ignored, but we never picked up on this inconsistency. Disgruntled as we always were at being pulled from play to get ready for bed, if Mum was in the right mood and could be persuaded to tell us a story, we actually enjoyed the "top an' tail" ritual. For one thing, it provided the two essential ingredients for storytelling: it put us all in the same room at the same time, and brisk toweling after vigorous applications of a soapy wash cloth, kept our mother's busy hands occupied. For she could never just talk. She had to be doing something useful at the same time. After Dad died, her story telling became a much more regular feature—perhaps because, as we got older, we became better listeners? Or did it help ease her still unaccustomed loneliness? What *is* clear, in retrospect, is that her stories became a kind of "glue" that helped to knit us together after the recent re-shaping of our family landscape.

For a long time there were no competing attractions for our mother's tales; going to bed was the only other item on the agenda, so we always egged her on, hopeful that she'd stretch out her yarns and delay bedtime. Even when we, eventually, acquired a radio—having moved into a house with electricity—what the radio had to offer usually lost out to a Mum-story, or to one of the poems she liked to recite. *Poems?* Before you get the wrong idea, let me give a sample. I don't remember all of it, but hopefully enough to give the flavor of my mother's repertoire:

The Prettiest Doll In the World
I once had a sweet little doll, dears
The prettiest doll in the world
Her cheeks were so round and so pink, dears
And her hair so beautifully curled.
I lost my sweet little doll, dears
As I played on the heath one day
Tho' I searched for a year and a day, dears
I never could find where she lay.
I found my sweet little doll, dears
As I played on the heath one day
With her face trodden in by the cows, dears
And her clothes ... ...
I still love my sweet little doll, dears
Tho' her hair is not beautifully curled
Nor her clothes ... ... , dears
She's still the prettiest doll in the world.

Another favorite was a long, blank verse ballad about a burglar caught in the act of stealing by the small child of the household that he is burgling. I remember only a chunk in the middle that went something like this:

> In her snow-white nightdress,
> From which peeped her dimpled toes,
> Stood Pet, her dolly held close in her arms.
> "Is you a Belgian refugee?
> 'Cos all those pennies are for you.
> And if you have a little girl,
> Please take my dolly, too.
> Your little girl will love her, I am sure."
> The burglar winced,
> And a memory came back to his mind,
> Of a little girl he'd loved, so long ago.
> But she'd died, and the world seemed empty,
> And people were unkind,
> So he'd simply let things go ...

The burglar, needless to say, becomes a reformed character as a result of this encounter. (This stuff has been fermenting in my head for decades!) But we kids were not a critical audience, and we lapped it up. The burglar ballad had the redeeming feature that it raised questions about Belgian refugees and got Mum talking about World War I. She was fourteen when that war started—one of the generation of girls for whom the young men they might have married never came back from the fields of Flanders. Sometimes she'd tell us about our father and how he'd fought in the trenches; how his best friend had died there, in the mud and the cold and the horrors of those trenches; how Dad had been gassed, which left him "very chesty," and how he was finally invalided out with a leg injury. "Prob'ly saved 'im from dyin' in the mud like 'is mate, that piece o' shrapnel ... " she always ended.

The boys often requested one of their favorites: "The dog story ... ple-a-s-e Mummy! Tell us about the dog." And Mum would be off, transporting us to the world she'd known when she was "in service" as a young girl still in her teens: "One o' me jobs was ta clean out the grates ev'ry mornin', then blacken 'em till they shone, an' polish the brass on the firearms an' fenders. Took 'alf the mornin' it did, 'cos there was nine or ten grates in that 'ouse. An' 'eaven 'elp me, if I stirred up any dust from all those ashes! The parlor maid would give me a piece of 'er mind, *an'* box me ears fer good measure. I'd 'ear about nothin' else fer days!

"Well, one mornin' I was blackin' the grate in the front 'all when the lady of the 'ouse, she come down the stairs an' scooped up her li'l dog, one o' those ugly Pekes, a yappy li'l thing with a scrunched up kind o' face. She started kissin' an' cuddlin' it, callin' it, 'my swe-e-et little sno-o-odlums!' Well ... when the cook, Bertha—a big fat ol' German woman, she was—saw the missus kissing the dog, she come rushin' up, snatched the dog out of 'er arms, an' shouted, 'Do not kees ze dawg Madame! 'E licks cats' ass'oles!'" This was the punch line we'd been waiting for, and we fell about laughing, though we'd heard this story a hundred times or more. Actually, the cook sounds more French than German, and no self-respecting cat ever let a dog that close to its rear end, but that was the story, according to Mum, and my carping comments did not sneak in until much later.

At other times we'd beg, "Tell us about when yew was a kid." For we loved this stuff, even if it was no more than a description of mealtimes in the large household of which she was a part in the early 1900's. "I was the twelfth o' thirteen," these stories always started. "So ya c'n bet yer boots there was no nonsense in that 'ouse! When food was ready, we was expected ta be there—an' ta eat what was put in front of us. Ev'ry bit. Gawd 'elp yew if ya didn't end up with a clean plate. Poor Lilly, she used ta eat like a bird, so she'd try ta slide some of 'er dinner on ta someone else's plate. Not the meat, mind ya ... jus' the spuds an' veg. An' when she got caught, they both copped it ... Lilly *an'* the one she give the veg'tables to.

"It was 'ard ta get away with anythin', 'cos our father sat at the 'ead of the table, an' 'e kept a pret'y sharp look out. A bit deaf 'e was, but there weren't nothin' wrong with 'is eyesight. O' course, there was no talkin' at the table. Not fer us young 'uns, anyway. There was two rules we daresn't break: 'Children are ta be seen an' not 'eard,' an' 'Speak when yer spoken to.' So mealtimes was very quiet—not like yew noisy lot! I s'pose, with s'many of us, it would've bin bedlam otherwise."

Mum's tree-climbing yarns were the top of the pops, and invariably started, "Like a bloomin' monkey, I was. Me father used t'say, 'I dunno, May … Yew should've bin a boy.'" Then she'd launch into some escapade involving the tree—gigantic, apparently—that stood close to the back of their house. We especially loved to hear about the time she snuck out of the house after her bedtime, but found her re-entry barred by her father. He had discovered her absence and was sitting, waiting and watching, at the foot of the stairs. "Give me the shock o' me life it did, ta see 'im sittin' there readin' the paper, waitin' fer me. I was in fer a real good 'idin' if 'e caught me. So I crept round the 'ouse, climbed up the tree, an' got in through the winder on the upstairs landin'. Me Dad, 'e sat there in the front 'all, waitin' an' waitin', till 'e got fed up an' went upstairs ta bed. 'E got the shock of '*is* life when 'e looked in an' found me tucked up in bed … sleepin' like a bloomin' baby. Well … pretendin' to, at any rate!"

Another tale was about her sister Lilly, a year or so older than my mother, and as feminine as Mum was tomboyish. This particular tale took place soon after their father, who ran his own business as a carter, had slipped on some ice, fallen under the horse and been badly injured.

"We was quite comf'tably off, till then," according to Mum. "But our Dad couldn't work fer months on end, an' all that time there was no money comin' in, so 'e 'ad ta start sellin' off 'is stuff. First the 'orse, then the cart. Broke 'is 'eart, it did, an' 'e was never really the same after that. Money got s'tight that we was all tryin' ta earn a few pennies, 'ere an' there, to 'elp out, but Lilly was dyin' ta get some ribbons fer 'er 'air. She musta bin about thirteen—jus' beginnin' ta notice boys, an' the boys was beginnin' ta notice Lilly, too. An' no wonder. She was a pret'y li'l thing. Very dainty, with a beau'iful creamy complexion an' lovely curly auburn 'air. Anyway, when our mother said, 'There ain't no money fer no ribbons', Lilly started ta whine.

"'But May's got money. Why can't I 'ave some too?'

"'Yew'll get money, m'lady … when yew go out an' earn it, like May does!'

"Well … that made me laugh," Mum always chuckled, at this point. "I knew the way I got that money wouldn't suit our fastidious Lilly … 'cos I'd earned it muckrakin'! Before an' after school, I used ta go around with a bucket an' shovel, scoopin' up 'orse droppins ta sell as manure. I earned a lot that way. An' when I give it ta me mother, she always said, 'Keep a bit fer yerself, May. Yew deserve it,' an' she always made me take some back. But sure as God made li'l apples, Lilly would never stoop ta pickin' up 'orse droppins. No mat'er 'ow much she wanted the money. An' I was right …

"'I couldn't do that!' said Lilly, wrinklin' up 'er dainty nose.

"'Oh, could'ncha?' said our mother. 'Well … yew'll just 'ave ta go without yer fancy ribbons then, won'cha, madam? A right Lady Muckless, yew are!'

"From then on, Lady Muckless—soon shortened ta Lady Muck—was Lilly's nickname. It was years before she shook it off, poor Lilly. It used ta make 'er so mad. She'd stamp 'er foot an' scream, 'May's the Lady Muck round 'ere—not me!'" This was another eagerly awaited punch line. It never failed, and we were still giggling about our Lady Muck Auntie Lilly long after we were in bed.

The only other sibling that ever figured in Mum's repertoire of tales was her sister Etty. Etty was much older than Mum, and they could have been taken for mother and daughter rather than sisters; both had straight black hair, green eyes, high coloring, were short and rotund, and loved a good laugh. Mum had a soft spot for Aunt Etty who, in her opinion, had had a raw deal in life. "Poor ol' Etty," she'd sigh. "She was never the same after she got 'it by a car one night. Ridin' 'er bike 'ome from work, she was, an' it was dark an' rainin' cats an' dogs. We don't know 'ow long she lay there before someone found 'er, but she was unconscious fer days, an' 'as bin simple-minded ever since. The blighter drivin' the car never even stopped. Jus' plain wicked, I call it … I'd like ta get me 'ands on that devil! Deserves ta be whipped from 'ere ta John O'Groats, 'e does."

The rest of the Wheatland family shunned poor simple-minded Etty, and this made Mum mad. "Oh, I know," she'd say, "Etty did keep 'avin babies she couldn't take care of … she was jus' too simple-minded ta know what was goin' on … an' too soft'earted ta say no. So the fellas, they took advantage of 'er. Four, she 'ad, an' never knew 'oo the father was—p'raps a different fella each time.

"The first was a li'l girl, Kathleen, an' our mother 'elped Etty ta look after 'er. That Kathy was the most beautiful child I ever set eyes on! Jet-black 'air an' vi'let-colored eyes … an' as good as gold … a real li'l angel. I remember, on 'er second birthday, we all sat laughin' an' clappin' as she danced on the ol' kitchen table in 'er first pair o' proper shoes. As pret'y as a picture, she was. Li'l did we guess she'd be dead within the month … measles, it was. Poor Etty, she was 'eart-broken. After that come the three boys, an' they all went into a Boys' 'Ome, 'cos Etty jus' wasn't capable o' lookin' after them. I know … it was an awful way fer those boys ta grow up. But I still say ya can't really blame poor Etty."

Mum was the only member of the Wheatland family who visited or wrote to Aunt Etty. Even her three sons refused to have anything to do with her when they grew up, and they didn't go to her funeral. But Aunt Etty found a way to ease the loneliness of her declining years. She opened her tiny flint-stone terrace house to a stream of sick and dying old men who were even lonelier than she was. She nursed each of them, in turn, through his final illness and made sure that each got what she called "a decent li'l burial." One had cancer of the mouth, and the stench was indescribable, but Aunt Etty tended him lovingly and cheerfully, dressing the hideous gaping hole in his face several times a day—and was his only mourner when he died. Poor Auntie Etty; in her last few years she went through a lot of mourning and a lot of funerals. "Jus' a good-'earted simple soul," as Mum always declared, and I like to think that Auntie Etty's later acts of mercy helped to balance out what the world at large perceived as the misdeeds of her younger days.

For some reason Mum's brothers never featured in any of her stories, but one day her brother George appeared, unannounced. I remember him as sandy-haired and tall, with a bit of a paunch. He was well dressed in a tweedy sort of way, and looked very healthy, as if he spent a lot of time in the open air. But the most remarkable thing about Uncle George was the fact that he sported a bow tie and spats, articles of clothing that I had never seen before. The cream-colored spats, which emerged from the bottom of his trouser legs and covered all but the toes of his highly polished brown shoes, were especially fascinating, and after he left, I asked what they were for.

"Gawd on'y knows! An' 'e won't split fer a pint, will 'e?" Mum laughed. "Daft things, I think they are. George jus' wanted ta look posh, I s'pose. Wanted ta make sure we all remembered where 'e works—at tha' fancy big 'ouse, dahn in Sussex somewhere. I ferget its name [Petworth House, in fact]—where e's the chauffeur fer 'Is Lordship. So now 'e drives around all day in a posh car. But mind yew, 'e ain't always bin s'grand. When 'e started there, 'e was nothin' but a stable boy an' spent 'is days cleanin' up after the 'orses. But 'e worked 'is way up ta be 'ead groom ... an' now ta chauffeur."

What a pity Uncle George didn't stay long enough to tell us about his life as a groom, I thought, and about the fancy cars he now drives—the boys would have loved it. But Mum didn't seem overly fond of her brother, so perhaps that's why he left soon after the statutory cup-of-tea-and-biscuit. And that was the last we ever saw of him.

It was hard to think of the Auntie Lilly we knew as a "pret'y li'l thing." By her early thirties, she'd already been a wartime bride, a widow with two small boys, and the mother of two more children by a second marriage. Her second husband, John, turned out to be "a real rot'er", and they were dirt-poor much of the time, partly because of the Depression and partly because of Uncle John's spendthrift ways. What little he earned was often spent on gambling and drinking before Auntie Lilly even got a look at it.

By the early 1930s, when they moved to the Dagenham Estate—from a much worse London slum than the Coin Street area—Auntie Lilly and her children had been through some very hard times. In my memories from our Dagenham days, she was already a worn-out, worried husk, alarmingly thin, and always in a state of high anxiety. The creamy complexion was still there, but the lovely reddish-gold hair had grown dull and frizzy, and thick myopic lenses reduced her blue eyes to faded small circles. She had the persistent cough of a chain smoker and, living as they did on the "rough" side of the estate, was perpetually worried about her children and the bad influences to which they might succumb. Her fears, it transpired, were unwarranted; all four of her children turned out just fine, despite those difficult early years.

The two older boys were treated very harshly by their hard-drinking stepfather, and each of them, on leaving school at fourteen, immediately left home and went to work as a pageboy in a London hotel. At the outbreak of World War II, Frank joined the army to be with his older brother, and, although they weren't in the same regiment, they spent the rest of the war together in the same POW camps in Germany and Poland after being captured at Dunkirk.

Poor Auntie Lilly. For five long years, she vacillated between sleeping better because her two boys were not actively fighting on some horrible battlefield and anxiety about the unknown horrors of a POW camp. Their censored letters told little of what was really happening; which was just as well, for this experience was no picnic. It left Frank with tuberculosis and stone deaf in one ear—the result of a brutal kick by a camp guard—while Ted came back shattered psychologically and never got over his wartime experiences. But at least Auntie Lilly got them both back and could hug and fuss over them to her heart's content.

It was years before I understood my mother's hatred of Uncle John. As a child, I liked him, because he played the piano, by ear, and used to challenge me to name countries and capitals. This put him several notches above any other relative I knew except for my beloved Uncle Dick, and I was blissfully unaware of his drinking problem until my wedding day when, after one whisky, there was Uncle John—out cold under the table. Auntie Lilly wept with humiliation, and Mum raged, "What did I tell ya? We shouldn't 'ave let 'im come!" For there had been considerable argument about this. Mum reluctantly let me include Uncle John on the invitation and afterwards confessed to having hoped that his job—a steward on luxury liners—would put an ocean or two between him and us on the day of the wedding. But it was a long time before I heard the full story—the many embarrassments and humiliations that Auntie Lilly had suffered—and came to understand why Uncle John had been such an unwanted guest.

◆   ◆   ◆

ADDENDUM

On the day of my mother's funeral, I was surprised to see Cousin Frank and his wife, Jess. I hadn't known that there was much of a connection between Mum and them, although, back in the late 1920s, Mum and Lilly had a lot to do with one another. Later I got in touch with Cousin Frank to ask him if he had any memories of my mother's Coin Street days. Did he ever!

I learned so much from his reply: much that was heart-warming and much that was heart breaking. His letter said that he and Teddie used to pay regular visits to Coin Street, walking all the way from Shoreditch, " ... hungry, barefoot and raggedy-arsed most of the time." They were so poor, he said, that Auntie Lilly couldn't keep them adequately fed, clothed and shod. He fondly remembered my mother and father for the welcome he and Teddie always got at number nine Coin Street, and for the wonderful, big meals Mum used to serve up for them—a far cry from what they got at home, apparently. "Auntie May was our second mother," was the way he put it. My father used to take them to the boxing venue, The Ring, in Blackfriars; the exact same treat that the Hodds gave me, a few years later, but unlike me, they loved it, Frank said.

When he was about eight and Teddie about ten, Frank wrote, the situation in Shoreditch was so bad that they were both taken from their home and put "in Care," where they were so miserable that they ran away and slept in doorways, stealing whatever food they could. They were caught after a few days and returned to the institution from which they had run away, and of course, punished for running away. At this point, Auntie May came to their rescue, he said; she signed them "out of Care" and agreed to take responsibility for them. What a responsibility for my mother—living in one room—to take on! I wonder whether she did it with the OK of my father? Knowing her, it's entirely possible that he didn't know until it was a *fait accompli*.

Eventually the two boys were able to go back to Auntie Lilly, but it was Frank's long-lived gratitude to my mother for all the things she did for them, that had brought him to her funeral. His younger sister Maisie had planned to be there too, but she had unexpectedly dropped dead of a heart attack only three days before, so Frank and Jess had to hurry back and make arrangements for *her* funeral, so they couldn't linger. Or I might have learned of Frank's Coin Street memories on the day of my mother's funeral.

Strangely, my mother never breathed a word about taking her young nephews out of care. Such a brave, generous thing that she did; yet she kept it to herself. Ashamed, perhaps, that her sister's children had been put in Care? Or didn't want us to know what a "softie" she was underneath that hard protective shell? She had talked about little Maisie spending a lot of time at Coin Street, but barely mentioned the boys' visits. In fact, she often said, "Teddie an' Frankie, they couldn't stay with us, becos' o' the noise. Their loud voices an' 'eavy boots clompin' around over Ma Tanner's 'ead—the ol' gal would've 'ad a fit! But Maisie was such a quiet li'l thing, so it was easier if we 'ad 'er over ta stay, jus' ta give poor Lilly a break.

"As a mat'er o' fact, Maisie was with us so much when she was a toddler that, yer Dad, 'e'd come ta think that Maisie must be mine! 'Specially with our names bein' Maisie an' May. 'E reckoned Lilly was jus' takin' care o' Maisie, 'elpin' me out till I could take care of 'er meself. Well, 'e waited till we was well set'led in Coin Street, then 'e got tired o' waitin' fer me ta tell 'im about Maisie. So one day 'e asked, 'An' when's li'l Maisie gonna come an' live with *us*?' An' 'e was real disappointed ta find that Maisie *wasn't* mine!"

In the light of more recent information, I think this Maisie story has to be amended. She was about five when my parents got married—not exactly a toddler. However, she would have been toddling four years earlier ... So my guess is that my parents set up house on Coin Street four years before they tied the knot in 1928 ... the four years that they spent in Ol' Ma Tanner's "second floor front," prior to my birth, according to Mum's story that always started: "I let this room ta two not ta three."

Chapter 15

Another New Address

LESS THAN A YEAR after Dad died we moved again—just a couple of blocks. But so many moves! Four, in less than three years; two almost within spitting distance. Oddly enough, I have no memory of any actual moving days. How did we get our stuff from one house to another? Did we hire a van? For the long-distance moves, we must have; for local moves, we most likely took several runs at it, pushing a cart piled high with our worldly belongings. Events like that would seem pretty memorable, so maybe I'm drawing a blank because we three were packed off to an aunt on moving days, to get us out from under everyone's feet.

Why did we make this last move, to 36B Aquinas Street, I wonder? (Contrary to dictionaries, Ack-win-ass was Waterloo's version of Thomas's last name.) We had gone from a four-story house to a flat that was smaller yet more expensive, so there must have been some compelling reason. Maybe it was simply to escape from a house that was haunted by sad memories. Or, perhaps, because this street was a notch up on Commercial Road. Though Peabody Buildings, just around the corner, were a different story, we soon discovered.

Aquinas Street was certainly quieter and cleaner, entirely residential apart from one small builder's yard; there were no warehouses, no paint factories, no newspaper printing plants, and no lines of horse-drawn dust carts. We were all glad to have left the flies behind, but we three missed the horses and the jangle of harness when they tossed their heads—and the friendly dustmen. However, Aquinas Street had a counter-attraction: on Saturdays, equally friendly taxi drivers sat in idling vehicles, in a slow-moving queue that stretched all the way to Waterloo Station. The line started just before mid-day, in readiness for fares who'd just finished work for the week and were in a hurry to get away for the weekend. The taxi drivers smoked like chimneys while they waited in line, as good a source of cigarette cards as the dustmen had been! By this time we were avid collectors of these cards and skilled negotiators in the art of swapping, but they were never a source of revenue like jam jars full of dead flies.

Uncle Bert moved with us, but Grampa Benson did not, so the family income had been depleted by whatever his contribution had been. This put us back on Relief most of the time, since rent now consumed about three-quarters of Mum's pension. Though happier when *not* on Relief, our mother didn't find Relief money shameful, any more than she'd been ashamed to take the dole when Dad was out of work. She regarded both as a sort of earned right for hard-working, honest folk like her and Dad, who always worked when work was available and struggled to make ends meet, "raise our kids right, an' stay out o' debt. Out o' the pawnshop, too. No mat'er what 'ard times we 'ad." What she couldn't abide was anything that smacked of charity; that, to her, *was* demeaning and shameful.

I remember, once, standing with her in a line at a local church hall, waiting for what she afterwards called, "their bloomin' 'andouts." I saw her lips tighten as she took the bundle of clothes pressed on her by the kindly, smiling, church ladies, all wearing neat tweed skirts, twin sets, and strings of pearls. "Never agin!" she stormed, as we walked home. "Not if I c'n 'elp it. I'd rather starve first! But I couldn't let yew three go through the winter without some warm clothes, now could I?" Then, after a pause for breath, "Did ya notice their 'ands? All them rings? I bet they ain't none of 'em ever done a good day's work in their bloomin' lives! An' they think they're bet'er than the likes of us! I'd like ta see *them* dahn on their knees, scrubbin' out ol' Wallace's fish shop ev'ry mornin' ... those 'ands wouldn't look all soft an' white, after a few days o' that!"

Our pricey new living quarters consisted of a living room (small), a kitchen (tiny), two bedrooms (one large, one small), and a hallway (long, but useless as a place to play, since we had to creep along it like mice, so as not to upset the tenants below). There was the usual one cold faucet in the kitchen and no bath; but we now had electricity—and an indoor toilet! The latter was closet-sized, to be sure, but a mere flick of a switch meant no more groping in the scary darkness, fearful that a long-legged spider was waiting to pounce the moment you reached the point of no return—with your knickers round your ankles, preventing a rapid retreat.

In addition, I no longer had to pass the house of Hazel-the-whip-wielder on my way to school, and leaky roofs no longer plagued us, so there was no weekly earful for the rent lady—the same long-suffering Mrs. 'Ouston, since this property, too, belonged to the Duchy of Cornwall. However, we had gone from seven rooms for six people to three-and-a-half-rooms for five; it seemed like we were always on top of one another, and it was hard to sneak off to another room to be on your own. But the very smallness of that cozy, easier-to-heat flat did give us a sense of togetherness, something we badly needed at the time, I think.

I have no idea what became of Old Grampa Benson. He didn't stay in the house on Commercial Road, so maybe he'd gotten too old and too blind and had to go in a Home. Or perhaps his wife (ex-wife? I never knew why they lived apart) finally took pity on him, and he went back to her. She ran a boarding house in Broadstairs for summer visitors and kept a parrot that resented the annual invasion so much that he screeched, "Chuck 'em aht, Muvva! Chuck 'em aht!" and had to be banished to the garden shed until the last houseguest had left. Or so Grampa Benson had told us, laughing so hard that the last "Chuck 'em aht" was always lost in a coughing fit.

Mum once took us to visit Mrs. Benson in her boarding house, perhaps, to discuss Grampa Benson's needs and make arrangements for him. Or maybe Bertie's grandmother simply wanted to see her grandchild, the son of her dead daughter; but, if so, it didn't lead to any further visits. All I remember is a long tedious bus journey and the poshness of tiny Mrs. Benson and her equally tiny semi-detached house—my first encounter with a dwelling that wasn't part of a row of attached houses. Everything was incredibly neat, including the diminutive gardens, one at the front and one at the back. Two gardens? For one house? That was an eye-opener. We were hugely disappointed to find that the famed parrot was no longer in the land of the living. But Mrs. Benson did verify Grampa Benson's account of the parrot's raucous, unacceptable response to her summer boarders, which cast doubt on any skepticism we might have entertained concerning his other yarns. To my shame, I don't remember asking what became of Grampa Benson when we moved. Or, if I did, what the answer was. Yet I had really loved that cheerful old man.

In the new flat, Uncle Bert slept in the big front bedroom, and the rest of us shared the smaller one. It was a crunch in there. Derek and I slept with Mum in the old brass-railed double bed—it took a while to get over my aversion to sleeping in the bed in which Dad died—and Bertie had a single bed to himself, because he was still a bed-wetter. My dollhouse perched on top of a small chest of drawers, and you had to move Bertie's narrow little cot to get to the drawers, which always stuck and made the dollhouse wobble alarmingly.

To this day, I fail to understand that sleeping arrangement; there was an unused, single bed in Uncle Bert's bedroom, and why didn't we four have the bigger room? However, our tight squeeze of a bedroom was nice and cozy, and we got used to it. It was an arrangement that could not last long, though: Derek was almost six, and I would soon be nine, so some time soon it would not be acceptable for us to share a bed. I don't know if Mum had a long-term plan to deal with that eventuality. She never mentioned one, and with so much on her plate, she tended to live one day at a time, assuming that somehow everything would work itself out.

Our flat was the middle one of three, and below us lived the Wilsons, an elderly woman with an invalid husband, so we had to be quiet all the time; there could be no shouting, no noisy games, no running or jumping. The linoleum-covered hallway that stretched the length of the flat was potentially a fabulous slide—better even than the expanse of lino in our Commercial Road bedroom—and a great temptation. But one of the first things Mum did was to put down a carpet runner and threaten us with the copper stick: "If I catch yew rollin' up that carpet, yew won't be able ta sit down fer a week." (We thought we'd seen the last of the copper stick, thought it was part and parcel of the old copper, but there it was, propped up in the corner of our new, copper-less kitchen.)

Carpet also stopped marbles rolling, which ruled out that game anywhere indoors, because a marble rolling across an uncarpeted floor sounded loud and clear in the flat below. Even the balcony off the living room was useless, because marbles rolled off the edge. Most of all, we missed our old back garden for grubbing around in, or for simply letting off steam. The iron stairs from our balcony led down to a small garden at the back, but it was for the ground floor tenants only. This seemed a waste of a good garden to us, since they never used it. The disadvantages of flat life rapidly became apparent to the three of us.

How dismayed Mrs. Wilson must have been when a single mother with a girl of eight and two five-year-old boys moved into the flat above the head of her poor paralyzed husband. But Mum's determined efforts made us good neighbors, and in the eighteen months we were there, Mrs. Wilson complained only once—on the day we learned that marbles played on linoleum was not the quiet game we had thought. In fact after a while, she begged Mum to relax a bit. "We enjoy hearing your kiddies having fun. It brightens up our day!" The Wilsons had no children of their own and were quite lonely, I think. But Mum kept us on a tight rein, wisely. If she'd given us an inch, we would've taken a mile—perhaps two.

One day the tortoise that Harry gave me when he found that Monty was worse than useless in his garden, crawled out of his box on the balcony and fell down into Mrs. Wilson's garden. Nervously, I rang her doorbell to ask if I could come down the back stairs to pick him up, but she insisted that I go directly to the garden through her flat. As I walked along their hallway—identical to ours—I was struck by the silence. Their heavy carpet muffled my footsteps, and all I could hear was the ticking of a clock somewhere. No wonder the sound of our rolling marbles had been so annoying!

Miraculously, given the ratio of earth to concrete, Monty had landed on a small flowerbed and was quite unharmed. Mrs. Wilson seemed as relieved as I was and gave Monty a piece of lettuce—a real treat, since lettuce was rarely part of our daily fare. She pointed out how difficult it would be to keep a tortoise from straying off a small balcony and suggested that he'd be safer if his official residence were her garden. "He'd be happier, too, I think. And find lots to eat," she added, smiling. I told her that, in Harry's garden, Monty ate the plants and ignored the weeds that he'd been purchased to consume. But to this she replied "I'm sure that'll be all right. I've no prized specimens to worry about." And so began a happier life-style for Monty and a quiet friendship between the Wilsons and me.

With always a touch of powder on her nose and never a hair out of place, Mrs. Wilson was not your typical Waterloo resident, and her smile reminded me of my first and favorite teacher, (how I still missed Miss Johnson!) Mr. Wilson, a thin, frail figure, was always propped up in bed midst a profusion of pillows, and he was quite the cleanest person I'd ever met (with the possible exception of small babies before they reach the drooly, spitting-up stage). His scalp gleamed pinkly through sparse silvery hair, and his hands, soft and white with shell-pink nails, were so different from the work-hardened, grimy hands of other grown-ups. It was clearly a long time since those hands had shoveled coal, chopped wood, polished shoes, or done anything that would make them grubby. Now, poor man, he could move only the left one, very, very slowly.

Conversation with Mr. Wilson was difficult. His speech was slurred and hard to understand, but I did the best I could, and, apparently, my visits helped to cheer him up. They had the opposite effect on me, however, and his room had a depressing smell, strangely sweet and scented. Sometimes, when I couldn't sleep, I lay thinking of the poor man in the bedroom immediately below—who also slept badly—and that cloying smell seemed to seep up into our bedroom. To my dismay, Mr. Wilson began to ask about me if more than a day or two went by without my stopping in to see them, and I was torn between the dread of ringing their doorbell and the guilt of deliberately walking past it.

A happy solution to this dilemma presented itself one day, when my arrival happened to coincide with Mrs. Wilson's daily session of reading the newspaper to her husband, and she asked if I would take over while she attended to something in the kitchen. I was delighted to oblige! Since Dad's death, that was something I really missed—reading the occasional newspaper he brought home when he found one left behind somewhere. Furthermore, reading the paper to Mr. Wilson alleviated the task of making conversation. Topics naturally arose from the newspaper, and, when you had some idea what he was talking about, it was easier to understand him.

That was the beginning of our regular newspaper sessions; and from newspapers we progressed to books. Mr. Wilson could hold a book unassisted if it was propped up with a pillow, but if he felt tired, he liked to be read to. There was always a pile of books on the bedside table, mainly about travel and adventure and history (probably historical fiction, because they were singularly uncluttered with dates and easier reading than any real history book I ever encountered). I loved reading aloud to Mr. Wilson. He was a much more appreciative audience than Derek and Bertie, and his attention span certainly beat theirs! As I started to read, he'd give a contented sigh and lie back on the pillows with closed eyes. However, he never fell asleep. If I hesitated over a word, his blue eyes popped open, and, after he'd helped sort out the difficulty, disappeared again, just as suddenly, behind his almost transparent eyelids. And I would continue reading.

Access to all that printed material gave me immense pleasure; though I do wonder how Mr. Wilson tolerated the mangling of the language of his precious books by my rough Waterloo pronunciation. Yet there was an element of relief when the door of their flat shut behind me and I walked away from its cloistered quietness and sickly smell. Without fail, Mrs. Wilson pressed three wrapped sweets into my hands as I left, one for each of us children, and I hadn't the heart to tell her that none of us liked them because they had such a strange scented smell. I lived in dread of one of the boys blurting out that we didn't like her sweets, and made them promise not to—on pain of death, if not worse.

The Wilsons' books puzzled me. There were so many of them, and they came and went with such regularity. I eventually reached the conclusion that they didn't actually belong to the Wilsons. But where did they come from? And where did they go? Mrs. Wilson sometimes mentioned a book being "due back at the lib'ry," but since I had no idea what a "lib'ry" was, I was none the wiser. Until one day, when I was down The Marsh shopping with Mum, I noticed a man coming down the steps of a solid-looking brick building carrying several books, and on the wall of the building, I saw an engraving in ornate lettering that made it difficult to decipher. But I suddenly realized it spelled **PUBLIC LIBRARY**, and a possible connection to Mrs. Wilson's "lib'ry" emerged.

"Mummy, is that where ya c'n get books from?" I asked, with rising excitement.

"Yeah. But it ain't fer the likes of us."

Her tone of voice meant that was the end of *that*. I knew from past experience that it was worse than useless to ignore her end-of-discussion voice; argument simply led to a hardening of her stance. So I let the subject drop, even though I was *so* tired of reading and re-reading the three volumes that constituted our entire collection of books—other than the set of Dickens, which was still beyond me. The tantalizing vision of an endless stream of books faded quickly, and we walked the rest of the way home in silence.

Mum's pronouncement that the Public Library wasn't for the likes of us—and, by implication, was only for posh people like the Wilsons—is how the word "public" acquired overtones of "elite" in my mind. Not that "elite" was then part of my vocabulary, but I got the message, and this notion was soon reinforced from, of all things, a comic book. We didn't have a dictionary, so my understanding of words was based entirely on the context in which I bumped into them, and it was in a comic book that I next noticed the word public. There was a serial strip about a fancy school, called a "public school," in which all the pupils were rich and learned Latin and French and rode horses, and their families had motor cars. The students lived at the school, except during "the hols," and their parents, called Mater and Pater, sent parcels of "tuck" to supplement what seemed to me an abundant supply of food provided at this swanky boarding school. This picture seemed to confirm that "public" meant "for posh people."

My misunderstanding did not come to light until about a year later when Hatfield Street School awarded me a swimming pass. Written on the free pass was, "For Admission to the Public Baths, Southwark." I'd never heard of South-war-k (which is how I read it). It didn't occur to me that it was the neighboring district that I knew as "Suvvak" (never having seen *that* written down). I assumed that the pass was for some swanky swimming pool that, like the Public Library, was not for the likes of us. I put the pass in my coat pocket, thinking that Hatfield Street School had made a foolish mistake, and forgot all about it. When Mum found it there a few weeks later, she wanted to know why I hadn't told her about it, and, more important, why I hadn't used it "ta go swimmin', fer free 'n all." I explained why I'd thought the pass was useless to me, and she was amused—but more than a little annoyed at all the free swimming I had missed out on.

"Ya got it arse back'ards, ya daft thing," was the way she put it.

"So why did yew say the Public Lib'ry ain't fer the likes of us?"

"'Cos yew 'ave ta pay fines if yew ferget ta take lib'ry books back on time. An' we ain't got money fer no fines. It's 'ard enough puttin' food on the table ev'ry day without *that*, thank yew very much!" she replied sharply.

The Library had, I discovered, been a contentious issue between Mum and Dad over the years; hence her unwillingness to get dragged into any further discussion when I first raised the question. I reckoned that if Dad had not prevailed in this argument, there was no chance that I would, especially since our income was now less than when he'd been alive. So, once again, I let the matter drop.

Having sorted out the meaning of "public" unless applied to schools—and here Mum couldn't help—I used the swimming pass happily, and frequently. For the Public Baths, Southwark, turned out to be the familiar Lavington Street Baths, to which the Hodds had taken me regularly. It was only about a mile away, and by now I was big enough to walk there by myself.

I never changed Mum's mind about the Public Library. Not until I was about thirteen did I get a library card, (prompted by the sheer necessity of access to books in order to complete a history project). But, by then I was an evacuee, no longer living under her roof, so in the final analysis, I suppose I did an end-run around my mother on this issue. Maybe, by that time she would have relented anyway, but I was spared that particular battle by the exigencies of wartime. I became a voracious devourer of the public library's offerings, and, needless to say, did sometimes let books get overdue and run up fines that I could ill afford. But it makes me sad—and angry—to think of all the reading that I missed out on all those years. Not to mention the reading my book-loving Dad missed out on, too.

◆　◆　◆

The morning of January 21, 1938 went by without comment. There was no "Happy Birthday!" and no mention that this was anything but a perfectly ordinary day. Which was just fine by me. For the past week I'd been churned up inside, dreading any attempt to celebrate, and as the day wore on, I began to hope that I was, indeed, going to be spared the misery of pretending to be happy about this birthday, the first since Dad died. It wasn't till the boys had been settled down for the night, and I was almost ready for bed, that Mum reached for her handbag, saying, "'Ere, Gwen ... I got somethin' for ya'. Somethin' special." She rummaged in her bag and pulled out a small bundle, wrapped loosely in newspaper, and my heart sank; she had remembered.

"I bought this with the last o' yer father's insurance money," she said. "There was a bit left over after I'd got the stuff we needed fer the flat, an' I thought you should 'ave somethin' special. Somethin' ta make up fer the rot'en birthday yew 'ad last year. I'm sure yer Dad woulda wanted yew to 'ave it. Solid gold it is ... eighteen carat ... not that cheap "rolled gold" rubbish."

I gazed at the gleaming bracelet on Mum's outstretched hand. It was my first piece of real jewelry, and I knew that I should be jumping up and down, saying "Oh, Mum! Thank you. Thank you!" But I couldn't. Even though I was bowled over by this extravagant present. Its very existence forced me to do what I was trying to avoid: forced me to acknowledge that Dad had, indeed, been dead for a whole year, that he was gone, and nothing could bring him back. I wasn't ready to deal with that.

Worse yet, after one glance at the bracelet, I knew that I would never wear it except in the company of adults—as a kind of duty, so as not to hurt Mum's feelings. But never, ever, would I wear it if there were the *slightest* chance of any other girls being around. For it was a large, adult-style bracelet, not a girl's, and I could already hear the sniggering it would provoke. I didn't know what to say, and simply nodded when Mum asked:

"Well? D'ya like it?"

"Put it on then," a bit impatiently. "Let's see 'ow it fits."

"Which 'and?" I stalled.

"It don't matter. Either will do."

The bracelet was too large to stay on my wrist, but Mum was not one to be beaten easily. "Jus' shove it up yer arm. I bought it big, so ya wouldn't grow out of it in a year or two." But even above my elbow, the thing was still too big and stayed in place only if you stuffed a hanky through it.

"Yew'll grow into it," declared Mum. (But I never did. Even when a hanky was no longer needed, the bracelet had to be worn either just below, or just above, the elbow, because it always fell off my wrist). We went into Uncle Bert's room, so that I could parade in front of the long wardrobe mirror to see how the bracelet looked on me. Decidedly silly, I thought—especially since I was wearing my nightie—but I was afraid to say so, for fear of hurting Mum's feelings. So it was a relief when she said, "O' course, it looks a bit daft with yer nightie!" and we had a giggle together. That broke the ice, and I did, finally, manage to say thank you and act like I was pleased with this special gift. We then folded the bracelet in the hankie and put it in one of the tiny drawers of the dressing table in Uncle Bert's room, drawers that usually held nothing other than stray safety pins and buttons. And in the drawer the bracelet stayed.

Even on the few occasions dressy enough to warrant the appearance of the bracelet in public, Mum seemed to have forgotten about it, and I was not about to remind her. I was too scared of bumping into one of the girls from the street with it held in place above my elbow by a stupid hankie. It seemed a shame, though: the bracelet was quite elegant if you looked at it closely, as I occasionally did, when no one was around. It was engraved with an interlocking geometric pattern of square zigzags—identical to the edge strip on our lavatory linoleum—an ancient design of Roman or Greek origin, I believe. If only it had been on a bracelet that sat prettily on the wrist, like those that other girls wore … I felt so guilty about my lack of appreciation.

The bracelet probably cost a lot more than we could afford, even if it *had* come out of what was left of Dad's life insurance; that welcome little windfall that had helped us through a rather desperate time.

"Thank 'eavens I kept that li'l insurance up!" Mum often said. "On'y a penny a week, it was, but sometimes it was 'ard ta scrape up that penny. Several times, when yer Dad was out o' work, I thought I'd 'ave ta drop it. But somethin' made me find the money from *some*where. Thank Gawd I did! 'Cos it's made a big difference … I couldn't 'ave bought the carpet fer the 'all. Or the radio, or the washin' machine."

Our newly acquired, much-prized radio was turned on sparingly "ta save wastin' money on all that 'lectric'ty," but we soon became devoted listeners to a program called *Monday Night At Seven.* We especially loved a comedian called Arthur Askey—"that silly little man"—and the mere mention of Arthur's girlfriend, Nausea Bagwash, was enough to make the three of us crack up. I wish I could remember more of the jokes, but only two still lodge in my memory banks:

> Romantic Scene #1: When gazing at a sliver of the moon, Nausea says, "That reminds me. I must cut my toenails tonight."
> Romantic Scene #2: Arthur asks, dreamily, "Nausea, what do you think lips are made for?" To which Nausea replies, "To stop our mouths from fraying at the edges."

Arthur Askey was a welcome addition to our lives, for all his silliness: indeed, *because of* his silliness. He made us laugh till we cried. Until, to our disgust, the show was changed to *Monday Night At Eight,* and that was too late for us; we were always in bed by eight sharp. No matter how hard we begged, "Can't we stay up? Just this once … please Mum. Pl-e-a-s-e!" it was to no avail, even during school holidays. Not till the ripe old age of ten, was I allowed to stay up till nine o'clock on Mondays, and this made the boys mad: "That's not fair! Why can't we stay up, too?" They often sneaked out of bed to listen from the hallway, but their giggling invariably betrayed them, and back to bed they shot when they heard Mum's chair creak as she got up "ta send those li'l devils packin'!"

The other recent acquisition, the washing machine, made a different kind of difference. A far cry from the motor driven, automatic, spinning wonders of today, it was simply a square tub on legs with an protruding arm that you swung by hand from side to side, making paddles swoosh back and forth to agitate the clothes. But it was Mum's pride and joy. It sure beat scrubbing every article on a washboard, and we three fought over the privilege of swinging the arm back and forth. The tub had to be filled manually—Mum missed the old copper for heating the water—but there was a hose for emptying it, which was a lot easier than ladling water from the copper with saucepans. We three begged to be allowed to drain the water into a bucket, but were firmly denied—the potential for disaster being enormous—and we thought Mum was so mean.

A wringer attached to the machine squeezed out more water than was possible with hand wringing, which meant less time with your hands immersed in a sink-ful of running cold water doing the rinsing. This was a particularly welcome feature for me, because that was *my* job if I was around on a Monday morning. A miserable job it was in cold weather. The efficient little mangle also squeezed out more water *after* the rinsing and eased the drying problem, which was acute, since there was only one short clothesline on the balcony. Wet washing was draped all over the flat on drying racks that were put round the fire after we went to bed, while big things, like sheets, hung on lines stretched the length of the hallway. We were in big trouble if we touched a wet sheet with dirty hands, and weak-bladdered Bertie, in his frequent, frantic rushes to get to the lavatory in time, was the chief offender; but he soon learned that even grubbying a sheet was less frowned upon than wetting his trousers.

The washing machine's down side was that it took up a lot space in the tiny kitchen, and we all acquired bruises trying to squeeze past—particularly nasty for the boys, because the corners were at face-level for them. But that primitive appliance took much of the drudgery out of Washing Days, and Mum was "as pleased as punch" with it.

We were now eligible for a free clinic, and for the first time in our lives, we all had medical coverage. After our first visit to the clinic, Derek was put on Cod Liver Oil and Malt because he was deficient in something, which was why he was always so pale; and I was put on thyroid extract because of a thyroid deficiency, quite a pronounced deficiency, which was why I was so overweight. But frail Bertie, who looked like he had deficiencies galore, was found to have none, so he wasn't put on anything—to his chagrin, and Mum's surprise. Bertie and I envied Derek his daily dollop of Cod Liver Oil and Malt, but he hated the stuff and had to be coaxed into opening his mouth for that sticky spoonful. "Can we 'ave a taste? Jus' a li'l bit, pl-e-a-s-e Mum," Bertie and I pleaded. We did get turns licking the spoon clean afterwards and kept careful track of whose day it was.

Thyroid pills made me lose *some* weight, but it was not the dramatic effect I'd been led to expect when the problem was first diagnosed. I also had to do without a second slice of bread and jam at tea, so I came to view the intervention of the medical profession with mixed feelings. What's more, the cough medicine from the doctor didn't work as well as Liquifruita, the over-the-counter stuff I'd been taking. (Liquifruita was an evil-smelling, foul-tasting, dark brown potion containing onions, garlic and syrup, that the Hodds all swore by.)

The combined aroma of Liquifruita down my throat and Vick's Vapor Rub on my chest was a potent mix, and poor Derek suffered when I climbed into bed beside him. "P-o-o-h … she stinks!" he'd grumble, holding his nose and rolling as far away as he could without falling off the other side of bed. But this smelly combination did help with the cough that plagued me every winter and got worse each year. London air didn't agree with me, any more than it had agreed with my father, said the clinic doctor, when Mum took me back to see if he had a stronger cough syrup. "I'm afraid there's nothing more I can do," he said. "Chronic bronchitis, that's what she's got. Just like her father. Get her out of London, and she'll be fine!" At night I often coughed until I was sick, and poor Mum had to deal with all that mess while Derek and I stood shivering, bare-foot on the cold linoleum, while she changed the bedding. Between my throw-ups and Bertie's bed-wetting, Mum washed a lot of bed linen and often said, "Thank Gawd fer me washin' machine. I dunno what I'd do without it."

Despite the inadequacy of the cough medicine, Mum was very happy with our newfound access to the clinic. "I wish we'd 'ad somethin' like this when yer Dad was alive," she sometimes said. "P'raps 'e'd still be alive, if we 'ad. That rot'en ol' Panel doctor wasn't up ta much." And then I knew I was in for one of her rants: "The last time yer father went ta see 'im, 'e just give 'im a bot'le of cough medicine, an' told 'im ta come back in a week, if 'e wasn't no bet'er. When yer Dad tried ta go back a week later, 'e collapsed before 'e got ta the end o' the bloomin' street, an' a coupl'a fellas carried 'im 'ome an' 'elped me put 'im inta bed. On'y three days later, 'e was dead. An' I blame that doctor. 'E shoulda seen 'ow ill yer father was, shoulda come ta see 'im at 'ome, 'stead o' makin' 'im go ta the Surgery on a bit'er cold winter day. An' I never did like the way 'is Panel patients 'ad ta go round ta the back door o' the Surgery an' wait in a cold, drafty corridor. But the private patients waltzed in through the front door an' got ta sit in a fancy waitin' room, with a nice, warm fire!"

Access to a Panel doctor had always been touted as a major benefit of union membership, but now there seemed considerable doubt as to how beneficial it had been, in my mother's mind, at least. It was a topic that she brought up with fair regularity, and one that I came to dread. My father's death was hard enough to deal with, without entertaining the possibility that he had died needlessly.

Chapter 16

Aquinas Street: Pros and Cons

OUR GARDEN-LESS FLAT MEANT that we were expected to "go out an' play" every free minute of daylight, unless it was raining, or we were sick. This notion was reinforced by the fact that Aquinas Street was an ideal playground; there was virtually no traffic, except on Saturdays, when the taxis lined up along the road. But they inched along s-o-o slowly, and rarely was there any traffic faster than the milkman's horse-drawn cart on its stop-and-go meander, delivering bottles of milk to individual doorsteps.

Because the street *was* so safe, there were usually lots of games in progress—mostly those that involved only two or three kids, but occasionally more elaborate games, like Kick-the-Can or Hot Rice, which demanded a level of cooperation not always obtainable. Given the abundance of brick walls that Waterloo had to offer, there were also countless games that involved throwing balls against those walls. Occupants of corner houses—boasting a broad expanse of blank wall—were amazingly tolerant of the constant thud-thud-thud of a bouncing ball next to their ears, but once in a while, one would come out flapping a folded newspaper, yelling, "Clear awf! Yer li'l buggers ... " And we soon got to know which walls to avoid.

People in corner houses were also potential victims of Knockin' Dahn Ginger. This was a game in which kids tied one end of a long piece of string to a doorknocker, ran round the corner and banged the knocker by pulling on the other end of the string. They then waited with bated breath for the occupant's reaction when he/she opened the door—only to find no one on the doorstep. The best targets for this game were the more irascible characters of the neighborhood; they were guaranteed to vent their displeasure in colorful terms while the concealed pranksters listened delightedly and struggled to control their giggling, so as not to give away their hiding place. Sometimes, and this was a real bonus, the victims didn't notice the telltale string tied to the

109

knocker and closed the door, thinking they must have imagined that someone had knocked. Enough time was allowed for the poor soul to get comfortably settled in a favorite armchair, and then the operation was gleefully repeated. Usually with even more dramatic results.

The inevitable end result was the loss of the string, once the victim noticed it, and long pieces of string weren't that easy to come by, so this limited the frequency of Knocking Dahn Ginger. Mercifully: for it was a cruel game. The victims were, all too often, elderly folks who couldn't give chase to their tormentors: people like Ol' Nell Panswick, the pigeon lady, who was a frequent target, because she fit the bill in every respect. Our mother disapproved of Knocking Down Ginger, so we were forbidden to play it, and I was secretly glad, though I faked disgruntlement. However, this taboo was yet one more thing that made us misfits on the street.

For those who had roller skates, the two roads connecting Aquinas Street to Stamford Road had enough of a slope to make for exciting skate rides: exciting but hazardous. In that city environment every mishap meant an encounter with something hard and unyielding: stone sidewalks, brick walls, iron railings and lampposts. There was nothing to soften a fall: no grass, no flowerbeds, no bushes, and no helmet or pad. That kind of safety did not rank high among anyone's priorities. To make matters worse, the leather straps that held skates onto shoes were apt to come loose and contributed to innumerable scrapes and sprains. Skates at that time had metal wheels and made a tremendous noise—another irritant for long-suffering grown-ups—but, as with the thudding balls, there was an amazing tolerance on the part of the adult world.

A bicycle was a rare treasure, and the fortunate owner of one was much in demand to provide the "drive" for a popular game that we called The Skate-Chain. A long chain of roller skaters hung on to a bike as it sped downhill and turned sharply at the corner halfway down, with the bike-rider pedaling like mad to maximize the challenge for the skaters to keep their hold going round that corner. Skaters who let go were objects of scorn from those who were further back in the chain—the ones who got flung off and went hurtling down the rest of the hill toward the railings of Peabody Buildings if the chain broke. A "weak link" was promptly demoted to the tail end of the chain, so your position in the chain was a measure of status. Much effort went into working your way closer and closer to the bike, and, once in the prestigious position at the head of the chain, you were sitting pretty, so to speak, because it was the least challenging spot in the chain. This seemed unfair to the likes of me, who never achieved this lofty status, but as Mum was fond of telling us, "Ta them that 'ath, ta them it shall be given."

Skate-Chain was the most exciting game in town, with the exception of getting a free ride by hanging on to the back of a moving lorry—a stunt that only the wildest boys pulled. But, to our great disgust, we three were forbidden to play it after Derek collided with the railings and needed several stitches in his forehead. (In retrospect, it is astonishing that the Skate Chain game led to so few visits to the Casualty Department of the hospital.)

Before long, however, Aquinas Street, that perfect playground, became a scene of misery for me. The kids here turned out to be meaner and fiercer than those on Commercial Road; they rarely let me join in any of the games, so I spent much of the time sitting on our front doorstep, watching them. I was bewildered by this hostility. I wasn't a fast runner, but when it came to skipping and ball catching, I was as good as most and better than others. Occasionally I *was* included: when one more person was needed, or if I had a skipping rope the right length or a ball the right size. On those red-letter days, I joined in and played just like one of the crowd, always hoping that this would prove to be a turning point. But the next day, I'd be back on the doorstep, a spectator again, baffled and miserable. These kids may be a cut above those on Commercial Road, I often thought, but they're a nasty lot; and the girls were worse than the boys; or did it just seem that way because I played mostly in all-girl games?

Things suddenly went from bad to worse when the Hendersons moved into the small row house immediately opposite our flat. Hazel rapidly became a popular figure, but was spiteful toward anyone who fell out of favor with her—like me, or anyone foolish enough to play with me. She quickly poisoned the waters, and the other chidren shunned me even more after her arrival on the street. However, Hazel never went so far as to repeat her whip attack. One encounter with Mum-on-the-warpath was enough, apparently.

Then began the name-calling, largely instigated by Hazel. However, the others didn't need much encouragement, and jeers of "Ol' Fat'y Arbunkle!" and "There goes ol' Fat'y!" soon followed me wherever I went. Even if I was sitting on our doorstep playing quietly by myself. When I could stand it no longer, I rang the doorbell and begged Mum to let me play indoors; but outside was the place to play, she said, and outside I was to stay.

There *were* a few blessed times when I didn't have to deal with the street: rainy days, after dark, in class at school, and when I was reading with Mr. Wilson. But my best escape hatch was with Louie and Harry, in their flat. Most Sundays I happily helped Louie in the kitchen and Harry in the garden, and, when the chores were done, amused myself however I pleased. There was no anxiety about being told to "go out an' play," and there was plenty to amuse myself with in their flat. Harry was still a collector of gadgets and silly wind-up toys, and there was an abundant supply of old comics—courtesy of Viley—unless Louie had gone on a "clearin' out" rampage.

Harry's latest hobby and passion was a collection of pet birds, which were an endless source of fascination to me. I even liked to help clean out their cages, but to Louie's house-proud eyes, they were "Messy fings!" The canaries were a lovely soft yellow, like lemon-flavored sherbet powder; and they sang a lot, filling the room with their song if several were in voice at the same time. Billie, a blue budgie, had a vocabulary of two or three just-distinguishable words or phrases, and was fun because he liked to sit on your shoulder, nibbling gently at your ear, chattering quietly, as if whispering a secret. But my favorite was Joey, a beautiful multi-colored European goldfinch. If Harry whistled a certain tune, Joey burst into song, a full-throated complicated song, that went on and on and on, with lots of variations. Just by himself, Joey could fill the room with his glorious, liquid warbling. I practiced for hours, trying to whistle the tune that made Joey sing, but never produced more than a pathetic breathy sound that Joey did not find inspirational.

Sometimes, if several of the birds were in full song, Louie would cover her ears and plead, "Aw! Fer Gawd's sake, shuddup, can'cha! I can't 'ear meself fink in 'ere," and Harry would put the offending bird to sleep by draping a cloth over its cage. This never ceased to amaze me. Birds go to sleep, instantly, just because it's dark? And how strange to think that one creature could have such total control over another! But when I mentioned this to Mum, all she said was, "Pity yew three ain't like that," and didn't find it at all amazing.

While Louie and Harry took their Sunday after-dinner kip, I happily read comics or did, and re-did, the huge Snow White jigsaw puzzle that they'd given me after we saw the film (my first brand new puzzle: no missing pieces!) Their afternoon snooze was a very special time for me. It was the only time of the week when I was completely alone, and I relished every quiet minute. Of course, it helped that Louie had primed me with sweets, had sent me round to Hood's Sweet Shop to get humbugs or toffees for Harry and a chocolatey treat—perhaps raspberry truffles—for Louie and me. Though I sometimes plumped for pear drops or something with liquorice.

Much as I enjoyed walking out of Hood's shop with those bags of pleasure-to-come, I dreaded entering it, because I was deathly afraid of Mr. Hood. He was a gruff old man and impatient if you dilly-dallied in making a choice from his vast and delicious selection; but it was the stuffed glove protruding unnaturally from one sleeve that made him truly fearful. I shuddered at the thought of being touched by it and couldn't keep my eyes off the stiff, black leather. Instead of concentrating on my choice of sweets I was always preoccupied, wondering how I could avoid having that "hand," brush against my skin. So I got yelled at on a regular basis in Hood's Sweet Shop and always emerged with a feeling of relief at having got *that* over and done with.

After Louie and Harry woke up, came Sunday tea—winkles and celery sticks and chocolate digestive biscuits—while we listened to a radio show, "beamed all the way from Lux'mberg," Harry told me, in awed tones. I had no idea where Luxembourg was, but gathered from his voice that it was far away. That, I supposed, explained why the reception was not always good, but made it all the more miraculous when the signal came through crystal clear. It was a commercial program, aimed at children, and regularly featured a group called, "The Ovaltinies," an obnoxiously, cheery, up beat bunch of girls and boys—though I didn't think them obnoxious at the time. They opened and closed the show with the song:

> We are the Ovaltine-ies
> Happy boys and g-i-r-l-s!
> At games and sports
> We're more than keen,
> No merrier children can be seen,
> Because we all drink Ovaltine
> We're happy boys and g-i-r-l-s!

This musical gem still runs through my mind sometimes—especially when I'm chomping on a stick of celery! My favorite part of the show was the weekly serial; I could scarcely wait to hear the next exciting installment and was beside myself if I missed a week and had to fill in the blank episode as best I could the following Sunday.

In addition to introducing me to radio programs from foreign countries, Louie and Harry often took me "ta the pictures," where I laughed till my sides ached at the antics of Laurel and Hardy or Abbott and Costello, and adored Shirley Temple pictures. How I envied that pretty, dimpled, dancing-and-singing doll of a child, with her mop of perfect curls. Oh! ... To be just *one* of those things. My favorite movie house was The Odeon at the Elephant and Castle, where, after the cartoons and The News and the B-picture, a brilliantly lit organ came up out of the floor, and an organist played—completely unconcerned—as he and the organ rose up out of the depths. When it was time for the main film, he stood and bowed stiffly in three directions, before—again playing unconcernedly—descending back down into the darkness. It was astonishing, and magical, as far as I was concerned.

The film *Snow White* was a huge disappointment. I thought all that animation was a silly way to make a picture. Drawing dwarfs was one thing, but real characters like Snow White and the Wicked Queen? That didn't seem right. I wanted my movie-people to be real.

However I no longer labored under the misapprehension that everything portrayed on the screen actually happened—as when I was first exposed to movies at the Saturday morning shows for kids. At that time, I couldn't imagine how any film star was persuaded to play a role in which he or she died. It seemed improbable that money alone would do the trick, no matter how much was offered. Unless they got paid a long time ahead, so they had time to enjoy the money before dying? Or did the filmmakers cheat and spring the dying bit on them as a surprise? I puzzled over this, until I realized that dead film stars re-appeared in later films. I felt decidedly letdown—all that sympathy lavished on dying heroes and heroines, only to find that it was all pretend! ("Ya daft thing!" said Mum, when I told her.)

My time with Louie and Harry became a dominant part of my life; I essentially lived from one Sunday to the next, impatiently counting the days and trying to ignore the street scene with its attendant difficulties. Then, out of the blue, I became the proud owner of a bike, when Viley got a spiffing new one, a racing model with low handlebars. She passed her old three-quarter-size bike on to me, and this did wonders for my standing on the street. I came to be in demand as the bike rider for The Skate-Chain (this being before Derek's head injury). I was ecstatic at this break in the clouds. There was no change in the street's acceptance of me in other games, but I was prepared to be patient and hoped for a gradual thaw. One evening, I came in after some exciting Skate-Chain rides and, while being "topped an' tailed," told my mother how much fun I was having now that the others let me play with them. "Don't be s'daft!" she said. "They on'y wan'cha 'cos ya've got a bike."

That burst my bubble in a hurry. I was devastated. But clearly, there was no sympathy to be had from my mother, so I held back the tears until I was alone. Fortunately, the boys were already asleep when I crawled into bed, and I had a good cry in the dark. (Writing about this, so many years later, I am astonished to find the pain inflicted by that blunt remark still there, still sharp and vivid). I knew, in my heart of hearts, that what Mum said was true; but I wasn't willing to face up to it. I persuaded myself that she was wrong and, for a while, continued to enjoy a modicum of popularity on days when the Skate-Chain game was possible.

The moment of truth came one day when teams for a big game of Kick the Can were being chosen. I looked around, saw that Hazel Henderson and Phyllis Turner (my two nemeses) weren't there, and plucked up the courage to ask, "C'n I play?" In response came a barrage of jeers:

"'Ow abaht *that*! Ol' Fat'y Arbunkle, 'erself! She wants t'play wiv' us?"

"Well ... we don't wanna play wiv' *yew*, Fat'y!"

"Why don'cha jus' clear awf!"

"Go a-way! Go a-way!"

And, in unison, they all took up the chant: "Go a-way! / Go a-way! / Fat'y! Fat'y! / Go a-way!"

I turned and ran. About a dozen of them, boys *and* girls, gave chase, and pursued me the length of the street, jeering, mocking, then—the final horror—throwing stones at me. Stones were a rare feature on those city streets, but on that particular day, there happened to be a pile of gravel outside the builder's yard. A few stones hit me on the back, but it was the ones that caught me on the head and face that really hurt. I ran for home as fast as I could and frantically rang the bell, then crouched down facing the door and protected my face and head with my arms. But the hail of stones had stopped, probably for fear of breaking the glass panes around the door, and everybody was running away when Mum opened the door and found me, hysterical and bloodied from a stone that had caught the side of my face. By the time she'd assessed the situation, checked on the damage and calmed me down, there wasn't a child in sight—which made her almost as mad as what they had done.

"The li'l buggers!" she fumed. "I'll 'ave their guts fer garters! 'Oo was it?" When I shook my head, mutely, she went on, "Jus' tell me 'oo it was! Come on, nah, Gwen. Why won'cha tell me?" and, after waiting hopefully, "Aach, ya silly thing! Yew get on me nerves, yew do."

For days, she pestered me for names, but I didn't tell her. I was afraid to. If she knew, and went on one of her rampages, "the street" would only hate me more. Things were bad enough without that. As it was, I couldn't face going outside, and, for a while, Mum walked me to and from school and didn't insist on me going outside to play. Eventually, however, we drifted back to the old routine, and I was, once more, expected to go outside. But never again did I join in any of the games, even when I was invited to join The Skate-Chain. I now knew that Mum was right: the other kids *did* only want me because I had a bike. A bitter pill to swallow, that was.

I began to feel more and more isolated: increasingly hopeless in a world where I had no friends; where no one liked to do the kind of things I liked; and where I had no one I could talk to about how I felt. In the Waterloo world you were expected to "pull yerself togevva an' jus' git on wiv' it." Feeling sorry for oneself got little or no sympathy, and as the weeks went by, I spiraled down into what I suppose was a depression. How I missed Dad! He'd always been my sounding board … I could see no hope that my situation would get any better and desperately wanted out. But I had no idea how to free myself from this trap. Then, standing on a chair one day, to reach a jar of jam from the back of the pantry, I noticed a small, dark blue bottle labeled POISON. It was on the highest shelf and had probably been purchased to deal with the mice that were sometimes a problem. I knew about poisons from *Grimm's Fairy Tales*, and my mind kept going back to the blue bottle with the white label. And every time, a bubble of hope rose up inside me …

One day I was feeling particularly despondent and happened to be alone in the flat, so I dragged a chair over to the pantry and, with the help of a couple of pillows from the bedroom, managed to reach the bottle. I stood on the chair, holding it in my hand … and have often wondered what I would have done next. Would I have drunk the contents of the little blue bottle? Or put it back on its shelf, content in the knowledge that it was there—within reach? I'll never know. As I stood on the chair, looking at it, I heard my brothers clomping up the stairs towards the door of the flat and Mum's voice saying, "Sh-h! Don't make sa much noise, yew two!" I hastily put the bottle back on its shelf, just in time, before they came stampeding down the hall, followed by Mum.

"Wa'cha bin doin' with tha' chair?" were her first words. "An' why the pillers?"

"Jus' what 'ave yew bin up to, m'lady?" she added, suspiciously.

"I fought I 'eard a mouse," I muttered, as I dragged the chair back to where it belonged. This was not exactly a convincing answer. I had a track record of running away from mice, not seeking them out, but to my relief, Mum didn't pursue the matter further. However, next time I looked, the bottle was gone; and it never reappeared on the shelf in the pantry. Neither did my mother ever refer to the incident. But she put two and two together, I think. She probably *had* noticed that I was depressed, even though no mention of it had ever been made. And maybe I didn't put the bottle back exactly as it had been.

For whatever reason, from that day on I was allowed to stay indoors if I wished. On cold days, Bertie and Derek took a dim view of this, but Mum turned a deaf ear to their cries of, "It ain't fair!" Occasionally, if Hazel and Phyllis were not on the street, I ventured out. But usually I kept myself busy indoors. I did puzzles and played Patience [Solitaire]; read *Grimm's Fairy Tales* for the three-hundredth time; or tried to knit—without dropping stitches or making them so tight that the needle broke when I moved them along (bone knitting needles then, not aluminum). I even filled in the blanks bits left in old coloring books; anything beat dealing with that miserable street scene. And gradually, as my world began to seem a bit more manageable, I felt less trapped.

To get me out from under her feet, Mum sometimes let me play in Uncle Bert's bedroom if he wasn't around, and this opened up a whole new world of games involving the long wardrobe mirror in that room. I became two people: the real me, and the reflected me. I had a friend, at last. Soon there were several, each with a distinctive voice; for the game changed from day to day, and my reflection got cast in a number of different roles. What's more, these were friends that I could mold as I pleased—although we did occasionally argue and get mad at one another! It took my mother a while to get used to the non-stop murmuring from Uncle Bert's room, and, at first, she regularly berated me:

"Wha'cha doin' in there?"

"Yew talkin' ta yerself agin? Ya mus' be goin' barmy!"

"Can'cha find somethin' bet'er ta do than talk ta yerself?"

"Gives me the willies, it do ... jus' lis'nin' ta yer."

And, one day when I was doing a better-than-usual job of the second voice, she called out, "'Oo's that in there with yew?" But she eventually reconciled herself to this strange behavior and let me be.

It was around this time that I learned how to iron, and this unexpectedly opened up a whole new chapter in my fantasy life. For practice, I worked on the rolled bandages that were kept in a couple of shoeboxes in place of too-expensive Band-Aids. All cuts and scrapes got bandaged, as did the boils that Bertie was still plagued with, poor boy. "All that poison, it's gotta come out," Mum would sigh. She predicted that this would take seven years, but Bertie was now almost seven, with no sign of abatement. Each spring and autumn he had a rough time for a week or two, unable to sit, stand, or lie in comfort; worse yet, the poor boy had to suffer the indignity of walking around covered in bandages, like a badly wounded soldier or a partially wrapped Egyptian mummy.

The soiled bandages had to be washed, ironed, and rolled up, ready for re-use, so a rapid turnaround was needed to keep the supply adequate at the peak of Bertie's episodes. And that's where I now began to play a role. At first I was put on rolling duty, but soon graduated to ironing, and I still remember the pride of my first successfully ironed bandage. It was a tricky business, ironing with an old flatiron heated over a gas flame. The iron needed frequent re-heating, and maintaining the right temperature—hot enough to do the job, but not so hot as to singe the fabric—was an acquired skill; as was unraveling the bandage in the path of the iron without letting the hot metal touch your hand as you guided the strip of tangled gauze. A number of burns preceded mastery of this skill, but the end result was immense satisfaction at getting through this rite of passage; it was right up there with the triumph of being allowed to wheel a neighbor's baby in its pram.

My new skill led to a whole new "mirror game." Now that I could help with the production of clean bandages, I was allowed to play with a few of them, and my mirror friends and I played nurses and hospitals, bandaging dolls till they looked like Bertie in mid-boil-season. This lent itself to endless variations, and dire emergencies and dramas got played out. On rainy days the two boys, cooped up in the flat, begged me to let them join in, but I jealously guarded the secret world that I'd carved out for myself in front of the wardrobe mirror. Of course, none of this did anything to improve my street-scene skills, but it gave me countless happy hours and made a big dent in the depression that had been threatening to overwhelm me.

◆　　◆　　◆

The summer holidays were always alarming to contemplate—six long difficult weeks with no school to provide a daily escape hatch from the street. But that summer, the summer of 1938, I received a respite when The Country Holiday Fund sent me away for a week, free of charge. The boys were too young, but I jumped at the chance when Mum raised the issue.

However, when the day arrived, it was with great trepidation that I set off for this adventure, because, in the weeks since signing up, there'd been the nagging fear that Hazel Henderson and Phyllis Turner might be going too. What would I do, if they were? Could I just walk away, at the last moment? It was not a matter that I cared to discuss with Mum, whose contempt for my timidity I knew only too well; so I sweated out my fears on my own. However, there was no sign of Hazel or Phyllis in the little crowd at the station, and my heart was lighter than it had been for a long time when I said goodbye to Mum and the boys and clambered aboard the train.

We were headed for Gloucestershire, and the train journey itself was a thrill; especially when we got beyond the city outskirts and were speeding through unfamiliar scenes of fields and cows and sheep and horses. We were each given a lunch box containing a sandwich, a fruity drink and an apple; after which, some time was spent giving solemn admonitions about the good behavior expected of us in the homes of kind strangers. The gist was that, under someone else's roof, you follow their rules without question or complaint, and special emphasis was put on the need to comply with the bedtime set by your new "parents." It seems that this issue had been troublesome in the past, probably because many kids were used to staying out quite late on long summer evenings.

Finally, we were each given another small package, containing a wash cloth, a bar of soap, a small brush with a long handle, and a flat tin of pink powder. None of us knew what to do with the little brush or the powder, dental hygiene not being part of the Waterloo scene, so we were given careful instructions on how to clean our teeth, and taken to the lavatory, a few at a time, to demonstrate that we had understood the instructions.

My Gloucester family consisted of an elderly couple and their granddaughter, Gloria, a girl about my age. They lived in a tiny cottage with a colorful flower garden, nestled among the hills with not another house in sight; it could not have been more different from the London scene I had left!

Grandparents had been distinctly lacking in my life, and these two were lovely and kind and gentle, so I enjoyed this novel experience.

It was unexpected to find no mother or father in this household, but nobody talked about Gloria's parents, and I got the feeling that nobody wanted to, so I didn't dare raise the subject. She was a beautiful slender child, with a pale complexion and a mop of tight, black curls that caused her considerable anguish every morning when her grandmother insisted on trying to bring some semblance of order to that dense tangle. How I envied Gloria: her pretty face and slender build, that glorious hair, her kind grandparents, the delightful cottage, the lovely garden, and her name, which I thought the prettiest I'd ever heard.

We got along well, Gloria and I. Most of the time we played in the garden, for I soon discovered that Gloria's grandparents were very protective and rarely allowed her to venture outside the garden. To her delight, because I was there to go with her, they let us roam into the field just beyond the garden hedge to pick wildflowers, as long as we told them first. And, once, they even let us climb to the top of the hill across the road. But this made them nervous because it took us out of their sight, and they were waiting anxiously at the gate for our return. I began to realize what a lonely child Gloria must be, with those overprotective grandparents in that isolated house. There were no children of her age around, and she obviously spent a lot of time playing by herself when she wasn't in school. In this paradise, she wasn't in any better shape than I was in the crowded, unlovely streets of Waterloo.

That Country Holiday Fund experience was a week of great happiness for me. For Gloria too, I think. "Come again next year!" they all said, when the time came to say goodbye, and I hoped that I would. But the last I ever saw of them was as they stood by the garden gate, waving me off.

Returning home was a bittersweet experience. I missed Gloria and her grandparents and the loveliness of the quiet countryside, and I dreaded having to deal with the street scene again; but it was good to see Mum and the two boys and all the Hodds. And that interlude in the country had made a difference. It had given me a glimpse of another world, one that I could conjure up in my mind's eye whenever I wanted an escape from Waterloo.

◆   ◆   ◆

ADDENDUM

A few years ago, I spent an afternoon wandering around Waterloo. The Cut and The Marsh were disappointing—glitzy, plasticky shadows of their former colorful selves. There were only a few "barrer boys," none of them yelling raucous invitations to come and buy unbeatable wares; no "cockles an' mussels" or live eels for sale; even the permanent shops seemed to have less individuality.

The Commercial Road that I knew had vanished completely. Soon after the war every building in that neighborhood was razed to make room for the Festival Hall, the National Theatre, and all the cultural facilities that make up the new South Bank. Gone are the ugly, dirty, old buildings that used to hide the river from Commercial Road. Now one can stroll along a riverside esplanade and enjoy the views of the river and the city on the opposite bank; and it is especially gorgeous at night, when all the lights are reflected in the water. There are few reminders of the old south bank, but the railway arches under which (or so we were told) the comedy team Flanagan and Allen slept—and which inspired their song "Underneath the Arches"—are still there, but chic shops now nestle snugly under them. (I recently learned that the actual inspirational railway arches are somewhere in Derby.)

Gentrification, I learned, had threatened to spread as far as Coin Street until The Coin Street Project, spearheaded by a group of determined locals, succeeded in preventing the entire area from becoming nothing but high rise buildings, expensive restaurants and luxury flats. They replaced the old run-down housing of the Coin Street area with new and better houses that remain within the means of teachers, nurses, bus drivers, retail workers, and the like. In much the same spirit, along Upper Ground the occasional pub was spared, along with Gabriel's Wharf (one of the few picturesque old buildings) and the OXO tower—now a culture center, complete with art galleries.

But much of that section of Waterloo *has* been gentrified, and properties fetch phenomenal prices. For instance, on the corner of Stamford Street and Coin Street, Jay's Confectioners, where the formidable Mrs. Jay scowlingly dispensed sweets and comic books after a careful scrutiny of your hot, sticky pennies—and where you were well advised to scrutinize your change—has become an expensive, trendy restaurant.

Aquinas Street looked unchanged at first sight, apart from the parked cars lining it on both sides. Closer inspection showed that the exteriors of all the buildings had been spruced up with fresh paint and scrubbed brickwork, and inside, as I learned when the lady living opposite our old flat invited me in for a cup of tea, there is now modern plumbing and central heating. This lady, it turned out, grew up on Doon Street, which used to back on to Commercial Road, and she went to school with Nell Weddinger, one of my stepsisters. I didn't let on that, in our Commercial Road days, we hadn't been allowed to play with "those rough Doon Street kids." And it was amusing to find that this particular Doon Street child now owned her cozy, little Aquinas Street house (Hazel Henderson's old house) and was sitting on a veritable little gold mine. I wondered, as I sipped my cup of tea in what had been the house of my nemesis, what my mother would have thought about this turn of events. Would she have been outraged or pleased by this Doon Street kid's improved circumstances? The latter, I expect.

The crooked, narrow road that led from Aquinas Street to Hatfield Street has been built over, and the school, now used "fer trainin' sailer boys," according to my Doon Street lady, is inaccessible. Peabody Buildings have been transformed into a fancy gated community, with its tall grim Victorian stone buildings scrubbed clean but otherwise left unchanged. However, they must have undergone changes inside; nobody would pay gated-community prices for the Peabody Buildings that I knew! I was always afraid to enter their unlit hallways and climb the dank, massive stone stairs that spiraled up, passing unspeakably smelly communal lavatories on every other floor.

The history of Peabody Buildings has a roller coaster quality, I recently discovered. They were originally built by George Peabody, the Peabody who sprinkled the East Coast of America with Museums, Institutes, and divers educational establishments. After settling in London in 1837 and amassing a considerable fortune, he made a $2.5 million donation to the City of London for the construction of moderate-rent housing to replace slum dwellings. I wonder how he would feel about the various transformations of his project. Would he be more outraged by its descent into a slum property in the 30's, or by its re-invention as a haven for the well heeled in the 90's? Or might he simply be pleased that his sturdy stone buildings had stood the test of time so well?

Chapter 17

Smoother Sailing

THE FOLLOWING YEAR WAS a lot easier. I was now ten, big enough to go places by myself, and as I gradually spread my wings, the problem of the street no longer dominated to the same extent. In particular, since none of the Aquinas Street crowd ever went to Lavington Street Baths, I made the most of my free pass and spent a lot of time there, by myself.

Why the school gave me that pass, I never knew. Maybe I was one of the few Hatfield Street School pupils who could actually swim—thanks to the Hodds. Now when I went swimming with them, the big challenge for Viley and me was daring to jump off ever-higher diving boards, and we did, eventually, summon enough courage to jump off the really high board. I was now too big for "the fellas" to toss me around, but we had a lot of fun swimming races, playing Tag, or just "muckin' abou'" in the water.

Swimming through one another's spread legs was a great favorite, but I learned the hard way not to do this with Harry or Georgie. They both had a bit of a mean streak and were apt to suddenly pull their legs together, trapping me underwater—even after swearing, "not this time, I promise!" When I got cross with them, they just laughed and teased, "Did'ncha notice? I 'ad me fingers crossed!" I tried to get the better of them, refusing to dive unless I could see their hands high in the air with all ten fingers splayed out; but, after behaving themselves for a while, they'd wait till I started to dive down before pulling their legs together. The more I spluttered, "But yew promised!" the more they laughed, saying, "Can't trust no-one these days, can ya?" It was difficult not to laugh with them; they were clearly having such a great time, even if it was at my expense.

Percy, the gentle giant, was the only one who could be trusted not to be sneaky. A real softie, he was, unlike his sweetheart, the hard-as nails-petite Rosie. What a study in contrast they made: Perce was blond and blue-eyed,

Rosie, dark and sloe-eyed; he was amiable and slow moving, she, sharp-tongued and brisk. But they got along famously—as long as he let her rule the roost. Round-faced Perce looked like an enormous pudgy baby, but he had muscles of iron, and I loved it when he came to the Baths, because only he could still throw me around like a beach ball.

Amazingly, Viley still let me tag along with her sometimes, though she must have been fourteen and ready to leave school. Together we joined a choir and sang in Queen's Hall once a week. I loved that large, circular hall, lined with gleaming, red-brown mahogany. (It was destroyed by fire, I think, in one of the early air raids of the war, so I'm doubly grateful to Viley for having introduced me to that lovely place, while it was still there to be enjoyed.) To my surprise, I enjoyed the singing, too; though there can't have been an audition, because neither of us could hold a tune; our contributions must have been drowned out, or kindly overlooked. It was the first time I'd been part of a group focussed on working together simply for the pleasure of creating something that was beautiful—yet transitory—and I found it to be a stirring experience. Of course, it didn't hurt that being the youngest choir member made me feel grown-up, helped boost my otherwise distinctly negative self-image.

Viley also took me on bike rides and introduced me to the group of adolescents that she hung out with near The Elephant and Castle—a decidedly less cultural scene than Queens Hall. In retrospect, I'm amazed that I was allowed to ride a bike across The Elephant and Castle, a complicated intersection of five or six wide roads, all laced with tramlines. There was less traffic then, but it was a very busy spot, and the tramlines were a special challenge to cyclists, because the gap between the lines was a perfect match for bike wheels. You had to take great care to cross each rail at a big angle, but we clearly learned to navigate with some skill, for I don't remember any of us ever coming to grief.

Viley seemed to exert a strong attraction on the boys—"Like flies to a blessed 'oney pot," was how Mum put it—and this gave me considerable pause. For Viley was definitely on the large side, though not as overweight as I was. She was "no oil paintin', that's fer sure," (Mum, again), and I somehow knew what she meant, though I'd never seen an oil painting and I doubt whether she had. However, the remark caused me to examine faces more critically, and as far as I could see, no one we knew was in that category—except for dead Auntie Mary. I loved Viley and felt that Mum was being unduly unkind to her, but on the other hand, Viley's undeniable popularity with the boys did give me reason to think that perhaps my prospects were not as bleak as I had come to suppose. I started to examine my face in the hand mirror that lived on the windowsill and decided that, feature by feature, I stacked up quite favorably with Viley. Yet nobody seemed to find me in the least bit attractive … She, apparently, had something that I didn't, and I was mystified as to what that something might be. It never occurred to me that the age difference between us might be a factor.

School continued to be a haven for me, though I no longer had the luxury of Mr. Slarks for a teacher, because I had "gone up." The playground still presented problems, and I still delayed entering it till the last moment—with disastrous results, one afternoon. I was waiting outside the gate for the whistle and realized that I needed to go to the lavatory. The lavatories were behind a wall, and I was scared to death of getting trapped there by one or more of my tormentors. So I waited till just before the whistle, in the hope that, by then, the lavatories would be empty … but I had waited too long. The whistle blew as I slipped behind the lavatory wall … Help! I'd be late getting into line, and nothing escaped sharp-eyed Mrs. Greenaway, the teacher on playground duty. Rather than face The Dragon Lady, as she was known throughout the school, I decided to stay where I was until everybody had left the playground. Then I could sneak in, unseen. It was a risk, but might work.

Embarked on what was my first deliberate attempt at law breaking, I waited anxiously until I could hear no more shuffling of feet, then crept along, hugging the playground wall—and got the shock of my life when I turned the corner. At the bottom of the steps stood Mrs. Greenaway, waiting, arms folded across her ample bosom, and I almost ran smack into her. *She must have seen me slip behind the lavatory wall* … My knees turned to jelly and my heart lurched, so violently I thought it must end up in my mouth (so *that's* what people meant when they said, "Me 'eart was in me mouf'"). Mrs. Greenaway transfixed me with her notorious steely-eyed stare and after what seemed forever, said sternly, "Come and see me before school on Monday morning. And make sure you're not late!" Then she turned and climbed the flight of wide steps. Flabbergasted, I stood there, stunned; then made my way to class where I was marked late, told off by my teacher, and had to "stay in" after school.

This happened on a Friday afternoon, and thus began a dreadful weekend. Mrs. Greenaway had gauged her victim well. For two long days and three long nights I tormented myself, wondering what punishment awaited me. The mere thought of climbing the steps, walking along the corridor and knocking on her door, made me feel weak, and the prospect of actually standing in front of her, waiting to hear my fate, was too much for my poor bowels. I spent a lot of time examining the ancient zigzag design on our lavatory lino that weekend …

I considered running away, but didn't know how to go about it. Where would I go? To Auntie Ada? No. She'd probably be cross with me for being so silly and would have to send me back, sooner or later. Anyhow, how would I get the bus fare? Were children allowed on buses without a grown-up? Gloria and Gloucestershire flashed through my mind, but that involved trains and even more expensive fares. I even considered going across the river to hide in one of the big London parks—and sleep in the bushes—but I wasn't brave enough for that ... Anyway, I'd soon be found by a policeman or a park attendant and brought back to face the music.

I slept very little that weekend. I was ashamed of "bein' in trouble" and daren't tell Mum, because she'd be really angry; not because of what I had done, but for what I hadn't done. The fact that I hadn't been able to face the prospect of encountering other kids in the lavatories would make her furious.

So I hugged my misery to myself until Monday morning, when I dragged myself to Mrs. Greenaway's room and stood quaking in front of her. I couldn't believe my ears when she said, mildly, "Well, I hope this will be a lesson to you." Then, more sternly, "And don't ever do anything like that again. You won't get off so lightly next time!" What a wily lady! She knew that she'd already given me the worst imaginable punishment, one that probably wouldn't have worked with any other student in Hatfield Street School. I wonder if, over that weekend, she savored the thought of my agonies? Whether she felt a twinge of pity? Most likely she never gave me a passing thought.

Soon after this incident I "went up" again and, to my dismay, found myself in Mrs. Greenaway's class. But she wasn't quite the dragon-lady of my imagination. She *was* strict and brooked no nonsense, but she was fair, except for one occasion on which she came down on me unfairly—in my opinion. My crime consisted of scooping a hole in an apple with my fingernail; the apple was sitting on the shelf under my desk, waiting for the mid-morning break, and Mrs. Greenaway came from behind, saw me scoop out a mini-morsel and put it in my mouth—and Pow! She hit me with a wooden ruler, so hard that the ruler snapped, and I was pretty upset. Not because I'd been hit by a teacher for the first time ever—probably an all-time record in Hatfield Street School—but because the punishment seemed way out of proportion to the crime. I almost told Mum about the broken ruler, but thought better of it. School was school, home was home; and Mum would probably have taken Mrs. Greenaway's side.

My street life changed dramatically—for the better—when two new girls moved into the area and were put into Mrs. Greenaway's class. Overnight, just like that, I had friends. *Two* friends! Neither lived on Aquinas Street, praise be! But near enough that we could easily get together. At long last, I had friends to walk to school with, and playground-avoidance tactics became a thing of the past; I now gobbled down breakfast and dinner, so as to spend as much time as possible with my new friends before the whistle blew.

Jean Sunnebank, the first to arrive, lived in The Police Buildings. This tall block of flats, exclusively for families of policemen, were built around a large, open area and provided a perfect traffic-free set up—a policeman's pay seemed to rule out any means of transportation faster than a bicycle.

Mrs. Sunnebank was a Nervous Nelly and wouldn't let Jean play on Aquinas Street, because of "all those rough boys from Peabody Buildings," (not to mention the rough girls, I thought), so we always played in that open area. This was just fine by me: I was only too happy to find an alternative to Aquinas Street. Georgie Harris—who'd had a few brushes with the law, I think—joked, rather nervously, "I s'pose I'd bet'er mind me p's an' q's, wiv' you bein' all matey wiv' coppers' kids, these days." But those matey coppers' kids were making a huge difference in my life. They let me join in whatever was going on, accepted me in a way that the Aquinas Street crowd never had, and I began to feel like a normal child again.

The other new girl, Marjory Strutt, lived on Stamford Street, and, like Jean, she had a younger sister Pauline. There the resemblance between my two new friends ended: Jean had a sweet round face and was a bit plump; Marjory's face was thin, and she was skinny and angular. ("All knees an' elbows, that girl," said Mum.) Jean was dreamy and solemn and slow moving, though no dummy in school; Marjory was quick and lively in every way—the way she thought and talked and moved. "'Er an' that mother of 'er's, they shaw live up ta their name, struttin' around, the pair of 'em!" was Mum's assessment.

Mum didn't like Marjory; but I worshipped her. How could I not? She had every attribute I longed for: she was slim, had gleaming blond hair (bangs, too—I was so envious), a quick mind and an equally quick tongue. Last, but not least, she laughed a lot; and made *me* laugh—something I hadn't done much of recently, except when listening to Arthur Askey or horsing around with the Hodds.

The two Strutt girls seemed to have an inexhaustible supply of elegant outfits with swirling flared skirts and matching tops. They were in interesting color combinations, gray with red or yellow, navy with red or white, all equally stunning and all hand-knitted by their mother, Marjory said. (Although Mum unaccountably snorted in a disbelieving way, when I told her this.) Inspired by these outfits, I laboriously learned how to knit basket stitch, a pattern often featured in them, and managed to produce several blankets for my dollhouse beds.

Because Stamford Street was a busy road with speeding taxis, heavy lorries and lumbering buses, we always played indoors when I went round to Marjory's flat. This, in itself, was a novel experience: I'd never before played in a friend's house! Like us, the Strutts lived in an upstairs flat, but the person below theirs was out during the day, so we didn't have to be quiet all the time. The row housing from which these flats were carved, had been built on a grander scale than any we'd ever lived in, so the Strutts' flat was nice and spacious; the rooms were large, the ceilings tall, and the stairs wide. Best of all, the tall, front windows opened onto a small balcony, from which we could watch the street below and wave to people in passing buses.

Marjory and her sister had a dollhouse (a fancy shop-bought one, not as nice as mine, I thought, but didn't say), and the three of us played with it for hours. Their mother gave us tiny squares of bread or apple, for tea parties with the dollhouse dolls, and I soon adored Mrs. Strutt as much as I adored her daughter. Like Marjory, Mrs. Strutt was tall and slender and quick—like a pair of elegant long-legged birds, they were—and she even wore make-up and high heels and earrings, which was a first for a Waterloo Mum, in my experience. In the Strutts' flat, I was made to feel so welcome and so safe, and it rapidly became a place where I loved to be.

Pauline Strutt was more like their father, a slow-moving, deliberate man of solid build, and he was away a lot "becos' 'e's an MP," Marjory said. I thought she meant a Member of Parliament and was duly impressed, but later found out that he was, in fact, a Military Policeman. To my mother, this was just another example of undesirable behavior on Marjory's part.

"The li'l liar!" she snorted. "I wish ya'd keep away from that show-arse of a girl, Gwen. She's no good, I tell ya."

I was never able to convince Mum that the MP error was entirely of my making. I'd never heard of Military Police, and MP meant only one thing: a Member of Parliament. I was astonished to find that my mother wasn't alone in her dislike of Marjory. And it wasn't just Marjory: the entire Strutt family met with disapproval. There was a lot of tut-tutting about "those Strutts," but especially about Mrs. Strutt. I heard mutterings that, "she's no bet'er than she should be," a remark that made less sense the more I thought about it.

What was so terrible about being no better than you should be? At worst, it seemed, you just weren't trying hard enough to *exceed* the world's expectations; to me, Mrs. Strutt seemed to be trying a lot harder than many of her accusers, and I wondered if I'd misheard. I made a point of listening carefully, but there was no mistake. That was, indeed, what was being said of Marjory's mother among the womenfolk of Waterloo, in tones indicating that her behavior was in some way reprehensible. I asked Mum one day what the expression meant, but all the answer I got was, "Yew'll find out ... sooner or later." Which wasn't much help.

Teachers at school also discouraged my friendship with Marjory and went out of their way to keep us apart, but approved of Jean and did their best to steer me in her direction. Much as I liked quiet, gentle Jean, in comparison with Marjory she was, truth to tell, a bit dull. It was Marjory that I adored. Perplexed and upset by the reaction of the adult world to this wonderful girl, who had literally lit up my life, I did my best to ignore all these silly grown-ups.

◆　　◆　　◆

During the Easter holidays Mum and I went to stay with Aunt Em and Uncle Dick for a week to help Mum recuperate from what she described as, "an operation ta fix up me insides, what got torn ta ribbons when Derek was born." The surgeon was Dr. Edith Summerskill, a well-known doctor and Member of Parliament who became a prominent player in the Labour government after the war, and was later made a Baroness. I mention this only because I find it quite remarkable that our free clinic gave my mother access to such a prominent doctor—long before the Welfare State, proper.

While Mum was in hospital, I stayed with Louie, and the boys went to Aunt Ada and Uncle Bill. Then Aunt Ada came up with the idea of keeping the boys a bit longer, to give Mum a chance to get her strength back; and Mum decided to go to Aunt Em's, taking me with her "ta give an 'and if I need one," she said, by way of justification.

The week that we spent in Shoreham-By-Sea has to be the coldest, windiest spring week in living memory. Not that we let that keep us indoors: my mother's idea of a rest cure was to sit on a pebbly beach wearing a coat, hat, and gloves, while I swam in the biggest waves I'd ever seen. It was probably quite dangerous; we were the only people on the beach, and Mum was in no shape to come to the rescue if I got into difficulties in those powerful waves.

It wasn't so bad at low tide when there was a strip of sand at the water's edge, but on our last day, the waves were breaking higher up the beach and carried with them lots of pebbles, some quite large. On that day, I had to admit defeat. The waves towered above my head, bombarding me with pebbles, and I had a mass of bruises to show for this foolhardiness.

Aunt Ada and Louie scolded Mum, when we got home. "Why didn'cha stay in the warm an' get a good rest, 'stead of sittin' on that windy ol' beach?" they wanted to know.

"We 'ad ta get out of Em's way ... she's s'busy with that shop, ya know," Mum replied. But this was nonsense. Aunt Em had *begged* her to stay in the warm, but my mother found it hard to be in the position of being taken care of.

She used me as an excuse: "Gwen jus' loves ta go ta the beach, yew know that." This was, at best, no more than a half-truth, and she knew it; but I held my tongue, so as not to make her look silly.

On those cold, windy days I would have been just as happy to stay home and spend time with Uncle Dick and Aunt Em. Uncle Dick was, after all, my favorite uncle, my chuckly, joke-telling uncle. He was a shopkeeper, a chimney sweep, *and* a fisherman with a boat—how could he *not* be the favorite uncle! I loved to watch for him to come home on his bike in the early afternoon, with his collection of circular brooms strapped to his back and his pale blue eyes looking oddly luminous in his soot-blackened face.

After he'd scrubbed away the soot, all but the traces that stubbornly remained in every line and wrinkle no matter how hard he scrubbed, his eyes no longer glowed in that ghostly way, and he was just plain old Uncle Dick again. Then I sat with him in his capacious armchair, and he'd tell time-honored yarns, including how, as a toddler, I used to make them laugh by saying, "Not 'arf, Mister Karko!" It was the nearest I could get to their name, Grasgey, and still made them laugh—though I never saw what was so funny about this example of childish ineptitude. I liked it better when he swapped jokes with me or started on his fishing yarns, which always ended with him pulling out the snapshot of him standing next to a fish almost as tall as he was.

Even while Uncle Dick was at work, I would have enjoyed helping Aunt Em in the shop. It was a corner grocery store that sold everything from soup to nuts—everything that didn't need refrigeration. When we heard the tinkle of the bell as a customer opened the shop door, Aunt Em would heave herself out of her comfy chair by the fire, and beckon me to come and help get goods off the shelves. As a treat, she sometimes let me make change, and I was in seventh heaven when she said I could weigh out sweets for a couple of children. This was even better than GWEN'S STORE! I decided, then and there, that when I was grown up I wanted to work in a shop just like this one.

◆　　◆　　◆

ADDENDUM

Marjory Strutt's name came up unexpectedly when I re-visited Aquinas Street a few years ago and was invited into what had been Hazel Henderson's house for a "cuppa tea". While reminiscing with the Doon Street lady who now lived in that house, we discovered a number of mutual acquaintances, and then she suddenly said:

"An' I betcha remember the Strutts! That Mrs. Strutt ... no bet'er than she should be, that one! The daugh'er, too ... soon as she left school. But ya could see that comin' a mile awf, couldn'cha? Always a brassy li'l hussy, she was. Like muvver like daugh'er ... as 'ard as nails, the pair of 'em. Made a fortune awf American soldiers, they did. The far'ver, poor fella, 'e come 'ome on leave once an' caught 'em bof at it—pickin' up Yanks dahn by Wat'erloo station. 'E jus' packed up an' left ... took the youngest gel wiv' 'im, an' they never come back. Then after the war, the uvver two left, an' we never saw 'em agin. Good riddance ta bad rubbish, we all said!"

I was stunned. But then I recalled something Mum had once told me toward the end of the war. She'd said that Marjory had "gone ta the dogs ... turned out ta be cut from the same cloth as that mother of 'er's." When I asked what she meant, she muttered something about "pickin' up Yanks," but I hadn't taken her remarks seriously, given that she'd always disliked Marjory and her mother. However, after what I'd just heard, I had to admit that there'd been more than a grain of truth in what Mum had said about Marjory. And in all the tut-tuttings about "that Mrs. Strutt," those many years ago. It was particularly startling to hear again that phrase "no better than she should be"—but it still doesn't seem to describe the behavior it was condemning and leaves me perplexed.

As I sat sipping my cup of tea in Hazel Henderson's old house, I felt a great sadness about what had become of the girl I'd worshipped, the glamorous creature I'd been dazzled by, the girl who, to me, had been to the rest of the Waterloo population as Stravinsky's Fire Bird Suite is to Musack. Marjory and I had lost touch at the outbreak of the war when I was evacuated. She and her sister stayed in Waterloo, it seems. With disastrous consequences for Marjory.

Chapter 18

Summer, 1939

In June, Louie and Harry took me with them to Ramsgate for a week. A seaside holiday! And a sandy beach! I could scarcely believe my luck. We had never been on a real holiday—only mini-holidays, visiting aunts and uncles on the south coast, where the beaches are pebbly and hard on bare feet. On bottoms, too, even with a blanket to sit on.

In comic books I'd seen pictures of seaside holidays: vast expanses of sandy beach, and all the fun things possible with more than a strip of firm, wet sand such as appeared for a short time at low tide on the Shoreham beach. That kind of sand, with its curious ribbed surface, was great for walking across with Uncle Dick, armed with a big bucket and shovel, looking for worm casts and digging up the worm under each cast for use as bait. And it was perfect for making "rivers"—when you dug a channel it immediately filled with water that rushed towards the sea—but hopeless for digging holes, because they quickly filled with a kind of slurry, and the walls collapsed.

A sandy beach and a whole week with Louie and Harry ... how lucky could a girl get! I was beside myself with excitement. But I felt badly for the two boys; they were understandably upset that they weren't coming, and we all knew there was no way Mum could give them a treat that matched what was in store for me. Particularly since they'd be in school, where I should be, too. How had Mum squared that with my teacher, I wondered. However, any pangs of conscience regarding the boys or school faded rapidly once we were on the train, rushing through the open countryside. It reminded me of the journey to Gloucestershire, and I thought about Gloria in her lovely, lonely world, and wished I could see her again. Over Louie's protests, Harry let me open the window and put my head out, but I got to enjoy the wind rushing though my hair for a few moments only before a piece of smut from the smoke of the engine lodged in my eye. So I arrived in Ramsgate, red-eyed and cross with myself; almost as cross as Louie was with Harry for letting me stick my head out the window.

To my surprise, we stayed in a real boarding house, not with some relative. It hadn't occurred to me that this holiday was going to be so posh! The boarding house was on a hill that led down to The Front, and the window of our third floor room overlooked the corner of a narrow alley and the window of a Humbug Shop. The humbugs were made in the window, to attract passers-by, so we had a perfect bird's-eye view of the operation. The humbug-man rolled out a striped "sausage," then worked along its length, making quick downward slashes at regular intervals with a sharp knife that squished the sticky sausage each time. He also turned the sausage a quarter turn between cuts, so the result was a row of humbugs with those mutually perpendicular "seams" on opposite sides—a shape that had long puzzled me. I never tired of watching this production of humbugs; it even made the occasional rainy morning welcome, because that meant no crowd of onlookers and an uninterrupted view of the shop window.

Viley, who now liked us to call her Violet (but we often forgot), came to Ramsgate with us, and so did her boy friend, Tom. He was one of the Elephant and Castle crowd and by far the handsomest of the bunch. With her straight, lank hair, fleshy face, and heavy build, how *did* Viley do it? (However, I took great comfort from the fact that appearance seemed not to matter if you were a nice, friendly person, like Viley.)

Looking back on that week, I do wonder how the sleeping arrangements were reconciled with pocket books and consciences. I never gave it a passing thought, at the time, but Louie, as the responsible older sister, would have been anxious to ensure no hanky-panky between the two teenagers. We may have had a girls' room and a boys' room … but more likely, we all slept in one room. After all, Louie and Harry footed the bill for everything, I suspect, and their means were pretty slender.

The weather was chilly and windy, but that didn't stop the five of us going to the beach, except for one day, when it rained solidly, non-stop. Despite chilly temperatures we swam, made sand castles, dug holes, played with a beach ball, rode donkeys, and watched Punch and Judy shows; in fact, we did all the sea-side things portrayed in my comic books and had ourselves a wonderful time on Ramsgate's splendid beaches. Blowing sand might sting our faces and get in our eyes, but we simply dug a hole, deep enough and big enough that we could all sit in to eat our sandwiches without getting a mouthful of sand with every bite. Harry and Tom did most of the digging, while Viley and I decorated the rim with small sandcastles and carved out seats in the walls, so that we didn't have to sit cross-legged all day.

Every night the tide removed all traces of the hole, and we had to start afresh the next day, like the man who made intricate sand sculptures only to have his handiwork washed away daily. I wept the first time I witnessed this. It seemed such a shame; his sand sculptures were so beautiful, and made with such care. I could see why he never stayed around to see his masterpieces disappear; or thought I could.

The owners of the boarding house, Mr. and Mrs. Brewster, treated their boarders like family, so we ate our breakfast and "high tea" (in the early evening) at a huge old table, with them and their other guests. Mr. Brewster was a Welshman, and I could have listened all day to his lovely, lilting Welsh accent. And he could have talked all day! About Wales, about fishing, about mining, about anything and everything. In Wales he'd been a coal miner, and to our surprise, was still a coal miner, here in Ramsgate, in a mine that went down under the sea. At first I thought he was pulling our legs. A coal mine under the sea? About as unlikely as the notion that pearls come from oysters (a "fact" that I still thought was a joke of the Hodds).

The fine, black dust embedded in every line and pore of Mr. Brewster's skin, especially on the back of his neck no matter how carefully he washed— just like my chimney sweep uncle—finally convinced me that he really did work in a mine. In many other respects, he and Uncle Dick were astonishingly alike: the same build and coloring, the same dark hair, the same light blue eyes that contrasted so strangely with their dusky coal-laden skin; they even had the same laugh, which invariably culminated in identical coughing fits. Both puffed on a pipe with the same staccato rhythm to get it going, then let it droop from the far right corner of the mouth. I loved the smell of Mr. Brewster's pipe and, when we got back to Waterloo, tried, unsuccessfully, to persuade George and Perce to take up pipes instead of their disgusting old fags.

After our high tea, we wandered the Promenade and the fun fair, Merry Something. (Merry England, perhaps?) We put pennies in machines and tried to grab prizes with a crane, but the prize you had your eye on always slipped out of the crane's jaws, and, at best, you ended up with some useless gewgaw. Always with the tantalizing hope of winning a prize, we rolled pennies down little ramps, tossed rings to ensnare targets, and threw beanbags trying to dislodge coconuts balanced on tall, eggcup-like supports. Harry and Tom liked the rifle range and the try-your-strength-can-you-ring-the-bell challenge, and we girls cheered them on, hoping they'd win something embarrassingly unmanly like a silly, stuffed animal and give it to one of us.

We were usually empty-handed at the end of the evening, but none of us minded much; we always finished up with an exciting ride on the Bumper Cars or braved the scary, giant roller coaster and soon forgot our earlier disappointments. Finally, to close the day in good style, we bought ice cream cones and ate them on the way back to the boarding house. Ice cream was a once-or-twice-a-year treat, so I was truly in heaven that week. Though I did, just occasionally, think guiltily about Derek and Bertie, and how much they would love all this.

The grand finale of our holiday was a day trip to Calais. We spent only a short time ashore, but long enough to learn that the French really did speak a different language and use different money and eat strange food—and had even stranger toilet arrangements. Their lavatories had no seats! You planted your feet on two foot-shaped platforms and peed into a hole, trying not to get your knickers and shoes and socks wet. This novel experience was accompanied by gales of laughter and was the one thing about France that none of us ever forgot. It also cleared up a mystery that I had been pondering for some time: Why did "French drawers" have such wide leg openings? Clearly, these extraordinary knickers were designed to help French ladies use the extraordinary French lavatories, I decided.

On the way back across the Channel we hit rough weather, and I disgraced myself by being seasick. Louie had planted me strategically next to the rail, so that I could be sick without making a mess; but when the moment came, I dashed across the deck into Harry's arms and threw up all over his new trousers. It was a long time before I lived that down with Louie. I'm not sure which of my offences was the more damning, the ruination of the trousers or the abrupt transfer of allegiance in a moment of crisis.

On the first day back at school, I was called into the headmaster's office and asked why I had not been in school the previous week. To my astonishment, when I told Mr. Pascoe that I'd been on holiday, he slumped in his chair and stared at me with tears in his eyes instead of being interested in where I'd gone and what I'd seen. In a choked voice, he explained why he was so upset. Apparently, I had missed something called the Preliminary Exam and, having no acceptable reason for my absence, would not be allowed to take the Scholarship Exam in September. The Scholarship Exam, it seems, was the golden key to a grammar school and any hope for a better future. Without passing that exam, he said I would go to the local secondary school with the rest of my classmates and, by implication, would have diminished hopes for a better future. By this he meant escaping from Waterloo, I supposed, though he didn't say so in so many words.

Mr. Pascoe had, apparently, nursed high hopes of me getting a scholarship to a grammar school and, to this end, had been working with me on the part of the exam where he anticipated that I would have a problem: the General Knowledge section. He suspected that in our household there were no books, no newspapers or magazines, and no radio; and he was right, except for our recently acquired radio. But I don't remember the radio being tuned to anything informative, and Mr. Pascoe's fears were well grounded: what I knew of General Knowledge would barely fill a thimble—and some of that was nonsense, thanks to the misinformation given me by the teasers of the Hodd family.

To remedy my ignorance about the world in general, I'd been meeting with Mr. Pascoe after school, and we discussed newspaper or magazine articles, and looked things up in a big fat encyclopedia in his office. That was my first encounter with a book devoted entirely to imparting information, and I was impressed that such a book should exist. At first I had found Mr. Pascoe rather intimidating. A tall, thin man, he held himself very upright as he slowly strode the corridors of the school, looking severe and remote—necessary attributes, I suppose, if he was to keep the unruly students of Hatfield Street in order. But after seeing his gentler side, I grew fond of him and came to look forward to those General Knowledge sessions. During the winter months when it got dark early, he had cut them short, because he didn't want me walking home alone in the dark, and I been quite cross about that.

When summoned to his office after my week at Ramsgate, I had assumed that it was in connection with our after-school sessions. And I was eager to share with him what I'd learned: the making of humbugs, the coal mine under the sea, and the trip to France (though I would leave out the strange lavatories). But the business of the Preliminary Exam drove all that out of my head. I'd never seen a man with tears in his eyes and felt terrible, felt in some way responsible.

As I walked back to class, and on the way home that day, I asked myself again and again: Why had my mother let me go to Ramsgate? Didn't she know how important the Preliminary was? I'd known vaguely about some impending exam; that was the reason for the General Knowledge sessions, after all. But I had no inkling of how much hung on it, or that it was slated to take place during our Ramsgate week.

Mr. Pascoe seemed to think that Mum knew all about it; that's why he was so shocked. But if Mum *did* know, what had persuaded her to let me miss that exam? Was it because I might never get another chance at a real holiday, if her life was anything to go by? Or because it was awfully hard to say "No" to Louie once she'd set her mind on something? Would Mum have knowingly jeopardized my future for either of these reasons? I couldn't bring myself to ask her when I got home that day; or in the days and weeks that followed. But they ran through my mind many times.

To my disappointment, the General Knowledge sessions now came to an abrupt halt, but on a couple of occasions, Mr. Pascoe pulled me out of class to take some tests in his office. They were given by a man I'd never seen before and were different from any test I'd ever taken. There were pages and pages of questions, and I didn't have to write out answers, just choose one from several that were given. I didn't like the fact that each page was timed and left no time to ponder a question. Sometimes I had to make a guess and *hated* doing that. (On my next encounter with a multiple-choice test, the Graduate Record Exam, some thirty years later, I had the exact same hang-ups!)

Mr. Pascoe never told me what these tests were all about, and I didn't see any other Hatfield Street kid taking them, which was mystifying. Why only me? But I certainly didn't ask for answers or express any objection. You just did whatever a teacher, especially a headmaster, told you to do; just "got on wiv' it," in true Waterloo fashion.

◆　　◆　　◆

When the summer holidays started there was no mention of the Country Holiday Fund, and I thought wistfully of Gloria and Gloucestershire, but didn't dare say anything for fear of seeming greedy. After all, I'd just come back from a splendid, seaside holiday. And, in any case, now that I had friends to call my own, I was in much better shape to deal with the street scene; the long summer holidays were not the threat that they had been a year earlier.

Mum's surgery had been a great success, and she was feeling so much better that she was able to work more often. Furthermore, I was now old enough to keep an eye on the boys for an hour or so—with a friendly neighbor as back-up in the event of an emergency—so she didn't have to give up her "li'l jobs" during the school holidays.

Consequently, our finances had picked up enough for us to go on an outing one day: to a new open-air pool in Brockwell Park that everyone was raving about. With good cause! It had everything one could desire: a huge pool with slides as well as diving boards; a playground with swings and seesaws; grassy areas for picnics and letting off steam, and even a place where you could buy an ice cream. The day was warm and sunny, and we three had such a great time that we didn't want to go home. On the bus back to Waterloo, we pestered, "C'n we go agin? Please ... pu-r-r-le-e-ese, Mum! C'mon ... jus' say Yes!" until she laughingly promised that she would. But added, in protest, "I 'ave ta save up, first. Money don't grow on trees, ya know!"

By the middle of August my thoughts began to turn towards school, and I thought guiltily about Mr. Pascoe and the upcoming Scholarship Exam that I would not be allowed to take. I also wondered, wistfully, about those lost opportunities for a better future, had I passed the exam.

Mum, too, must have been thinking about this when we went down The Cut one day to exchange a large number of flimsy Co-op tokens—values ranging from a farthing to a shilling—for the more solid tokens worth a pound each. As we stood watching the girl in the little corner kiosk sort the tokens into piles of ten and slide each pile into the appropriate "bowl" carved into the surface of her desk, Mum said, "Nah there's a nice little job yew could do, Gwen. Yew'd enjoy that, wouldn'cha? A nice warm office all ta yerself ... it beats scrubbin' floors on yer bloomin' 'ands an' knees, I c'n tell ya!" And added, a bit defensively I thought, "I bet'cha it don't need no grammar school education, neither."

I had always admired the lovely polished wood and scooped out bowls of that kiosk desk, and had noticed the nice clothes and beautifully cared for hands of the young lady; so I knew that this job was undeniably better than those that my mother had to settle for. And, truth be told, I had enjoyed sorting out all our tokens the night before—a combination of button games and playing shop—but I doubted that this job would stand the test of time. I somehow didn't think it would rank high in what Mr. Pascoe thought of as "a better future." For one thing, it clearly did not pave the way for an escape from Waterloo; this young woman was still trapped in The Cut's Co-op shop, however quiet and cozy her little kiosk might be.

I'm afraid my mother was disappointed by my lukewarm response to her idea of a good job. I knew that it put her on a guilt trip over the Preliminary Exam business, and I felt bad about that; but I could raise no enthusiasm for this job. Although a couple of years earlier, it probably *would* have seemed attractive.

By late August, our finances were adequate for another outing, but the weather wasn't warm enough for open-air swimming, so we went to Kew Gardens instead. The boys were not exactly enthusiastic about all those trees and flowers and greenhouses and got bored once they'd tired of running around like mad things in the wide open, grassy spaces.

But then we wandered into a wooded area and discovered what a wonderful place it was for hide-and-seek, and they perked up. So many trees had trunks big enough to hide behind, and we were having such a good time that Mum had difficulty persuading us to stop for our picnic. Until she told us what she'd packed: banana sandwiches in Hovis brown bread! And Tizer (a bright orange, fizzy drink that left lips, tongues and teeth equally bright orange)! That made us settle down quickly.

Mum had picked out a huge tree with dense dark green foliage and immense spreading branches, the like of which I'd never seen. The branches were like a roof, and it was as if we were in a house without walls. As we sat under that "roof", munching on banana sandwiches and taking swigs of Tizer from the bottle—watching that no one took more than their fair share and shrieking with laughter at our orange tongues and mouths—it would have been hard to find three happier kids.

Knowing, with the benefit of hindsight, how soon we would all be embroiled in the war, I am glad that the last month of peace ended on such a happy note for our little family. By some miracle, our mother had managed to keep it intact since being left a widow with three young children and very meager resources. We had none of us fallen apart at the seams, had each worked our way through the loss of Dad and the various traumas that had followed, secure in the knowledge that our feisty Mum was there doing battle for us. She richly deserved a memory such as that picnic under that magnificent tree, and her small moment of triumph the next day, when she reported to Louie, "As 'appy as sandboys they was!"

PART II

From Pillar to Post

Chapter 19

Down on the Farm

SEPT. 1ST 1939. I am standing with my two brothers in a long line of children from our school. We are waiting to be taken to a train that will, after we've said goodbye to parents, take us to some unknown destination out of London. Each child stands beside a suitcase: some suitcases are old and battered, some new and shiny, bought hurriedly because there'd never before been any need for a suitcase.

A piece of string is draped around each child's shoulder, from which a cardboard box hangs; it rests awkwardly on stomach or hip or buttocks, and there is much adjusting of the string, trying to find the least uncomfortable arrangement. Inside the box is a weird-looking gas mask; we have all peeked, of course, and recoiled from this rubber-snouted device, giggling nervously. I know about gas from tales of The Great War, know that it had left my father "all chesty," and it is both comforting and scary to have this unfamiliar thing hanging around my neck.

"Yew'll be safe from air raids," our mother had explained. "An' don'cha worry, even if there is a war, it won't be fer long. It'll be over in three or four weeks, they say. So ya'll just 'ave a nice 'oliday in the country. An' all fer free!"

And that was all we were told. I had no idea what an air raid might be, and there had been no discussion about us leaving London if war broke out. At the age of ten-and-a-half, I was old enough to have noticed the word "war" creeping into the talk of grown-ups; but the only wars I knew anything about were the trenches of World War I and Grampa Benson's soldiers on horseback in bright red uniforms and plumed hats in distant lands. Both seemed remote and foreign, and I couldn't imagine war playing itself out on the streets on which we played.

It was a long time before I knew that there had been a choice regarding the evacuation scheme, that every family made up its own mind about sending its school-age children out of the city with their teachers. Neither did I know that our mother could have come with us, like Kennie Norton's mother did, to help take care of Hatfield Street School's evacuees. Our Mum would have enjoyed doing mending and scrounging around for things like extra clothes or blankets, and she would have been good at it. I felt a stab of betrayal when I first realized all this, because there was nothing to keep our mother in London: no regular job, no husband. But at the time I meekly stood in line with Derek and Bertie, and later, the question was one that somehow, I couldn't raise with her.

Bertie, still a Mummy's Boy, was upset at going away without Mum, but he merely whimpered as we stood in line, afraid no doubt, of being teased by the other boys if he broke down and cried like the little five-year-olds. But most of us were amazingly stoic about leaving home for parts unknown. Was the ploy of "a nice 'oliday in the country" working its magic? Partly. But if we had anxieties, we were certainly not about to show them—after years of being told "ta jus put up wiv it," no matter how rotten a hand you'd been dealt. What's more, every child in that line was excited at the prospect of a ride in a train—a first for many—and when we reached the main line station, couldn't help but be awed by the high, vaulted, echoing roof and the great expanse of glass.

Midst the shrieking of whistles and hissing of steam from huge, black engines, the younger children cried and clung to their mothers when the moment came to say goodbye. But soon after the train got under way, most of them forgot their tears in the excitement of exploring the contents of a small box that each child had been given. At first our teachers tried to restrain us, pointing out the label that read: To Be Opened In an Emergency, but once the first cry of, "Cor! Look! Choc'lit!" rang through the train, they knew it was a lost cause.

Those boxes were irresistible—it was like an extra Christmas—and most were opened while the train was still gathering speed. By the time fields of grazing cows and sheep had taken the place of grimy city buildings, everything edible had been sampled and consumed, if it passed muster. Not much did. The contents of the boxes were generally judged a disappointment, especially the chocolate, which was dark and bitter, not a patch on Cadbury's Milk bars.

A slab of hard, chewy, brown stuff —iron rations, somebody said, but most of us thought that sounded daft—was widely declared to be inedible after one jaw-breaking bite. The few who actually liked it, crammed their pockets to overflowing with half-wrapped discards, and one or two ate so much of the stuff that they were sick. Our teachers earned their pay that day.

Another source of wonderment was the long-handled brush and tin of pink powder in each box. I had been initiated into the rituals of dental hygiene when I went to Gloucester with the Country Holiday Fund, but leery of taunts like "Jus' listen to 'er! Proppa Miss Know-All!" I chose not to share this knowledge. Eventually Micky Chapman waved the toothbrush in Mr. Waters' face, wanting to know: "An' wha's this fing for, then?" and Mr. Waters explained. I don't think his audience was convinced, because Mr. Waters was a bit of a tease and played practical jokes, so I doubt that many toothbrushes were put to good use. Some kids, hoping the pink powder might be like strawberry sherbet, sampled it by sticking in a dampened finger; most were rapidly disillusioned by the gritty texture on their tongues, but a few hardy souls claimed to like its pepperminty flavor.

By the time we reached our destination—Sturminster Newton, a small market town in Dorset—the only unsampled things in the emergency boxes were tins of corned beef and sardines, battered and misshapen by unsuccessful struggles to open them.

After Sturminster Newton, we went by bus to the village of Lydlinch where we all clustered in the afternoon sunshine on the Common, next to the Village Hall. While grown-ups made plans to sort out housing, we were free to run around and let off steam for the first time that day. And let off steam, we did; the coarse grass was covered with running, jumping, leap-frogging, cartwheeling youngsters, laughing and yelling and shoving.

The little ones stood rather miserably at the edge, not daring to join in this wild scene; but for the bigger kids there were cows to chase (and cow pads to learn about), bracken in which to hide, hedgerows to scare birds from, and a small pond to throw stones into. The resident ducks, which had been placidly paddling, flew off to the astonishment of those who thought ducks only swam, waddled and quacked. A few kids gave chase, but, outstripped by the airborne ducks, they soon came panting back. However, when Georgie Morten fell in the pond and almost drowned, this newfound freedom came to an abrupt halt. To prevent further mishaps, we were herded into sheep pens that someone rustled up, until we were taken, one family at a time, into the Village Hall to be matched up with a host family.

Inside the hall, we stood on a stage in front of rows of seated local people who had been "volunteered" by some government official to take as many evacuees as their house was deemed capable of absorbing. A few biographical details of the family on display were followed by the question, "Who would like to take these children? Please raise your hand ... "

It amounted to a public auction in which no money changed hands. For me, a shy, self-conscious, overweight ten-year-old, it was excruciating to stand on that stage with my brothers and hear a lady describe us in an unfamiliar, soft, West Country drawl: " ... a nice little faaamily ... a girrl of ten and two boys, eight and seven. We'd rrreally like to keep them togetherrr, if we caaan ... the two boys arrr so yooong."

Then came the wait for someone to "bid." *Please ... let someone want us ... S'pose no-one does ...* These thoughts raced through my head during a lengthy silence, but finally, we heard the lady say, "Oh go-o-d. Thank you *verry* much! The Goulds, bain't it?" *Will Mrs. Gould know about Bertie's bed-wetting,* I now worried. *Or will I have to explain it to her?*

In all fairness, a real effort was made to keep evacuee families together, under what must have been very difficult circumstances; but with big families there was little choice, for few local families had a house large enough to take more than two evacuees. But we three were lucky. The Goulds had a huge attic space that easily held three beds—small canvas affairs and not the height of luxury, but at least we were together.

Which was just as well. I think Bertie would have fallen apart completely without me as his substitute Mummy. As it was, he cried himself to sleep that first night. I considered crawling into his bed to give him a cuddle in his misery, but the beds were very narrow; also, there was the thought of waking up in the morning with a wet nightie and having Mrs. Gould think I was a bed-wetter, too. She hadn't known about Bertie's bed-wetting when she raised her hand at the "auction," but she found the rubber sheet and the note that Mum had put in his suitcase, so I didn't have to explain the situation to her, thank goodness. I felt really sorry for Bertie, sobbing in the dark—darker than anything we city kids had ever experienced—that first night away from home and kept myself awake, offering words of comfort until he eventually dropped off to sleep.

Sharing a bedroom was nothing new to the three of us, and having separate beds was an unexpected luxury, even if they were only fold-up canvas cots supplied by the government, I think, in this well-thought-out evacuation operation. Our new bedroom stretched across the entire width of the old farmhouse immediately under the thatched roof; it was a far cry from the poky bedroom in Aquinas Street that we'd shared with Mum, and never had we enjoyed so much elbowroom. The rustlings from above scared us at first, but the little creatures in the thatch seemed to pay us no attention, and we soon learned to pay no heed to them.

Mum's last words had been, "Now, Gwen ... look after yer brothers, an' make sure the three of ya stick together." I don't know if the boys were listening, but in this new setting they let the Bertie-an'-Derek unit expand to include me, and the three of us did everything together—for the first time in our entire lives. Perhaps, overwhelmed by the separation from Mum, they simply latched onto me as the only familiar figure in these unfamiliar surroundings. Or was it the isolation of the farmhouse, there being no other children within a mile or so?

Whatever the reason, once we'd put behind us the trauma of leaving home and not knowing when we'd next see our Mum—and the humiliation of the sheep-pens and auction started to fade—we had the time of our young lives for a few glorious weeks. Together we explored all the new, exciting things to be found on a working farm deep in the country: open fields; hedgerows with wild flowers and bird nests and blackberries; a clear rippling stream to wade in; minnows and frogs to catch in jam jars; trees to climb; apples to pick; cows, hens, ducks and horses to feed; butter to cream; and an endless supply of wild farm kittens that, in response to the unaccustomed attention from the three of us, purred like the idling taxis so familiar to us on Aquinas Street.

We were disappointed to find birds' nests empty; not knowing that by September, baby birds had long since learned to fly and were no longer living at home. In the evenings swarms of silent swallows swooped and darted, catching insects in their open mouths—Mrs. Gould told me—before disappearing back into the thatch of the roof. If one of the Hodds had spun a yarn like that—birds in mid-flight, catching flies in their mouths—I would have dismissed it as a tease, but I had no reason to suspect Mrs. Gould's veracity, and my admiration for these graceful creatures knew no bounds. They brought to mind my ceramic swallows, relics of the old blue pram, and I wished that I'd hidden these treasures in my suitcase, despite the prohibition on toys. No one would have noticed. And they would have given me great comfort.

There were a few negatives in this idyllic scene: stinging nettles; a terrifying monster of a bull; a farm dog that was a snappy creature, more used to snipping at cows' heels to hurry them along than playing with children; and an unlit, smelly outhouse at the far end of the garden that was worse than our Commercial Road lavatory—which did, at least, flush. In addition, the farm had no electricity, so we missed the radio; and oil lamps and candles made the place spooky after dark. As September advanced, we also discovered that after the sun went down, the old farmhouse, with its stone floors and gaps under the doors, was chilly and drafty.

The Goulds were very kind, but they were newly-weds with a farm to take care of, so they had little time to spare for us. We were pretty much left alone as long as we didn't go beyond the farm gate and kept clear of the duck pond and the bull. There was no fear of us disobeying the injunction regarding the bull! He was a massive, black creature that we could hear snorting and bellowing, restlessly pawing the ground in the barn where he spent most of the time. On our very first day, we saw three strong men unsuccessfully wrestle with him in a small enclosure, trying to get him back into the barn; then watched with bated breath, as they scrambled over the fence to get away, when he broke loose and charged with lowered horns.

After that, simply hearing him bellow was enough to make us run for our lives, and I had a recurring nightmare in which this fearsome beast was underneath my bed, his every breath making the bed rise and fall. Waking from this nightmare and in that halfway stage between sleep and wakefulness, not knowing whether I was still dreaming, I lay in the dark, afraid to move or breathe until I could be sure that the bed was not, in fact, rising and falling.

When I asked Mrs. Gould why they kept such a dangerous animal, she said, with her soft burr, "He's a vaaalu'ble stud. Lots o' farrmerrs loik to use 'im ferrr theirrr cowwws." This left me none the wiser; a stud, to me, was a little button-like thing that men put in their shirts, but I didn't like to bother this busy lady for further details. She'd already taught me so much: how to churn butter, where the hens liked to lay their eggs in the hedges and odd spots around the farmyard, and how to collect an egg without breaking it. I loved it when the egg was still warm from the hen's body, but although Mrs. Gould showed me how to reach under a hen that was still sitting on an egg, I never mustered the courage to put my hand under that clucking, scolding bundle of feathers, with its nasty, pointy beak.

After a few tries I'd even learned how to milk a cow. I never fully conquered my fear of the threatening hoofs, but loved the smell of the warm milk and the sound it made, spurting into the can when the can was near empty. The Goulds' cows were various mixes of black and white, and I discovered to my surprise, that all cows were "she's" and really did say "Moo," just like the books said. I'd never known whether this was a fanciful fiction. This probably meant that sheep said "Baa," but the Goulds had no sheep for me to check this out.

I was delighted to find that each cow had a name, one that matched her in some way: Frisky, Dot, Bumper (given to bumping you gently) and Moaner (she moaned quietly while being milked). Our favorite cow was Old Gran with her twin calves, though to our disappointment, the calves were too timid to let us pet them. Old Gran was very docile and even tolerated us on her back when we could cajole Mr.Gould into heaving us up. It was an uncomfortable, knobbly ride, and scary, because Old Gran's horns were too far away to hold on to, but we wouldn't admit to being scared and pleaded daily for a ride.

We had two favorite spots on that farm: The Hill, where we played King-O'-The-Castle, and a minnow-filled stream. Unbeknownst to us, The Hill was a turfed-over mound of cow droppings—many months of cowshed scrapings—as we discovered when Derek climbed to an over-hanging tree limb and jumped. He went right through the crust and found himself in *you-know-what* up to his armpits! Bertie and I managed to pull him out without ourselves going through the crust, and, a very smelly threesome, we slunk back to the house.

We cleaned up as best we could under the cold-water pump, which was the only source of water other than the horse-trough or the duck pond. Poor Mrs.Gould. She had to get buckets of hot water going for baths in front of the fire, so that we'd be fit for human company—even farmhouse company that was accustomed to some pretty pungent odors. The Hill was declared out of bounds after this episode, though this was probably unnecessary; it had lost some of its charm now we knew what lay beneath that innocuous-looking grassy surface.

The stream was a much cleaner source of amusement, and it was pure delight for us city kids. I had read about streams and brooks, but could never quite picture what they were really like. My experience of moving water had been the breaking waves of the sea, and the slow-moving, swirling River Thames with its broad expanses of mud at low tide. This little rippling stream was so different. About six inches deep, it was crystal clear, not brown and muddy like the Thames, and it didn't taste salty like the sea. The lack of tides was also a puzzle, but I somehow knew that I was unlikely to get an explanation from either of the busy Goulds, so I didn't bother to ask.

You could see every pebble on the gravelly bottom of that stream and every minnow that foolishly swam over the shiny treacle-tin lids that we put on the bottom. On top of each lid we laid a jam-jar on its side, with a piece of string around the neck, and at each minnow sighting, we yanked up on the string. Sometimes we were lucky; other times, luck was on the side of the minnow. But we usually ended up with a goodly collection of the gleaming little fishes, and sad experiences with jars of very dead minnows taught us to return them to the stream before we went back to the house.

Mrs.Gould scolded if we got our clothes too wet—the boys *were* rather prone to falling in—but happy hours messing around in that stream were well worth a scolding. We tried not to get too wet, too often, however, for fear that the stream might also be put off bounds. After the first few days, the three of us fell into bed every night, tired, happy, and rather grubby, because we simply sluiced off the worst of the dirt under the hand-pump. Hot water might have helped but was a rare commodity, and baths were even rarer, because Mrs.Gould was a very busy lady, much too busy to pay close attention to our personal hygiene. And it certainly wasn't high on our list of priorities.

The Goulds had no radio and took no newspaper, so we were unaware that the country was at war with Germany until Mr.Gould went to the weekly market in Sturminster Newton, several days after the declaration of war on

September, 3. Not that we three realized the seriousness of this news. It was not followed by any changes in that peaceful Dorset scene—no bombs, no booming of guns, and the cows still had to be milked on time—so it didn't spoil the wonderful time we were having on that farm, in the glorious weather that bathed England throughout that September.

Mr.Gould used a horse-drawn cart for his market trips, and we were allowed to await his return at the end of the lane, beyond the farm gate. He would help us climb up into the cart, and we rode with him the rest of the way, one of us scrambling down to open and close the gate; an honor we regularly fought over. Bumping along the rough track and watching the steady movement of the old horse's powerful haunches was *the* highlight of our week.

On one of those rides, Mr.Gould spurred Betsy into a trot, and we were introduced to a startling, new fact of life: that horses fart! *And* they are gloriously unconcerned about it—there's none of that, "It wasn't me!" nonsense. The first time we heard old Betsy trumpeting away in time with the clip-clop of her hooves, we could scarcely believe our ears; we fell about laughing, so hard it's a wonder we didn't fall out of the cart. Even dour Mr.Gould, who rarely cracked a smile, laughed hard enough that he had to take the pipe out of his mouth—a rare event, indeed.

The first two or three weeks of evacuation really were, as Mum had said, like a summer holiday, but eventually school intruded on our little paradise. While we'd been romping about the farm, the three teachers who'd come with us, had been busy locating a building, sorting out supplies, and arranging daily transportation for seventy or so students scattered over about a hundred square miles.

For our schoolhouse, they'd settled on the Village Hall in Lydlinch (the scene of the auction), and this was far enough from the Goulds' farm that we found ourselves in the novel situation of taking a bus to school. In order to catch the bus, we had to walk across two fields, through a small wood, then cross a stream on a couple of planks—a deliciously adventurous way to start and end every school day. It was a far cry from the dreary, treeless streets that we'd walked every day in Waterloo, and, much as we resented the intrusion of school, the three of us loved that walk.

In the mornings, we had to be careful not to get distracted, lest we miss the bus, and I was constantly nudging the boys along, telling them there wasn't time to look for bird nests, chase rabbits, or climb trees. But one morning, it was I who got distracted. There had been hoarfrost overnight, and the fields were transformed: every leaf, every blade of grass, was outlined with a coating of frost, white and fluffy in the shade, sparkling with rainbow colors where the morning sunlight fell on it.

Enchanted by this delicate, glistening world, I dallied so long, wondering at the myriad patterns of frost, that I missed the bus. The boys, who could have cared less about this wondrous whiteness, hadn't waited for me, and I was panic-stricken when I found them, and the bus, gone. I slowly realized there was only one thing to be done: I had to walk to school. It was a couple of miles, and I wasn't sure of the way, but did recognize enough landmarks to get there—eventually.

Then came the embarrassment of explaining why I was late. "I was lookin' at the frost on the grass ... " sounded pretty feeble, but Mrs. Greenaway, the Dragon-Lady, seemed almost amused, and she let me off lightly. My punishment was to write out, in my best handwriting, "I must not be late for school" three hundred times. I had wondered, as I trudged along, whether I was going to "get the cane" for the first time ever; and I kept thinking of the time that Mrs. Greenaway had broken a ruler on me. A caning by her was a frightening prospect, so it was with a feeling of having got away with murder that I gave up several lunch breaks to write out my "lines."

School ate into the endless free time we'd enjoyed at first, but on weekends we still romped and explored to our hearts' content until the day our mother suddenly appeared, unannounced. She was carrying two heavy suitcases full of warm clothes for us, now that it had become clear that the war would last more than a month, as so many had kidded themselves, back in August.

We were, of course, overjoyed to see her and eagerly showed her all over the farm. She was happy to find us happy, impressed by my newly acquired cow-milking skill and very pleased that Derek's stutter had improved. It had been steadily worsening, though Mum had always maintained that, "the clinic doctor said he'll prob'ly grow out of it once 'is life set'les down agin after losin' 'is father." However, she was appalled to find the three of us covered with scabies and impetigo, which had come into full bloom a couple of days before her arrival. Scabies blisters clustered in every crack and crevice— knees, elbows, fingers and toes—and the impetigo was mainly on our heads, which made hair-brushing difficult, so we probably looked more scruffy and neglected than we really were. Poor Mum. Was it possible, she wailed, for the children she'd sent off clean and neat, with gleaming well-kept hair, to be reduced to scabby, tousled, dirty little ragamuffins, in such a short time?

Scabies and impetigo were only too familiar to mothers in Waterloo. There were always a few children excluded from school with one or the other after a visit by the school nurse, otherwise known as Nitty Nora, because she also examined heads for lice and nits. We three had never been sent home with a note from Nitty Nora, which was a matter of no small pride to our mother since these three scourges all carried the stigma of being "dirty." In our nightly "top-'n-tail" procedure, Mum's sharp eyes would have spotted the first scab or blister, and once a week we were put through a de-nitting torture with a special fine-toothed comb and a dark cloth draped over our shoulders—for ease in spotting any combed-out tiny white nits. Poor Bertie, with his snarly, curly hair, "screamed bloody murder," so he was always "nitted" first, to get it over with.

Outraged at our condition, Mum let fly at Mr.Waters, our new headmaster. (Mr. Pascoe had stayed in Waterloo with the un-evacuated part of the school). Come to think of it, how did she reach Mr.Waters? Nobody had phones, there was only one bus a week, on market day, and I'm sure she didn't hire a taxi. She'd have to be at death's door for that! Did Mr. Gould take her in the horse and cart? She certainly didn't ride in the school bus. That would have been the ultimate in humiliation, and I would have remembered *that*. By the same token, how did she get from Aquinas Street to the Goulds' remote farm? At the time, it didn't enter my head to wonder about any of this!

The upshot was that, within a day or two, we were whisked away from the farm and taken to Sturminster Newton, where a lovely old house had been converted into an impromptu hospital especially for evacuees. It was overflowing with impetigo and scabies cases, for the epidemic was on a scale unknown in grubby, old London—where, ironically, some of us were not cared for as well as we had been during our sojourn in this healthy country setting. Were they perhaps different strains, Dorset varieties of these diseases, against which London-acquired immunity was not effective? Or was it that our Dorset "mothers" were not as familiar with the early warning signs as their city-dwelling counterparts? Had our teachers, perhaps, come to rely too much on the sharp eyes of Nitty Nora? Midst the upheaval of those early months of the war, probably *no one* was paying enough attention.

We three presented the hospital with a unique problem. There were two scabies wards, one for girls and one for boys, and two gender-based wards for impetigo. But … where to put us, who had both? Finally, it was decided to forget the gender issue and put us in our own mini-ward, a charming upstairs room with pretty flowered curtains and a matching cushioned window seat. *And* a small bookcase full of children's books. I had a marvelous time on that deep window seat, reading all those books and looking out the window into the branches of a huge old fig tree that grew so close to the window it was as if you had climbed up into the tree itself. It reminded me of an illustration in my *Anderson's Fairy Tales*, and when tired of reading, I daydreamed my way through the story of *The Elder Tree*, imagining myself hidden in its depths.

Bertie's autumn crop of boils chose this singularly unfortunate time to erupt, so he was a mess. These outbreaks were always painful ordeals, but on top of itchy, scabby impetigo and even itchier scabies, the poor boy was in terrible shape for a week or two. After that, none of us felt ill, and the only thing that really bothered us during the rest of our "hospital" stay were the cries that came from a room just down the hall, where little Helen Green lay, shrieking with pain. She had a bad case of rheumatic fever, and even though the bedclothes were draped over a cage to keep their weight from pressing on her pain-wracked body, she moaned and screamed, day and night, "Mummy! M-u-m-m-y! M-u-m-m-y! *I w-a-n-t my M-u-m-m-y ...* "

In comparison, our problems seemed trivial: the non-stop itching, the scabs you weren't supposed to scratch, and the horrible cod-liver-oily smell of the stuff we were bathed in daily to treat the scabies. That smell pervaded our clothes for months afterwards. But even trivial problems have a way of being hard to live with twenty-four hours of every day, and we missed the stream and the kittens and the freedom to roam that we'd enjoyed on the farm. Derek and Bertie, energetic young boys confined to one room—and not fond of reading—got very bored and did a lot of bed bouncing. Derek's bed ultimately collapsed and had to be replaced, after which, we were kept well supplied with comics.

On the whole, we had a good the-three-of-us-together-time, in that hospital, with its kind nurses and excellent food. But it was to be our last such time together. Never again did we all sleep under the same roof, let alone in the same room, as we had for as long as we could remember.

◆　◆　◆

Addenda

In the summer of 2004, I visited Laycock Abbey, not far from Sturminster Newton. There wasn't a great deal left of the Abbey after Henry the Eighth and his daughter Elizabeth were finished with it, but it makes a lovely ruin. Of particular interest to me, was a display featuring photos and documents related to the evacuees in that area during World War II. Many of the documents were written by the grown-up versions of those evacuees, and their accounts of being chosen by local families were remarkably similar to my description of our auction in Lydlinch. I had sometimes wondered whether memory had dramatized those events, but it seems not.

However, for these children, their school was not a lowly village hall, but the romantic ruins of Laycock Abbey. What a fabulous experience! I wonder how they kept their attention on spelling and multiplication tables when surrounded by those thick, ancient walls and elegant, arched windows. More recently, Laycock Abbey again served as the backdrop to school life: this time for the students of Hogwarts School, during the filming of a Harry Potter movie. A school for wizards? I wonder how the nuns for whom the Abbey was originally built might feel about this.

◆　　◆　　◆

Decades after we left the Goulds' farm, their old horse, Betsy, was the unlikely means of reconciliation between Derek and me. We had become rather alienated, and it didn't help that the Atlantic Ocean now lay between us. Or that, in the course of a troubled life, Derek had withdrawn into what seemed a truly impenetrable shell—though a thick wall of dense fog might be a better description. At least with a shell there's hope of a crack opening up, but however you flail at fog, it forms again … instantly.

I'd almost given up trying to reach Derek, in any real sense, and decided not to bother visiting him and his wife when I next went to England. But, in the end, I couldn't *not* visit him. Our mother had died a few years earlier, and I couldn't bear to think that I'd essentially lost my brother, too, my only remaining connection with Dad. And, thank goodness I gave it one more try, because something had changed, and we were able to chat about this and that in something approaching a normal manner.

One topic that came up was our early childhood. Curious to learn how similar—or dissimilar—our recollections were, I asked Derek, "What do you remember about our father?"

He shook his head slowly. "Nothin', really. The only thing I c'n remember is bein' lifted up by someone, so I could see 'im, in 'is coffin."

I was stunned. It hadn't occurred to me that he'd never really known our father—had been too young when Dad died to have formed clear memories. My little stock of early memories of our father is an important part of who I am; and I felt such sadness for my brother who had none, other than that one image of a pale face in a coffin.

Probing further, I tried to find just where Derek's memories began. Did he remember places we'd lived? Commercial Road and switching Grampa Benson's salt and pepper? Aquinas Street? Our pet tortoise? Hatfield Street School? Being evacuated? We drew a blank, until we got to the farm in Dorset. Then a few vague memories surfaced, as I mentioned some specifics: the bull, the wasp nest we found, and the manure "hill" on which we played King O' the Castle. But the real breakthrough came when I asked: "Do you remember riding in the horse cart and discovering—"

"That 'orses blow off!" Sixty-year-old Derek fell about, laughing helplessly, just like the seven-year-old Derek had on making this momentous discovery. We *both* fell about with laughter—again. Together. After all those years, those blank, empty years, my brother and I had a good laugh together. The fog had lifted, finally, and it felt *so* good. After that, we were able to talk in a way we never had before, and it turned out that Derek did have some memories—things like The Sliding Game and The Stair Game—but hadn't known where to place them. Then he suddenly remembered something I'd forgotten: Mum's near-apoplexy when Bertie swapped his bike for a pile of old comics and Bertie's indignant cry, "Bu' I 'adn't read all of 'em!" Of course, deaf to Berties's protests, Mum had dragged him and the comics around Peabody Buildings, found the wily kid who had his bike and undid the swap.

When we parted that day, I felt content that we had broken through whatever the barrier had been; I would have been much less content had I known that it was to be the last time we ever met. For my brother died three years later, and I wasn't told of his illness until it was too late. "There's no need fer Gwen ta know," he'd said. "I don't want 'er comin' all across the Atlantic fer nothin'. We'll let 'er know in good time, if it's necessary." But they didn't. So I treasure all the more our last meeting; that brief episode in which we shared a few early memories and had a good laugh together. But it remains a matter of deep regret that there were so few such episodes in our sixty-four years as brother and sister.

Chapter 20

Village Life

WE STILL LOOKED BLOTCHY but were declared no longer contagious, and it was time to say good-bye to all the kind, friendly nurses. The three of us had chatted happily about re-exploring the Gould's farm, until Mum wrote to say that when the question of returning there was raised, she'd declared, "Over my dead body!" We were bitterly disappointed, but set off for pastures new, clutching our suitcases, hoping that another farm awaited us.

The two boys lucked out in this respect, but it proved impossible, this time, to keep the three of us under the same roof. That felt all wrong. But at least the three of us were in the same small village; and Derek and Bertie were together—that was the most important thing. Their billet was only a few minutes walk away from mine, and their new "parents," the Veals, always encouraged me to spend time with the boys. But I fretted about having failed to follow Mum's admonishment to "make sure the three of ya stick t'gether" and was glad of the daily ride on the school bus as a way to keep an eye on Derek and Bertie. I was especially worried about Bertie, but motherly Mrs. Veal had taken his bed-wetting and pernicketty eating in her stride, and both he and Derek seemed to settle in quickly. I finally stopped worrying about them when it became clear that the main thing that bothered them was having to board the school bus and waste precious hours in school.

The Veals were an older couple whose grown children had long since flown the nest, but they were both large, boisterous, jovial souls and somehow found the energy to take care of two small boys as well as a farm and a pub. Their farm had no animals other than a few dogs and chickens, but the pub—the only one for several miles—was a very busy place. Mr. Veal, with his loud cheery voice, heavy tweeds, and expansive belly embellished by the inevitable watch chain, was the quintessential country publican; a man superbly well matched to his chosen occupation. And buxom Mrs. Veal was an equally good fit as the wife of this farmer-cum-publican.

I, however, found myself in a very different situation. I was billeted with an eighty-one-year-old widow, tall, lean, masterful Gran Miller, who lived alone in a drab council house in the middle of the village. She was intimidating, this sturdy, blue-eyed, apple-cheeked, straight-backed lady with the sharp tongue; not given to smiling a great deal, she seemed stern and remote, but her bark was worse than her bite, I soon discovered. With her tanned, leathery skin and firm stride, she was unlike any eighty-one-year-old I'd ever met. Especially when she marched down the garden path, armed with a garden fork to dig up potatoes for dinner. I was accustomed to the old ladies of Waterloo, pale and stooped, too fat or too thin, shuffling around in carpet slippers! But Gran dealt briskly with all the housework, cooking, washing and ironing, *and* did her own gardening. She double-dug that heavy Dorset clay, maintaining a steady crop of flowers and vegetables, and we were cutting cabbages and digging parsnips well into the winter.

Gran's house was a distinct let down after the Goulds' picture-perfect thatched farmhouse, but it was in keeping with most of the village of Pulham, which was nothing more than a string of undistinguished structures that straggled along a road. The only buildings of any interest were the pub, the church, and two picturesque cottages, one of which was an abandoned thatched affair opposite Gran's house. The other, the cottage that housed the village shop and post office, was remarkable more for the profusion of roses that covered its walls than for its architecture, which may or may not have been admirable; it was hard to see under all that plant life. The pub, the Veals' pub, was part of a sprawling old house of mellow honey-colored stone, set well back from the road against a dramatic background of tall trees in which a host of raucous crows made their home. But Pulham's most beautiful building, to my untutored ten-year-old eyes, was the old, gray, square-towered Norman style church tucked away down a narrow side road, a well-hidden secret, seen by few except those who worshipped in it every Sunday.

Like all villages, Pulham had its share of gossip and gossips. Gran paid no attention to either, unlike her daughter-in-law, Connie, who spent a lot of time down at the shop, picking up every juicy story. Many of these reached my ears through Connie's daughter, Josephine, and from the amount of re-cycling that went on, I gathered that the pickings were pretty slim. Nobody in Pulham had a father who regularly got "nicked fer breakin' an' enterin'" like Jimmy Greene of Peabody Buildings; or a mother who was "no bet'er than she should be," like Marjory Strutt. Pulham's tut-tutting mostly revolved around the wanderings, mental and physical, of an old lady who lived alone and was goin' "bonkers," and the shameful goings on of a family that lived next to the post office. This household had a father who drank too much and a slut of a mother who compounded her sins by adding another baby to their brood every year. I felt so sorry for their skinny, unkempt offspring. They were shunned by all the village kids, who got their ears boxed if they talked to them. And I knew, only too well, how it felt to be ostracised. But at least, if these unfortunate children stayed in plain view of the ear-boxing parents, they could avoid teasing and taunting such I had endured in Waterloo.

Soon after we'd settled in Pulham Mum came to visit, armed with jars of Vick's Vapor Rub and bottles of Liquifruita, "fer when yer cough starts, Gwen, it bein' November already." Of course she'd really come to check out our new billets, to make sure we weren't being "neglected" again. Apparently she liked what she saw and didn't go storming off to Mr. Waters. In fact, she and Gran positively approved of one another. "Yew've lucked out this time, Gwen," said Mum. And after she'd gone back to London, Gran remarked, with a satisfied nod, "A rroight decent, rrespectable body, thaat motherr o' yewrrrs." High praise indeed from this woman of few words, who didn't hold a high opinion of evacuees or their parents.

Every once in a while, the latest evacuee horror story—kids swearing, fighting, or yet another outbreak of head lice—would trigger a good old rant from Gran about "disgrraceful parrents," and "filthy 'omes." These blanket condemnations of Londoners made me uncomfortable and angry. I knew they were warranted in some instances, but I longed to tell her about Louie and Harry and the Hodds and the Wilsons, and was sorely tempted to remind her that she'd said that Mum, at least, was a decent respectable body. But I held my tongue.

Josephine, daughter of Connie, lived next door to Gran. I was older by a couple of years, but Josephine and I became close friends, in part because we both had desperate need of a friend. Josephine's life in this village was lonelier than mine in Waterloo had been, for there were no girls her age other than the "untouchables" next to the post office. My recently acquired Aquinas Street friends, Marjory and Jean, had stayed in London, and the only girl *my* age in Pulham was the dreaded Phyllis Turner from Peabody Buildings, so I needed Josephine as much as she needed me. As a windfall from the upheaval of war, we both suddenly had a friend, and, an extra bonus, one that lived next door.

Unfortunately, there was a worm in my windfall: Josephine was an incorrigible troublemaker; she specialized in fibs whose only point seemed to be to get me into trouble, silly stories about something I'd said or done, or not said or done. When we played in her house, Connie believed her daughter's fabrications and angrily sent me packing; but in Gran's house, Josephine's shrewd old grandmother saw through the lies and sent *her* packing. After it became apparent that I was no match for the wily Josephine, Gran put her foot down: "If yew an' Josephine want ta plaay, it'll be in *this* 'ouse. So I can keep an eye on the two o' yew."

This simplified my life enormously. I hated and dreaded the nasty incidents with Connie. She was a more practiced troublemaker than her daughter, and I rapidly came to fear this tall, large-boned woman with the black hair, swarthy face, and witch-like profile, who always stood closer than was comfortable and loomed over in a scary way when she was talking to you. Connie's presence filled rooms the moment she entered, and she dominated everyone. Everyone except Gran; there, Connie had met her match. And although Gran never said much, she clearly didn't like her daughter-in-law any more than I did.

Along with her trouble-making propensities, Josephine had also inherited her mother's jutting jaw; but she had been blessed with a soft, round face; pretty, gray-green eyes; and a lovely, creamy complexion. Nevertheless she was "a plain li'l thing … " as Mum said to me, in her blunt fashion, after meeting Josephine for the first time. "A pity she didn't get the father's good looks, like 'er brother." Unbeknownst to Gerald, the handsome brother, he was the first member of the opposite gender to set my young heart a-flutter; it was unbeknownst to me too, until I realized the implications of the fact that I cried myself to sleep the night he broke his arm. However, the handsome Gerald showed not the slightest awareness of my existence, and I never told a soul about my fluttering heart, not even Josephine. Especially not Josephine.

The good-looking father was Gran's only son, and I gathered that it was a great disappointment to her that George was still a farm hand and hadn't "bettered 'isself," like her two daughters had. Vera married well and lived in a "big 'ouse down Poole waay," a posh resort area on the Dorset coast; and Meg's husband owned his own farm in Buckland, a few miles down the road. I never met Vera, so her visits to Gran must have been few and far between, whereas Meg's were, if anything, too frequent. She came pedaling in every Sunday morning to sing in the church, and very thin the choir sounded when Meg was not there to add her rich soprano. I loved to watch this big blond woman singing; she looked so happy, doing what she knew she did so well.

However if, on any day but Sunday, Meg's sit-up-and-beg bike came squeaking down the front path before being propped up against the wall of the house, Gran snorted, "Meg … agen!" and put the kettle on. Within seconds, in would burst big-bosomed Meg, tears running down her plump cheeks, and out tumbled the story of her latest domestic disagreement. It was hard to reconcile the happy Meg, the joyous singer filling the church with her beautiful voice, with this unhappy woman who regularly pedaled several miles in all weathers to pour out her woes to a not very sympathetic mother. I felt sorry for the unhappy Meg and thought Gran very hard-hearted; the most she gave her daughter, before sending her back on her bike to patch things up, was a cup of tea and a clean rag to mop up her tears.

Gran's house was curiously bare. There was none of the accumulated clutter that old ladies with grown families usually have: no dark, much-handled pictures of children and grandchildren; no chipped souvenirs from seaside resorts; no collection of clocks telling different times—several with hands frozen at the hour when the wind-up mechanism gave up the ghost. And there was very little furniture: a table, a sideboard, a high-backed fireside chair and a pouf in the living room, and a massive bed in Gran's bedroom—the only piece of real furniture I ever saw upstairs. The second bedroom was kept locked, and my little back room must have been empty before my arrival on the scene, because it contained only a fold-up canvas bed (government supply, again) and two cardboard boxes to hold my clothes.

Adding to the mystery of the scarcity of Gran's belongings was the derelict, still picturesque, thatched cottage across the road, in which she had spent her entire married life. Josephine and I were intrigued, but forbidden to go anywhere near it, and Gran firmly cut off all questions. This made our imaginations run wild. Had fire destroyed all Gran's possessions? Was the place haunted? Maybe someone mad was locked up in there? Had it been the scene of an unthinkably terrible disaster? *A murder, even?* Delectable shivers ran down our spines as we tossed these ideas back and forth, and it was a huge temptation to sneak into the cottage garden to look around. But the gate was padlocked, and we never plucked up courage to do more than peer through gaps in the tall hedge; peeks that revealed only a jungle of tall weeds and a house with no sign of fire or anything other than the neglect of disuse. We tried pumping Meg and Josephine's father about the house in which they'd spent their childhood, but they too clammed up. So there the cottage sat behind its tall hedges, just across the road, taunting us on a daily basis, and we never did satisfy our curiosity.

My barely furnished bedroom was decidedly bleak in comparison with our lovely room in the hospital. Instead of the deep window seat from which I'd imagined myself among the branches of the old fig tree, I now had a small window that looked out on a rough pasture and unexciting back gardens with the usual assortment of crudely nailed-together rabbit hutches, wire-netted chicken runs, and rows of vegetables. The pasture was never used for grazing; and I always hoped that one morning I'd wake up and see cows or sheep or horses, their heads down, chomping away at the hummocky grass.

However, despite the room's shortcomings, I did rejoice in the novel experience of having a bedroom to myself. Unfortunately, Gran grew suspicious if I spent much time up there alone; solitary occupations like reading were not what she considered "naach'rral" in a girl my age. In any case, there was nothing to read in Gran's house except for the big, old, family bible; nothing to sit on in my bedroom (other than the sagging camp bed); and no light to read by (there being no electricity in the house). The candle that I took up every night was to be extinguished as soon as I was ready for bed, so I spent very little time luxuriating in this newfound privacy, other than the miserable week when I was confined to bed with German measles and jaundice.

Josephine was made to visit me every day in the hope that she would catch German measles, "because it's good ferrr a gurrl," and we both thought this a strange notion, given the miserable time that I was having. But her visits were a godsend; they relieved the tedium of hours of Patience [Solitaire] with comparatively exciting two-person games like tic-tac-toe, but one day, she unkindly brought a small hand mirror and showed me what an un-pretty sight I was—red spots against an orange-yellow background. I vowed to retaliate, but the opportunity never arose, because she didn't catch German Measles *or* jaundice. Curiously, apart from that episode, I was extra-ordinarily healthy all winter, with no hint of bronchitis and, therefore, no need for Vick's or Liquifruita; those smelly remedies, thoughtfully provided by my mother, sat gathering dust on the bathroom shelf, and never again did I have need of them. Apparently the Clinic doctor had been right; getting me out of London had done the trick.

Gran's routine varied little from day to day, and every evening she and I settled down in front of the fire after tea, with the oil lamp burbling gently and throwing its soft light over nearby objects, leaving the rest in shadow. Gran did mending—her own, and that of the family next door—while I played Patience or amused myself with yet another splendid collection of old buttons. To my dismay, I soon discovered that button games had largely lost their charm; they'd never failed to while away a lonely hour or two, and it came as a shock to realize that, now eleven years old, I'd outgrown them. It was my first Peter Pan moment (though I didn't make Peter's acquaintance until introducing him to my own children, many years later).

Fortunately, House, a game that Josephine and I invented that winter, soon filled the hole left by button games. We happily cut pictures out of old catalogues: pictures of houses, people, children, clothes, tables, beds, prams, toys, bikes, and pets, which we propped up to make "houses" that we furnished and filled with "families.' We took care of those families through many vicissitudes, vicissitudes that came fast and furious, for our family members were remarkably prone to serious illnesses and major accidents. (Interestingly, in that quiet corner of Dorset, the war seemed so remote that never once did it enter into the dramas that were played out nightly on the floor in front of Gran's fire.) When bedtime came, we stored everything in shoeboxes and jealously guarded our ever-growing treasure troves. This game saw us through many long winter evenings, and even when spring brought longer days and warmer weather, we often begged to stay in and play House; but Gran firmly shooed us outside to get some fresh air.

The highlight of a typical Pulham week was Saturday morning: that was when I took the boys to the Post Office and cashed the shilling postal order that Mum sent, as regular as clockwork. After buying a stamp for our thank-you letter (the school required each child to write a letter home on Monday afternoon) the rest of the money went for sweets that we carefully shared out, down to the last jelly baby. We'd never before had pocket money, never had so much to spend on such a regular basis; I secretly chalked this up as positive fall-out from this evacuee business. And so did the boys, I suspect.

But, inexorably, after Saturday came Sunday. And Sunday was Church Day—all day. Gran insisted that I go to Sunday school, the Morning Service *and* the Evening Service. In Sunday school the children were all younger, and it was a huge bore, as were the too-long sermons in the adult Services. I resented all this enforced religion. Apart from Meg, no other member of the extended Miller family went to church, and it seemed most unfair. Particularly since I wasn't from a church-going family. Come to think of it, I don't remember the question of my faith ever being raised. Not that I would have been able to help, beyond a vague memory of once walking in a parade wearing a white dress and a veil. But for all Gran knew, I could have come from a devout family of Catholics, Baptists, even Buddhists … Of course, there wasn't a church of any denomination other than Church of England within walking distance, so I don't suppose it would have made any difference.

Most of all, however, I resented Gran's insistence on my wearing one of her hats to church, since mine was deemed unsuitable. Not suitable? My Deanna Durbin hat? I was inordinately proud of that hat, with its dramatic curved brim; it was my first hat with any pretense to being a fashion statement. I was outraged, but had to swallow hard and wear Gran's "old-lady's" hat every Sunday. When Spring arrived, and other girls appeared wearing fancy straw bonnets, my resentment threatened to boil over, but thoughtful Meg came to the rescue with a flower-trimmed, wide-brimmed affair that must have been at the back of her wardrobe since she was a girl. But I was enchanted and wore it happily until the weather forced a return to Gran's ugly old felt thing.

Despite my church-going disgruntlement, I grew to love the ritual in Pulham's simple old Norman church, so lovingly decorated with flowers, or sheaves of wheat, or bare branches, depending on the season. As when I'd sung in the choir with Viley, I still couldn't hold a tune, but enjoyed belting out the hymns and hearing the organ fill the church to its rafters with wave after wave of sound so intense that you could *feel* it in your bones. I especially loved it when the choir did its fancy stuff, with the sopranos singing high notes that made my throat ache just to hear them. And there was the language of the King James' Bible, the cadences of which linger in my head to this day and still evoke an emotional response whenever I hear them. Yet I didn't then understand much of what I was hearing; and am now a devout atheist. Powerful stuff, that language: the committee responsible for it knew what they were about. (It's hard to believe that something so splendid came out of a *committee!*) That weekly immersion in "church" also gave me a sense of belonging. It came largely from familiarity, I think: familiarity with the liturgy, with the people who came to worship every week, with the whole predictable scene. It is probably an important factor in religious faith for many; for me, though, it wasn't enough to prop up faith in the long run.

Gran was not an early riser, and she prepared my breakfast the night before so that I could get myself up and off in time to pick up the boys and catch the school bus. This scheme was not a success. My bowl of porridge, left overnight in the oven above the fireplace, was no longer warm by morning; it had become a gelatinous, gray lump that made me gag with every spoonful. I couldn't add extra sugar to make it more palatable, because Gran had already sweetened it and put the sugar bowl away—sugar being tightly rationed. In all fairness, on the first day of this regimen, Gran had asked, "Werrre yewrrr porrridge still warrm, this morrnin'?" Like an idiot I said yes, thereby condemning myself to an-ordeal-by-cold-porridge every morning, and as time went on, it became harder and harder to tell Gran that her solution to the warm-breakfast problem was a failure. I struggled with those bowls of cold porridge for many mornings but, in the end, routinely flushed them down the toilet.

Until the day Gran discovered traces of porridge clinging to the toilet bowl, and I had to confess that this had been the fate of my porridge every morning. She was angry about all that good food going to waste, and hurt because, as she saw it, I'd been deceiving her, effectively telling a lie, on a daily basis. I understood her anger. That's exactly how Mum would have reacted to the waste of a bowl of good porridge. But, for reasons that still mystify me, I made no attempt to make her understand the basis of my "lies." I simply stood, mutely, enduring her tongue-lashing. I didn't explain that I hadn't wanted to hurt her feelings by mentioning that the porridge idea didn't work, and didn't want her to feel she had to get up every morning to cook it (because she wouldn't let me use the stove). When the storm subsided, it was agreed to forget the warm-breakfast idea. Bread-and-butter-and-jam was all I needed. But Gran never forgave my "deceit," and from that day, there was a coolness that hadn't been there before.

"Cold an' damp ... just like our Dag'n'am 'ouse," was Mum's comment on her first visit to Gran's council house. (Indeed, the two houses were almost clones, apart from the absence of electricity in this one) But when Spring brought warmer weather, the general chilliness of Gran's house became a thing of the past, and longer days meant more time spent outdoors, anyway.

Josephine and I did a lot of walking that spring. She introduced me to magical things like nodding catkins, the soft silkiness of pussy willow buds, banks studded with primroses and cowslips, vivid carpets of fragrant bluebells in the woods, hawthorn hedgerows loaded with blossom. Of course, there was also the menace of innocent-looking stinging nettles and the fear of snakes where delicate white snake flowers hid in long grass (according to Josephine). But the positives of the Dorset countryside far outweighed the negatives: there was so much loveliness; so much freedom to roam; and none of the street-miseries that had made a recluse of me in Waterloo.

After Josephine had her tenth birthday, we were allowed to walk to Meg's farm, about four miles away, and it was on those walks that I fell in love with winter landscapes, came to love the beauty of bare trees silhouetted against the backdrop of fields and sky. Not that I was aware of this burgeoning love affair as I chatted away to Josephine; but it is those Dorset lanes and fields and skies that pop, unbidden, into my mind's eye, whenever I am thinking about winter and what it brings in its wake.

On our first visit to Meg, I was nervous about meeting her husband, the man who so often reduced her to tears and sent her pedaling over to Pulham. But Will turned out to be a very nice man; he taught Josephine and me how to play Draughts [Checkers], but he was a bit gruff and rough-and-ready, and I wondered whether *that* was the heart of Meg's problem. Their farm was disappointing in that it had no cows or ducks, but there was a goat, Butter, and one look at his wispy, narrow beard cleared up the long-standing question of why pointy beards are called "goatees." I loved Butter's coat, so unexpectedly coarse, and his eyes, so strangely yellow and glassy, and I even enjoyed cleaning out his stall before feeding him some mushy stuff and taking him to the orchard. There Butter munched his way through the fallen apples, thereby reducing the number of wasps that otherwise plagued the farm. It was simply amazing what that animal would eat. He once tore a ribbon off Josephine's hair and snatched up a sock that I'd taken off to remove a pebble—sock and pebble, both, disappeared down Butter's throat! His endless capacity for springing surprises was another thing I loved about him.

After leaving Butter in the orchard on my first visit to Meg's farm, I wandered to the top of a slight rise and heard whimpers coming from a small shed. Inside, I found a beautiful collie dog, straining on a heavy chain and wagging his tail so vigorously that it wagged his whole body. He rolled on his back and licked my face in ecstasy as I tickled his tummy—which was the scene that greeted an astonished Will, who'd rushed in panic to the shed on discovering that I hadn't returned from the orchard. For, he told me breathlessly, Jock was a vicious dog. Especially with children. That's why he was kept chained in a locked shed. Their son Billy had teased the poor dog mercilessly as a puppy, he said, and he and Meg felt so guilty for letting this happen that they couldn't bring themselves to have Jock destroyed. They just took great care to keep him safely locked up if not with them, and Will was horrified that they'd slipped up on this occasion.

To Meg, Jock's behavior with me was nothing short of a miracle, but Will maintained that it was because I'd been blissfully unaware of the dog's history, so he hadn't picked up the scent of fear on that first encounter. Will was right, I thought—the notion of miracles being hard to take seriously—but kept my opinion to myself for fear of hurting Meg's feelings. Jock was always gentle and friendly with me, but he erupted into wild-eyed frenzy if Josephine was there: he strained at his chain, barking and snarling and baring his teeth, a different animal, entirely. Will always accompanied me to the shed, just to make sure ... before leaving me to play with Jock, but I never could spend as much time with the poor creature as I would have liked, because Josephine got sulky if I stayed too long.

Interspersed with these engrossing country experiences, there was school, of course. The under-sevens must have gone to the local Primary schools, but three teachers and the seven-to-eleven year-olds—about seventy of us—managed to fit into our one-room schoolhouse in Lydlinch Village Hall. It was a very different experience from the self-contained classrooms of Hatfield Street, though not as chaotic as one might have predicted. The best part of each school day was the bus ride. It took us past farmland, through villages, across Lydlinch Common, and even gave us a glimpse of the Squire's house, a grand mansion set way back in a fenced park where a herd of dappled deer grazed.

That daily journey made me aware, for the first time, of the continual changes wrought in a landscape by the seasons: a ploughed field suddenly full of bright green shoots that slowly changed to heavy-headed golden wheat—only to be suddenly reduced to stubble and ploughed back into the brown earth; and the changes in the bracken on the Common, from fresh green to crisp golden-brown, then transformed by winter rains to a soggy, slippery, black mess and impossible to play in until the green of Spring returned. In the city, evidence of the seasons—gradual changes in temperature and day length; the Easter transition from winter woollies to white ankle socks and cotton frocks; and the deliciousness of fresh peas in early spring after a winter of cabbage—had always been much less dramatic.

One misty autumn morning, as the bus was crossing the Common, we heard the call of a horn and caught glimpses of a fox hunt: bright-jacketed riders on horse back, and milling, baying hounds—a sea of wagging tails. We begged Mr. Fipps, the bus driver, to stop, so that we could watch for a while, but he said, "An' maake yeew all late ferr yewrr schewel? That's morr than me job is werrth!" and kept going. We often teased and taunted Mr. Fipps, and after this incident the jibes came with greater frequency and ferocity, until the poor man complained to the headmaster and threatened to quit. I'm not proud of the fact that I joined in this harassment and saw this limited world, the microcosm within the confines of a school bus, as a rare chance to safely become one of the gang. But I had the grace to be ashamed of myself when Mr. Waters gave us all a scathing dressing-down, especially when he took me to one side to say, "And *you*, of all people! I would've expected better of you, Gwen Redfern." However I was enormously relieved that he'd taken me to one side; it was not a comment that I wanted any other kid to hear.

The only break in the school routine that I remember was an outing to a small river near Sturminster Newton (the River Stour, a glance at a map now tells me). There was a beachy spot midst the tall rushes that elsewhere lined the banks, and our teachers had rustled up enough swimming costumes [bathing suits] for us all. The sun was bright and the water warm and clear once you got away from the little beach where wading feet had stirred up the soft, slimy mud bottom. Swimmers could keep their feet clear of that squooshy riverbed, but mud oozed through your toes when you tried to stand, and the non-swimmers were not happy. Until Mr. Robinson, the only teacher with the courage to appear in swimming attire, saved the day by clowning around in the water with them, taking their minds off what was happening in the region of their toes.

I'd never swum in a river and was enjoying this novel experience—despite the strange, earthy smell—when I saw a brilliant flash of blue. The bird, a kingfisher I later discovered, disappeared among the rushes, and as I trod water hoping for another glimpse, I found myself eyeball to eyeball with another river creature—a water rat! It looked *enor*mous, like the mouse that once sat on my pillow, and I swam back to the beach as fast as I knew how. Startled to find what a difference a current made, I was thankful, even in my panic, that I had the current *with*, not against, me.

The only other excursion took place some time in the spring, when a few of us in the top class were told to be ready for the bus on Saturday morning, because we were going to Sherborne to take the Scholarship Exam. Was I really supposed to go, I wondered, after all the fuss about missing the Preliminary? Maybe I had lucked out, and midst the chaos of the war nobody had noticed … Anyway, Mr. Waters said nothing, and questioning an authority figure was not exactly common practice, so I decided he must know best and didn't ask.

We left early Saturday morning with the long-suffering Mr. Fipps at the wheel of the school bus, each of us clutching a brown paper bag lunch. Our destination was Sherborne Grammar School, about twelve miles away, where we were joined by lots of other evacuees. I didn't recognize this ancient school as one of the public schools for rich kids that I'd read about in comic books; neither did I see any students other than we Scholarship-Exam-takers, so maybe it was their Easter "hols." However, I was awed by the thickness of the honey-colored stone walls everywhere, and as I sat taking the exam, I kept wondering, "This is a *school?*" It seemed more like a fortress, or perhaps a castle ... a beautiful castle ... with lovely arched doorways. We ate our paper bag lunches sitting on an extensive lawn under a tree, which reminded me of our picnic in Kew Gardens the summer before the war ... less than a year ago ... it seemed much longer ... and so far away. Lunch over, we were summoned back into the school for the second part of the exam, then given a drink and an apple before getting back on the bus. And we all promptly dismissed the whole excursion as the waste of a perfectly good Saturday.

With the arrival of the long summer holidays, my blissful fun-filled days were interrupted only by church on Sundays. Since Gran took no newspaper and had no radio, I was scarcely aware that there was a war going on, apart from the gas mask that had accompanied me to school every day and now sat gathering dust in a corner of my bedroom. The summer stretched ahead, an endless stream of days resembling my stay in Gloucester with Gloria; the only blot on this near-perfect landscape was Phyllis Turner, who lived only two houses away. When I first arrived in Pulham, my heart had dropped to my boots at every encounter, but I'd carefully avoided eye contact, and she'd left me alone. Now, however, we were both outdoors a lot and, after warily circling one another, the dearth of girls our age in Pulham eventually drew us together. I discovered that, in the absence of Hazel Henderson (who'd stayed in London), Phyllis was no longer the mean creature I'd known in Aquinas Street; and she found that I was not the hopeless "brainy goody-goody" she had thought. To our mutual surprise, we became good friends and, with Josephine, were soon inseparable. "Two's company, three's a crowd," didn't seem to apply, perhaps because Josephine was in awe of Phyllis—the most dominant personality and the oldest in our trio. Was it this that kept her trouble-making propensity in check? Or did an eyewitness make it more difficult to invent convincing fibs? A bit of each, probably.

We wandered the lanes and fields, picked wild flowers and berries, made flower chains, scared rabbits and ground-nesting birds, and even the occasional fox. Phyllis taught Josephine and me how to climb trees and, with less success, how to do cartwheels. On rainy days, we played in Gran's shed, listening to scratched records on a wheezy old wind-up gramophone, and I taught them how to knit. We made a lot of "scent" that summer, by soaking rose petals in water scooped out of the rainwater barrel outside the back door. Undeterred by results that were invariably disappointing, we always assumed that the next batch would smell less like rotting rose petals and more like the real perfume that is sold in cute little bottles. I wonder whether Josephine and Phyllis remember that wonderful summer as fondly as I do? Indeed, do they remember it at all?

Autumn brought new country delights: scuffing through dry, rustling leaves; the challenge of hide-and-seek in crisp brown bracken where every movement now made a give-away noise; and the search for horse chestnuts, or conkers, as we called them. All of this was a great novelty to us city kids. In treeless Waterloo there'd been no rustling leaves, no bracken, and no chestnuts lying on the ground waiting to be picked up and released from their prickly protective casing. The game of Conkers took the school by storm and—a rare event—even leapt the gender barrier. Its rules were simple but rigid: the goal was to crack one shiny, red-brown chestnut dangling at the end of a string, by swinging at it with another conker-on-a-string, and the prior score of a cracked conker was added to the score of the survivor of this encounter. String length was a matter of choice, but each miss counted as a swing, so it was a game of skill and the competition was fierce. We searched assiduously among fallen chestnut leaves, hoping to find a "champ," and since no one could document their conker's score, there were occasional cries of "Gor … come awf it! Yew rot'en cheat, yew!" But, by and large, an informal honor system worked amazingly well, considering that these were rough street-wise youngsters, unaccustomed to obeying rules. It seemed different if the rules were of their own making.

That autumn Mum's letters started to mention air raids, and one contained the proud announcement that she was now an Air Raid Warden; we were duly impressed, but had only the vaguest notions of air raids and no idea what an Air Raid Warden did. But one week, her letter-with-postal-order failed to arrive. We got no sweets that Saturday, and Gran had to give me a stamp for the weekly letter home. I was uneasy, but didn't say anything to the boys, and it wasn't till Mum's next letter that we learned the cause of the hiatus. It was nothing less than a bomb—a real bomb—that had landed on our doorstep and buried itself without exploding. The residents of the area had to move out for about a week, until the disposal squad came to de-fuse the bomb and remove it, and Mum's letter went on:

> No one got so much as a scratch from that bomb
> but you will be sorry to hear Gwen that Mr. Wilson
> died when the ambulance evacuating him crashed

> into a fire engine in the blackout. Killed instantly
> he was. A merciful release for both of them if you
> ask me and Mrs.Wilson says shes moving away. To a
> happier life than she had in Aquinas Street I hope.

I was indeed sorry to hear about poor Mr. Wilson, but I didn't want to think that Mum was right about the happy release bit. The Wilsons were happy with one another, I had thought, despite his invalid state. Though Mrs. Wilson *would* probably be glad about moving away from Waterloo. It had never been a good fit for them.

That bomb finally brought the war closer to home for the three of us: someone we knew was dead because of it, and that was *our* doorstep and *our* mother who could have been killed if the bomb had exploded. But Mum had clearly survived to tell the tale, and with the carefree optimism of childhood, we soon stopped worrying about bombs and air raids and re-immersed ourselves in the all-engrossing world of Conkers.

In late October Mum brought down some new winter clothes and a few of our toys. The boys were delighted to see their favorite tip-up lorry and fire engine, but I was embarrassed to be re-united with my Shirley Temple doll. Without realizing it, I'd grown out of dolls after a year without one; the cutout pictures of babies and children in our House game had supplanted them, but I couldn't tell Mum that. Not after she'd bought a new frock for Shirley Ann and lugged her all the way down on the train. Feeling quite a fraud, I feigned pleasure. We were very excited to see Mum, of course, and she was especially pleased to find that Derek's stutter was almost a thing of the past and Bertie's September eruption of boils had been a mere smattering. "What did I tell ya? I always said 'e'd grow out of 'em, didn't I!" she said triumphantly.

After one glance at the knee socks that Mum had knitted for the boys, I knew something was wrong. Their green and orange border was identical to the border on Josephine's new gloves ... Next morning, the boys waltzed in wearing their new socks, and I could tell from Gran's face that she, too, recognized that border. As did Mum when Josephine appeared wearing the gloves—which had been knitted for me and sent in a parcel, along with oranges that were hard to come by in Pulham. Cunning Connie had, apparently, intercepted the parcel and kept the contents; other parcels too, we figured out later.

Mum was livid. "I'll 'ave 'er guts fer garters!" she spluttered (showing, to my relief, uncharacteristic restraint by omitting the adjective "bloody"). This colorful threat seemed new to Gran, and she let out a great guffaw, but then turned serious and managed to dissuade Mum from marching next door to do battle with Connie. "Do-o-n't ye go an' spoil things ferr the shorrt time yewrrr with yorrr kiddies. I'll deal with Connie afterrr yewrrr gone. She won't do nothin' loike thaat agen. I give ye me wurrd." Mum reluctantly agreed, after I reassured her, in private, that Gran really did know how to deal with Connie. "But from now on I'll send yer parcels ta the Veals', just in case … " she vowed, still seething.

The day before she left, Mum dropped a bombshell of her own. She and I were standing in Gran's garden, and it must have been late afternoon, because it was beginning to get dark when she said, "There's somethin' I 'ave ta tell ya, Gwen. I'm gettin' married agin' … ta Jack Weddinger. Yew prob'ly remember 'im … "

Jack Weddinger? The Jack Weddinger? I certainly did remember him. I stared at her in disbelief, trying to reconcile this news with all the stories I'd heard, back in our Commercial Road days, about "that Jack Weddinger." We then lived a few houses down the street from the Weddingers, and after Dad died, Mum took a little daily job helping the bed-ridden Mrs. Weddinger. Every day she'd come home with some story about poor Aggie and "that devil of a man," and how mean and vile-tempered he was, "'specially when 'e'd bin on the booze." When Aggie died, the only surprise in the neighborhood was, "'ow long she'd lasted, the poor soul … wiv' tha' devil ta put up wiv'."

Now my mother was telling me that *she wanted to be the second Mrs. Weddinger?* My face must have spoken volumes, because Mum went on, "But 'e's not like ya think, Gwen … all those things Aggie Weddinger use' ta say. Now I know 'is side of the story, an' she was no angel, I c'n tell ya!" I had no desire to hear Aggie's faults, or her husband's newfound virtues. So I said nothing, and Mum continued, "An' 'e brings in a good income ya know. Steady, too … 'e's a qualified 'lectrician an' there's plenty o' work fer 'lectricians these days, with all the bomb damage. There's a telephone in the 'ouse too … the one Aggie made 'im put in. It's still there. Ya'll enjoy that, won'cha? An' yew'll really like 'is girls when ya get ta know 'em."

Girls? I remembered no girls in that house. But it turned out that there were six of them, most married with children of their own. None of them now lived with their father, but *six step-sisters?* And an unknown number of nieces and nephews. I was about to become a step-aunt, several times over. I was not thrilled at this news. I'd always wanted a baby sister to counterbalance the two boys. But six grown-up sisters was not what I had in mind, even though I'd given up on the baby sister idea after Mum had her operation, and the doctors said she couldn't have any more children.

As for a telephone, I couldn't imagine why I'd enjoy that. I'd never used one, didn't know how to, didn't even know anyone who had a phone except for doctors and people in Shirley Temple films. Having the phone installed had been Jack Weddinger's one redeeming act, in my mother's eyes, because it had meant that the first Mrs. Weddinger could phone for her doctor when she was "'avin' one of 'er bad turns.'" I was surprised to hear that it was still there, since Aggie died some time ago, but I couldn't muster any enthusiasm for a telephone. It certainly didn't compensate for the unwelcome injection of Jack Weddinger into our family circle.

It was the unexploded bomb that had thrown my mother and Jack Weddinger together: they were both on Air Raid Warden duty when it landed, and he let her stay in his house till she could get back into her flat. Thus began the great romance ... Mum tried to reassure me that this momentous step would be a good one, good for us three *and* for her. But it was hard to absorb the notion of a new father in the short time that we stood together in Gran's garden in the deepening dusk. I couldn't help but be reminded of the other occasion when the two of us had stood together in the dark unlit corner outside her bedroom in Commercial Road, and she told me that I'd just *lost* a father.

I went indoors for tea with a heavy heart; a feeling that persisted next morning when we all got together at the Veals', and Mum broke the news of her impending marriage to the boys. They were too engrossed in their truck and fire engine to pay much attention, and not till she said, "Well ... I've gotta go an' catch the train ta go back 'ome now," did they tear themselves away to give her a hug and a kiss. Bertie shed a few tears when she left, but he was no longer the Mummy's boy of a year ago. He'd done a lot of growing up in the past year. We all had.

◆   ◆   ◆

ADDENDA

Recently I heard a harmonica referred to as a *hand organ*, which gave me pause; I'd always known harmonicas as *mouth* organs; a *hand* organ was a hurdy-gurdy, or barrel organ. It had two big wheels, so that it could be pushed around the streets, and a handle that the organ grinder turned to play music for a monkey to dance to before coming round with its tiny hat to collect money.

Then I began to wonder: might a *hand organ* also mean an organ with bellows driven by a hand pump? I'd seen one like that, somewhere ... And—instantly—I was back in Gran's living room, and there, in the middle of one wall, I could "see" a small organ with a hand pump down near the floor. This was the room that I had remembered as *bare and devoid of all but the minimum of furniture?* How could I have forgotten an exotic thing like an organ! I was always uneasy, for reasons I couldn't explain, when describing the bareness of Gran's furnishings, but am truly astonished to discover *why*.

I remain at a loss to understand such a lapse in memory. I had looked at that organ every day, and it even got used once. Indeed, that memory came flooding back as soon as I remembered the organ itself: Meg's full voice filling the room, Gran pounding on the keyboard, and Josephine down on her knees pumping away—until she cried, "That's enough! I'm t-i-e-r-r-red!" Unless my memory is playing more tricks, it never happened again. Probably because a lot of things had to fall into place at the same time: Gran in the right mood and her arthritic hands not acting up; Meg in the right mood and not in a hurry to pedal home to fix Will's dinner; and last but not least, Josephine in the right mood and available to pump. In all likelihood, the temperature had to be right as well, because Gran didn't like to sit far from the fireplace on cold days.

It was I suppose, akin to having all the planets of the solar system aligned—but for that very reason, should have lodged firmly in my memory banks. Why did it take the mention of a hand organ to make it pop out from wherever it had hidden for decades. Mysterious stuff, memory.

◆　　◆　　◆

I re-visited "my" corner of Dorset some sixty years later, expecting big changes and lots of development, but found only a smattering of new houses and buildings. The most marked difference was that the trees were bigger!

Lydlinch Village Hall looked exactly as I remembered it—even inside, I discovered, on peeking through the windows. The only exception was the little back room where Mrs. Greenaway had taken all the girls of "that age," just a handful of us, to alert us to the changes that were soon to take place in our bodies. Its conversion into a kitchen was the only evidence of the passage of time in Lydlinch, though the Common did seem a bit smaller and its grass rougher, and there was no trace of the pond that Georgie Morten had fallen into. Otherwise, it was as if the clocks in that village had been turned back sixty years. Similarly, the Goulds' farm was pretty much as I remembered it, apart from a new roof on the barn and a general tidying up of the farmyard. The strip of garden, full of hollyhocks back when we sat in the sun and played with the kittens, was no longer there. Those hollyhocks were lovely, just right for that spot, and their absence made the farmhouse look too stark, too neat. A pity, I thought.

In Pulham the post-office-cum-village shop had reverted to being just a pretty cottage covered with an abundance of roses. But the other change, a sad one, was that the church had fallen into disuse and now sat, hidden from the road and surrounded by tall weeds, looking forlorn and abandoned. Never again will its rafters ring to the thunderous peal of the organ and to voices like Meg's. And never again will an impressionable, musically ignorant eleven year-old thrill to those sounds and be swept away by the language of the King James Bible. It seems such a sad loss. I suppose the villagers have cars these days and can drive to distant towns for their place of worship—and for shopping. Probably they see these as changes for the better. But I suspect that the sense of community that prevailed in the crowded little post-office shop, and in the church when the congregation joined voices, has been lost forever.

Why so few changes in the area? Is it too far from London? But Dorset is a much sought-after part of England. This particular corner is less dramatic than others, but that, presumably, would be reflected in lower prices. And the more spectacular areas are only a few miles away. Those miles prevented us from exploring them on foot, but they are only moments away in the age of the automobile. A likelier explanation, perhaps, is the Town & Country Planning Act, enacted soon after the war, which decreed that agricultural land should stay that way. If that's the case, then three cheers for a far-seeing piece of legislation.

Writing about that year in Pulham has made me realize how special it was. It allowed my street miseries to fade, and, for the first time since I recognized that I was a misfit and came to rely on the company of adults or "mirror friends," I was free to be a child again. Just in time; just before the complications of puberty. The Dorset countryside also awakened in me a sense of wonder at things like delicate primrose petals set against such fleshy, quilted leaves, and raised the question: *Why* all that beauty? Much of it lay so carefully hidden and so rarely seen, by human eyes, at least. (Do any other eyes *see* beauty?) In particular, I remember an exquisite, white spider sitting on Queen Anne's-lace, completely invisible until it moved. That spider was *so* hard to see; its beauty seemed such a *waste*—to me, who at the time knew nothing about protective coloration and the value of that pure whiteness to the spider.

Chapter 21

New Terrain

IN MY DREAM SOMEONE was dropping heavy furniture overhead. As I gradually wakened, the loud bumps continued, and I could hear the drone of a faraway engine. I slowly became aware that I was sitting in the dark in a moving car, the one that had stopped at Gran's house this morning. Or was it yesterday? Had I been in this car all night? So much had happened on what had started off as a perfectly ordinary Saturday morning.

The appearance of the strange car had created quite a stir, because the only car in Pulham was Doctor Honnington's. But stranger things were yet to unfold. A man and a woman climbed out of the car, knocked on the door and announced to a startled Gran that they'd come to take me to a new school. They showed her a lot of official-looking papers, but Gran didn't read all that well (if she could read at all—I was never sure), so she sent next door for her son to sort this out. He promptly dispatched *his* son to fetch Mr. Robinson from the far end of the village, and Josephine came running across the field where Phyllis and I were playing, with the breathless message, "Coome 'ome quick, Grran says."

It transpired that I had passed the Scholarship Exam; the day in Sherborne had not, after all, been a waste of a good Saturday! And my mother, as one of her choices (should I pass the exam), had checked off the school to which I was being transferred. I was to join the evacuated part of that school, Honor Oak Grammar School, in Reigate, Surrey ... *today* ... that's what all those papers said.

Mr. Robinson decided to consult with the headmaster, so he got on his bike and rode over to Kings Stagg where Mr. Waters lived; Mr. Waters promptly jumped on *his* bike, and they rode back to Pulham and pored over the papers with the two strangers. Neither Mr. Waters nor my mother had been informed that I'd passed the exam; in the confusion of wartime,

172

apparently, the paperwork to them had not kept up with paperwork to the new school. No one had access to a telephone, and in any case, it was now after mid-day on a Saturday, so London County Council Education officials were unlikely to be at their desks. This left the decision up to Mr. Waters and Mr. Robinson. After lengthy deliberations they concurred that the paperwork was legitimate; these two strangers *were* authorized to take me. *Then and there.* The two strangers were anxious to get started a soon as possible because of the blackout, and you could almost "see" them thinking that enough time had already been wasted with all this bicycling back and forth.

When told of this decision Gran looked at me in dismay. I was muddy from playing in the field, and there wasn't time to get the fire going to heat water for a bath. So I was dispatched to the bathroom with a kettle of hot water for a good head-to-toe scrub down, while Gran found a change of clothes and packed the rest of my belongings. She was upset because most of my clothes were dirty—this being Saturday, and washing day not till Monday; in fact, I had the impression that she was more upset by *this* than by the thought of saying goodbye to me ...

By early afternoon we were ready. Shirley Ann wouldn't fit in my suitcase, so there I was, about to go to a new school, to the grammar school of Mr. Pascoe's dreams, carrying a stupid doll—in full view of the small crowd attracted by the car and all the to-ing and fro-ing of teachers on bikes. Hugely embarrassed to have Shirley Ann tucked under my arm, I hurried up the garden path, but as I was stepping into the car, I suddenly remembered Mum saying, "look after yer brothers, an' make sure the three of ya stick t'gether." I stopped dead in my tracks and asked Mr. Robinson, "Bu' what abaht me two bruvvas? Me Mum said we was ta stay t'gevva."

This started a whole new set of deliberations. What *should* be done about the two boys? Should they stay in Dorset with people they knew: their teachers, their friends, and the Veals? Or should we be kept together as a family? The paperwork made no mention of younger brothers. What *would* be best for them? What a difficult decision for those two male teachers in their still-new role as *in loco parentis*! After much soul searching, they decided that the right thing was to keep the three of us together. And off they went on their bikes again to break the news to the boys and the Veals. The boys, too, were grubby and had to be cleaned up, so there was further delay before they joined me and Shirley Ann in the car with their hurriedly packed suitcases; and the tip-up truck and fire engine.

Things had happened so quickly. There'd been no time to think about the implications of all these hurried good-byes to those we'd lived with for the past year; in particular, the likelihood that we might not see any of them again. (We never did.) Neither had there been time to dwell on the fact that we had no idea where we were going, since the names Reigate and Surrey meant nothing to us; no idea what our new schools would be like; no idea who we'd be living with. But was there, perhaps, a silver lining? Was there a chance that we'd all three be under the same roof again?

The excitement of a ride in a car took the edge off our anxieties for a while, until it got dark, at least; then Derek and Bertie, mercifully, fell asleep. I sat there, in the back seat next to the sleeping boys and finally had time to ponder the changes we were about to encounter, including the troubling thought that Derek and Bertie could get separated. In addition, I'd have to start all over again in the friend department—not exactly my strong point—and I sadly added Josephine and Phyllis to a growing list of left-behind friends. Only then did I remember that I hadn't said goodbye to Phyllis; I'd simply hurried back to Gran's house. And I started to cry, silently, so as not to wake the boys, because I didn't want them to know that I was upset. The irony of shedding tears because I might have hurt the feelings of my old nemesis, Phyllis Turner, was not lost on me, and it made me smile even as I wept.

Eventually I, too, must have fallen asleep, until woken by the loud "bumps" of my dream. By the time I was fully awake, I realized that the heavy things being dropped could not be furniture. "Is tha' bombs?" I nervously asked the man driving the car.

"Sh-h-h," he whispered. "We don't want to wake the others, do we?" and then reassured me that what I was hearing was only anti-aircraft guns.

"What are they shootin' at?" I whispered back.

"German planes." (What an idiot I was, not to realize what anti-aircraft meant. But the man let my stupidity pass without comment.) "Can you hear the planes up there? The guns are trying to shoot 'em down, so those devils don't get through to London with their bombs."

"S'pose they do shoot one down. It could fall on us ... "

"We-l-l, it could, I suppose. But don't worry about that, my dear child," he said, kindly. (Dear child? I'd never been called that, before!) "I've driven through quite a few air raids, and a plane hasn't fallen on the car yet!"

So this is what Mum meant when she talked in her letters about air raids, I thought, but our driver was so calm and relaxed that my fears abated somewhat. I then asked about the broad beams of light that were sweeping across the sky, sometimes hitting a cloud, sometimes disappearing into the darkness, sometimes glinting off fat, sausage-shaped, silvery things. He explained, still in a whisper, what searchlights and barrage balloons were for, but I couldn't for the life of me, see how a benign-looking, soft balloon could stop a low-flying plane. However, I didn't like to tax his patience after he'd so generously answered all my questions, and we lapsed into silence. As we continued on through the darkness, listening to the guns and the drone of bombers, I wondered whether to wake Derek and Bertie to witness these dramatic events. But I let them sleep on, since I didn't know how much further we had to go, or how much it might frighten them.

When the car finally came to a halt, we were unloaded into a grand-looking house and handed over to a motherly lady who settled us down for the night. I had to go through the Bertie-wets-the-bed routine and give the lady his rubber sheet, which was pretty embarrassing; but better than having to tell her about a wet bed the next morning. Our drivers had disappeared into the night before I realized that they were leaving, so I didn't get to thank that nice man for being so kind when I woke in the middle of the air raid.

Next morning we were shaken awake by a young woman and learned that the motherly lady of the night before was no other than the Mayor's wife. We'd slept in the house of a Mayor? Yes, and we would be seeing His Honor at breakfast, "if ya don't take all day ta get washed an' dressed," the young woman said rather sharply. Downstairs, nervous at the thought of breakfasting with a Mayor, we were astonished to find ourselves sitting at a table with an elderly man wearing shabby slippers and a dressing gown with egg stains down the front. Our expectations for Mayors derived from the radio program *Toy Town*, in which "Mr. Mayor, Sir" never went anywhere without his heavy gold chain of office, and this disheveled gentleman, whose glasses kept sliding down his nose, was a big disappointment. But Mr. Mayor soon won us over with a couple of Knock-Knock jokes before disappearing behind his paper again. At which point, motherly Mrs. Mayor chatted with us and tried to put us at our ease.

I was not at ease, however. I didn't know what to do with all the knives and forks and spoons, or which plate I was supposed to put my toast on. There was a fancy arrangement for toast, with the slices stacked upright in a little silver rack. But the toast was cold and leathery, not warm and crisp and buttery like the toast we made at home by holding the bread close to a red-glowing fire on a toasting fork and buttering it as soon as it was golden-brown, so that the butter melted into it. I was also deeply embarrassed by a grubby bandage on my hand, covering a deep nick from a rusty old wheelbarrow. In the rush and confusion, I'd forgotten to ask Gran for a clean bandage, and I now tried to eat with that hand hidden under the table.

Before long, Mr. and Mrs. Mayor went off to church, and we were handed over to another lady with a car, who was to take us to our new billets. Another car ride! The novelty still gave pleasure, but we weren't happy to hear that we were going to three different houses. "We couldn't find anyone who could take more than one," the lady said. "But the houses are close to one another. I'm sure you'll be all right."

So we *were* going to be split up. I thought, guiltily, about Mum's exhortation and came close to saying, "My Mum said … " But didn't. I felt so powerless. What could I say to the lady driving the car that would change the outcome? What would Mum say if she were here? Would she be really cross with me for not making some kind of protest? Poor Bertie and Derek. I was worried about both of them. They'd never been apart except for a disastrous week that Bertie spent in the Isolation Hospital when he had scarlet fever. A nurse had to carry him, kicking and screaming, into the ambulance, while Dad carried Derek, also kicking and screaming, back into the house. For the entire week, Derek had not stopped crying except when he fell asleep, exhausted. But I could hear him sobbing, little convulsive sobs, even as he slept, so I expect Bertie did much the same. Of course, I now comforted myself, they were then only four years old, and now they are eight. So maybe they'll be all right.

This car ride took us through towns separated by big grassy hills with bright white paths meandering across them, and patches of countryside that were very different from Dorset's great flat stretches of uninterrupted fields and hedgerows. Here there were many more buildings and wires and poles and railway lines, and it was hard to tell where one village or town ended and the next began. The only big expanse of green drew a comment from our otherwise taciturn driver: "That's Earlswood Common. And we're almost at Nags Head, where you'll be staying—so you won't be far from this lovely Common. The big building over there, the one among the trees, that's the Earlswood Asylum—one of the biggest in the country."

I wished the lady hadn't mentioned the asylum. The thought of all the poor, shut up, crazy people sent a shiver down my spine. It spoiled the otherwise pleasant thought of living near a Common; like when Mum used to point out Bedlam Asylum, "where they lock up all the loonies," which she did, without fail, whenever we walked by the lovely park-like grounds that surround the infamous local madhouse of South London.

Nags Head—a straggle of houses and shops named after its only pub— turned out to be a kind of overgrown village, with small Victorian houses along the main London-Brighton Road and off-shoots of more modern housing on either side. In addition to the pub, Nags Head boasted the usual village requirements of a store, a church, and a school, but there was no real center and, I came to learn, no sense of "belonging" as there'd been in Pulham. It was also much drearier: no rose-covered thatched cottages, and no beautiful, mellow, stone buildings. The Nags Head church, like its Pulham counterpart, was tucked away down a side road, but it was an ugly, shed-like building, with worn linoleum on the floors, ordinary windows, and an old beat-up piano. Every week, as I sat enduring another version of Sunday school,

I sorely missed Pulham's lovely church, with its thick, stone walls and stained glass—and Meg singing her heart out over the rich tones of the organ.

Our new billets were indeed close to one another—at most, five minutes walk apart—but I wished that the boys' houses had been within sight of one another. However, neither of them broke down when we left them with their new hostesses, which was a good sign, I hoped. My new billet was in the house of my dreams, semi-detached and modern, with an indoor bathroom and hot water. How lucky could a girl get! Mr. and Mrs. Phipp seemed kind, well-padded, comfortable-looking people, and once we got over our initial shyness, Geoffrey, their little four-year-old, and I were soon on good terms.

The lady with the car said someone would come the next morning to take me to my new school, and off she went. Mrs. Phipp then took me up to my bedroom and explained that another evacuee would be arriving soon, so we'd have to share the room—*and* the double bed. "I hope that'll be all right," she said, anxiously. "Oh, of course it will," I reassured her, thinking, little does she know that in Aquinas Street I shared a bed with Mum *and* Derek! Neither could she know that this was the most luxurious bedroom I'd ever seen: it had a carpet, matching bedspread and curtains, and a dressing table with cute little drawers and a mirror. In any case, had she really thought that I would—or could, under the circumstances—say anything to the contrary? I found out before long, that this was Mrs. Phipp's way: she used her own nervousness to disarm you, and it was an immensely successful strategy.

The next morning, at eight o'clock sharp, there was a knock at the door, and there stood a lady to take me to my new school. She assured an anxious Mrs. Phipp that there was no need to worry, "I'll make sure she gets home safely." And off I went, with my gas mask slung over my shoulder and a paper bag containing a sandwich, an apple and a penny for milk.

The journey wasn't exactly straightforward. It involved a change of buses, and you had to keep a sharp watch out for the bus stop outside the Reigate County School, which was our destination. But it wasn't until we'd passed through big entrance gates and started walking up a long curving driveway from which we got our first glimpse of the school itself, that I began to feel overwhelmed. I was going to school in that imposing looking building, with the huge expanse of lawn? I wasn't sure that I was up to this. Later that day, when I realized that I was the only member of the class not in school uniform, I *knew* that I wasn't up to this; a certainty that was reinforced at lunchtime in the cafeteria, when I saw that the entire school was in uniform. I wanted to run and hide, ashamed of my home-made frock, the garment that had so delighted me when Mum had brought it to Pulham a couple of weeks ago. As I sat, listening to all the chatter and feeling sorry for myself, it finally dawned upon me that there was not a boy to be seen. There were only girls in this school … This was a novel idea, and I wasn't sure how I felt about it; boys were rough, but girls could be so mean. However, mulling this over did at least take my mind off the issue of school uniforms.

After lunch, the lady who'd brought me to school came into class and handed me a note, on which she'd written the bus numbers and where I had to get on and off. This could mean only one thing: she wasn't going to take me back to the Phipps' house; I had to manage the return journey on my own. I almost cried at the very idea, but held back the tears, determined *not* to start life at a new school by crying on the very first day.

Soon I was in a panic for an entirely different reason: the French teacher was absent and had left a test for us to take! A *test*? In *French*? I'd picked up four French words on our Calais trip: *wee, nong, seevooplay* and *mairsee* but had no idea how to spell them. In any case, this limited vocabulary was not going to be much help. The substitute teacher said, sympathetically, "Just do the best you can, dear," but never will I forget that test on the irregular verbs on page 29 of the French book. I knew what a verb was and what it did, but was mystified as to how a verb could be irregular—it made no sense whatsoever—and to my utter mortification, for the first time in my life I handed in a blank paper when the bell rang. At the end of the day, I went to the cloakroom to get my coat, convinced that, having failed so miserably on my first day, I would surely be thrown out of this school. And part of me was quite relieved at the prospect.

Not till I looked at the lady's note to see where to go to for the first bus, did it dawn on me that I had no money. In my pocket was the shilling postal order Mum had sent, but in all the excitement of Saturday morning, I hadn't gone to the Post Office to cash it. I sat in the cloakroom with the useless postal order, wondering what to do, and my spirits sank even lower when I realized that it was completely dark outside (this being November).

Eventually a teacher noticed me and asked what I was doing, still in school, so late. It was the absent-minded biology mistress (I later learned), and she offered to lend me the bus fare upon hearing my tale of woe. But there was nothing smaller than a five-pound note in her handbag. (A *five-pound* note? I'd never seen one before and immediately concluded that teachers must be very rich.) At that point, I was shocked to see her eyes begin to tear up—adult tears being a rare occurrence in the world of Waterloo—but I subsequently learned that softhearted Miss Franklin shed tears so easily that she was fondly known as Weeping Wilhemina. A sweet, kind woman, she habitually took the troubles of the world on her well-padded shoulders, but had such a low distress threshold that she suffered deeply and sighed frequently. Further rummaging in her voluminous handbag failed to produce the two pennies that I needed, and her tears brimmed over as she directed me to the Office—the last door on the left at the end of the corridor, my dear—where Mr. Coster would give me the money.

When I got to the door labeled Office it was closed, and I was too shy to knock on the door, so I sat in a classroom and waited for Mr. Coster to emerge. Two women came out and hurried off, eager to get their buses home, I presumed, and I was getting more and more worried, for it was, by now, very late indeed. When a third woman emerged, turned off the Office light and locked the door, I couldn't help but burst into tears. Whereupon she noticed me sitting in the dark classroom and came over to find out what was the matter.

"I'm lookin' fer Mr. Coster!" I wailed.

"We-l-l … and you've found me. What is it you want?" she said brusquely.

To my astonishment, I had indeed found the person I was seeking. Her name was Miss De Costa. I'd never met anyone with a French name, and on this, my first day in an all-girls' school, I hadn't realized that the staff were all female, too. She grudgingly unlocked the office, extracted sixpence from a little tin moneybox, exactly like the one I'd left behind in Aquinas Street, and wrote down my name, admonishing me sternly to return the money the next morning, without fail.

We walked to the bus stop together, and I was glad of her company, however reluctantly given, for the long driveway was now pitch dark, and she had a torch [flashlight]. Its beam was feeble, she explained, because most of its light had to be blocked on account of the blackout; feeble it might be, but I kept wondering how I would have managed that twisty driveway if I'd been alone with no light. It was my first experience of navigating in the blackout, and mighty scary it was. At least there were no guns booming. Yet. But it was terrifying to realize that I might have to deal with my first air raid when alone on unfamiliar buses in unfamiliar surroundings. Nobody had told me what to do if the siren sounded before I reached the safety of the Phipps' house …

However, I did successfully change buses and made it back safely; but very late indeed, because in addition to the earlier delays, I missed the Nags Head bus stop in the dark and had to walk back from the next stop. Predictably, the Phipps were extremely anxious: she was weeping, and he was about to go on his bike to the police station to enlist their help. I think he was relieved that he now didn't have to—it was a dangerous business riding a bike in the blackout. Mrs. Phipp dried her tears and started scolding me for being so late, until she heard my story. Then her anger was re-directed toward "that woman … she ought to be reported … how could she just walk away, leaving you there … without any bus fare!" Like me, Mrs. Phipp had understood that the lady was going to accompany me back to the house, but I don't think anyone ever reported anything to the authorities, though Mrs. Phipp kept saying, "someone should."

My roommate-bedmate arrived a few days later. She was a skinny, round-shouldered girl with glasses and freckles, called Belinda. We got along all right, though I felt like a baby elephant next to her, and she wasn't happy about us sleeping in the same bed. It wasn't me that she objected to so much, as the idea of having to share a bed with anyone. She was accustomed to a room of her own and a bed to herself. As far as I was concerned this bed, even with two of us in it, was more comfortable than the narrow folding canvas things I'd slept on in Dorset. My biggest problem was the main line London-Brighton railway line that ran along a high embankment at the bottom of the garden. Belinda was used to train noise just outside her bedroom window at home, so this didn't faze her at all, but after the quiet of Dorset at night, the clatter of high-speed trains rushing by kept me awake.

When I learned that Belinda had a twin brother, I assumed that she must miss him horribly, but she didn't seem to; not as much as Bertie and Derek were missing one another. Neither of them had settled well, and I'd begun to think that maybe they should have stayed in Pulham; they'd been so happy with the Veals, and would not have been separated. Mercifully, they both went to the same school, the local Nags Head Primary school, and were in the same class, or they would have been even less happy.

Mrs. Phipp was always very kind to us, but Belinda and I soon learned what a tense, anxious lady she was. Her pretty face was a mass of "worry lines" that made her look old, a lot older than her husband. She was always fussing and worrying about something or other; though it seemed to me that she had precious little to worry about, with her comfy house, a nice little boy, and a husband who adored her. Belinda and I did our best to wash the dishes and put everything away *exactly* as decreed, but Mrs. Phipp always found fault, which made us tense and anxious, too. Especially Belinda, who was inclined that way to begin with. Fortunately, Mr. Phipp was an easy-going soul who teasingly shrugged off what he called his wife's "miseroos." He was not exactly a handsome fellow—"he's got a face like a potato," said Belinda, rather unkindly I thought, though it *was* a very apt description—but I envied little Geoffrey this kind and playful father who romped with him every evening after work. I did *not* envy the child his fusspot of a mother.

The Reigate area was not a target for air raids, but it lay between the South coast and London, so bombers heading for London often flew over it. Consequently, the war was now very much a part of our lives: we often heard the wailing of sirens, followed by a repeat of what I'd heard in the car, the drone of planes and the booming of anti-aircraft guns. Nothing more dramatic than that happened, and we got used to it. Even Mrs. Nervous Nellie

Phipp had reached the stage of sighing, in exasperation, "Oh no! Not again!" before shepherding us all into the small cupboard under the stairs, the safest place in the house, we were told.

It was much more exciting when the siren wailed during the school day, and we filed, in silence, with our gas masks and whatever else we could grab, into the County School shelters underneath the lawn. They had to be the most exotic shelters in the whole of Great Britain: a labyrinth of naturally occurring tunnels, deep under ground, that ran for miles; all the way to the coast it was rumored. In earlier times these sand caves were used by smugglers, said those with strong imaginations, but I don't know their origin or history. They certainly made a dramatic change from the classroom while we waited for the "All Clear" siren. Of course, a mere air raid was not allowed to disrupt our education. We sat cross-legged on the sandy floor, and our lessons continued as if nothing untoward was happening, despite the fact that some of us had not managed to grab so much as a pencil, let alone a notebook. The enthusiasm of Miss Busby, the gym mistress, had to be curtailed after her class did handstands against the wall of the "gym" tunnel, and a big chunk of the ceiling fell. From that day on, Buzzer (as we called her, on account of her rasping saw-mill voice) was restricted to calisthenics and running-on-the-spot exercises, much to everybody's disgust; we all hated calisthenics.

When the siren sounded in the middle of lunch, we were allowed to take our plates with us, and learned that a fine dusting of sand fell steadily from the high ceilings of the tunnels, helped, perhaps, by the excited chatter of several hundred girls. Those gritty lunches were reminiscent of eating sandwiches on a windy day at Ramsgate, though not as much fun. On one occasion the lights went out, and the blackness in those tunnels put the blackout above ground to shame. We sat paralyzed with fear, in part because of the intense darkness—if the absence of light can be said to be intense—and in part because we didn't know what had caused it. Had a bomb fallen on the school? Had a tunnel collapsed? Were we trapped underground? After the initial cries of surprise, a strange hush settled over us as we sat staring into the darkness, straining to see something. A few girls started to cry, and teachers with dimmed flashlights picked their way among the seated bodies, trying to locate them and give comfort as best they could. I don't know how long the lights were out, but it seemed like forever, and on that occasion we were actually glad to hear the All Clear siren and file back to our classrooms.

We evacuees, about two hundred of us, shared the County School building with its rightful occupants. It was a tight fit, but the two schools did not combine classes; each went about its business as if the other didn't exist. What a nightmare it must have been, dovetailing all those classes, particularly for subjects like gym and art, where special rooms were needed. To ease the crunch, Honor Oak students had the day off on Monday, the afternoon off on Thursday, and went to school all day Saturday; the Reigate girls had the usual Monday-Friday schedule, with a half-day on Wednesday. Thus, each school had the building to itself one-and-a half days a week, but we evacuees felt cheated; somehow, Monday off didn't have the same feel as Saturday off.

This arrangement made it difficult for me to see the two boys. It was dark when I got home from school, so Sunday was the only day all three of us were free, but between Sunday school and taking care of Geoffrey while the Phipps went to church, my Sundays were pretty much spoken for. It was also difficult to know *where* to get together with the boys. Neither of their new "mothers" asked me in, unlike warm-hearted Mrs. Veal; and I did not feel comfortable asking Mrs. Phipp if the boys could come to *her* house. The only way we could get together was to go for a walk, but in November the weather wasn't always co-operative, and neither were the boys. Going for a walk was not one of their favorite activities. As a result, I didn't see much of them during our first week or two in Nags Head, and Bertie was whisked away to a Home for Problem Boys before I knew that he was having serious difficulties. His bed-wetting, apparently, had got a lot worse, and his hostess wasn't prepared to deal with it any longer.

I don't know to what extent Bertie's deterioration had been due to the fact that, since leaving Dorset, he and Derek no longer slept under the same roof; but the sudden removal of Bertie from Nag's Head certainly had a profound effect on Derek. He rapidly went from bewildered anguish to tight-lipped anger at the world in general, and it got harder and harder to get a word out of him. It was a while before I found out how to get to the Home to go visit Bertie—it was a tricky journey involving three buses—but Bertie didn't exactly welcome me with open arms: it was Derek he wanted to see. Poor lad, he clearly wasn't happy at the Home, and I felt so sorry for him. On my next visit Derek came with me, and Bertie excitedly showed him around, pointing out the good climbing trees and the best hiding places. It was lovely to watch them having fun together again, but our visit was cruelly brief, and the parting was hard on them both. I wondered, afterwards, if it had been a good idea to stir up their feelings like that. Maybe I shouldn't take Derek next time? However I never had to answer this question; by then Derek, too, had left Nags Head, so I went alone—and had to break that news to Bertie

◆　　◆　　◆

At first there were only a handful of students in my class at school, but new girls slowly trickled in as the authorities found out where they'd been evacuated to with their elementary schools and made arrangements for them to come to Reigate, just as they had with me. We compared notes one day and found that we'd been scattered all over England, Wales and Scotland, so it must have been a monumental task, gathering us up. That trickle of new girls soon meant that I wasn't the only one without a school uniform or a satchel in which to carry my books, and I felt more at ease. Truth to tell, I rather enjoyed carrying the books in my arms, with the French book on top because I wanted the whole world to know that I, Gwen Redfern, was learning French, just like the posh kids in the comic strips!

The Honor Oak version of schoolwork was very different from that of Hatfield Street School: we had "subjects," each with a different teacher, were expected to take notes in a Rough Notebook, and had homework every night. It was altogether a more serious business, and I liked this, though it took a while to get used to the homework bit. There was also the little matter of pen-and-ink. Pencil was not accepted for anything other than rough notes, and I was ill prepared to deal with the problems attendant on pens: treacherous nibs that unpredictably released puddles of ink or sprayed it in all directions; ink that smudged if not quite dry; blotting paper as elusive as Mr. Slarks' cane; papers ruined by a leaky bottle of ink; permanently ink-stained fingers and clothes. Hatfield Street School's pencil-only policy made for a very messy start at Honor Oak.

One of our weekly assignments was a composition, and it didn't take long for Miss Brophy, the English mistress, to discover that I had, essentially, two languages: one for speech, the other for writing. From my mouth came the bad grammar and sloppy pronunciation of Waterloo, and from my pen, the correct grammar and archaic vocabulary of the fairy tales of Andersen and the Brothers Grimm. I handed in compositions sprinkled with "quoth he" and "come hither", and "marquises" traveled "leagues" in search of "fair damsels." Miss Brophy took me under her wing in after-school sessions to address these problems. Expanding my written vocabulary into the twentieth century was the easier task and would probably have happened anyway, given the broader reach of the reading material to which I was now exposed. Changing the speech patterns was harder. I was by no means the only girl with a working class accent, but for Miss Brophy to have singled me out, I was probably more in need of help than most. With practice I learned to make the right sounds, but was reluctant to employ them in public, hideously embarrassed at the thought of "sounding posh," and it took a while to overcame this hurdle.

The letter *h* gave me huge trouble. I felt incredibly self-conscious pronouncing that sound. And so many words needed it—innocent little words like *had* and *hit* and *he*. But slowly I developed a comfort level with all this speech stuff and got to the point where I could say *hello* instead of *'ello*, and *bath* instead of *barf*, without even thinking about it. Then it dawned on me that some *h*s are silent. That threw me for a loop. How could you know if you'd not seen *and* heard the word? There seemed to be no rules. The final blow was to discover that, in French, hs are as silent as in Waterloo! For a long time, reading aloud in English or French was a miserable experience. I was so afraid of being thought a fool if I sounded an aitch that was supposed to be silent, or left silent one that should be sounded. Indeed, for years I unknowingly made just such a fool of myself, referring to *high teeth* instead of *eyeteeth*—on the assumption that all those Waterloo mums had dropped the *h* when discussing the teething problems of their offspring!

At Christmas, Derek and I went home for the holidays, since we were now only twenty miles south of London, about an hour on a Green Line coach—a lot quicker and cheaper than the two hundred-mile journey from Dorset. We were so excited to be going home, for the first time in fifteen months. Though it was not the place we still thought of as home, the Aquinas Street flat, because Mum was now married to Jack Weddinger. The knot was tied the day we were whisked away from Pulham, so our home was now *his* house on the corner of Upper Ground—the corner where Dad had collapsed on his way to the doctor, I couldn't help thinking.

Two other worries nagged at me, as I sat on the coach. In Waterloo German planes wouldn't just fly over us: London was where they *dropped* their bombs. And what would we be expected to call the stepfather we were about to meet? Dad? What else *could* we call him? Certainly not *Jack*. I didn't like the idea of calling this man, a virtual stranger to us, Dad.

Both worries were justified. There *were* air raids, and they *were* scary and a lot noisier than raids in Reigate. As well as guns and droning planes there were exploding bombs, sometimes very loud, which inevitably prompted someone to voice the thought that was in everybody's head: "That was a close one." Just as inevitably, this was greeted with rolled eyes and, "We all know that, ya daft thing!" or words to that effect. Even more terrifying than *hearing* an explosion, was to *feel* it, directly, through your feet, but as we sheltered in the basement, Derek and I played cards a lot and tried not to think about what was going on. As for the second worry, we were indeed expected to call our stepfather Dad. This *was* difficult but rarely necessary, as it turned out. For there were two Jack Weddingers: the over-friendly, smarmy fellow who'd just come back from the pub in a good mood after a few beers, and the surly, quarrelsome man who'd drunk whisky instead of beer; or had no money to go to the pub, even for a beer. The friendly fellow talked a blue streak, and it was hard to get a word in edgeways; the surly one was best left alone. So we skated around the "Dad" issue by rarely addressing our stepfather directly; we merely responded if he spoke to us.

Jack Weddinger's house was exactly the same as the one we'd lived in when our father died, apart from the fact that this one had electricity, and the big front basement hadn't been filled in, so it served as the main living room. Another welcome difference was that, in this house, we used toilet paper instead of squares of scrap paper threaded on a loop of string. Was this because of improved finances, now that the head of the household had a regular, relatively well paid job? Or had our stepfather put his foot down when it came to using cut-up scrap? Either way, it was a relief not to worry about someone having inadvertently cut up a bag that had contained pepper—as I once did. I happened to be the one who suffered the consequences of that carelessness and can vouch for their extreme unpleasantness!

I found it quite disturbing to be in a house identical to the one that we used to live in. There were so many daily reminders of our life as it had been, and half-forgotten memories kept surfacing. In particular, it was impossible to pass the dark corner outside Mum's bedroom, in which she now slept with her new husband, without being transported back in memory to the identical dark corner—a few houses down the road—where Mum told me that Dad had died. There was no avoiding that corner; it was a spot that I had to pass several times a day. So it was just as well that we didn't also have to deal with saying, "Dad, this … " and "Dad that."

On Christmas morning there was a satchel at the foot of my bed, "real leather … put yer nose in an' take a sniff!" said Mum. I was delighted, by the satchel *and* by its smell. The novelty of prominently displaying my French book had worn off, and I was tired of books and papers getting wet when it rained. But, for Derek, not even waking to find that the Father Christmas he no longer believed in had left him the toy tank of his dreams compensated for the absence of Bertie. We had both assumed that Bertie would be home for Christmas, too, and on the Green Line bus Derek had chatted happily about what the two of them would do over the holidays. He was devastated when it turned out that Bertie wasn't going to be there, not even for Christmas Day.

"Bu' why not?" he kept asking Mum.

"'E couldn't come. That's all … " was the only answer he got. Eventually he stopped asking and moped around, half-heartedly playing with his new tank.

When I went back to school after Christmas there was a school uniform in my suitcase, folded *very* carefully, so as not to crease the box-pleated skirt. I felt self-conscious in its new-stiffness, but no one other than me gave it a second thought, and I thankfully blended into the background. However, the cost of the uniform had left my mother in shock. She was used to making our clothes out of remnants or discarded clothes from the Hodds, but now everything had to be a special design in navy blue and red. From the pleated skirt to the brimmed felt hat with school hatband and the tie—which took me forever to learn how to knot—nothing was make-able at home, out of scraps. Fortunately by the time we made that first trip to the uniform store in Peckham, my scholarship grant money had come through—about three pounds a term I think—not enough to cover this initial outlay, but it helped.

Similarly, when spring arrived there wasn't enough to buy a school blazer or a straw hat, and since we weren't allowed to go coat-less or hat-less in public, I had to sweat out hot days in all my winter stuff. Eventually the grant money kept pace with the uniform expenses, and I got the coveted blazer, complete with school badge on the pocket. I felt so proud of myself in that blazer but was glad that I didn't have to walk to school every day through the streets of Waterloo in this get-up. Just thinking about the taunts it would provoke, made me cringe. The summer uniform was more relaxed—a plain cotton frock of any solid, pastel shade—and here Mum saved a ton of money by making mine. But I'm afraid I envied the girls who had the "official" frocks bought from the shop in Peckham.

To my astonishment, not every girl was happy to don the school uniform: Jean Richardson, a quiet unobtrusive girl, startled us one day by climbing on her desk, ripping the school band off her hat, screaming and yelling about this "rotten school" and its "stinkin' ol' uniform." She was stamping on the offending hat, now crushed beyond recognition, when a couple of teachers arrived to help Miss Franklin—who'd been endeavoring to teach us everything there was to know about leaves when Jean erupted. Poor Weeping Wilhemina was not designed to deal with crises of this nature: she simply stood there, tears filling her faded blue eyes, and remonstrated feebly, "Jean, my dear … p-l-e-a-s- e Jean … " until the other teachers carried Jean, kicking and screaming, out of the room. And that was the last we ever saw of Jean Richardson. In rowdy Hatfield Street School, I'd never witnessed a scene like this, and I found Jean's outburst very disturbing. I'd come to think of Honor Oak School as a calm, peaceful oasis and had assumed that all my classmates were, like me, delighted with it. However, the Jean Richardson fiasco faded, and things settled down again.

In the fullness of time, I got the school routine sorted out; or, perhaps, *it* sorted *me* out. I really enjoyed the greater variety of subjects, things like French and Science that hadn't been part of the Hatfield Street scene. Indeed, I was beginning to feel comfortable in this new life, both at school *and* at home with the Phipps, when it was disrupted by an unfortunate incident.

The incident involved, of all things, a rice pudding. On the fateful day, Mrs. Phipp was out when we got home from school and Belinda wasn't feeling well, so she went to lie down for a while. I did my homework, feeling quite virtuous for such diligence, and then, suddenly, I felt ravenously hungry, as only a rapidly growing eleven-year-old can. I poked my nose into the pantry to see if I could find an apple—Mrs. Phipp often gave us one after school, so I didn't think she'd mind—but my eye fell upon a dish of leftover rice pudding. I love rice pudding, especially cold rice pudding; and the temptation was too great. Just one spoonful, I thought. I scooped up a spoonful, then guiltily washed the spoon and put it away to remove all traces of my crime. But, to my dismay, evidence of the missing spoonful remained in the shape of a "dent" in the pudding. I hadn't realized that this would happen. I could think of no way to undo that dent, so I closed the pantry door and hoped that no one would notice. I hoped in vain. When Mrs. Phipp went to fetch the pudding from the pantry, she shrieked, "Who's been eating my pudding?"

"It was like Goldilocks an' the Three Bears!" Belinda giggled, in bed that night. "I could hardly keep a straight face." I was too guilt ridden to see the funny side of this scene, and it was certainly no laughing matter as far as Mrs. Phipp was concerned. When I admitted to being the culprit, my confession seemed to whip her into a greater frenzy. She kept on and on about how could I be so deceitful … sneaking around the house like a thief as soon as her back was turned … she'd never be able to trust me again … what had she ever done to deserve this? She was a genuinely devout Christian lady, and it seemed that I had somehow deeply wounded her, right to her spiritual core. I was baffled as to how a spoonful of rice pudding could wreak so much damage. Again and again I told her that I was sorry—really, really, sorry—and hadn't meant to upset her. But whatever I said only made things worse, and eventually I just sat there, not knowing what to do or what to say. She worked herself into such a hysterical state that Mr. Phipp gave her some aspirin, took her upstairs and sat with her till she fell asleep, while Belinda and I did the washing up in silence, put little Geoffrey to bed, then went to bed ourselves.

By morning I hoped the storm would have blown over, but Mrs. Phipp was still red-eyed and weepy when we left for school. And when we came home. By the following day the tears were gone, their place taken by tightly compressed lips and a lot of heavy sighing, and I thought maybe this was the time to tell her, once more, how sorry I was. Well … that was a big mistake. She turned the water works on again and was still crying when Mr. Phipp came home. I'd often heard of an "atmosphere you could cut with a knife" and now knew, first hand, what it felt like.

I racked my brains for a way to put things right, but in the end there was no need. On Sunday morning Mr. Phipp quietly told me to pack my suitcase, because he was taking me to a new billet. "You're going to some friends of ours, the Sharps. They live just round the corner, so you'll still be near your brother." As we walked to the Sharps' house, I longed to tell Mr. Phipp how sorry I was to have upset Mrs. Phipp. I badly needed to hear this gentle, potato-faced man say something like, "Yes. I know you are, my dear ... " but shame for what I had done, and fear that his reply might not be what I wanted to hear, kept me tongue-tied and mute, and we walked along in silence, parting with no more than an embarrassed, "Well ... goodbye then."

When I saw Belinda in school the next day, she said, "Mrs. Phipp's still on about that stupid rice pudding. I can't stand it any more. So I've written to my Mum and Dad to come an' take me home." Which they did, adding enormously to my guilt. For I now worried that, because of me, Belinda was back in London and might die in an air raid. All on account of a spoonful of rice pudding. Never in my wildest dreams could I have imagined consequences so dire.

◆　　◆　　◆

Addendum

Why was I allowed to take the Scholarship exam? Had nobody noticed, in the confusion of wartime, that I hadn't sat the Preliminary? Was *this* what rescued me from the consequences of that omission—consequences that had brought tears to Mr. Pascoe's eyes? Or was it, perhaps, Mr. Pascoe's doing? Those strange tests that I took in his office ... were they used to make a case to the authorities on my behalf? And did he ever know that I *did* pass? That his efforts to make a dent in my ignorance of General Knowledge had not been in vain? I like to think that *someone* told him. But as with many of my questions, I'll never know the answer.

Chapter 22

Life with the Sharps

LIFE WITH THE SHARPS meant a return to the discomforts of the late-nineteenth century, because their house was one of the small semi-detached Victorian dwellings that lined the main road through Nags Head.

Like most houses in which I'd lived, it had one cold faucet, no built-in bath, and an unlit outside toilet—reminiscent of the spider-filled darkness of our Commercial Road lavatory. After enjoying modern plumbing for the past year, it was back to hauling in a tub from the back wall for a bath in the kitchen. And this kitchen had the added disadvantage of being the main thoroughfare to the back door … The Sharps' lavatory did actually have a light socket, but was without a bulb. When I asked about the missing bulb Mr. Sharp explained, "the door's got gaps b'tween the boards, an' the air raid warden kept warnin' us that we 'ad ta fix it, so we just unscrewed the bulb." Adding insult to injury, there was no covered way to the toilet; when it was raining, you chose between getting wet *en route*, or coping with a clammy, clingy raincoat in that confined space.

There was no light in my bedroom either. For some reason, when the house was "modernized" wiring wasn't extended to that small back room. And I couldn't even take a candle up to bed, as in Gran's house, because the Sharps hadn't bothered to put blackout curtains in a room that was rarely used before my arrival on the scene. Getting undressed in the dark didn't bother me, but I did miss reading in bed—a luxury I'd been introduced to by Belinda. I also missed the Phipps. I had liked that family, despite Mrs. Phipp's fussiness. My new "parents" were brusque, almost surly, and I felt that I'd paid a high price for that spoonful of rice pudding.

Mrs. Sharp was a no-nonsense lady, no matter who she was dealing with: her husband, her two boys, me—or even the King of England himself, I imagine. ("Sharp by name and sharp by nature!" was Mum's verdict on

189

meeting her.) Mr. Sharp, a mechanic of some sort judging by his oily overalls, was a stolid fellow of few words, more at ease dealing with machines than real live people. He took his wife's prickliness in his stride, and when she started a rant, he simply shrugged his broad shoulders and opened up the paper or went to see to the chickens that he kept at the end of the garden.

They had two boys, as different from one another as chalk is from cheese. Teddy, a skinny sensitive four-year-old with a peaked, mournful little face was very handsome, like his mother, and he had her "edginess" as well. Robbie, however, still a round-faced toddler, was as chunky and stolid as Mr. Sharp in appearance and in temperament.

Teddy often had a hard time with his mother's take-it-or-leave-it approach to parenting, and his way of coping with a bad day was to bottle up his distress until his father came home. On those days, as soon as Mr. Sharp came through the door, Teddy ran to him and clung tight, burying his sad little face between his Daddy's legs. They seemed to have a silent pact. Without a word on either side, Mr. Sharp would gently free his legs, crouch down to let the boy climb on his back and, with Teddy nuzzling his neck, give him a piggy-back ride. If the weather was fine, they hunted for eggs in the hen house, picked a lettuce from the garden, or went down the road for a paper, but on rainy days, they settled for the unheated front room to be off by themselves. Whatever transpired during those sessions, it calmed Teddy down, and life in the Sharp household was restored to its customary uneasy version of peace. Stolid little Robbie would probably develop a shrug-it-off strategy like that of his father; but when I knew him, his only recourse was to bawl lustily when his mother was too hard and unrelenting for his liking. He had a very healthy pair of lungs, and when he and Mrs. Sharp had a disagreement you could hear his protests from the bottom of the garden.

As I did my best to navigate these shoals, with varying degrees of success, I often wondered what the Sharps had been told by their good friends, the Phipps. Had Mrs. Phipps branded me in advance as "a thief," "a deceitful little hussy and not to be trusted"? The Phipps would surely have given some reason for throwing me out of their house, but nothing was ever said, so I didn't know quite where I stood. However, the first time the teacher responsible for overseeing the Nags Head area came on one of her regular visits, she and Mrs. Sharp were closeted in the front room for a very long time. Before leaving, Miss Frampton wagged her finger and cautioned me sternly to be on my best behavior. That I took to mean that she knew all about the rice pudding—not an auspicious beginning to my relationship with my history mistress.

Monday, as in most British households, was Washing Day for the Sharps. Hence, on my day off from school, I found myself in an unheated kitchen, up to my elbows in cold running water, doing the rinsing. It was not my idea of fun, an opinion shared by every Honor Oak girl who found herself in the same boat. This turned out to be most of us, and our mumbling and grumbling usually peaked on Saturdays when we had to go to school and our "free" Monday loomed just over the horizon. I can't speak for the others, but given the choice, I would have preferred an extra day of school to a morning at the kitchen sink. For to my delight, it was fast becoming apparent that I "fit" in this new school in a way that I never had in Hatfield Street School. At last! I was in a world of like-minded girls, girls with whom I had interests in common and who laughed at the same things. But even more important, I was in a bigger pond and no longer top of the class. Indeed, I was far from the top and could comfortably blend into the woodwork—to my immense relief.

Gym classes, however, were another story. There, I was miserable, horribly aware of being the fattest girl in the class. In the entire school, probably. In particular, my inability to turn upside down on the wall bars seemed to provoke the wrath of the gym mistress; it was as though she believed I failed at this task deliberately. I did, once, actually succeed, to the surprise of everyone—myself most of all. But Miss Busbey got so excited and had the class do so many exercises in this ridiculous position that my hands could no longer support my weight, and I fell on my head with a mighty thump. After that, I *did* deliberately fail to upend myself on those stupid wall bars, and The Buzzer, determined to get a repeat performance out of me, pestered me mercilessly. Gym was not my favorite class; neither was I her favorite pupil.

My only other classroom anxiety was the English mistress's propensity to assign a poem once in a while, in place of an essay. I could not do this: I simply froze when I tried to write poetry. Why, I'm not sure, other than a vague feeling that poetry bared the soul in a way that prose did not. I struggled with those assignments but never produced anything worth handing in. Not hand in an assignment? At first, the idea was terrifying. I wondered what the consequences might be, but anything seemed preferable to handing in a part of myself in the form of a poem. When I discovered that the consequences were nothing more than raised eyebrows and a few caustic comments from Miss Brophy, I simply learned to steel myself in preparation for the eyebrows and comments. I had just started to worry about how I would explain the equally caustic comments that would appear on my report card, when I noticed that one of my friends often dreamed her way through classes, scribbling poems in her Rough Notebook. Or even on the back of her hand.

"How can ya do that?" I asked Elaine, in awe.

"It's easy," she replied. "A lot easier than writing stupid essays. I *hate* doing those!"

The upshot of this conversation was that Elaine and I entered a pact: I'd write essays for her, and she'd write poems for me. She was getting the better deal, since the assignment was usually an essay, but I didn't care. Anything to avoid having to write poetry. Not until I settled down to writing the first "Elaine" essay did it dawn on me that it had to be credibly from *her* pen, not mine. Thank goodness my essays were no longer sprinkled with archaic vocabulary! Nevertheless, I had to write two essays on the same topic with two distinct voices; I had to "be" Elaine, wear her shoes, so to speak. I tried to imagine what it would be like to be tall and thin, with straight black hair, dreamy pale blue eyes and a long turn-up nose; to be someone who could run swiftly and was supremely indifferent to what other people thought or said about her; someone who, with a shrug and a lazy laugh, brushed off things that would have bothered me for days. I admired Elaine tremendously and often wished I were more like her; now, almost weekly, I had to pretend that I *was* she!

Of course Elaine had a similar problem, but less often, and Miss Brophy had no poetry samples in my voice, for comparison. That first "Elaine" essay required several re-writes, and it was with much trepidation that I gave it to her to copy over before handing it in. We were always nervous when Miss Brophy handed back our papers, but she never suspected either the "Elaine" essays or the "Gwen" poems. It was, I suppose, cheating. But that never crossed our minds, and we continued the subterfuge, becoming more and more proficient in our "other" voices as time went on. This nefarious practice came to an abrupt halt at the end of the school year, because Elaine didn't return after the summer holidays. I missed her horribly, missed her lazy laid-back ways and laconic comments; I'd never before known anyone quite like that. But the loss of her poetry-writing skills was not the disaster I feared at first, because Miss Brophy, too, failed to re-appear in September, and no other English mistress was as fond of poetry assignments as she had been.

Not long after Christmas, Mum took my brother back to London. He'd been getting into all sorts of trouble, in school and out. There was talk of a broken window, of Derek acting up with his hostess, and his teachers—when he wasn't playing truant. He'd never settled down after Bertie was taken to the Home; his stutter had returned with a vengeance, but I wasn't aware of any of this, because he'd become so withdrawn that I could hardly get a word out of him when we went for walks together. I was a bit jealous about Derek going home, leaving me in Nags Head by myself. But I didn't envy him being in London with all the air raids; or living with our stepfather, from what we'd seen of the man at Christmas.

That Christmas had been a turning point for Derek, I think. The fact that Mum had clammed up whenever we asked about Bertie suggested that he might no longer be part of our family. That was how I interpreted her silence, and Derek too, I suspect, judging by his demeanor throughout the entire holiday. Sadly, Derek and I also clammed up and never talked to one another about *why* Bertie hadn't come home. Or why nobody ever talked about him. Whatever the reason—or reasons—Bertie's sudden disappearance from our family marked the beginning of a rapid downward spiral for Derek, and he retreated further and further into himself. Of course it must have been even harder on Bertie, poor boy. He was separated not only from Derek, but from everyone who had been family to him.

I still don't know what really happened that Christmas. Was it simply too difficult to get permission to take Bertie out of the Home to visit someone living in a heavily bombed area—someone who wasn't his real mother? Or did our stepfather say, "I'll take on your two, but not the other one. Let 'is own father take care of 'im!" It would not have been totally unreasonable (or out of character). But I do know how glad I am that, when Derek and I visited Bertie in the Home, we none of us knew that it was—to the best of my knowledge—the last time the two boys saw one another.

◆　　◆　　◆

Sometime in the Spring of that year a new "home" was found for Honor Oak School, a large house, called Rosemead, and we reverted to a normal Monday-Friday school week. This was a relief to everybody—with the possible exception of the hostesses who now had to do their own rinsing on Mondays. We walked to the County School once a week to use the science labs, but not, thank God, the gym. No more wall-bars for Buzzer to torment me with! That weekly trip reinforced our preference for our cozy, new setting over the County school's standard, utilitarian building. We *did* miss the exotic sand-tunnel-shelters, however; now, when the siren sounded, we trekked to boring, above ground, windowless, reinforced brick shelters, built where there had been lovely flower beds in Rosemead's heyday, we were told.

There was something neat about having school in an elegant house with an impressive main staircase and two narrow, spiral back staircases. Above what had been the stables there was a very large room, called "the ballroom", though it had no chandeliers or fancy décor. We used it for assembly, art, music, gym, and as a place to gather after lunch on wet days. Those rainy lunch hours were noisy, chaotic affairs, and with about two hundred bodies packed into the ballroom, the windows were soon streaming with condensation. The walls were always lined with girls sitting on the floor and chatting, doing homework, or playing quiet games like Ick-Ack-Ock. Others let off steam with energetic games of Tag, and the more sophisticated tried to dance to music provided by an old wind-up gramophone. To this day, a Benny Goodman recording conjures up that crowded, sweaty scene: pairs of pimply girls in school uniform and klutzy shoes, struggling to master the intricacies of the waltz, the quick step and, for a bold few, the fox trot—whilst dodging those who were racing around trying not to get tagged.

Our teachers now attempted to pound algebra and geography into our heads in high-ceilinged rooms with fancy moldings and big bay windows overlooking the garden. The lighting was inadequate, except for the desk immediately below the ornate center light fixture, and there was no central heating. In cold weather we had to rotate our seating at least once per lesson, to prevent those near the small gas fire being burnt to a crisp and those near the drafty windows being frozen in their seats. Another cross that our teachers bore, bravely for the most part, were blackboards on rickety easels and the mischievous spirits who rigged them for immediate collapse at the first stroke of a chalk stick. Seasoned faculty members always checked, but inept or overwhelmed teachers, those poor souls who seemed to bring out the cruel streak in every schoolgirl, were prime targets and provided a regular source of entertainment.

Soon after the move to Rosemead Miss Brophy, in yet another burst of creativity, introduced The Glove Game into our English class; as a treat, she said. But it was a game guaranteed to throw me into a panic. Miss Brophy started to tell a story and, after a few sentences, stopped and threw a glove to one of us; the recipient threw the glove back and continued with the story until Miss Brophy threw the glove to someone else. "Just say whatever comes into your mind … let your imagination take over," she said brightly, to put us at ease. Easier said than done … for me, this game was nightmarish. I often lay in bed making up stories, letting my fantasies take over, exactly as Miss Brophy was suggesting; but I considered that fantasy life to be a very private part of me—a troubling part that I'd never shared with anyone, not even Marjory Strutt or Elaine.

It was sheer torture to sit in class knowing that, at any moment, that brown leather glove might land on me, and I would have to pick up the story. The scary thing was that you had no control over this story. There was no way to prepare your contribution ahead of time, no way to know what twists and turns the story would have undergone by the time the glove landed on you. There was something dreadfully permanent about the publicly spoken word: it could not be crossed out, torn up, or erased. It was irretrievable. The first time I "got the glove," the heroine was trapped in a dungeon—and I was trapped in my seat, paralyzed with fear, and unable to say a word for what seemed like forever. Eventually Miss Brophy came to my rescue and threw the glove to someone else, but I was left with a deep sense of failure. And shame. It was depressing to discover that I was, apparently, so different from other girls, those who could blithely share the products of their imaginations with the world at large. I could do it on paper, but not in public. And certainly not spontaneously. To my surprise, Miss Brophy never took me to task over this incident, and neither did it evoke any comments from my classmates. So I thanked my lucky stars, and did my best to put the entire episode behind me.

The Glove Game was played as an end-of-the-week treat, and I came to dread Fridays. One particular Friday, I woke up and realized that Miss Brophy hadn't thrown the glove for a couple of weeks, so she almost certainly would throw it today, and the thought was so unnerving that I decided not to go to school. Play hooky? Me? Law-abiding Gwen Redfern? But I was desperate. Whatever the consequences, anything seemed preferable to The Glove Game.

Appalled by what I was contemplating, I left the house as usual, turned down the first side road, so as not to meet any of my friends, and just kept on walking. I spent a miserable, damp, hungry day roaming around Earlswood Common, and selected the remotest and narrowest footpaths, because I was afraid that I'd be seen and asked what I was doing there. It would be so obvious that I wasn't supposed to be wandering the Common in the middle of the day in my school uniform. I had to guess what the time was, but managed to meet up with Margaret Hill at the end of the day as she was walking home from the bus stop, and I swore her to secrecy. I went up several notches in her estimation for my daring—if only she'd known how cowardly I'd felt all day—but when she pointed out that I'd have to have a note for Monday morning I almost fainted with fear. I hadn't thought about this. Margaret came to the rescue by forging a note for me, and went up several notches in *my* estimation because forgery was a brand new concept to me.

I think Margaret was delighted to be involved in a secret of this magnitude and regretted not having been part of what she saw as an exciting escapade—if only she'd known how dreary that day had been. I got away with it. The note was accepted without question, but my criminal activities had been in vain; Miss Brophy had not been in school that day, so no glove had been thrown, and I now faced the following Friday with an even greater probability of it happening. However I never again played hooky. It was even more nerve-racking than playing The Glove Game, I decided. Eventually I learned the tricks of the trade and could come up with acceptable contributions to the story, but they didn't come from letting my imagination run wild, which was the whole point of Miss Brophy's game.

One morning Margaret and I were walking to school, because every bus had been full, as always on rainy days, when she pointed to a tall-steepled church and remarked, "That's where I go to church."

"Cor! Ya lucky thing," I said. "I'd love to go there instead of the ugly little church where I go for Sunday school."

"*Sunday School?* You still go to Sunday school! Why don'cha ask if y'can come to St. John's with me?"

When Margaret told me that St. John's had an organ and a choir, that settled it. I *would* ask the Sharps. At worst, they could only say no. To my delight, they agreed readily, and thus began another episode in my love affair with church ritual, and with religion itself. St. John's was grander than Pulham's little church, with a lot more stained glass and ornate carved woodwork and fancy candlesticks. Not till I looked at the steeple from close quarters, did I realize how tall it was, but it was disappointing to find that you couldn't see up into that slender spire from inside. It was a High Anglican Church, so the service, too, was more elaborate than in Pulham, with much swinging of incense and something called "taking communion." But the basics were common to both: the psalms, the hymns, and the use of The King James Bible. The music at St. John's was fabulous, the organ and the choir both more powerful than their counterparts in Pulham. Even Meg's voice wouldn't stand out in this lot, I thought to myself, the first time I heard them going full blast. But the congregation here lacked the closeness that had been such a remarkable feature in the Pulham church, where everybody had known everybody, as had their parents and grandparents before them. I missed that, but *loved* going to church with Margaret. One day I asked her what communion was all about, and she explained it to me; as best she could, since she herself had never taken communion.

"Why not?"

"'Cos I've not been confirmed. But I will be soon. When I finish me confirmation classes."

"Oh! I was confirmed when I was seven."

"At *seven?*"

"Yeah. Soon after we moved back ta London. I wore a veil, an' a white frock that me Mum made 'specially fer the confirmation. An' I walked in a parade." As I spoke, another memory unexpectedly emerged, and I added, "The grown-ups in front o' me were carrying a statue of a lady on their shoulders, on a kind of platform. But halfway down the street, the statue fell off an' broke into lots o' pieces, an' everyone started crying!"

"That must've been the Virgin Mary," said Margaret. "No wonder they were upset! But that means you must be a Catholic! And you *must* 'ave gone to confirmation classes. Or you couldn't have been in that parade."

But there memory failed me, though I think Margaret was right; nobody gets confirmed without some preparation. However my preparation clearly hadn't "stuck." I was even hazy about what religion I'd been confirmed in, though I later learned that, as a baby, I was baptized into the Catholic Church, so Margaret was right about that too.

As time went on, I got quite a thorough grounding in the tenets of the High Anglican Church as we trudged across Earlswood Common. Margaret was keen for me to join her confirmation class and become a fully fledged High Anglican, so that I could confess my sins, take communion to get God's forgiveness and put my spiritual world in order every once in a while. This was not her language, exactly, but that was the message I extracted. I was sorely tempted; but the more I mulled it over, the more reluctant I felt. I saw all kinds of problems, especially as regards the First Communion. Did you have to confess every sin you'd ever committed up to that point? What about ones you'd forgotten? Did you have to pay for them later? Actually, the whole sin-confession-forgiveness business smacked of a cheap cheat, a way to get yourself off the hook. But these were trivial concerns in comparison to the reservations I had about an All-Seeing God, let alone the notion that a wafer was Christ's body and wine his blood, and that was "seriously real," according to Margaret, "not something you just pretend."

After much agonizing, I decided that I couldn't join Margaret's church. I could not believe in this God, or in communion, or in sinning and heaven and hell. I finally admitted to myself that my reasons for wanting to join the church were the wrong ones: the beautiful building, the music, the surplices, and the swinging incense—all the rituals. Last, but by no means least, I wanted to be part of this so that, once a week, I could sit back and let the language of the King James Bible roll over me. I had came close to being seduced by all that lovely stuff and felt sad at having to walk away from it. Equally sad was the return to the dismal church that the Sharps attended. Though I was now allowed to attend the adult service instead of Sunday school.

◆　　◆　　◆

I often looked after Teddy and Robbie, to the extent that my mother thought that Mrs. Sharp was taking advantage of me. Usually I didn't mind, because I liked those two boys. But I *had* minded when Mrs. Sharp kept me home from school for a couple of weeks when they both had chickenpox. I got hideously bored trying to keep two spotty, itchy, cranky children amused, with no schoolwork to keep me busy and no school chitchat to liven up each day. There were no books in the Sharp household (my rebellion against the library taboo being still a year away) until the next door neighbor, friendly, buck-toothed Mrs. Sunderland, came to the rescue and invited me to see if there was anything on her bookshelves that I would like to read. Was there ever! She had a shelf full of Elsie Dinsmore books, and I devoured them, one by one. Volume after volume dealt with the trials and tribulations of Elsie, a motherless girl with golden ringlets and large brown eyes. She had lots of adventures and was given to petulantly tossing her golden curls, a ploy guaranteed to melt the heart of a doting father who was, in any case, always anxious to make up to his daughter for the loss of her mother. I became seriously addicted to Elsie Dinsmore and was devastated when I reached the end of the final volume.

Then I discovered a massive tome called *Castle Lacy* on Mrs. Sunderland's bookshelves. This told of the tumultuous life of the Lacy family, twelve in number, who lived with their stern, widowed father in a crumbling old house on a wild and barren moor. The ten year old boy of this family was the hero: a mischievous, stubborn child, but brave, loyal, generous and, of course, loved by everyone once his latest prank had been resolved and seen to have been inspired by the noblest of intentions. He had narrow escapes from locked rooms in abandoned houses, leaky boats, old mine shafts, encounters with gypsies … the list was endless. This was heady stuff, and I lapped it up. And the best part was that *Castle Lacy* took longer to read than four or five Elsie Dinsmore books.

When I'd exhausted Mrs. Sunderland's library, I went through it again, and again. These fictional worlds had become virtually essential to me, and in an effort to perpetuate them, I lay in bed and wrote my own version of *Castle Lacy*. It was called *The Moat* and featured a large family living in an ancient mansion with a moat, complete with drawbridge, and an Elsie-like girl as a visiting cousin. It was "written" entirely in my head, without help of pencil and paper, in part because I didn't want to risk anyone ever reading this product of my imagination. But there were, also, two more pragmatic reasons: there was no light (or blackout curtain) in my bedroom, and paper was in desperately short supply at that stage of the war. In school, every square inch of our Rough Notebooks had to be filled before we were given a new one. This entailed boxing off the existing writing and using the spaces between the boxes until they too were filled, which made it extremely difficult to study from one's notes! Writing an ambitious novel in one's head was equally difficult, and it is not surprising that *The Moat* was never completed.

Just before the end of the summer term, Mum wrote to say that I couldn't go home for the holidays, because—Surprise! Surprise! She was expecting! It seems the doctors had been wrong in their pronouncement that she couldn't have any more children. However, her letter went on: "It's too risky for the baby to be born normally so its got to be a Cessarian. Im not looking forward to another operation, but its safer they say." Apparently, this meant that we already knew the exact time at which this baby would be born on August 28, 1941, (it was news to me that there was ever any doubt about the exact time of arrival of a baby). The prospect of a new baby was (almost) enough to compensate for the disappointment of not going home for the summer holidays, but I was now *really* jealous of Derek; he'd be there for this great event, and I wouldn't. It seemed most unfair.

The summer dragged by, and I waited impatiently, hoping against hope that the baby would be a girl—I'd wanted a baby sister for as long as I could remember—but August 28 came and went, with no word from Mum. Then another week. I was beside myself, frantic to know what was happening. Had the operation not worked? Had the hospital been bombed? Had Mum and the baby been killed? *Why hadn't anyone written?* School had already started again before a letter came, and, to my relief, it looked like Mum's handwriting; so even before I tore open the envelope, I knew that one of the things I'd dreaded had not happened. The letter read:

> Well Gwen you got your baby sister all right. Her name is Maureen Jean like Louie wanted and because she was a Cessarian she didnt have to fight her way out so shes just beautiful not all red and wrinkly like most babies when theyre born. The nurses call her the little princess and show her off to all the other patients in the ward. Sorry I didnt write earlier but Ive been very ill pneumonia they say and have got to stay in hospital a bit longer. I am getting better though since they put me on this new sulfur drug the miracle drug they call it. Dereks staying with Auntie Ada and Uncle Bill bless them and as soon as Im well enough you can come home and see your new little sister. Hope you can read my writing. Love Mum

I was ecstatic. I wanted to see my long-yearned-for baby sister— *immediately*! But Mum's handwriting, which usually flowed smoothly and gave the impression that the letter had been written without stopping to take a breath, was indeed all over the place, very scratchy and wobbly. This gave me pause. It was scary to realize that she might have died. I swallowed my impatience to see the baby, consoling myself with the fact that Derek hadn't seen her yet, either. Finally, came the day when I sat on a bus that was taking me to see my baby sister for the first time, barely able to contain my excitement.

Mum was waiting at the bus stop, but exasperatingly, Maureen Jean was asleep in the pram and stubbornly slept all the way home. I wanted her to open her eyes, so that I could see what she *really* looked like and, perhaps, coax a smile. In due course, I got to hold her in my arms and examine every inch of her delectable little body; I was especially entranced by the tiny toes and delicate pink fingernails and, during that all-too-short weekend, was rewarded with innumerable smiles. All of which made it exceedingly hard to go back to school on Sunday afternoon, and my envy of Derek knew no bounds. Yet ... I didn't ask if I, too, could come back to London. By this time I knew that I really did fit in the Honor Oak world. And how much this mattered to me.

Back in the world of Nags Head, I wasn't really happy; but neither was I desperately unhappy; not enough to pick up and settle in yet another new household, as Mum had hinted. Four different homes in two years were enough, and I was not eager to make it five. However I was beginning to agree that Mrs. Sharp did "use" my services too freely, but I was hardly in a position to say "No". I was sometimes tempted to, especially on Wednesday afternoons—my half-day from school—when she just assumed that I would look after the boys while she went to the pictures with Mrs. Phipp. Much as I liked those boys, especially that little butterball, Robbie, I did want the occasional half-day to myself and resented the fact that my availability was taken for granted.

In this I discovered, I was not alone; many of us evacuees had the same bone of contention. In retrospect, complaining about invasions of our free time seems so petty against the backdrop of a war, but for us twelve-year-olds it was a major source of discontent; we fledgling adults, which was how we were beginning to think of ourselves. After all, we now traveled on buses by ourselves *and* darned our own socks! We were itching to do things on our own, in our own way; yet, truth to tell, most of us were scared stiff at the prospect. Especially me. I was less ready than most; not eager to embrace those pesky changes that Mrs. Greenaway had told us about in the back room of Lydlinch Village Hall. They had come to me early as far as I could judge from the absence of burgeoning breasts in any of my classmates, and I was hugely embarrassed at what was happening to me; I did my best to simply ignore the whole thing whenever possible.

The Wednesday afternoon issue suddenly intensified when a James Mason film came to town, and I pleaded with Mrs. Sharp, "Please let me go, just this once. All me friends are going!" Her response was a definite, "Nope. That's *my* afternoon out!" which left me seething with resentment. I'd once caught a glimpse of James Mason in a trailer for another film and was bowled over by his plummy, husky voice. I yearned to sit in the dark of the cinema and luxuriate in that sensuous, stomach-churning voice. I wanted it so badly that I went to the James Mason picture on Wednesday afternoon—without telling Mrs. Sharp of my intention. I knew she'd be doubly furious because I hadn't told her; there she'd be, her hat and coat on, waiting for me, and how humiliated she'd be when Mrs. Phipp appeared, ready for the pair of them to set off for the bus stop. As I paid for my cinema ticket that afternoon, I felt like the proverbial worm that had finally turned and firmly shut my mind to the consequences, determined to enjoy my precious hour or so with my heartthrob, James Mason.

The storm broke the moment I walked into the house. Mrs. Sharp, still decked out in her going-to-the-pictures finery, met me at the door, arms akimbo, eyes flashing. Under any circumstances she had a striking, though slightly lop-sided, face, with huge, dark blue, slightly protruding eyes atop a proud Roman nose. But she looked extraordinarily handsome in her rage.

"An' just where 'ave *yew* bin?" she spat.

Did she really want me to answer that question? If I *did*, would that enrage her more? More than if I didn't? The latter, apparently, because as I hesitated, her face turned red, and she flailed with clenched fists as if having a hard time controlling the urge to lash out at me.

"Answer me ... yew lyin' li'l bitch!"

It hardly seemed an opportune moment to ask how I could have lied, if I hadn't actually *said* anything. But there was nothing to be gained by further delay, so I told her what I was sure she already knew,

"I went to the pictures. Like I said I wanted to!" And added, defiantly, "It was time I had a turn!"

I don't know which part of my reply infuriated her the most, but it unleashed a torrent of epithets, a listing of the grand totality of my undesirable characteristics and offensive behaviors. I was, it seems, deceitful, lazy, dirty, slovenly, insolent, careless, never offered to help, always had my nose in a book, didn't make my bed properly or keep my room tidy ... The tongue-lashing went on and on, continuing into the evening ... and the following evening.

I was astounded at Mrs. Sharp's list of unsettled scores. Was I really like that? In bed at night I did a lot of soul-searching and concluded that most of the accusations were unfounded, though I did plead guilty as charged when it came to sticking my nose in books, not making my bed carefully, and having an untidy bedroom. The charge of carelessness was also warranted. I had, after all, broken two cups and a plate in the year that I'd been with the Sharps. More serious was the day I took a sleeping Robbie in his pushchair on an errand, parked him outside the shop, and then forgot that he was there. To make matters worse, I'd re-immersed myself in my book, and who knows how long the sleeping Robbie would have been parked outside the shop if Mrs. Sharp hadn't noticed his absence. *That* was bad. But it was the only serious offense I could think of, other than my recent illicit wallowing in the charms of James Mason.

I managed to hold my tongue throughout these lengthy harangues until Friday morning, when Mrs. Sharp was still screeching at me. Then the dam broke, and a no-holds-barred shouting match developed, with Teddy and Robbie crying in the background. I'd never shouted at a grown-up before and was astonished at myself. But I couldn't stop.

Eventually—already late for school—I tried to run out the door, but Mrs. Sharp lunged at me, screaming, "Oh no, ya don't Ya li'l bitch! I'm not finished with yew yet. Not by a long chalk!" She grabbed the strap of my satchel, and I pulled away, crying, "Let go of me!" In the ensuing tug of war the strap broke, and I ran off down the road with the book-filled satchel under my arm—only to see the taillights of a bus disappearing over the brow of the hill. I ended up walking to school and was, of course, very late, so I was given after-school detention. That was the least of my worries.

On that long walk I did plenty of thinking, and one thing was clear: I couldn't go back to the Sharps. Not after the way I'd yelled at her, and the nasty things she'd screamed at me. It was out of the question to even *think* of it. *I'd have to run away.* The only place I could go was home—to Mum. Which meant that I had to raise money for the fare. I spent the day scrounging from my friends—pennies here and pennies there—and after school I went to detention, then made a mad dash to catch the local bus, the first leg of my running-away journey. When recounting this story to a group of friends, many years later, one of them said, wonderingly, "You went to *detention*? When you were planning to *run away*?" And for the first time, I realized that it *was* a little odd. But it simply never occurred to me not to go to detention, any more than it had crossed my mind not to go to school after the horrible fight with Mrs. Sharp. Which, I suppose, gives a measure of how law-abiding I was, and how remarkable it was that this worm had finally turned.

Unfortunately, the worm got careless. In the rush for the bus, I fell down Rosemead's elegant staircase and twisted my ankle. Miss Franklin happened to be standing at the bottom of the stairs and, in true Weeping Wilhemina fashion, oozed sympathy and tears as she helped me to a chair and put a cool wet cloth on the rapidly swelling ankle. She decided, on the basis of the swelling, that it was just a sprain and helped me hobble to the bus stop, with my broken satchel under my arm. She insisted on riding all the way to Nags Head with me, and I couldn't tell her that I really wanted to take the Green Line bus to London—in the opposite direction—because I was in the middle of running away! She came as far as the Sharps' front gate, but there, to my relief, she left, after I assured her that I could manage the rest by myself. I didn't want a still-angry Mrs. Sharp to burden Weeping Willy with the litany of my crimes. She would have been a basket case, and I didn't want to be responsible for *that*, too.

To her credit, Mrs. Sharp swallowed her anger when she saw my ankle and restrained any impulse to shut the door in my face, but she didn't put herself out to help with awkward things like getting upstairs and undressing in the dark. Next morning Mrs. Sunderland, who'd been a nurse, took one look at my leg and said it ought to be checked at the hospital, but there was no one to take me till Mr. Sharp came home at noon. He wasn't exactly pleased to spend his Saturday afternoon helping this pesky evacuee on and off buses and waiting around for x-rays, which revealed a break, just above the ankle. After more reluctant waiting, for the cast to set, he finally got back to what was left of his customary Saturday afternoon of puttering around with the chickens and the garden.

Crutches, supplied by the hospital, made it easier to get around, but clearly my running-away scheme was now on hold. My only hope of escape from the glacial atmosphere that prevailed, was if Mum responded to my letter begging her to come and take me home, so I hunkered down and concentrated on learning when, and how, to use the crutches.

There were some hairy moments, the hairiest being on the first night. I had groped my way to the lavatory in the dark and propped the crutches against the wall outside—in that confined space, they were worse than useless—and was about to sit down to do what I had come to do, when something large and feathery flapped in my face. Startled, I lost my balance and fell against the door, which wasn't properly fastened and flew open ... and out I pitched, with all my weight on the freshly set leg. My shriek of pain brought everyone running, including the Sunderlands. In the excitement, they forgot about the blackout and left their back door open, and the light from the open door fell on me like a spotlight. I don't know which was worse, the pain or the embarrassment of being seen by all those people with my knickers round my ankles. (Mum roared with laughter when I told her, "Caught with yer drawers down, eh! Talk about a spotlight on charm!") I ended up feeling rather foolish, because the flapping creature turned out to be nothing more than a chicken that Mr. Sharp had slaughtered that evening and put on the lavatory door to "hang," or whatever it is that one does to freshly killed animals before they can be eaten.

Once back in the house, Mrs. Sunderland was worried that I might have un-set the break, but no one was eager to set off for the hospital again that night. In any case, there was considerable uncertainty about the time of the last bus, and it was decided that we'd wait till the morning. By that time the pain had subsided, and the chicken incident was deemed to have done no lasting damage, but the next few days were difficult, to put it mildly. I was definitely a *persona non grata,* one who could no longer help much around the house. Once again I endured an atmosphere that could be cut with a knife, until Mum finally arrived and took me back to London.

It was not an easy journey. I was still learning the art of crutch-management, and Mum had to cope with a three-month-old baby, a suitcase, a strapless book-filled satchel, Shirley Ann and a doll's pram. The pram had been my "big" present the Christmas before the war—an embarrassment from the moment I set eyes on it. Mum had wanted, so badly, she told me, to give me a present; had wanted, just for once, that there should be something on Christmas morning that wasn't from the ever-generous Hodds. It had given her enormous pleasure to surprise me with the pram —a folding pram, the height of fashion. The only pity was that it had come too late: I was almost ten, too big to play with prams, but didn't have the heart to tell her that. Two years later, when she insisted that I take it to Nags Head "ta give ya something ta play with there," I was equally incapable of protesting that the pram was now even less appropriate. I can't begin to describe how stupid I had felt, wheeling that wretched pram from the bus stop to the Sharps' house, hoping I wouldn't bump into any of my friends. It had, of course, sat in my bedroom, unused other than to provide storage for Shirley Ann—also unused.

However, on our journey back to London, the pram finally came in useful. It was big enough to accommodate Maureen Jean, Shirley Ann *and* the broken satchel, and, when folded flat, could be stuffed into the luggage hole on buses. Getting on and off buses was tricky, and the walk from the last bus stop seemed interminable, but we finally reached Upper Ground without the complications of an air raid, something we'd both silently dreaded. My escape plan could not be said to have gone without a hitch, but I had, finally, got away from Mrs. Sharp!

◆　　◆　　◆

A cast and crutches complicated the dash down to the basement when the siren wailed, but this paled before the delight of spending six weeks with my little sister: six, glorious, unanticipated weeks! Derek and I doted on that baby. We did everything except feed her (she was breast-fed, so that was Mum's department), and, of course, played with her whenever she was awake. "Yew two ... yew'll spoil 'er rot'en!" Mum complained, in a voice that meant she really didn't mind. The only unpleasant task was giving Maureen her daily spoonful of cod liver oil, the smell of which—like the scabies medicine that had left our clothes so smelly—made me nauseous. How could anyone swallow the stuff? But Maureen did, *and* smacked her little lips afterwards. Both cod liver oil and rose hip syrup were government issue for children under five, to ward off vitamin deficiencies from limited supplies of certain foods: things, like oranges, that don't grow in Britain and couldn't be imported in wartime.

I learned how to make my mother's version of a pacifier, for she had a thing about "those dirty ol' dummies. I've seen a mother pick one up awf the ground an' put it straight back in the baby's mouth!" She didn't approve of thumb-sucking either. Her baby-calming technique involved knotting a hard boiled sweet [candy] in a clean hanky for the fussy infant to suck on, taking care to knot it so there was no danger of the baby swallowing the sweet. Maureen wasn't in the least bit interested in the first one I made, and when Mum saw what was happening, she said, scornfully, "Ya daft thing! She's not gonna suck on a dry 'ankie! Yew 'ave ta put it in yer own mouth first an' make it wet, so she gets the taste o' the sweet straight away." It seemed to me that her version of a pacifier had health hazards, too, but I kept my own counsel.

Another task that became mine, since I was pretty much housebound, was to gently rub Maureen's head with special oil to clear up her eczema, which was the result of wearing a fluffy angora bonnet. I found it hard to accept that this otherwise perfect little body could have developed such a blemish, and it was a relief to see the scaly patches yield slowly to my ministrations. On the basis of this soothing operation, I now knew, with absolute certainty, that when I grew up I wanted to be a nurse and look after babies; gone were my dreams of working in a shop like Auntie Emmy's!

After Christmas it was time to get my cast removed, but doctors at Waterloo Hospital shook their heads and refused to be responsible for a leg that was not accompanied by x rays and had been set in another hospital. Mum begged and pleaded, and they tried x-raying through the cast but didn't get a clear enough picture, so we had to go home with the cast still in place. My mother was not one to take defeat lying down; back we went a few days later, and she finally found a doctor who reluctantly took the cast off, after she'd agreed not to hold him or the hospital responsible if there were problems. Fortunately all was well; the only unexpected feature was the collection of knitting needles that clattered to the floor when the cast dropped away. They'd been the only things long enough to scratch the itch down by my ankle, I explained, to the amusement of the doctors and nurses, and, once dropped, were impossible to retrieve without standing on my head.

Soon after that I went back to school. But not to the Sharps. Mum had discovered a married cousin, the son of my father's oldest brother, who lived only a few miles from Reigate, and she'd arranged for me to stay with him and his family. Oddly enough, the possibility of me staying in London never came up for discussion. To my relief. I might have said yes, for fear of hurting Mum's feelings by saying no. What I really wanted was to get back to the

Honor Oak scene, despite the strong pull of a little sister in London. (But it was *so* hard to kiss that baby good-bye when the time came to pick up my life as an evacuee—one of the hardest things I'd ever done.)

Carrying my mended satchel and, by now, rather battered suitcase, Mum and I took the train to Merstham, where Cousin Reg lived (having, mercifully, and without discussion, left the doll's pram and Shirley Ann behind in Waterloo). It was my first train journey since going to Dorset, two years earlier, and I was looking forward to watching the scenery change from city to countryside. But the windows were now covered in sticky mesh as protection against flying glass, and all you could see was a vague blur rushing by. When the train approached a station, you had to peer through a small rectangular hole in the mesh to see the name of the station, and I was thankful to have Mum along, or I would have been fearful of missing my stop. I was not alone in that fear, apparently. There were posters all over the carriage with cartoons showing a passenger peeling away the mesh round the hole and, emanating from an unseen mouth, a balloon that contained the following admonition:

> Pardon me for the correction
> That stuff is there for your protection.

To which exasperated riders had responded with variants of:

> Thank you for the information
> I'd rather see the ruddy station.

The train was crowded, so Mum and I weren't sitting together, and, without the distractions of chatting or watching scenery, I fell to wondering what lay ahead as the train clickety-clacked along, speeding me towards yet another new "home." Would it be easier to live with relatives than with strangers? Or were there family complications that I knew nothing about? At least this time, as I first dipped my toes into these untested waters, Mum would be with me, and that was a comforting thought. At school, would it be easy to pick up where I left off, almost two months ago? Or would I have to start all over in the friends department? Then an even bigger question loomed. Was I, strictly speaking, still an evacuee? Did living with family—even family that I hardly knew—disqualify me? Even if nobody in officialdom noticed, would I feel a fraud, a fake, just pretending to be an evacuee, while my schoolmates coped daily with the problems attendant upon being the real thing?

◆　　◆　　◆

ADDENDUM

Over the years, my mother doled out occasional snippets of information about Bertie as she learned them from one or other of her siblings: news that his father had re-married and, a few years later, that Bertie had joined the navy and got married. But—as far as I know—there was never any attempt on her part at a regular correspondence with him, let alone a reunion. I find this quite extra-ordinary, given the love and care she lavished on him throughout his fragile, early months and always-difficult childhood at a time when her life was fraught with plenty of other difficulties.

But, in the same vein, neither Derek nor I made any attempt to get in touch with Bertie; and I never asked my mother why he disappeared so completely, as far as we were concerned. Which leaves me with a lot of regrets concerning my lost "brother." And forces me to acknowledge that we were, all of us, a pretty strange lot.

Chapter 23

Next Stop, Merstham

IT WAS HARD TO tell how large the village of Merstham was, because to the south there was no clear point where it ended and the next town began. However to the north, where a small side road dipped down and a faceted church steeple could be seen poking above the trees, you were suddenly in open country.

Along that small side road there were thick woods to the left, while on the right, towered Hastings Hill, part of a chalk ridge that stretches from East to West for many miles. I was just thirteen when I first set eyes on Hastings Hill and fell in love with chalk hills. That love was later re-kindled by the South Downs of Sussex, where I was to spend some of the happiest days of my life hiking the steep, smooth slopes on which the grass was kept short and devoid of shrubs or trees by hungry rabbits. On Hastings Hill, as on all chalk hills, the footpaths stood out as narrow, white scars; and if you followed the one that wound its way upward toward the back fold of the hill, you reached a wood that, in the spring, was so thickly carpeted with bluebells it was impossible not to crush a few, no matter how carefully you trod. Once, when there with only the dog for company, I sat for a long time gazing into the deep blue, elongated bells lined up along the stem of every flower, each bell smaller than the one below and nodding in the breeze, giving fragrant joyrides to foraging bees ... until Rickie began to whine. He was impatient to move on and explore new territory.

The rest of Merstham was not equally enchanting, visually. From the cluster of picturesque buildings that straddled the main road in the old village, a row of nondescript houses led downhill to a much larger collection of newer, but equally nondescript, dwellings. This was South Merstham, and it sprawled across the clay plain that stretches from the foot of the chalk hills to a sandstone ridge. The houses in South Merstham were, for the most part, modest and semi-detached, with small-ish gardens; some dated from the Victorian era, while others, built more recently, afforded their occupants the comforts of indoor plumbing. I was not destined to enjoy such comforts during my sojourn in South Merstham, for the house of my Cousin Reg was a clone of the Sharps'—even to there being no light or blackout curtain in my small back bedroom.

Happily, there the resemblance ended. In stark contrast to Mr. Sharp, my cousin was a stocky, feisty bantam of a man, quick to anger, but equally quick to forgive and forget. He spoke his mind in no uncertain terms, so you knew exactly where you stood with Uncle Reg, as I called him because of the age difference between us. It was harder to "read" Aunt Mary, his wife, a tall, big-boned woman, who was quiet and reserved and had none of Mrs. Sharp's uncomfortable edginess. When we knocked on their back door, Mum and I were greeted with a cheery, "Oh! Auntie May and Gwen ... come on in ... it's so good to see you!" and I immediately thought, "This looks like it's gonna be easier."

And it was. Aunt Mary, did occasionally retreat into herself and avoid eye contact for a few tight-lipped days, but if left alone, she would quietly tackle the backlog of ironing or mending and somehow work through whatever was troubling her. When we heard her throaty chuckle again and saw her broad, eye-crinkling smile, we could all breath freely again; old Aunt Lil, her mother-in-law, stopped sighing and clucking under her breath, and Uncle Reg resumed horsing around with their little daughter, Jackie. Fortunately these tight-lipped episodes were rare, and of course, I knew nothing of them that first day in Merstham, as we sat chatting and drinking the inevitable cups of tea before Mum had to rush back to feed Maureen.

But it wasn't simply that I was dealing with less prickly personalities in Cousin Reg's household: these folks were family; and that seemed to help a lot, even though I did not know them well to begin with. I *had* met old Aunt Lil, just a couple of times, when we visited her flat in Dulwich and Bertie and Derek made a nuisance of themselves, running noisily up and down stone stairwells and along balconies. But I remembered her as a fat, cross, sloppily dressed old lady with an untidy mop of hair, and I was surprised to find that she was small, not particularly cross, neatly dressed, and wore what was left of her dark brown hair scragged back into a tight tidy little knot. Such is the stuff of memory ... (Or had Aunt Lil's recent cataract operation—at that time a lengthy ordeal, during which the head was held motionless with sandbags—played a role in this transformation? Maybe, because Mum did comment that she had lost some weight.) Aunt Mary I'd met only once: she had visited us in Aquinas Street, just before the war, and while we had tea, little Jackie, then about a year old, had slept in my doll's pram—the embarrassing pram that

I'd happily just left behind in Waterloo. Jackie was now three, but clearly recognizable as the solemn, blond baby with huge gray eyes that I'd wheeled in the doll's pram, back and forth, along the hallway of our flat.

As for Uncle Reg, to the best of my knowledge he and I had never met. However I had heard a lot about him. He was one of the stream of nephews and nieces who spent time with my parents in their one room on Coin Street, and like all the visiting nephews, he was always given a square meal and taken to the boxing venue at The Ring, Blackfriars. He loved going to The Ring, he told me one day, as I helped him polish the shoes of the entire household, a daily chore that he always took upon himself. He'd been "a nach'ral li'l boxer" and was boxing seriously by his mid-teens, but a promising career was cut short when he dove into a river to help a drowning man, hit his head on something, and sustained a gash that went from his eyebrow to the back of his head. "When I come up, I 'fought me 'air was fallin' in me eyes, till I flipped it back an' found it was a flap o' skin!" he said, on the one occasion when he let himself be persuaded to talk about it. "An' it needed s'many stitches, it put the kibosh on me ever boxin' agin. It was the end of the swimmer, too, the poor devil."

In Mum's opinion, Uncle Reg was lucky to have escaped a boxing career. "At least 'e didn't get cauliflower ears an' end up knocked silly like s'many of 'em," she said to me—but not to Uncle Reg. I'd often heard the diving story from her, and it was probably connections like this that made it easier to live with family instead of strangers. We didn't have to start from scratch; they knew things about me and mine, and I knew things about them and theirs. They knew all about Bertie and my Dad, and I knew that old Aunt Lil's only girl had died at the age of two, and that, of her eight boys, only four were still alive. I even knew that her Joey, crippled by polio, died when he was about fourteen, and her sailor-son, Richard, was killed when a crate slipped out of the jaws of a crane and crushed him as he was going ashore. Already-existing threads like these provided a sense of belonging; with strangers it was hard to start weaving connections when you had no threads to start from. Thus, it had taken best part of a year before I learned that the Sharps had lost their first baby—another son, a whopping fourteen-pounder at birth—and that Mr. Sharp's mother had been very ill for most of the year that I lived with them.

There were undercurrents, of course, in this Merstham family. For instance, Aunt Lil bore a deep grudge against Aunt Mary's sister, Hope. She was convinced that Hope was responsible for the fact that she was now in Merstham and dependent on her son and daughter-in-law, instead of living independently in her own London flat. And Aunt Mary always felt compelled to defend her sister, though she was the first to admit that Hope had quite a track record as a meddlesome stirrer-up of mischief. I often got a blow-by-blow account of this family feud from old Aunt Lil; but only if we were alone in the house.

"When I was in 'ospital wiv me cataracks," the story always started, "tha' there 'Ope—a born trouble-maker she is—went over ta Dulwich an' emptied aht me flat. She 'ad all me furniture, ev'ry stick of it, sent dahn 'ere ta Merstram." (Aunt Lil's pronunciation was distinctly idiosyncratic). "Said she 'ad to. 'Cos wiv me eyes sa bad—almos' blind I was before me operation—I wouldn't be able t'live be meself agin. Spesh'ly in London, wiv the air raids an' all. The nerve of 'er! It weren't none of 'er business! It should'a bin left ta me, me an' my Neddie, 'cos my 'ome was 'is 'ome, too. They all seem ta ferget tha'.

"When Georgie fetched me 'ere, fr'm the 'ospital, an' I saw all me stuff in *this* 'ouse, ya could'a knocked me dahn wiv a fevver. All o' this," indicating the furnishings of the room we were sitting in, "is mine, ya know, Gwen. Gettin' knocked abaht, while *their* stuff sits in the bloomin' front room, as good as new. 'Cos they 'ardly ever use tha' room, do they? Got their 'eads screwed on the righ' way, they 'ave! So 'ere I am ... wivou' a roof ta call me own ... fer the first time in me married life."

Aunt Lil was always weeping at this juncture and had to push her coke-bottle post-cataract glasses up to mop away the tears coursing down her oddly shiny and un-wrinkled old cheeks. But her weepy spells were short-lived, and after returning the damp hanky to the pocket of her pinafore, she'd shuffle into the kitchen in her comfy felt slippers and put the kettle on for a cup of tea; that never-failing source of comfort.

Apart from "'igh days an' 'olidays," Aunt Lil's compact form—a possible prototype for a set of nesting Russian dolls—was always enveloped by that wrap-around pinafore, or another, identical one. Once when I was home from school on a Monday, I discovered that she was not her usual compact self on Washing Day while her "buskies" were hanging on the line to dry; and I suddenly understood why she, just like Old Ma Tanner, sometimes creaked. I couldn't imagine being encased in those full length corsets, but vanity invariably won out over comfort, and as soon as her body armor was dry, Aunt Lil rushed upstairs to put it on and came down looking more at ease than she had all day.

Before long, I became old Aunt Lil's scribe. "I never go' much schoolin'," she'd explain, at the drop of a hat, to anyone whose ear she could bend. "'Cos it costed a penny a week. Tha' was a lot'a money back then, an' sometimes there wasn't enough fer all of us t'go. Uvver times I stayed 'ome an' looked after the li'l ones, so me muvva could go out an' earn a bit. Wha' wiv one fing an' anuvva, I do know 'ow ta read—s'long as the words ain't too long—bu' never did ge' much writin'. Jus' enough ta sign me name. So I 'ave ta git someone t'write me let'ers ta Neddie. Me poor boy. Bin in the army ever since the war started, 'e 'as."

Her correspondence was not extensive, and Uncle Reg helped her with anything official, but that weekly letter to her youngest, and only unmarried son, preyed on her mind. Uncle Reg worked nights and did lots of overtime, because he was in some kind of war work, so it was rare for him and Aunt Lil to be awake at the same time, and she was much too proud and prickly to ask Aunt Mary. She didn't want any daughter-in-law of hers to know every word she wrote to Ned, the only son with no interfering wife to complicate their relationship. She could read well enough to make out Ned's letters to her, but had to dictate her replies, and this was far from satisfactory, because, in that small living room, there was always someone around to hear every word. In winter especially, when it was the only heated room, that was where Jackie played, and we all chatted, knitted, listened to the radio, did ironing and mending and homework—and ate all our meals.

Eventually, lack of privacy for Ned's letters caused Aunt Lil such distress that she taught herself how to write. She did this by reading every newspaper she could put her hands on until she bumped into the word that she didn't know how to write. It was a laborious process, but she did get to the point where her written vocabulary was extensive enough for her correspondence with Ned. After I moved away from Merstham, I received a few letters from this remarkable old lady. They were moving in their simplicity and always had the amusing ending " … and god bless You," leaving no doubt as to the relative importance of the deity and the letter recipient to old Aunt Lil!

On my first day of school, I saw three Honor Oak uniforms in the queue at the bus stop and knew, immediately, that I was not the lone evacuee here in Merstham. As good luck would have it, Peggy, Joan and Lorna, the wearers of those uniforms, became my good friends, and we spent all our spare time together. We did nothing in particular, just wandered the streets of Merstham, in rain or cold, after dark in the blackout, it didn't matter to us. Only an air raid or not being allowed out because we were sick or "in the doghouse," prevented our nocturnal ramblings. We did a lot of laughing and giggling and chattered non-stop, mainly school chitchat. We discussed teachers and friends, and who had a "pash" on whom: they were girl-on-girl pashes, mostly, with just an occasional girl-on-teacher crush—like poor Vera Tait, whose fair skin turned an extraordinary shade of pink, down to her waist we speculated, whenever the gym mistress hove into view.

We let the war intrude on this silly schoolgirl stuff only if there'd been some direct impact—as when Joan's cousin was killed in North Africa—but it so happened that none of us had a father in the armed forces, or a brother old enough to be called up. In view of the battles being fought, and what was happening to our families during the almost nightly air raids on London, our featherbrained behavior now fills me with shame. Even allowing for the fact that our ages ranged from twelve to fourteen—arguably the most irresponsible years of the human condition—it seems monstrous that we could relegate the war to back-stage. But we did. Our time together, inconsequential as it may now seem, was tremendously important to us, and was perhaps, an essential part of our survival strategy as adolescents in that difficult time.

At this stage in the war, air raids were a significant part of our lives, because bombers chased by fast-flying and highly maneuverable fighter planes, dropped their bombs at random to improve their own maneuverability, and many of these incidents took place in the skies over the Reigate area. In school we scurried to windowless shelters, but at home the whole family packed itself into the cupboard under the stairs, including Rickie, who whined non-stop if we left him out. This cupboard also served as the food pantry, which prompted old Aunt Lil to joke (always), "Oh well ... we won't go 'ungry will we? Even if Jerry keeps us 'ere all nigh'!" Which, in turn, prompted the rest of us, including little Jackie, to roll up our eyes (always). Air raids were not considered a valid excuse for incomplete homework, so I was allowed to sit under the low-wattage bare bulb that hung from the ceiling of the pantry until I'd completed my assignments. Then I swapped places with Aunt Mary, so she could have a look at the day's paper.

When I went home to London for the Easter holidays, I found a Morrison shelter installed in the basement. It was a large, reinforced steel table (strong enough to withstand falling masonry, but not a direct hit), with wire mesh sides that gave protection against chunks of flying debris. Big enough to sleep the five of us, it took up most of the living room, but certainly felt safer than simply sitting around in the basement. Our stepfather had rigged up a couple of light bulbs inside the shelter, so we could read or play cards, and the radio was usually left on, so it was a great improvement on the Merstham arrangement. Of course, the need for a real shelter was also greater here.

At this point in the Blitz, fire from incendiary bombs was perhaps the biggest hazard, and the building opposite our house, where *The Star* newspaper was printed, was frequently in flames. Like all buildings on the riverfront, it was an easy target, especially on moonlit nights when the river was clearly visible from the air. We spent a lot of time, and much of our tea and sugar rations, doling out cups of tea to exhausted firemen, but, to our disgust, Derek and I weren't allowed to help till after the All Clear had sounded. However, *The Star* fires were puny compared with the blaze from the paint factory just down the road: *that* was a fire to remember. The flames made a great roaring noise as they leapt up, trying to lick the clouds, it seemed, and in the end, the firemen had to let that fire burn itself out. Everyone was worried that if it were still burning when darkness fell, it would act as a beacon for the next night's wave of bombers, but fortunately, at dusk it was simply a smoldering heap.

Back in Merstham after the holidays, memories of those fires haunted me as we huddled in the pantry during air raids, but all I could do was hope against hope that everybody in Upper Ground was safe. At times, I regretted having forfeited the use of prayer by walking away from Margaret's God.

Quite apart from this newfound familiarity with air raids, my general awareness of the war increased because Uncle Reg insisted that we all listen to the BBC news programs, especially the evening nine-o'clock news—unless nine o'clock found us sheltering in the pantry. Major developments in the war always evoked, "Oh, me Gawd! " from Old Aunt Lil, and her hands flew up to cover her mouth, as if she'd uttered a naughty word. Bad news she dealt with by rocking in her chair, wringing her hands and humming mournfully; good news, she celebrated by jumping up, grabbed with both hands the face of whoever was nearest and planted a great smacking kiss full on the lips of that fortunate individual.

Because Uncle Reg worked nights and was rarely present for the evening news, it became my responsibility to make a note of major changes on the war fronts so that we could update the war map that was pinned on the wall next to the radio. Sometimes "our" red pins retreated with such depressing regularity that Aunt Mary would say, "I don't know why ya keep that thing up on the wall, Reg … It's bad enough that we have ta listen ta what's happenin', without lookin' at it all the time, as well." And it was a constant reminder to poor old Aunt Lil that Neddie, her baby, was somewhere out there near one of those red pins, perhaps being shot at or bombed that very moment. After gazing at the map, she usually retreated with quivering lips and moist eyes to her seat by the fire, where she did a lot of hand wringing and quiet humming. For me, the nightly ritual of listening to the news—always preceded by Big Ben striking the hour—provided a potent link back to pre-war life in Waterloo when I'd lain in bed, listening to Big Ben. Now, after the ninth solemn boom had died away and before I settled down to my note taking for Uncle Reg, I silently said, "Good-night," to the folks in Waterloo—who had probably heard Big Ben as they, too, tuned into the news.

It was around this time that my love affair with radio began. Unlike today's plethora of stations, there were only two from which to choose: The BBC Light Program and The BBC Home Service. In this particular household, the brown Bakelite box that held pride of place on the sideboard was tuned to the Home Service for the news and *Children's Hour* at five o'clock—an important part of the day for little Jackie. But when it came to music, The Home Service wasn't to Aunt Mary's liking. She couldn't stand "all that classical stuff," and the radio was quickly switched to The Light Program for

Vera Lynn or Bing Crosby crooning wildly popular songs like "The White Cliffs of Dover," or "We'll Meet Again."

However, on Saturday nights, it was back to the Home Service for a full-length radio play on *Saturday Night Theatre*, to which Aunt Mary and I were devoted listeners. It followed the nine o'clock news, and as soon as the news ended, Aunt Lil would announce that she'd taken her "sasprins"—two aspirins that she took religiously every night—and was going to bed early. This was a strategy born of necessity, because she rapidly lost interest in the play and started humming, or chatting about this, that, or the other, and landed herself in Aunt Mary's black book for days. After "the ol' lady" had heaved herself up the creaky stairs, Aunt Mary and I settled ourselves in happy anticipation of our weekly treat. And for the next hour and a half we were transported to some other place and some other time, with people we'd never met, who sometimes did or said things that were beyond our wildest imaginings—unless the siren wailed and forced us to rouse those already asleep and crowd into the cupboard under the stairs. We once tried leaving the radio on as we huddled in the cupboard, but it didn't work. The illusion had been shattered and could not be restored. Radio plays require attention to every nuance of sound; anything less, and it is impossible to conjure up a mental image of the characters and the drama being acted out.

The advent of TV renders that internal imagining unnecessary, and, though radio drama survives as a sort of threatened species, something valuable has been lost, I think. To this day, I prefer listening to stories on the radio, rather than on TV. Music, too: it is distracting and annoying to have one's attention directed by some unseen cameraman to a close-up of an instrumentalist's fingers, however dexterous, or the conductor's profile, however dramatic. The illusion of the concert hall can only be restored by closing one's eyes. Or by tuning in to a radio in the first place!

In school I had, by now, caught up on all the class work I missed as a result of the broken leg fiasco, but socially I was getting nervous. The cause of my anxiety was the addition of Latin to our curriculum. I'd quickly come to love this new language; it was so satisfyingly "square," rather like Algebra with all those definite rules. But the problem was that I found Latin easy and saw danger ahead, the danger of inching my way to the top of the class if I wasn't careful. With still-raw memories of my Waterloo street problems, I knew, very emphatically, that I didn't want to deal with the social implications of *that*. However, the danger didn't seem imminent, so I pushed my fears to the back of my mind and let myself simply enjoy learning Latin—and French, which I also loved. French, however, was harder, so it did not pose the same threat.

Much of my pleasure in these languages came from poring through the dictionaries we'd been given; I could hardly believe that someone had taken the trouble to list all those French and Latin words and their English equivalents. (A year or so later I discovered, with equal delight, that someone had compiled a dictionary of the entire English language: *all* its words and all their *meanings*. I no longer had to put a new word on hold in my head until I bumped into it in some other context. I could simply look it up!)

◆　◆　◆

As summer approached, it was hard to contain my excitement at the prospect of six long weeks with "my" baby—which is how I'd come to think of Maureen Jean. She was, effectively, my first child, and I couldn't wait to hold her and cuddle her and listen to her laugh. But when that long-awaited moment arrived, and Mum opened the front door, I knew by her face that something was wrong. Nothing catastrophic, it turned out. It was simply that Maureen wasn't there for me to cuddle, because Louie had taken her out and wasn't back yet. But Mum was upset. "That Louie!" she said crossly. "I told 'er ta get back with Maureen before yew arrived. An' she said, 'Don't be silly. O' course we'll be back in time fer Gwen. We're on'y goin' dahn The Cut fer a few odds an' sods.'"

I told Mum that it really didn't matter. But it did. I'd imagined that moment so many times and didn't know how to keep the disappointment out of my face. And what followed was worse. Louie finally arrived and sat herself down in Jack Weddinger's chair—the chair that none of us dared ever to sit in—but, instead of relinquishing Maureen to my out-stretched arms, she wrapped her own arms round the baby and hugged her tight, crooning softly. Then she held Maureen up at arms' length and jiggled her, saying, "C'mon! Give us a smile, then … " and, when Maureen crowed with delight, "T-h-e-r-e! That's my girl, that's my Maureen Jean … yew jus' tell 'em! Yore Louie's baby, aincha … me li'l sweet'art!"

I felt as if Louie—always so loving, always so generous—had physically attacked me, had plunged something sharp and hurtful deep into my chest. The feeling that filled my rib cage wasn't pain, exactly; more like everything had drained out, leaving only a hollow emptiness. Never had I felt deliberately betrayed by an adult, a trusted adult, at that. I was speechless. So was Mum. We both just stood there, watching Louie play with Maureen, until finally Mum said, "Why don'cha let Gwen 'old 'er, Louie. She's 'er sister, after all. An' it's bin a long time since she's seen 'er."

Whereupon Louie, in a bit of a huff, said, "Well … 'ere she is, then. Take 'er!" and thrust Maureen towards me. Of course, after an absence of several months, I was a stranger to the bewildered 11-month-old, and she turned back towards Louie, who promptly cuddled her again, crooning, "There ... see! It's yer Louie ya want, ain't it, me luv'ly one!"

I didn't wait for more. I ran upstairs and lay on my bed, crying. A little later I heard the front door slam as Louie left, and from the vehemence of that slam and the absence of cheery good-byes, I assumed that she and Mum had parted on less than their usual friendly terms. Of course, it wasn't long before Maureen and I picked up where we'd left off at the end of the Easter holidays, and I did indeed have a wonderful summer with "my" baby. But I never regained the unquestioning trust I'd always had in Louie, after that glimpse of her cruel streak. I'd known for a long time that she liked her own way and could get pretty sulky if crossed; but deliberately cruel? No way. That had been a nasty surprise.

Within a day or two, it was clear that my mother's honeymoon period was over, and she was paying a high price for choosing to disbelieve what Jack Weddinger's first wife had told her. Not that there had ever been much of a honeymoon; things had felt uncomfortable that first Christmas, when the marriage was then less than two months old. The anticipation of a new baby had given it a new lease of life, but the new lease had been sorely tried by the fact that Mum had presented Jack Weddinger with his seventh daughter, not the son he'd been longing for. The first Mrs. Weddinger had been blamed for her supposed inability to produce a son, but wife number two had already proved herself capable of bearing a male child, and Jack Weddinger's understandable disappointment had turned to bitterness.

Sadly, he didn't see Derek as a ready-made surrogate son. On the contrary, much of his anger was directed toward Derek, and he led the poor boy a dog's life. Derek could do nothing right: if quiet, he was berated for being sullen, and if talkative, was told, "Shuddup, can'cha! Yore big enough ta knew yer place, be now ... Just speak when yore spoken to!" If Derek was sitting in the living room, he was accused of, "'angin' around an' nosin' inta everyone's business," and of being secretive, "up ta no good, sulkin' away up there" if he stayed in his bedroom.

Derek's way of dealing with all this was to spend his free time riding the Underground. He bought the cheapest ticket from Waterloo station and kept changing trains until, eventually, he'd exit the Underground one station away from Waterloo and walk home from there. During the summer holidays, he often took a sandwich and some lemonade and spent the entire day "ridin' the rails." As a result, his knowledge of the London Underground was formidable, and he became the authority people consulted when they weren't sure of the easiest way to get from A to B. At first, I worried about him being trapped underground in the event of an air raid, until Mum pointed out, "Ya daft thing! The Underground's where people go fer shelter … it's safer than stayin' in yer own 'ouse! Real deep, those tunnels are."

Riding the Underground was an ingenious solution to Derek's problems on the domestic front, but it meant that we saw very little of one another except at breakfast and teatime. And then our stepfather was glaring at us across the table, begrudging every slice of bread and butter that we consumed. Mealtimes were really miserable affairs, and I was secretly glad that, unlike Derek, I didn't have to deal with this scene all the time. At the end of the holidays, I'd be heading for Merstham with a sigh of relief—even though it meant saying goodbye to Maureen until the next holiday. The realization that I would actually be *glad* to leave the little sister I'd so longed for, stirred up a deep anger in me. Why, oh why, had Mum married this man? The first Mrs. Weddinger had *told* her what he was like … so she *knew*. My already-existent mother-directed rage expanded into something stronger and deeper-rooted, and it continued to grow as I piled on each of my mother's new "sins." The vehemence of my feelings got to be quite scary, but I tried not to dwell on them and reluctantly reminded myself that there would never have been a baby sister had there been no marriage.

That summer, I made the most of every opportunity to play "mother" to Maureen. At the weekly Baby Clinic, it was I who undressed her to be weighed and examined by the nurse, although, if she needed to see the doctor, Mum took over. "What a lucky little girl you are!" the nurse used to say to Maureen. "It's not many babies that have *two* Mummies!" And Mum would sniff, pretending to be hurt, "Yeah … she don't want nothin' ta do with me while 'er big sister's around!" and we'd all laugh, except Maureen, who was too busy playing with the watch pinned to the nurse's uniform. The simple act of wheeling Maureen in her pram gave me such delight, that I never passed up a chance to go shopping with Mum, and—an added bonus—she would sometimes launch into one of her stories. On the way *to* the shops, she was always pre-occupied, figuring out how to get the most for every penny and every food coupon; on the way home, no such weighty matters occupied her mind, and that's when the tales got told.

On one occasion, we went home by a different route, because Mum had heard that a tobacconist on Waterloo Road had cigarettes. Like all imported goods, cigarettes were scarce during the war, and, the latest rumor had it, the next government budget would slap yet another big tax on cigarettes. Mum didn't approve of smoking, but she was not one to lose the chance to save a few pennies, *and* there was the hope that cigarettes would be a sure-fire way to put her hard-to-please husband in a good mood. When she emerged from the tobacconist shop and tucked two large packets of cigarettes in with the rest of the shopping at the bottom of the pram, she said triumphantly, "Gold Flake. The ol' man's fav'rites. That should keep 'is nibs 'appy fer a few days!"

As we turned towards home, she suddenly said, "That's where I met yer father" and pointed towards a Sausage & Mash shop underneath the railway bridge by Waterloo station. Having eaten out only once, the time we had tea with Mrs. Marsh and Betty, I thought this a pretty glamorous beginning for my parents, for I'd always been attracted to Sausage & Mash shops where the servers all wore those tall, white chef hats. The trickling condensation on their steamy windows made them the epitome of warmth and snugness, and I often hoped that, one day, we'd turn in out of the cold and sit at one of the small, oilcloth-covered tables midst all that steamy heat and tuck into a heaping plate of sausage-and-mash. But we never did.

"Yeah ... that's where it all began. An' where it darn near ended, too!" Mum chuckled. Apparently, she'd just started working there when my father came in with one of his pals, as they did regularly, once a week. Mum took their orders and called them down to the cooks, but she had to stand on a box to reach the speaking tube that went down to the kitchen.

"Well ... when yer Dad saw that, 'e turned to 'is mate an' said, 'Whadda pity ... a nice-lookin' gel like that ... with Duck's Disease.' An' made sure 'e said it loud enough fer me to 'ear, too!" she said, still indignant at the memory.

"I didn't know what 'e was talkin' about, but 'is buddy laughed 'is bloomin' 'ead off, so I knew I was bein' made fun of. Not ta be outdone, I said, 'Bet I could cook yore goose, mate!' This made the pair of 'em laugh even more. An' made me wonder whether I should'a kept me mouth shut. 'Stead o' tryin' ta be sa clever.

"When things got slack, I asked me pal, Elsie, what Duck's Disease was, an' she just looked at me an' grinned. 'Yew don't know ... ? It means yer arse is too close ta the ground, me luv!'

"'The cheeky bugger!' I said. 'Just wait till I see 'im agin ... I'll 'ave 'is guts fer garters! I 'ope 'e don't expect me ta serve 'im next time 'e comes in ... I'd rather lose me bloomin' job!'

"I meant it, too. When yer Dad found out 'e'd upset me, 'e tried ta say 'e was sorry, but I wasn't 'avin' any more of 'is nonsense. So I didn't serve 'im, even if 'e was the on'y customer in the shop. I just stared right through 'im, like 'e wasn't there. That got 'is dander up awright! An' bein' a stubborn Irishman, 'e started comin' in more often. Two or three times a week, an' kept tellin' me 'e was sorry, but I didn't budge an inch.

"Elsie warned me, 'Yew be careful, May ... if the manager notices, ya'll get the sack, treatin' a customer like that.' But like I told 'er, I'd rather lose me job than serve that cheeky blighter.

"'Strewf, May … Yore a stubborn thing … ' Elsie said, an' she walked away, throwin' 'er 'ands up in disgust.

"Well … the manager 'ad noticed. An' 'e said ta me, 'Yew seem ta be good fer business, May. That bloke comes in several times a week now. P'raps we could find another fella fer ya!'

"'Fellas like that I c'n do without, thanks,' I told 'im.

"Bu' I thanked me lucky stars 'e didn't give me the sack. This went on fer quite a while, then yer Dad talked to 'is pal, an' 'is pal talked to Elsie, so Elsie said she'd try, once more, ta get me ta make peace. 'Enough's enough, May!' she ended up. 'An' 'e seems like a nice bloke … Alf says 'e's real sweet on yew, too. An' I c'n b'lieve it, the way 'e comes in 'ere all the time, only becos o' yew. Yew'd be a fool not ta give 'im a chance. It was on'y a joke, after all!'

"So finally I give in, an' the four of us, we all started goin' out together— Elsie an' 'er fella, yer Dad an' me. After Elsie moved away, yer Dad an' me we kept together, an' then it seemed daft fer us both ta be payin' rent, so we decided ta git married. 'E was stayin' in the 'Ostel fer Workin' Men—a rough ol' place, it was, an' yer Dad 'ated it. I was livin' with Alice and Joe and their kids—three they 'ad then, an' it was a squeeze in their small 'ouse, I c'n tell ya! So we found the room in Coin Street—not far from the Sausage & Mash Shop, so I could get ta work easy—an' we put up the banns.

"Auntie Ada an' Uncle Bill was pleased as Punch when we told 'em. They'd bin telling yer Dad, 'Ya gotta good one there, Joe. Don't let 'er get away!' An' of course, they'd bin tellin' me not ta let a good fella like Joe give *me* the slip. 'It's abaht time 'e settled dahn,' they told me. 'Over forty, 'e is, so 'e's 'ad a good run fer 'is money!'

"An' 'e did settle dahn. Six years we was in that room. It was a bit crowded after yew was born, but we was 'appy enough. Specially after 'e give up goin' ta the pub with 'is pals. I told 'im, after the fight 'e 'ad with the foreman at the OXO place, it was me, or the booze—take it or leave it!" I'd heard veiled references to the OXO story before, but at this point we were rounding the corner to Upper Ground, so I knew I'd have to wait for another day and another shopping excursion when my mother was in the right mood.

There were some bad air raids that summer. One morning, after a night with a lot of "close ones," we went down The Cut and discovered that one of our regular shops was a pile of rubble. Nothing was left of it, or the flat above, but part of a staircase still covered in carpet, clinging precariously to the wall of the adjacent building. We joined the small crowd staring at this scene of devastation and saw a young soldier frantically digging through the rubble with his bare hands. A couple of policemen were trying to persuade him to stop, to leave the search to the experienced crew that was already there, those who had the training and equipment. "Lookin' fer 'is wife an' baby, 'e is," the woman next to us murmured. "It was their firs', too. An' 'e'd jus' come 'ome on the compash'nate leave ta see 'em bof' ... poor devil ... bin at it all night, 'e 'as ... 'e won't give up."

Later we learned just how terrible it had been for that young soldier. He was one of Perce's mates, and they'd been together at the pub when the bomb fell. "Eddie'd just got 'ome, that evenin'," Perce told us. "An' Lizzie, 'is wife, told 'im 'e might as well go an' 'ave a beer wiv 'is pals while she set'led the baby dahn. A right one fer 'avin' a good time while ya could, was Lizzie. 'Make 'ay while the bloomin' sun shines,' was 'er mot'o. She nevva let the war, or nuffink else, get 'er dahn. Poor Eddie! 'E'll never fergive 'isself fer not stayin' 'ome tha' nigh' ... fer leavin' Lizzie ta die by 'erself ... 'er an' the baby. 'E wishes 'e'd died wiv' 'em, an' I reck'n 'e'll jus' frow 'isself in front of a German bullet, firs' chance 'e gets."

Indeed, Eddie did his best to get killed at every opportunity that came his way, Perce told us a couple of years later when news came that Eddie had, finally, got his wish. However, it had taken many battles and an Italian bullet, not a German one.

"'Ow's yer Mum 'oldin' up with all the raids?" Mum asked Perce that day. "I ain't seen much of 'er lately."

"It's jus' terrible fer 'er," he said, shaking his head. "She can't 'ear the sirens, an' sometimes the firs' she knows about a raid is the thud she feels frew 'er feet—*after* the bloody bomb's 'it the ground. So she's a bundle o' nerves. We keep tryin' ta send 'er out o' London, bu' she don't wanna go wivout Dad an' me. 'Cos then she'd 'ave no-one ta talk to."

Poor Mrs. Lake. She was born both deaf and dumb, and with the best will in the world, it was impossible to understand her agitated clucking, despite the head shaking and hand-flapping that she added in an attempt to be understood. My mother was the only person who seemed to intuit what she was on about, or managed to smile and nod as if she did, and respond with some remark. Whereupon, Mrs. Lake's face was wreathed with smiles, and the excited clucking was renewed with greater vigor. Needless to say, the poor soul eagerly latched on to Mum whenever they met, and I used to dread the sight of this large lumbering lady bearing down on us. Throughout the ensuing clucking and flapping, I'd stand to one side, uneasily shifting my weight from one foot to the other, not knowing where to look and hoping for anything—even an air raid—that would cut this short.

Worse yet were the days when Mrs. Lake took it into her head to get me in on this "conversation." Bending down from her great height, she'd bring her face close, sometimes so close that I got sprayed with spittle from that clucking mouth. Pity and fear of my mother's anger and disgust kept my feet glued to the ground, while every fiber of my being wanted to turn tail and run.

Mum invariably came to the rescue with a comment like, "She's just sayin' 'ow smart yew look in yer new frock," and Mrs. Lake would pull back, beaming from ear to ear. Listening to Perce tell of the unique problems faced by a deaf mute in a time of war, I was doubly ashamed of my cowardly turning away from her overtures, yet acutely aware that if she turned the corner at that very moment, I would not be able to behave any other way.

Later that summer there was a truly terrifying air raid: perhaps the worst of the war in our corner of London. I was halfway down the stairs on my way to the basement when there was a tremendous explosion and, through a gap that suddenly appeared under the front wall of the house, I saw the area railings and a sliver of sidewalk lit up as bright as day. The stairs under my feet and the wall under my hand swayed and trembled; I had time to think, "It's goin' ta fall on top o' me," and a vision of that young soldier searching the rubble flashed through my mind. But instead, the house simply dropped back down, still intact—though I could hear falling plaster and breaking glass. It was as if I were dreaming, and I stood there, not quite able to believe what I'd just witnessed, until Mum came and pulled me down the remaining stairs into the shelter with the rest of the family. Next morning we assessed the damage, and it was remarkably light: there was some fallen plaster, a number of broken windows, and the front door, under which I'd seen the brightly lit paving stones, was jammed so tight that it had to be re-hung. And that was it. Those old Victorian row houses were sturdier than they looked!

The rest of the neighborhood, however, had not escaped that lightly. For this "bomb" was actually a land mine designed to create widespread destruction. It had fallen on the Eldorado Cold Storage Plant, a large refrigerated warehouse about two blocks from our house, destroying much of that six-story building and doing extensive damage to everything within about a block. What was left of the Eldorado plant blazed for days, despite the efforts of relays of firemen, and in the end, the fire was left to burn itself out. During which time, the warehouse having been full of refrigerated meat, the local residents got to "enjoy" the aroma of barbecued meat—pretty tantalizing, considering their meager meat ration. "Gor blimey! 'Ow many weeks rations d'ya reckon're goin' up in smoke there!" people lamented, as they cleaned up the damage to their houses; the lucky ones who still had a house to clean up. But for these long-suffering folks there was worse to come. Before the smoldering fire was cool enough for firemen to tackle any kind of clean up, the charred carcasses began to rot, and a much less attractive smell pervaded the area for weeks.

The summer holiday came to its inexorable end, and I had to deal, once again, with the opposing pulls of home and school. This time the rotten meat smell added to the glad-to-leave-London pull, but with so many pluses and minuses on each side, one more or less was hardly significant. However, the atmosphere at home had been steadily deteriorating, and the pull of school had been growing stronger. Honor Oak was no longer my "new school": it had become simply "my school," a school in which I felt established academically and even socially to some degree. For I now had a nucleus of steady friends, in school and out, for the first time in my life. Uncomfortably aware of this gradual shift in favor of school, I felt *so* guilty, such a traitor to my mother and my brother and my little sister, that I hardly dared acknowledge it, even to myself. But despite this inner turmoil, come the beginning of September off I went, ready to start the new school year, my third at Honor Oak. Having weathered the Third Form and the Lower Fourth, I was now in the Upper Fourth, which sounded much more important!

However, I did have one big issue to resolve in the coming school year. My last report card had been alarmingly good for someone whose goal was to never again be top of the class, and I was fearful that my new social standing would be seriously jeopardized if this continued. The problem had nagged at me all summer, and I'd decided to try deliberately getting some bad grades: I'd fool around and make no effort in subjects that didn't matter, to balance out good grades in those that did. All that remained was to sort out which mattered and which didn't; but based on what? I had no idea, other than a vague gut feeling that led me to classify Math, Latin, French and English, as important (and just happened to be my favorite subjects, where good grades came almost despite myself). In history and geography—possibly important, I dimly sensed—I would alternately do my best and then my worst, on a term-to-term basis. Science was in a category all by itself. I vaguely recognized its importance, but my grades fluctuated in a way that I couldn't seem to control, so I would have to adopt a wait-and-see approach. The remaining subjects, including Art and Music, I deemed unworthy of any effort on my part. (Oh! The arrogance of an ignorant thirteen-year-old!)

This plan might fix the problem of the escalating grades, but I wasn't sure that I could actually put it into operation, and as the train neared Merstham, my anxiety level peaked to near-panic level at the thought that I might fail in this endeavor.

◆　　◆　　◆

ADDENDUM

I recently learned that Maureen had been promised to Louie in the event that Mum hadn't survived the birth of this "surprise" baby. It was a possibility that had to be taken seriously, by all accounts. I do wonder if

Jack Weddinger was aware of this arrangement; and whether he would have honored it, especially if the baby had been a boy. However, when Maureen told me of this promise, it made sense that it was Louie who had chosen her names, Maureen Jean. And the scene in which Louie tried to hold on to Maureen, declaring, "Yore Louie's baby, ain'cha. … me li'l sweet'art!" also made a sad kind of sense.

It also helped to explain why, of all the babies that she took under her wing, so fiercely and possessively, Maureen was the only one that Louie stayed in touch with to the end of her long life. To my knowledge, there were at least four babies that she'd taken over; taken over and doted on, giving each in turn lots of time, love, and affection; showering each with generous gifts—until a new baby appeared on the scene. I suppose I was lucky to have been whisked away from Louie's world by World War II before my replacement appeared. I imagine the sudden switch would otherwise have been very hurtful. Although, given that my successor was my baby sister, how could I have begrudged Maureen what I had enjoyed for so long?

As with many additions to family lore, this little nugget of information about the promise made to Louie, leads to a new question: What about Derek and me? What were the plans for us in the event that Mum didn't survive Maureen's birth? I don't suppose, for one moment, that we would have stayed with Jack Weddinger. But where would we have gone? To Auntie Ada and Uncle Bill? Aunt Emmy and Uncle Dick? I never heard a whisper of any such arrangement from any of them. Or from Mum. Just one more to add to the growing list of questions to which I'll never know the answer.

Chapter 24

Staying Put

The Poor Grades Plan was a success. I had to work hard at not working, had to steel myself when it came to deliberately not handing in assignments, even in subjects that I'd so cavalierly deemed unimportant. But both came more easily with practice, and I was gratified to see the desired poor marks at the top of returned papers, with, "You can do better than this!" scrawled across the top.

In Art and Music, where teacher expectations were low, such comments were notably absent, but Miss Frampton soon became perturbed. My history papers were returned covered in red-inked sarcasm, and I came to dread the comment, "See Me! *TODAY.*" It always led to an uncomfortable confrontation, with Frampie wheezing—as always, when excited or upset—and fixing me with an icy glare as I stood, first on one foot, then on the other, while she waited for me to explain, "What's going on here, young lady?" Little did she know how impossible it was for me to do this. And she probably would not have believed me, had I told her. A mumbled, "I dunno," or a sullen silence exasperated her further, and an epic battle of wills raged all term. However, when the history Final Exam results were posted on the door of the classroom, facing the hallway for the entire world to see, my name was gratifyingly far from the top. And Miss Frampton's comments on my report card were blistering.

The next term it was geography's turn for the Poor Grade Treatment, and Frampie may have believed that my improvement in history was the result of her scathing comments. In which case, she had a rude awakening when it was history's turn again, and our battle was renewed. Bug-eyed with frustration, she was now always on my case. Even when I was with my friends in the center of town, her hat—a bright cerise affair—was often spotted, bobbing briskly along above the heads of other people, headed straight for us.

That conspicuous piece of headgear served as a useful early warning system if we happened to be breaking one of the myriad school rules concerning public deportment. It gave time to put school hats back on heads, or dispose of whatever forbidden fruits we'd been illicitly consuming when the cry of "Frampie!" was raised.

On one notable occasion, however, she wore a different hat, and we barely had time to stuff half-eaten ice creams into blazer pockets before she was on top of us. She must have been in a rare good mood (on account of her new hat, perhaps), because she stopped to chat, but I fear we were singularly unresponsive as we stood, trying not to stare at one another's pockets, just hoping she'd go away soon. Fortunately, she bid us goodbye before melted ice cream started to ooze from our pockets, but our relief at escaping punishment for the crime of eating on the street was considerably diminished by the need to spend next week's pocket money getting our blazers cleaned—not to mention the loss of our ice creams. Ice cream was a rare treat at that time.

One day, at the peak of Frampie War II, I was so mad at her that I vowed to myself: "On the next test I'm gonna get a nought. That'll show her!" I would have been hard put to explain just what this was supposed to show Miss Frampton, and it slowly dawned on me how hard it would be to get a zero: I had to know the material well enough to *know* my answers were wrong! Undeterred, I studied for that test harder than for any test I've ever taken, and since nobody but me knew of my vow, this has to be quite the silliest thing I ever did. I succeeded beyond my wildest dreams: out of a hundred points, I scored minus one—the consequence of two spelling errors. However, Miss Frampton trumped my moment of triumph. "Well done, Gwen Redfern!" she said, as she handed the paper back, her lips twitching in the nearest approach to a smile known to them. She knew! She'd figured out what I was up to; *that's* what my hard-earned zero had shown her. This display of acumen raised Frampie several notches in my estimation, and I sometimes wondered whether my negative score had done the same for me in her eyes, because there was a slight thaw in our frosty relationship after that episode.

I suppose it was a measure of my comfort level as part of Uncle Reg's family that relatively trivial matters, like the Frampie Wars, came to dominate my world. I now enjoyed the luxury of feeling sorry for myself about problems that, at the Sharps', had barely registered. Why else would the unpleasant smell that regularly pervaded the Redferns' house loom so large in my Merstham memories? The same smell had, with similar regularity, pervaded the Sharps' abode, but had paled in comparison with other concerns. In both houses, the smell was produced by a bucket of boiling vegetable scraps being reduced to a repulsive, mushy mess that was then mixed with meal and fed to the chickens in the wire-fenced run in the back garden. The chickens were invaluable because they augmented the egg rations and, ultimately, the meat rations, so one could hardly complain about the smell. But it was a major grumble that I shared with Peggy and Joan as we roamed the streets of Merstham; for they, too, had chickens at the bottom of their garden, as did many households during the war. All of them must have endured that horrible smell, because I never heard of anyone purchasing special chicken food.

Another Great Grumble that we shared was the lack of privacy in houses where one's ablutions were performed in a kitchen that was the general thoroughfare for all traffic. It was an embarrassing business for us "growing girls," and especially hard on Peggy who had grown up in a house with a proper bathroom. Joan and I had always lived in rotten old housing with inadequate facilities, but that had been before we hit puberty. Now we, too, found it hard to live with the ever-present fear that some male member of the family would appear at an awkward moment. When I complained about this to my mother, she showed no sympathy whatsoever. "Ya'll 'ave ta put up with it, me lady, an' do what everybody's *always* 'ad ta do. Ya jus' wash down as far as possible, an' up as far as possible. Then, if nobody's around, ya wash possible!" She laughed like a drain at this old joke and expected me to do the same, but I didn't think it funny. Neither did Peggy and Joan. But Mum was right about one thing: we *did* just "'ave t'git on wiv' it," in true Waterloo fashion.

In school, Peggy and I were in the same class and became part of a tight little foursome with two non-Merstham girls, Maggie and Beryl. We were surprisingly tight, given what an odd mix we were: the tall and the short, the skinny and the plump, the athletic and unathletic, the academic and the non-academic. Peggy alone mourned the fact that her hair was dead straight, and Beryl was the only one with cause to lament the absence of a bosom. I would gladly have swapped my boring brown hair for Peggy 's gleaming coppery locks, and my all too ample bosom for Beryl's miniscule "pimples." My over-abundance was a cross that I bore very reluctantly, so I was astonished when Maggie one day grabbed my hand excitedly and rubbed it back and forth against her blouse for me to feel the satiny texture of her first brassiere. She was *pleased* at this turn of events? This was hard to believe. In response to a note from Aunt Mary, my mother had recently dug out an old brassiere for me (old only in the sense that it had been purchased for a special event, then lain in a drawer until another occasion should demand that she "dress up"). I loathed that garment. When squeezed into it I felt as if I was wearing a placard that announced to the world, "I now have to wear a brassiere." Yet it did no more than flatten me, which was just as well. I would have died a thousand deaths had it made me stick out as Maggie's did—to her delight.

Despite my head start in the bosom department, Maggie was way ahead when it came to the opposite gender; she soon gave up on me and Peggy in this regard and stopped steering the conversation towards boys when we were around. Beryl provided more fertile ground, and the pair of them often peeled off and huddled together, whispering and giggling, leaving Peggy and me to chatter about matters that we *did* know how to handle. It slowly became apparent that teachers disapproved of this aspect of Maggie's behavior, though she was a favorite in other ways, because she was such a good student. I began to wonder whether this somehow explained why she was at Honor Oak. For Maggie was not a true evacuee. She lived with her family in Epsom, a long bus ride from Reigate, a very scary ride during air raids, she said. Her brothers went to their local school, so why did her parents put their thirteen-year-old daughter through this ordeal? Maggie, when asked, simply shrugged and said, "I dunno, really. But my Dad thinks Honor Oak is a good school for me." The presence of Maggie in the evacuee world of Honor Oak School eased my initial concern that living with relatives might mean that I was not quite the genuine article.

Over the Christmas holidays I made the acquaintance of two of my married stepsisters. Milly was the spitting image of her father, but there the resemblance ended, and I liked her a lot. She was a bubbly, no-nonsense lady with three children, but had the misfortune to fall in love with a man called Dilley. "Milly Dilley ... sounds so silly!" murmured Derek, and we both guffawed. "Don't let the ol' man 'ear yew two takin' the mickey out'a Milly. She's 'is fav'rite, ya know." said Mum sharply. Milly was Mum's favorite, too, but her sister, Beatrice, was an entirely different kettle of fish: a sober-sided lady who rarely cracked a smile, and her little daughter was cut from the same mold.

We spent a lot of time with Beatrice during those holidays, because she was a dressmaker and was making two frocks, one for Mum and one for me. The material came, coupon-free, from a bolt of cloth that Georgie Harris had thrust on me one day. "Hmm," Mum had sniffed, fingering the fabric. "A nice piece o' cloth. Black-market, o' course, an' prob'ly nicked ... jus fell off a lorry, as they say! But," she conceded, "it's a nice color, ain't it?" And it *was*. A deep blue-gray that somehow avoided looking dreary.

My frock turned out really well, but Mum's was too big. "Makes me look like a bloody sack o' potaters tied up in the middle!" she snorted angrily and refused to wear it, despite the fact that clothes were rationed and her wardrobe was not exactly extensive. She seemed to think that Beatrice had deliberately sabotaged her dress, "just fer spite, the toffee-nosed bitch!" And she invariably added, "Acts like 'er shit don't stink, she do! I never *did* like that one. So diff'rent from Milly." To her dying day, my mother bore Beatrice a grudge about that dress—a grudge of which Beatrice was, I trust, blissfully unaware.

We spent Christmas Day with a friend of our stepfather, which was a big departure. Mum was accustomed to spending the day quietly at home, and I'd always gone to the Hodds if I was in London. But my mother's new marriage had changed a lot of things, including our relationship with the Hodds. We saw much less of them now and there was no more popping in for cups of tea. Louie was the only one we saw regularly—but only because she doted on Maureen, I suspected. I still went round to the Hodds' when I was home during the holidays, and they were as friendly as ever if we bumped into them, but they no longer played a large role in our lives. Perhaps they figured that they weren't needed now that Mum had a husband with regular wages, wages larger than she'd ever known in her life. Or maybe they'd homed in on another needy family ... that was highly likely. But I missed them all, a lot.

Mum had never met the man who'd invited us over for Christmas Day, and she was leery of an arrangement made in a pub somewhere, without her knowledge. And, as soon as we walked into the flat of this friend of our stepfather, we all—except, perhaps, for the two men—knew that this was a bad mistake. The man was a bachelor, a paunchy, greasy, loud-mouthed, drinking buddy with a hateful personality. At first he was all Hail-Fellow-Well-Met, but after a few drinks, he started making pompous statements in an angry way that seemed to invite a challenge. Nobody, not even Mum, dared take him on, and this led to long, uncomfortable silences, broken only by expressions of frustration from Maureen, an active toddler for whom the small flat was like a cage, full of things that weren't to be touched or climbed upon.

The day was saved from total disaster by the discovery that our host was the Caretaker of the huge building in which his flat was located, and there were miles of empty corridors where Maureen could run to her heart's content. For this immense place housed a school called City Lit, according to Mum, but that sounded a strange name for a school, so she probably had it wrong. (Years later, I learned that I had maligned her: its full name was—still is—the City Literature Institute, and it plays an important role on the educational/cultural scene.) The school was, of course, devoid of students over Christmas, and this gave Derek and me an excuse to escape from that miserable flat to look after Maureen while she let off steam. We happily played "chase" with her for a bit, then watched admiringly as she practiced her still-inexpert jumping skills. I couldn't have imagined a stranger way to spend Christmas Day than in those dimly lit corridors, lined with locked and silent classrooms and echoing to a toddler's squeals of delight! "Gor! I could've brought me new roller skates!" said Derek. And, indeed, in those long corridors he *could* have tried out the present left at the foot of his bed that morning. (The Father Christmas nonsense had been resuscitated, because Mum wanted Maureen to have her fair share of all that make-believe.)

Eventually Mum came to fetch us, saying, "It's time ta go 'ome, thank Gawd!" But this was not to be. As we were putting on our coats the siren sounded, and we were trapped in that flat for another couple of hours; very tedious hours, with nothing to do but listen to the boom of guns, the whine and thud of bombs, and the clanging of fire engines and ambulances as they raced through blacked-out streets. Fortunately, our host's responsibilities included the role of Air Raid Warden for that large building, so we saw nothing more of him till the All Clear sounded, and we then made a speedy departure in case the siren started to wail again.

It was now well after midnight, and after standing at the bus stop for a while, Mum said, "Let's walk. It'll be warmer than waitin' in the cold fer buses what might not come. There ain't many this time o' night anyways. An' after a raid like we just 'ad, it might be hours!"

"That's all right fer yew," said our stepfather. "Yore not carryin' the bloody baby! She's out fer the count. Fair wore 'erself out, racin' those corridors, she did."

Maureen had indeed exhausted herself and was sound asleep, her head lolling on his shoulder, and there was no way those little legs would take another step that night. After Derek and I offered to take turns carrying her, we set off on foot—and Maureen never woke, even when being transferred from one shoulder to another. In the final stretch, as we were crossing Waterloo Bridge, an awesome sight brought us to a silent halt. The city was ablaze. In every direction, there were continuous walls of flames, too broad and extensive to be single buildings on fire. Accustomed as we were to the darkness of the blackout, it seemed like it must already be daybreak for there to be so much light around; yet we knew that the sun wouldn't rise for several hours yet.

"The buggers must'a dropped 'undreds of incendiaries," said our stepfather.

"More like thousan's," said Mum, and then she gasped, "Oh, me Gawd ... lo-o-k ... over there!"

She was pointing at a wall of fire on the south bank of the river, a bit downstream of us. It took a few moments to register that *The Star* building was in flames again, but this blaze was huge, much bigger than any previous fire at that ill-fated building. The implications raced through my mind, as I'm sure they did for each of us. Did we still have a house to go home to? Was it, too, a blazing inferno? What would have happened to us, had we stayed home that day? Trapped in a burning house? ... I shuddered. What about the Chapmans, next door? Was their house on fire too? Were they all right? And,

I'm ashamed to say, I thought regretfully of the knitting bag I'd been given for Christmas; there'd been no time to do more than open the zipper and admire the yellow wool and new needles that Mum (a.k.a. Father Christmas) had thoughtfully put inside. And Derek probably harbored similar thoughts about his unused roller skates.

Shaken and subdued, we pressed on across the bridge and discovered to our astonishment that, by some miracle, our house was still standing, intact, just as we'd left it that morning. It was only the buildings across the street, those bordering the river, that were engulfed in flames—*all* of them, not just *The Star*, this time. We couldn't get near our house because of the fire fighters and their equipment, so we went round to the Hodds (of course! Where else would one go in a time of trouble?) There we laid Maureen, still asleep, on a bed, and drank numerous cups of tea till our stepfather came to say that we could now get into the house. We then dispensed yet more cups of tea to weary firemen, and when we finally tumbled into bed, it was already daylight, daylight dimmed by thick palls of smoke.

All too soon, after that, it was time to head back to school, and as the train carried me away from London, I realized that it was exactly a year since I had been introduced to the world of Merstham. That was the longest I'd stayed in one place since being evacuated! And a good year, it had been, thanks to Uncle Reg's family; and to my mother, for ferreting out these relatives.

◆　　◆　　◆

One blustery night soon after my return, Aunt Lil, bereft of buskies and teeth and clad only in a nightie, shook me awake and told me to go for the midwife—a new little Redfern was about to make an appearance. I'd never been out alone at that time of night, so I was glad of Rickie's company as I battled with the gusty wind in the pitch dark. He was a cute little Cairn-like terrier mutt, but his bark was fierce, and in the dark no one would think that he was so small, I reasoned. On the way back, I mulled over Aunt Lil's unexpected pronouncement: a new baby … was that why Aunt Mary had got so fat, so suddenly … why she got tired and cranky in the evenings? No one had mentioned a baby, though. And I hadn't made the connection (at age fourteen, my ideas about babies and how they were produced were astonishingly vague). Several other mystifying events now fell into place: the recent installation of a bed in the front room, frequent visits by Aunt Mary's parents, and piles of unfamiliar-looking laundry.

Our mission accomplished, Rickie and I were sent back to bed, both of us. To my bed, no less. "I don't wan' tha' dog under me feet," said Aunt Lil, now fully dressed (buskies, teeth, and all), running around, heating lots of water on the stove and airing things in front of the fire. "So jus' take 'im up up wiv' yew, Gwen. That'll keep 'im out o' me way." Rickie must have thought he'd gone to Dog Heaven: first, an unprecedented walk in the middle of the night and, now, being sent upstairs to sleep on my bed.

Before I went to school the next morning, I was allowed a quick peek at the new addition, a little girl, name still undecided. I'd never seen a spanking new newborn before and hadn't realized that they came so tiny. When I said something to this effect, Aunt Lil snorted, "Tiny? She was nearly seven poun's!" as if this were an all-time record. "Big enough fer 'er paw muvver, that's fer sure. Righ', Mary?" This remark made no sense to me; such was the depth of my ignorance about childbirth. But there was no reply from Aunt Mary, who seemed upset and looked as if she'd been crying. Perhaps she'd wanted a boy and was disappointed to have a second daughter? Or maybe giving birth always had this effect? (Was Mum like this after Maureen was born? It was six weeks after the event when I first saw her, so I had no way to judge.) However, I noticed that Uncle Reg and Aunt Lil were also subdued, so maybe they had all hoped for a boy. In which case, I felt, it was a bit rough on that little girl, who'd had no choice in the matter of her gender.

Norma, as she was named, was a beautiful baby: neat and compact, with a surprisingly grown-up little face, and she had a perfect rosebud of a mouth, the lips so clearly delineated that they looked as if they'd been painted on with a fine brush. She was the spitting image of Uncle Reg, with a low forehead and straight brows that almost met over the bridge of the nose—a characteristic of all Aunt Lil's offspring. And Aunt Lil never let anyone lose sight of this. "A real li'l Redfern, this one is!" she'd crow on a regular basis, as she dandled her new little granddaughter. Aunt Mary soon got fed up with this refrain, and the implication that the other granddaughter, favoring her mother's side, was somehow inferior. But there was no stopping the old lady, and as time went on, her flagrant favoritism towards Norma became quite an issue.

There was a strange feeling of angst in the house for several weeks after the birth of this baby. Aunt Mary was weepy, and there were lengthy visits by her family, with endless *sotto voce* discussions in the front room, where the fire was lit every day—a highly unusual state of affairs—and from which Aunt Lil, Jackie and I were clearly expected to absent ourselves. Strange too were the frequent trips to London by Aunt Mary and Uncle Reg and the baby, trips that no one ever talked about—in front of me, at least. From the general murmuring in the front room I several times caught the words "specialist" and "consultant," so I supposed there must be something wrong with this seemingly perfect little baby; but I knew better than to ask. Then, one day, I thought I heard Aunt Mary's sister say, in her braying voice, "We-e-l-l, all I c'n say is it's a good thing ya chose a name like Norma ... where all yew 'ave ta do is add an *n*.'" She laughed raucously, and someone said, "Shuddup, Hope! It's no laughin' mat'er."

Add an *n* to Norma? Norman? But that was a *boy's* name. This made no sense at all. I finally broke my rule about keeping family stuff in its own separate compartment and confided in Peggy, the most loyal and trustworthy of my friends. She had no quick answers, but did put into words a startling thought that had flashed through my head: "It sounds as if they're not sure whether it's a girl or a boy … " We gazed at one another, not able to wrap our minds round this preposterous idea. Then, sounding relieved, Peggy added, "Well, *you* should know! You must've seen this baby without a nappy." And I realized, for the first time, that I hadn't. Never had I seen Norma undressed. I'd offered to change her when she was fussing, but Aunt Lil always elbowed me aside with a gruff, "No … that's *my* job." Yet she knew that I was perfectly capable of dealing with small babies and dirty nappies, having had lots of experience with Maureen. Neither had I ever witnessed Norma being given a bath, though I saw plenty of evidence that the baby bath had been put to good use. Peggy and I mulled over these fragments of "evidence" and finally decided that uncertainty about the baby's gender could not possibly be at the root of the recent goings-on. That was just too improbable for words; there had to be a simpler explanation. We concluded that Norma probably had a problem that required consultations with a specialist, a problem the family didn't want to talk about, but nothing *that* bizarre. I must have misheard Hope's remark.

Feeling relieved, I swore Peggy to secrecy (for I felt that I had, in some obscure way, betrayed Aunt Mary and Uncle Reg), and we agreed to never again refer to the matter unless there were new developments that cleared up the mystery. Nothing definitive happened to resolve the question, however, so Peggy and I never did discuss it further, and it gradually faded as the household slowly returned to normalcy. The journeys to London with the baby became fewer and then ceased; family visits reverted to their usual frequency; the front room was restored to its customary fire-less chill; there were no more conversations that suddenly stopped the moment I entered a room; and Aunt Mary's eyes were no longer red-rimmed. And, of course, Norma never was re-named Norman. Indeed, she grew into a lively, wiry little girl, with silky, straight blond hair that contrasted dramatically with thick, dark lashes and eyebrows—a little girl who always knew exactly what she wanted and how to get it. Especially from old Aunt Lil, her Nana, who was just crazy about this "proppa li'l Redfern."

◆   ◆   ◆

When it was geography's turn to be neglected again in accordance with the Poor Grade Plan, Miss Skinner started giving me a hard time. My ill-prepared assignments caused the fair-skinned Skinny to flush with indignation, from the top of her scalp, pinkly visible through sparse white hair, down to where her skimpy cleavage disappeared into the flounces of her blouse. Most dramatic was the effect on her "wattle," which always turned a deeper pink and swayed tremulously when she was excited. (A favorite sport was to get Skinny talking about meteorology, a subject guaranteed to get her all worked up. She would stand in front of the class, eyes closed, going on about air movements and illustrating them by waving her arms and fluttering her long slender fingers. Growing pinker by the moment, she'd intone, "the hot air rises ... and the cold air comes *f-i-l-*t-ering down ... " while we struggled to suppress our giggles. At the end of the war, as she slid gratefully back into the retirement from which she, and many of our teachers, had been enticed because of wartime shortages of teachers, she probably wondered about the extra-ordinary interest in meteorology evinced by the Upper Fourth that year.) But Skinny was not one to mess with; she fought back, hard, against my Plan, and when she began to make noises about getting my Scholarship revoked, I became seriously worried.

Then came the Bus Ticket Scandal. Some foolish girl left a notebook lying around: a notebook in which she had recorded the state of her finances. In it was listed, "Income, bus tickets --- 7d." Under questioning, she revealed that she had been selling some of the free bus tickets that she'd been allocated because she lived too far away to walk to school. We all did it. Much of the time the buses sailed right by because they were full, so we had to walk and had a lot of bus tickets left over at the end of the week. It seemed foolish to throw them away, so we sold them at half price to girls who weren't eligible for free tickets. It was a win-win situation for all parties, we reasoned: the Bus Company provided the same number of body-miles, so to speak, but to different bodies.

We were most indignant when accused of being involved in a criminal scheme. *Criminal?* Just selling a few leftover bus tickets? We were nonplussed by the concept of committing fraud against a nebulous entity like a Bus Company, which we saw as a sort of ghostly *deus ex machina* that, somehow, put buses on the roads, assigned numbers, and decided which bus went where, and when. But the school was serious about our ticket-selling enterprise being fraudulent and didn't buy into our argument that income so derived helped pay for the shoe leather worn out by all the walking that led to the surplus of bus tickets in the first place. We were hauled in front of the headmistress and given dire warnings of expulsion if we even *gave away* our leftover tickets. It seems that the fine print, which we had blithely ignored, said *Non Transferable*.

When Skinny learned that I was one of the delinquents in this brouhaha, a gleam came into her blue eyes (an astonishing bright blue, they were), and she saw it as extra ammunition to get my Scholarship revoked unless my work improved. This left me with no choice. I had to pull up my socks in geography, to assuage her wrath. As a result, I went back to London for the Easter holidays with good marks in geography *and* in history. And a sinking feeling in the pit of my stomach about the collapse of my Plan.

After the holidays I was in a real funk. I had no new plan to prevent my grades from spiraling up. A tight knot formed in my stomach as this did indeed begin to happen, and I expected at any moment to feel the cold winds of ostracism. Then, out of the blue, a solution presented itself in the form of an elaborate disciplinary system introduced by that year's prefects. ("Bunch of martinets!" I overheard one teacher mutter when the scheme was announced to the school during Assembly, and I duly filed "martinet" in the part of my brain where new words lodged, waiting to have their meaning confirmed or refined.) The gist of the new disciplinary measures was that an infraction of school rules earned the transgressor an Order Mark or a Discipline Mark, depending on the seriousness of the infraction. Fifteen Order Marks or three Discipline Marks in any one term landed you in deep trouble: the risk of expulsion.

At first I paid little heed to this announcement, since I wasn't in the habit of breaking school rules on a large scale. But it created quite a buzz, and speculation started as to which of the naughty girls in the school would first find herself in danger of expulsion. As I walked home that day, it dawned on me that this new system gave a clear-cut measure of naughtiness ... *It protected one from the danger of inadvertently stepping over the mark*. It might now be possible to *safely* join the ranks of the naughty, with the attendant popularity that this label carried! Would it work? Would a "naughty" label negate the unpopularity that went with being at, or near, the top of the class? I wasn't sure. But it was worth a try! The elation that flooded through me, making my knees all wobbly after I reached this decision, surprised even me; and made me aware of just how large the issue of social rejection had started to loom. I felt like I was walking on air ... but kept reminding myself that this new scheme might fail, might be even shorter-lived than its predecessor had been.

Thus began a new and exciting phase in my life. I carefully controlled my rate of acquisition of Order Marks and Discipline Marks, maximizing their number yet avoiding risk of serious trouble. For the first time ever, I acquired the labels "naughty" *and* "popular"! Plan B worked beyond my wildest dreams, and I was able to relax about my scholastic level, at long last.

What a relief it was to simply let the chips fall where they may, academically. And what fun I had! The new discipline scheme became a great game. We almost dared prefects to catch us breaking rules (playing hide-and-seek behind the air raid shelters, and other such acts of derring-do. It all seems so petty, in retrospect!)

The Order Mark totals were read out at Assembly on Monday mornings, with the goal of shaming the Forms with high totals, but this backfired, and a lively inter-class rivalry for the highest total developed. I became a major contributor to my Form's success in this competition, and my popularity grew by leaps and bounds. The unexpected success of Plan B left me dizzy with joy, but the prefects who initiated the new discipline scheme must have regretted doing so. We ran them ragged while having a lot of fun at their expense, and the school-rule breakage rate must have been at an all time high—not exactly what they had in mind. However, their new scheme had provided me with the perfect solution to my problem, and at the end of term I took home a good report card without enduring butterflies in my stomach.

◆ ◆ ◆

The memories that persist from the summer of that year, the year of 1943, are of long walks through London streets. Many of the streets had great gaps, like missing teeth, with shells of houses and piles of rubble; but a few were oddly intact, the only signs of war being heavily taped windows; and side streets like Aquinas Street had window-less, brick air-raid shelters along the middle of the road and were almost unrecognizable.

My mother and I must have walked miles that summer, always in search of some off-the-ration delicacy, oranges or bananas or broken biscuits—anything to relieve the monotony of the wartime diet. All it took was a whisper that, "Benner's dahn the Boro's got bananas," and off we trotted, with Maureen in the pram and her green ration book in Mum's handbag. For bananas, though not rationed, were reserved for the under-five crowd, those with a green ration book. Sometimes we got there too late, and Mum would grumble, "Waste o' bloomin' shoe leather, that was!" as we retraced our steps; but a successful excursion put her in a good mood for days.

Our most distant foraging trips were to a biscuit factory where, once in while, broken biscuits [cookies] were to be had. We rarely purchased packets of biscuits, because that meant parting with precious coupons needed for canned goods—corned beef, baked beans, sardines, or tins of fruit—deemed more important than biscuits. So the mere mention of coupon-free broken biscuits sent us hurrying to join a long line of fellow ration-supplementers, and Mum was doubly triumphant when I was with her because I could pass as an adult, and we went home with two bags of treasure. If you've never experienced the pleasure of catching a whiff of the mixed aromas emanating from a paper bag full of broken biscuits, then dipping your hand in not knowing what delicious fragment will emerge between your fingers, it's probably impossible to convey how much more exciting it was than simply taking an unbroken cookie out of a packet.

It was especially pleasurable to adolescents like Derek and me, at our most ravenous for sweet things at a moment in history when sugar, honey, jam, syrup, and even sweets themselves were rationed. Our mother seemed to understand this craving. For the mid-day meal on Thursdays and Fridays—meatless days because the week's meat ration had been exhausted—she made pancakes, or a suet pudding steamed with treacle at the bottom of the bowl, or a Spotted Dick with plump moist raisins embedded throughout. These became our favorite days of the week: not only was our sugar-need being met, but our stepfather was safely at work, so the meal was not eaten under his malevolent grudging glare, and we could savor these yummy puddings to the full.

Mum was not a particularly good or imaginative cook, but her pancakes were out of this world, bearing no resemblance to the soggy, heavy things produced by a pancake mix. I don't think mixes were available then, but she would have spurned them, in any case. And with good cause. From flour, eggs, milk, and some vigorous whisking with a large fork, she produced a thin, golden, crispy pancake, more like a crepe I suppose, which we sprinkled with lemon juice and sugar before rolling it up and adding just a little more sugar on top. To this day, I salivate, just thinking about those pancakes. During the war lemons were hard to come by, and we made do with a sharp-tasting jam, gooseberry or rhubarb, so Mum's pancakes were not always up to her pre-war lemony version. On the other hand, before the war this delectable treat had been served only once a year, on Shrove Tuesday; now we had pancakes with fair regularity. What we lost on the swings we won on the roundabouts!

For Mum, the quest for off-ration goodies was the motivation for our long walks, but for me, simply pushing my baby sister in her pram was a treat in its own right. I was more entranced than ever by Maureen, now that she was a freckled two-year-old with huge blue eyes, long curling dark lashes and an engaging grin. She was just learning to string words together, and I was fascinated. How did she do it? In school, French and Latin had to be pounded into our thick heads in a systematic way, along with written and oral exercises. Yet this little thing, exposed to the English language in a more or less random fashion, picked it up with no apparent effort, no exercises, no prior knowledge of grammar, no acquaintance with verbs, nouns, and adjectives—and she made fewer mistakes than we bumbling schoolgirls did. When I mentioned this to Mum, she shrugged impatiently and said, "I dunno. Bu' I did it, an' yew did it. *All* babies do it, ya daft thing!" She could see nothing remarkable in a two-year-old's acquisition of language. But for me, it was—and still is—wondrous, despite Naom Chomsky's ideas about in-built brain wiring. In fact, that makes the whole business even more intriguing.

In the countless miles that we traversed that summer, my mother and I, we also covered many of her stories. Some were familiar re-runs, which I was only too happy to hear again, but a few new stories surfaced, including one about my parents' early days together before I was born. This was a time of which I knew very little, other than a few scraps and shreds suggesting that they'd been happy, "tho' we did 'ave our stormy days," Mum always added. This was hardly surprising: my mother was temperamentally disinclined to pass many days without waxing indignant about something or other, and my father, apparently, had quite a temper, "'specially after a few beers." This particular story spilled out as we were walking past the OXO tower, near Blackfriars Bridge, and she suddenly announced:

"Yer Dad used ta work there. A bloomin' good job it was, too, till 'e lost it after 'avin' a fight with the foreman. 'Ad ta go ta court, 'e did, becos 'e broke the fella's nose. A nasty piece o' work 'e was, tha' foreman. 'E'd bin givin' short money ta one o' the men—a poor devil what was a bit simple in the 'ead—an' when yer Dad found out, 'e saw red an' went fer the foreman. A real Irish paddy yer father 'ad, but then 'is mother was Irish, so that's 'ardly surprisin'. An' 'e was big an' strong, then, so 'e made shaw that foreman thought twice b'fore shortchangin' any o' the men agin! When the magistrate 'eard what the fight was about, 'e let yer father off with a warnin'. Said 'e might'a done the same thing 'isself!

"Bu' yer Dad lost 'is job at the OXO plant an' 'ad ta go back ta the buildin' trade. Which wasn't as reg'lar an' didn't pay as well. It was outside work, too, in all weathers, which didn't do 'is chest any good. After that, I told 'im I wasn't goin' ta put up with 'im gettin' inta fights. If 'e wanted ta keep *me*, 'e 'ad ta keep 'is temper too. An' from that day on, 'e jus' stopped goin' ta the pub. An' never let 'is temper get the bet'er of 'im agin. A good 'usband 'e was. A good father, too. Never once did 'e s'much as raise 'is 'and ta yew three kiddies. An' the boys could be li'l devils at times! Auntie Ada always says, 'I don't know 'ow ya did it, May, bu' yew shaw tamed Joe!'"

◆　◆　◆

At the end of the summer I slid, more or less seamlessly, back into the routines of my Merstham life, where one of my responsibilities was taking care of a dozen or so rabbits that dwelt in cobbled-together hutches against the garden fence. Their sole purpose in life seemed to be to eat as much as they could, as quickly as they could, and to produce baby rabbits with equal rapidity; my job was to encourage them in these activities, so as to keep a plentiful supply of rabbit meat on the Redfern table to supplement the meat ration. To this end, I kept their hutches clean and lined with straw, and gathered enough dandelion leaves and vetch to accelerate the process. I rather enjoyed roaming the nearby fields and hedgerows, filling sacks with all this green stuff, but I was never able to swallow a mouthful of what was left of those furry, trusting, nose-twitchers after Uncle Reg had broken their necks and Aunt Lil had skinned them. Epecially those that had been born and reared on my watch. When rabbit was on the menu, I became a vegetarian.

My dandelion foraging paid off handsomely when I learned that the government paid good money for rose hips (to make rose hip syrup for British babies) and acorns (for feeding British pigs), because I knew where abundant sources of hips and acorns were to be found. Having sworn my friends to secrecy, the four of us supplemented our pocket money substantially. It was seasonal income, of course, but this probably helped to sustain the excitement.

The quest for hips (the vegetable variety?) also aroused the interest of a group of three boys from our "brother" school, the evacuated half of St. Dunstan's School for Boys. We'd been vaguely aware of them in their navy and white uniforms, going to and from school; especially the tall, blond, pimply one, who always rode his bike to school and was taunted by us from the back window of the bus when it overtook him on a hill. They, like us, were keen to augment their pocket money, and they took to following us when we went out armed with empty sacks. We were mean and never led them to the "good" spots, but they continued to dog our footsteps well after the hip-and-acorn season was over, and eventually we got on friendly terms with them—surprise, surprise! There was no pairing off however, to my relief; I dreaded the certain prospect of being the "left over"girl. (Possibly all four of us felt that way. But we never discussed it.)

The boys were more generous than we had been and introduced us to *their* closely-kept secret: a disused sand quarry with a deep pond and railway lines and some rusty old hopper cars that had been used to transport loads of sand to waiting lorries. It didn't take long to devise an exciting game that we called Riding-A-Hopper, which entailed clearing the rails of wind-blown sand, then putting our shoulders to a hopper and pushing it as far as we could up the hill before clambering in and being carried back down. There was always the question of where it would come to a halt ... *before* reaching the pond, hopefully. We were always braced, ready to leap out, but it never proved necessary, though we had some close calls. It was an exhilarating, clunking, clattering ride—and hideously dangerous. Apart from the chance of ending up in that deep, deep, pond, I now shudder to think that if one of us had slipped as we were pushing the hopper up the hill, the rest of us could not have held it in place. There was space for only one person to lie flat between the narrow gauge rails, and the others could not, all of them, have scrambled out of the hopper's path. We never discussed these dangers, but were well aware of them, I think. Which is probably why we solemnly swore never to divulge this secret place, especially to the adults in our lives.

It turned out that we girls were a necessary part of Riding-A-Hopper, because seven shoulders were required for the pushing-uphill part. This did make us wonder to what extent our maidenly charms had played a role in the boys' overtures ... but we had such a good time at the quarry, that we didn't let this bother us. Actually, six shoulders would have sufficed had they all been male, but, like us, our St. Dunstan's trio didn't seem interested in getting together with their local peers. This was a curious feature of all evacuees, I now realize, though I never gave it a moment's thought at the time: we tended to stick together and not mix with local kids; and they, likewise. Josephine was the only exception that I made in my six years as an evacuee; and that didn't really count, because she was essentially part of the family I was living with. Why such clannishness? I don't know. Each school certainly tried to foster in its students a sense of pride in their school, though there was none of the pep rally rah-rah-rah of an American High School; the British version of that time focussed more on "dignity." Most likely, the reluctance to establish "mixed" friendships was due, on both sides, to the fact that being an evacuee was necessarily a transitory business, we all hoped.

Even when our numbers were too low for Riding-A-Hopper, we were drawn to the quarry like iron filings to a magnet. With its mini-caves and occasional outcrops of sandstone rocks, it was a fantastic place to explore. You could even try your hand at cliff climbing, being guaranteed a nice soft landing on the sand. Although the still black waters of the pond conjured up enticing images of jumping in and splashing around, we were limited to skipping stones across its smooth surface until the weather warmed up.

A major school event that autumn was Parents' Day, and for weeks I looked forward to showing off my little sister to friends and teachers, but the day was a disaster from beginning to end. Maureen had a cold and was whiny and cross from being woken up to get off the bus; not a word could be coaxed out of her, whereas Maggie's little sister, Katy, was on top form, chatting and singing and dancing on request. Even Maureen's new coat, purchased for the occasion and—as always—"bought on the big side, so she c'n grow into it," didn't look as nice as Katy's, which fitted her to perfection. Katy was about a year older than Maureen, so I should have been prepared for her superior accomplishments, but I was mortified to see all the girls clustering around this dimpled Shirley Temple of a child, ooh-ing and aah-ing, and ignoring Maureen who spent the day clinging to Mum's neck.

The greatest mortification came, however, when I glanced down and noticed my mother's shoes: so shabby and worn, with their trodden-over heels. She'd done her best to make them presentable, but no amount of polish and elbow grease could hide the fact that they were on their last legs, literally. I knew that Mum had done her best to put on a good show for me, but I couldn't wait for that wretched day to come to an end. And shame, that I was ashamed of feeling, welled up in me.

At the end of term, I arrived home for Christmas to find my mother ill in bed with erysipelas. This highly infectious skin disease is extremely painful, and the slightest movement made Mum, usually such a stoic, scream and sob. Sharing a bed had become unthinkable for her, so she'd already abandoned the marital bed for the spare bed upstairs, but the tiniest vibrations of the floor, impossible to avoid no matter how carefully you crept across the room, reduced her to a wailing huddle of pain. Never had I heard such shrieks, not even little Helen Green's, when she lay in that evacuee hospital with rheumatic fever. To spare Maureen as much as possible, I made Derek take her out of the house during the day when the weather permitted, and it was, in some ways, a relief when Mum was taken to hospital on the morning of Christmas Eve. But, in my head, I can still hear her screams as she was carried down the stairs on a stretcher and put into the waiting ambulance. The arrival of an ambulance had attracted the usual little crowd, but even these spectacle seekers were subdued by Mum's agony.

Arrangements had already been made for us—of course—how could I have thought otherwise, I guiltily asked myself? But I *had* wondered, and it was a huge relief to learn that we would not be staying with Jack Weddinger— whose response to this crisis had been to spend more time than usual down the pub. Maureen and I were to go to Louie's, and Derek, to Auntie Ada's. Our stepfather shouted and hollered about being left to his own devices over Christmas, but Louie told him in no uncertain terms, "If yew fink I'm gonna cook Christmas dinner fer *yew,* yew've got annuvva fink comin', mate! I'll 'elp wiv the kids till May gits 'ome, bu' yew're big enough an' ugly enough ta take care o' yerself!" Helped by the fact that he was a wee bit beer-befuddled, she whisked the three of us out of the house before he fully realized what was happening. However, she was afraid that he might, lawfully, chase after her and re-claim Maureen, the only one of us that he cared about. And for a couple of nervous days, we dreaded every ring of the doorbell. We weren't allowed to visit Mum in the isolation hospital, and this was hard on Maureen who was too young to understand why her Mummy was suddenly not there.

But Louie got regular bulletins on Mum's slow improvement, so we were able to relax on that score, too, and concentrate on making the best of this disrupted Holiday.

Harry was, by now, in the Air Force and hadn't scrounged any Christmas leave, so Louie had been planning to spend Christmas Day with Aunt-mum and what was left of that crowd. For it was a diminished number that sat around Aunt-mum's big oval table these days. Viley, now married to her Tom, was with him on some army base; Georgie was on yet another army base, but without his comfort-loving Kitty, who wasn't about to be shuffled around at the whim of "some ol' gen'ral." Maureen and I were, of course, welcomed with open arms by big-hearted Aunt-mum, but on Christmas morning we woke to find Maureen covered in big, blistery spots—a full-blown case of chicken pox. She was decidedly cranky and not even interested in the few toys that Louie had rushed out to buy the night before, just so that there was *something* from Father Christmas in the poor child's stocking. Aunt-mum brought round some dinner and Christmas pudding and mince pies, but it was a singularly un-Christmassy Christmas Day; the worst yet, I think, though not as strange as the previous one in the echoing corridors of an empty school.

Two days later I, too, had chicken pox. And jaundice, reminiscent of when I had German measles in Pulham. At mealtimes, the mirror over the fireplace gave me an uninterrupted view of my spotty, yellowed visage, and I begged Louie to let me sit in Harry's seat with my back to it. But she said firmly, "Nope … that's 'Arry's seat. I'm savin' it fer 'im … when this bloomin' war is over." So I had to endure the spectacle of my un-pretty face every mealtime, whenever I looked up. When Mum came out of the hospital, we dreaded dealing with the man of the house, who was probably spitting mad still, but he actually seemed pleased to see us and came as close to purring as I ever heard; for a week or two, at least. But by then I had escaped and was back at school.

That otherwise bleak Christmas did yield one very pleasant surprise in the form of a parcel from Betty Marsh, the girl with elegant clothes and unbitten fingernails, with whom I'd sat through an uneasy tea several years earlier. There was a note inside suggesting that we write to one another, and, to that end, the parcel contained a leather wallet holding matching paper and envelopes—and a splendid fountain pen with a *gold* nib, no less! Betty, apparently, had just finished college, whatever that was, and was now a teacher of Domestic Science (one of the Unimportant Subjects in Plan A; I'd have to be careful not to let *that* slip, I thought). She also enclosed a postal order for a bottle of ink, so she *really* did mean for me to write back.

At first, I had no idea what to say to this girl-now-teacher. *A teacher?* So quickly? Teachers were, by definition, old; yet it seemed like yesterday that she and I, both schoolgirls, had sat in a restaurant, not knowing what to say to one another. Happily, her letter was full of excited chit-chat about her new school and the girls she was teaching, so I was able to respond, more or less in kind, from my perspective as a student in what sounded like a similar school. The new fountain pen was pure delight: it didn't snag on the up-strokes, nor flood on the down strokes; neither did it run out of ink every few words like an ordinary pen. Not many girls had a fountain pen, let alone one of such high quality, so it was a wonderful status symbol—my first since acquiring Viley's old blue bike in Aquinas Street. I've no idea what prompted Betty to start this correspondence with me, but I did come to enjoy it. It gave unexpected glimpses into school-life as seen by a teacher, though I doubt whether I, viewing it from the other end of the telescope, added anything that Betty didn't already know from her own time at my end.

Back in school, after Christmas, we were introduced to a new teacher and a new subject: physics. The teacher, Mrs. Bamber-Bowtell, was an eccentric lady more commonly referred to as Mrs. B, but *never, ever,* to her face. We didn't dare, even the boldest among us, for we were all in awe of Mrs. Bamber-Bowtell. In our ill-lit Rosemead classroom, with no equipment for demonstrations, Mrs. B managed to bring the difficult topic of electro-magnetism to life. She simply did a lot of swaying and hand-waving to illustrate what was happening to the electrons in a piece of copper wire that she pushed and pulled through the imaginary fields with which she had filled the room. Since this large-bosomed lady seemed to wear no brassiere, there was also a lot happening in the region of her free-flowing breasts, so her exertions engendered plenty of interest and amusement, even for those whose imaginations were not sparked by electro-magnetism. But I was captivated by Mrs. B, by her deep, sonorous voice and by her passion for her subject; for the first time, I found myself excited by science—though most of my classmates groaned at the very mention of physics.

However, the school event that most absorbed my class, the Lower Fifth form, that spring, was our production of a mini-opera, *Papageno*—a loose adaptation of a sub-plot of Mozart's *The Magic Flute.* It was a bold, demanding venture for a cast of fourteen- to fifteen-year-old girls, but we were fortunate in having an able, ambitious music teacher, and enough singers with good voices to pull it off. I had expected an opera to be a ho-hum affair and was pleasantly surprised to discover that I thoroughly enjoyed it. Of course, I was not one of the singers, not even a member of the chorus, but I got involved backstage, and Mozart's music lodged itself firmly in my head, though I was unaware of this until some years later.

According to Uncle Reg's colored pins, the war was going rather better by this time, the spring of 1944. But in our corner of England, it suddenly impinged on our lives in ways that were hard to ignore when the Germans started sending flying bombs. They were targeted on London, but often exhausted their fuel before reaching London and fell in the Surrey area. The nasty thing was that there was no warning: no siren, nothing but the drone of the doodlebug's engine in the sky. Oddly enough, you were safe as long as you could hear that drone. The moment the engine noise stopped and the sky was filled with an eerie silence, you knew that the bomb would start its downward trajectory and it was time to take cover—or, at least, fling yourself on the ground as protection against blast. The only successful product that ever emerged from my Domestic Science class—a pastry-wrapped apple dumpling, of which I was inordinately proud—was reduced to a splatter on the sidewalk when Peggy pulled me down to the ground during one of those nerve-racking silences.

Then came news that Aunt Mary's brother was Missing In Action. His plane had failed to return from a bombing mission over Germany, and a pall of gloom spread over the house. Aunt Mary's eyes were permanently red-rimmed, and old Aunt Lil spent hours standing at the window humming, hugging Norma and rocking to and fro. Until, one day, I walked into the kitchen and the pall was lifted: Aunt Mary's brother was alive, after all! "We don't know if he's hurt. An' he'll be in a German prisoner o' war camp 'til this bloomin' war's over. But at least he won't be up in a plane gettin' shot at, night after night," said Aunt Mary, smiling through her tears, tears of joy, this time. "We'll all sleep better, knowing that. 'Specially me poor ol' Mum and Dad. They've bin worried stiff about him fer months, now."

After that, a lot of things happened, very fast indeed, and by mid-July my Merstham world was a thing of the past. First came a two-week stint at a Farming Camp in Lincolnshire with my class, which was our small contribution to the War Effort. Accompanied by a group of Italian prisoners-of-war, we picked potatoes and weeded carrots—backbreaking tasks, whether working your way along an endless row of potatoes or an equally endless row of carrots that appeared to stretch to the horizon in those flat, hedge-less, red-soiled fields. As a change from school routine, it was fun. But the food was terrible. Especially lunch: everyday, it consisted of some horrible cheese (made by straining sour milk through muslin) between two great "doorsteps" of dry bread. The smell of that cheese made me gag if it came within an inch of my nose, let alone my mouth, and I must have lost about ten pounds. This was, no doubt, good for my waistline, but it left me pretty cranky. On carrot-weeding days, I was hungry enough to scrape the dirt off a carrot or two, but the result was an unsatisfactory gritty mouthful.

Then, in the middle of the second week, as if sleeping in wooden cabins with all your friends, weren't excitement enough, Maggie was suddenly whisked away and sent home. In disgrace, we were told. We were never told what she'd done, and the rumor mill jumped into high gear, with whisperings of misdeeds with an Italian prisoner-of-war—something about "fraternizing." (Nobody was sure what that meant, since it didn't seem to have anything to do with a brother, as suggested by our knowledge of Latin.) The remaining members of our foursome closed ranks and did not divulge what we now suspected might be evidence of Maggie's "crime": her occasional disappearances during the lunch break. We hadn't thought much about them at the time and weren't sure that they had anything to do with a POW, but out of loyalty to Maggie, we kept quiet. We were upset, though, and would have been much more upset had we known that we'd seen the last of our friend. For Maggie did not return to Honor Oak School—and we never learned why.

Meantime, I had other things on my mind. My mother's weekly letter failed to arrive, and I tried to convince myself that she'd simply forgotten I was at Farming Camp. But as the days ticked by and there was no forwarded letter from Aunt Mary, I got worried and couldn't help thinking of the other time this had happened: when the unexploded bomb landed on our Aquinas Street doorstep. Toward the end of the second week, at the peak of the Maggie crisis, a letter finally arrived—in Mum's familiar handwriting, but from an unfamiliar place.

What was she doing in Sussex, I wondered, as I tore the envelope open—and learned that my fears had been justified. A flying bomb had destroyed the top three floors of our house, but praise be, everybody had been in the basement shelter and had escaped without as much as a scratch. Indeed, Maureen hadn't even woken! Seeing all the rubble surrounding the Morrison table the next morning, she had simply lisped, "Oh-h! What a meth!" Finding replacement housing in bomb-damaged London had proved to be impossible, Mum said, so the family had gone down to Hove (on the South Coast, just outside Brighton). The coast area had been evacuated in the early days of the war, but danger of invasion across the Channel was no longer a threat, so it had been opened up, and housing was available there. "Will let you know our new address when we find something," the letter finished, and with that, I had to be content.

After farming camp, I arrived back in Merstham to find Aunt Lil again ensconced at the window, humming and rocking back and forth with Norma clutched close. "With good cause, the poor ol' soul," said Aunt Mary. "Her Neddie's bin killed. In Italy. After all these years ... since the war first started, he's bin fightin'. An' just when we started to think the war was almost over, an' she was lookin' forward to him comin' home fer good ... " Her eyes brimmed over, and she could say no more. Five-year-old Jackie was bewildered by the sudden preoccupied air of all the grown-ups in her life, and I did what I could to create diversions for her. We fished for minnows and went to the park where she made rapid progress in the arts of "pumping" a swing and making daisy chains. But flying bombs had un-nerved Aunt Mary to the point that she rarely even turned the radio on—for fear of missing that telltale drone and its sudden cessation—and was reluctant to let Jackie out of her sight. So I couldn't get the poor child out of that house of sadness very often, except to help me feed the rabbits. This she loved to do, so the rabbits did rather well. And I spent a lot of time scavenging for extra greenery.

I don't know how old Aunt Lil would have survived without Norma to cuddle and rock. At first, Aunt Mary generously surrendered her little daughter to the grieving old lady, though she did sometimes mutter, "That baby'll get spoiled rotten!" But then Aunt Lil got it into her head that Hope was to blame for Neddie's death: "If that 'Ope 'adn't given up me flat, me poor Ned would've bin given one o' them compash'nt 'xceptions. An' would've bin 'ome takin' care o' me, all fru' this bloody war ... 'stead o' bein' in Italy." Uncle Reg tried to tell her that—at best—Neddie would have been granted compassionate leave, not an exemption from military service. But nothing could shift the Hope-is-to-blame bee that was lodged in Aunt Lil's bonnet, and before long, Aunt Mary's sympathy for the old lady turned sour. The atmosphere in the house then grew so fraught that it was a relief to leave it behind every day when I went to school.

How long this lasted, I don't know, because the days of Honor Oak School in the Reigate area were numbered. Indeed, they had dwindled to one, we were told at Assembly one morning. The school was to be re-evacuated the following day because of the flying bombs, and we were dismissed from school immediately, to give us time to get ready for our departure the next morning for some destination unknown. Everything had to fit on the luggage rack of a train—or bus, no one knew which—so we were to bring only one suitcase and a satchel. No more, it was stressed. Apart from our gas masks and ration books, those essential wartime items. Walking home from school that morning, we were pretty subdued and scared. Yet, somewhere deep down, we couldn't help feeling excited. Where were we going? It had to be quite far, we agreed, to be beyond the reach of doodlebugs. Scotland? Yorkshire? Wales? (Possibly Gloucester, I wondered. Was there a faint hope of seeing Gloria again?)

"Maybe even Canada," Peggy hazarded. "Some kids I used ta know were evacuated there." That gave us pause. And made us realize that it might be a very long time indeed before we'd see our families again. Then more mundane concerns surfaced:

"Oh-h, I hope we don't go by bus ... I always get sick on buses."

"Me, too!"

"D'ya think St. Dunstan's will go to the same place as us?"

"We won't half miss the quarry."

"Rosemead, too! It's been a great place for a school ... "

"Great for Sticky Toffee, too!"

(Sticky Toffee was a "tag" game in which everyone who'd been caught joined hands, so the chain of catchers grew longer and longer, and more and more unwieldy—yet harder and harder to evade. Rosemead's big lawns had provided the perfect setting, and it had been the game of choice at lunchtime for quite a while.)

"Will all our teachers come, too?"

"I bet Skinny and Collywobbles won't ... they like that cottage of theirs too much."

"And Isaiah won't leave her old Mum. Or her budgie, that she's always on about!"

Inoffensive little Miss Wilson had acquired the nickname "Isaiah," the first day she set foot in the school. One glance at her lop-sided face had started the giggled whispers: "Look! One eye's 'igher than the other!" Initially cruel, in the thoughtless manner of schoolgirls, this nickname became a term of affection as we grew to love this gentle soul, who blushed so easily and struggled so valiantly to teach us Mathematics.

"Which teachers d'you hope *don't* come?"

This agreeable topic carried us all the way home, allowing us to avoid the *dis*agreeable aspects of the changes we faced the next day. I lay in bed that night, after a weepy evening with the Redfern family, and marveled at having been at the same address for two and a half years—a lifetime record! And I drew comfort from the thought that tomorrow's journey, to another unknown place and another family of strangers, would be undertaken in the company of my friends. This time, I wouldn't have to start all over again with *everything*: location, family, teachers *and* friends.

◆　　◆　　◆

ADDENDUM

Not long ago, I read an article about babies born with indeterminate gender and realized that the hypothesis with which Peggy and I had wrestled and firmly rejected was not as preposterous as we had thought. Whether it was, in fact, the correct explanation for all the "goings-on," after Norma was born, is another question, one of many to which I will never know the answer; and I am more than happy to leave this one unexplored. As far as I know, Norma grew up to be a perfectly normal girl. According to Aunt Lil's great-granddaughter Gillian:

> [Norma] married Bruce [who] owned a fish and chip shop in a parade of shops on an estate [development] on the outskirts of Hertford ... I popped into the shop one day, and Norma was working there. She reminded me so much of the "Old Lady," [Aunt Lil] little and round, but she had a very beautiful face and lovely dark hair. Sadly Norma died some years ago, and I have now lost touch with that side of the family.

Dark? The Norma I knew was so blond. Though she did have those dramatic dark eyebrows and lashes. But like Gillian, I had lost touch with that branch of the family and didn't know what changes the intervening years had wrought. I, too, felt saddened that Norma, she of the lively personality and lovely face, had died so young. It seemed wrong that she, for whose birth I had fetched the midwife one wild, dark night, should be dead while I was still alive.

Chapter 25

Off Again!

"IT'S WALES! WE'RE GOING to Wales!" The cry ran the length of the train, carried by excited girls racing along the corridor. They stopped to open the door of each compartment, hoping to be the first with this news, and great was the disappointment if greeted by a chorus of, "Tell us something we don't know!"

We tried to picture what our destination might look like, but our collective knowledge of Wales was limited to the fact that it was mountainous and in the West, as far West as you could go without a boat. Patty Morgan, who had an uncle in Wales, said, "they have funny long names for places an' speak Welsh."

"A different language? Ya mean they won't understand us?"

"Will we have to learn Welsh?"

"Depends what part of Wales. In South Wales everyone speaks English, I think," said Patty. That gave a crumb of comfort to those not eager to burden their overtaxed brains with yet another foreign language; with any luck, we might end up in that part of Wales.

"And they sing a lot, my uncle says."

"*Sing?* Why?"

"I dunno … but they have lovely voices, he says."

"It rains a lot, too." Again according to the Welsh uncle.

"Because of the mountains, perhaps … Remember Skinny … 'the hot air rises and cools … and then comes tri-c-k-l-ing down'!" Suddenly, we were all waving arms and wiggling fingers, Skinny fashion, giggling at the memory. But in other respects, we were as uninformed about mountains as we were about Wales. None of us had ever seen one, and an argument developed as to how tall a hill had to be before it was a mountain. The guesses ranged from three hundred feet to ten thousand feet, but Skinny wasn't around to ask; as predicted, she had stayed in Reigate, along with several other teachers.

Later we were told that we'd be billeted in pairs where possible, and that we could choose our "partner," as long as we chose *sensibly*. We all knew what that meant. Troublemakers would *not* be put together, and we did not need to be told who the troublemakers were. Peggy and I looked at one another in delight. We could live in the same house. Something we'd often wished! However, a solemn discussion then ensued among the girls of the Lower Fifth, and after lengthy deliberations, a consensus emerged that it would be better if "best friends" were not together; it might be too much of a good thing, it was felt; their friendship could be jeopardized.

When I look back, this seems an extra-ordinary conclusion for a bunch of fifteen-year-olds to reach, in a train *en route* to an unfamiliar new world. It was perhaps a wise one: friendships did seem to get frayed when best friends chose to live in the same household. On the other hand, teen-age friendships are tenuous at best, and maybe those who chose the sacrifice of separation had a point to prove. For it *was* a sacrifice. When Peggy and I decided to split up and swap partners with another twosome, I remember the sense of relinquishing a splendid opportunity and of doing something that was somehow noble in the interest of friendship. Of course, we had no idea whether there was any real basis for our sacrifice, and it was with considerable trepidation that each of us embarked on living at close quarters with a girl we didn't know particularly well.

In Cardiff we changed to a smaller and slower train, and soon the countryside became hillier, causing us to wonder whether these were mountains that we were now looking at. As the valley narrowed, we had to crane our necks to see the top of the hills (mountains?) on either side and sensed that we must be nearing our destination; the excitement mounted, mingled with apprehension about this world we were about to enter. Our destination turned out to be Tredegar, a small mining town in South Wales where everyone did speak English, to the relief of those not fond of foreign languages. I have no recollection of how we were matched with host families, though had there been an "auction," as in Dorset, I think I would have remembered.

In my first distinct Tredegar memory, I am standing in a narrow hall with Kay Warmley, meeting our two Welsh "Aunties," and am suddenly aware of the difference between Kay's gleaming new luggage and mine—the shabby suitcase that I'd carried to Dorset five years earlier. Upstairs in our bedroom, it became clear that there was a huge difference in the contents of our cases, too. Mine contained one outfit in addition to my school uniform, while Kay's had several, much fancier than mine. I began to have grave misgivings about this partnership. In Reigate I'd known Kay only in school, always in school uniform, and I had never suspected that she might be posh. Later that evening, when the Aunts were asking about our families, it transpired that Kay's father was the headmaster of a grammar school—a boys' version of Honor Oak. My heart sank. I felt out of my league, not sure that I knew how to handle this. Perhaps I should have stuck with Peggy, after all.

However, it was Kay who had the biggest adjustments to make. With her background, it was hard for her to get used to working class folks like the Aunts. Then there was the issue of the bed: she and I had to share a bed, a capacious double bed, but Kay was horrified that the two of us were expected to sleep in it. Every night she did her best to create her own "space" in its voluminous feather mattress, reminding me of Aunt Etty's old dog, and the way he spent ages going round and round in circles, treading down the bedding to his satisfaction before settling down at the foot of her bed. The mattress Kay had to work with was too soft and yielding to maintain the separation she carefully created, and to her chagrin, we invariably woke to find ourselves snuggled together in the central hollow created by our bodies. Eventually, we figured out that if we wedged the bolster (a bed-wide tubular kind of pillow) between us, it made a satisfactory divider, and Kay became (almost) reconciled to the proximity of our sleeping bodies.

Of course, the Aunts too had to make adjustments and get used to the invasion of their quiet household by these two "galumphing gurrt gurrls," as Auntie Megan called us, in her lovely lilting version of English. So infectious was the cadence of this local accent, the rising pitch at the end of each phrase making every statement sound like a question, that I was soon echoing it. By the time I'd added, "look you, mun," and "whateffa!" and "indeed t'goodness!" to my repertoire, I was often mistaken for a local, "not wan o' they 'vacuees frrum London." This error was compounded by the fact that I bore a Welsh name. The Aunts were tickled pink to discover that Gwen was really Gwynneth, not Gwendolyn, but equally disappointed to learn that I had not one drop of Welsh blood in my veins; the nearest connection was my father's dying buddy in the trenches of Flanders. And they were pretty disgusted that my parents hadn't known how to spell the name. "It's G-w-y-n-n-e-d-d, look you, whateffa!" expostulated Auntie Blodwen. They refused to use the shortened version by which I'd been known all my life: to them, I was Gwynnedd-bach and Kay was Katy-bach. She was furious that such a liberty should be taken with her name, and when out hearing of the Aunts, she'd splutter, "I hope my mother never hears them calling me Katy! She'd have a fit. She chose Kay because it was a name no one could mess about with—she thought!"

Aunties Blodwen and Megan never knew of Kay's nightly ordeal and frequently reminded us how lucky we were to have the most comfortable bed in the house, *and* the warmest room—over the kitchen where the coal-fired range was kept going day and night, summer or winter. Not that there was much difference between the seasons in the rainy mountains of South Wales. (Patty Morgan's uncle was right about the rain.) In this valley, coal was provided at very low cost to miners and their families—an old-style fringe benefit—and since the Aunts' father had worked in the mine all his life, his daughters enjoyed a generous supply that kept their big old range well stoked. At some point—"t'was for a song, look you," said Auntie Blodwen—the two sisters had purchased the little stone house in which they'd lived as children, and were, quite rightly, proud of how well they "kep' it up, look yew!" They'd even added a hot water system and a full-sized bathroom, which was music to my ears—as was my delight to theirs. I think Kay wondered what all the fuss was about, but I hadn't known such luxury since being cast out in disgrace over the rice pudding. It was also a novelty for me to live in a house owned by its occupants, and I was enormously impressed by these two sisters. How my mother would love to be the owner of this little house, I often thought. There'd be no more hassles about repairs with the rent-lady.

The house in question was on Albert Terrace, one of many such terraces that stepped up the mountain-side, leaving a green cap that revealed the shape of the mountain beneath this slate-gray encrustation. Each terrace was a long row of identical houses, packed cheek to jowl with no alleys or gaps, tiny houses with tiny, low-ceilinged rooms, two up and two down, and an outside toilet; few of them had an extra bedroom over an added-on bathroom, like the Aunts' house. I had never been in a house so tiny, yet it had the largest door key that had ever hung on a string around my neck; about seven inches long, it was, and it weighed a ton! The front door with its brightly polished, brass knocker, opened straight on to the street, but at the back, a long, narrow garden climbed steeply up to the stone wall of the next terrace. In that strip of black earth, the Aunts grew a few vegetables, prominent among them, leeks, of course (the vegetable of choice in Wales). To Kay's dismay. She hated leeks.

Auntie Megan, plain and mousy, was the tiny, stay-at-home, spinster sister; Auntie Blodwen, big-boned and statuesque, was a widow and went to work every day over in the next valley—doing something of major importance in the pay office of the steel works of Ebbw Vale, we were told repeatedly. "We-l-l, look you! Somewan 'as ta bring 'ome the bacon, don't they now!" she would say. "And poor Megan-bach, she's not up ta that, are ye m'gurrl? The Good Lorrd, He saw to it that she was prrovided ferrr when He took my Dai-William frrum me beforrr we'd any littl'uns." She was a handsome woman, with a thick head of wavy, dark hair, which, every night, she released from the head-hugging braids in which it had been confined all day and allowed to tumble down. Almost to her waist it fell, and Megan then brushed those gleaming tresses with long, patient strokes while the two sisters sat by the glowing embers of the fire.

It *was* a lovely sight, that hair, but woe betides us if we didn't make enough appreciative noises, and it verged on the suicidal to draw attention to the occasional gray hair midst all that glossy splendor. For Auntie Blodwen was a vain woman, and sharp-tongued if displeased; though she always masked the sharpness with honeyed tones and deep-dimpled smiles. Her other vanity was a throbbing contralto singing voice, which drove Kay to distraction. "All that horrible *wobb*ling," she'd say, of Auntie Blodwen's powerful vibrato. "I never want to hear another ruddy hymn in my life! One of these days, I'll tell her to shut up, I swear I will!" I said a silent prayer that Kay would do no such thing; my rice-pudding offense would pale in comparison, and I could picture the two of us out on our ears in a matter of seconds.

Auntie Megan suffered from epilepsy, which had profoundly affected her in many ways, from stunted growth and sparse hair to a slightly impaired intellect. However, she seemed content with her role as chief-cook-and-bottle-washer for her older sister. And, now, for Kay and me, too. I had the impression that she actually enjoyed having us "two gurrls" around; perhaps we made her feel more needed during the long days when Blodwen was at work. With Kay, she had a jocular, teasing relationship, especially when Kay got on her high horse about something or other and flounced around, as she was apt to do. Auntie Megan would then prance about on her skinny, stick legs, grinning from ear to ear, and give a near-perfect imitation of Kay's every movement, from her twitching hips to the nervous toss of her head. Kay was always annoyed at first, but usually ended up laughing at Auntie Megan—and, therefore, at herself. Sometimes, in more serious mode, Auntie Megan would put her hands on her hips and stand, all 4'10" of her, blocking Kay's path. "Anotherrr bee in yerrr bonnet? Indeed t'goodness, Madame Katybach!" she'd say. And Kay had no choice but to swallow hard, smile weakly, and back down.

However, while she took all this with good humor, Kay once confided in me: "Sometimes Auntie Megan flirts with me. And I don't like that."

"*Flirts* with you?"

"Yes. She gooses me when I least expect it. Only when Auntie Blodwen's in the house, so I can't say anything without making a big stink."

"Gooses … ?"

Kay's explanation left me relieved that I, apparently, did not tickle Auntie Megan's fancy. For one thing, I would have had no name for her way of demonstrating that fancy, and I was rather surprised that this well-brought-up headmaster's daughter did.

Kay had many more "run-ins" with the Aunts than I did: in part, I think, because this was her first experience as a true evacuee, living in someone else's house, having to fit in with their ways. In Reigate, she had something more akin to a boarding-school experience, living with about a dozen Honor Oak girls in a small hostel that had Mrs. Bamber-Bowtell as matron and Mrs. B's husband as ... I'm not sure what. Housemaster? A sort of father figure? "An old lech, that's what he was!" according to Kay. "Always putting his arms round our shoulders ... Ugh! He'd stand at the bottom of the stairs, calling out, 'Alice, my deah!' and sometimes *three* Alices would come running ... Mrs. B, the cook, and one of the senior girls. The old goat!"

But in addition to being new to this evacuee business, Kay simply had more spunk than I had, and like my mother, was impatient with my tendency to accept whatever came my way. "Why don't you ever stand up to them? Why do I always have to be the one?" she'd say crossly, and I couldn't help thinking how happy Mum would be if I were more like Kay. I suppose if I'd told Kay about the rice pudding, or my failed attempt to stand up to Mrs. Sharp, she might have understood my avoidance of confrontation. But I responded with no more than a shrug, and that really got under her skin. She'd flounce out of the room, saying, "Oh, you're *hopeless!*"

I always suspected that Kay was the Aunts' favorite. Or did I just think they favored her because they were always on about my bitten fingernails and slouched, bosom-minimizing posture? They held up Kay's shoulders-back, self-confident carriage as the model I should emulate, and I smarted under this comparison, valid though I knew it to be. I'd mutter to myself, "It has to help that Kay is taller. And slimmer. Can't they see that?" But in my heart of hearts, I knew that this was a feeble excuse.

However, Kay had her own crosses to bear. In particular, there was her father's disappointment in her scholastic ability and lack of enthusiasm for things academic. She wanted, oh so badly, to do well, to please him, and she worked hard to improve her grades, but there wasn't much she could do in the realm of whipping up more enthusiasm. Part of her father's chagrin lay in the fact that both his daughters wanted to work in what he saw as non-academic fields: caring for young children (Kay) and domestic science (her sister). He'd come from a poor family and had scrabbled his way to the top, or pretty close to the top—a respected headmaster of a good grammar school. He was frustrated because his girls were not interested in opportunities that he'd worked so hard to make sure they had.

"He says, 'Why, oh why, do you both want to spend your lives cooking and sewing and wiping babies' runny noses? That's what I wanted to help you get away from!' And how can we answer him?" Kay said to me, sadly. "He'd be so happy if just one of us got a report card full of Very Goods, instead of Fairly Goods ... But we can't be what we're not. I sometimes think he'd love to have you for his daughter!" I told her how much *my* mother would love to have a daughter with *her* spunk, but she refused to be consoled.

Kay's other cross was her poor eyesight, which necessitated thick glasses that perched awkwardly on her high-bridged nose—it always looked as if she was *following* her glasses, rather than *wearing* them. They kept her from being pretty—a fact of which she was painfully aware. She probably came into her own with the advent of contact lenses; then the world would see what I saw every night when Kay took off her glasses: her spectacularly large eyes, of a blue so pale that you sometimes thought they had no color. Yet, they were definitely blue, not green or gray.

Arriving in Wales in mid-July gave us the entire summer holidays to explore Tredegar, but we found precious little for girls our age in this gritty coal-mining town. There was a remarkably ugly clock tower in the middle of a shop-lined square, and, down the hill, a picture house and a park with the mandatory, formal flowerbeds and bandstand. But the shops sold uninteresting, everyday things, the bandstand rarely featured a band, and we could afford to go to the pictures only once in a while. Kay and I regularly met up at the clock tower with Kathleen and Peggy (her best friend and mine), and the four of us roamed around the town, in rain or shine, just as, in an earlier foursome, Peggy and I had wandered the streets of Merstham. Except that, now, we usually split up, Kay with Kathleen and Peggy with me, but always stayed within hailing distance. Peggy and I had never had so much one-on-one togetherness, because our Merstham group had always roamed as a foursome. We found it so pleasurable that we did wonder whether we'd made the right decision on the train.

One gloriously sunny day the four of us ventured further afield and explored the green cap that began where the terraces of stone dwellings stopped. We scrambled over the rough, tufty grass to the highest point, threw ourselves to the ground, panting, and sat looking down on the town spread out below. There were glimpses of more distant mountains beyond the Tredegar valley, and turning around, we expected to look down over Ebbw Vale, but were surprised to find that we were not at the highest point after all. On the far side of a small dip, yet another summit beckoned us, but we decided not to tackle it that day and sat, lazily picking out all the landmarks of Tredegar. We could see a few vehicles, even people, going about their business, some on foot and some on bikes; but despite all this evidence of a man-made world, there was a wild, isolated, top-of-the world feeling up there, in that treeless expanse of green. We headed back to it whenever we could, but discovered, the hard way, that it was bleak and cold on a rainy day. And the Aunts were so cross about having to drape our wet clothes around the fire to dry, that we limited our mountain explorations to days when the weather was fine—or, at least, dry. But dry days were few and far between in those Welsh mountains, even in the summer.

One by one, as parents came up with the train fare, back to their families the girls of Honor Oak went, for what was left of the summer holidays. Ostensibly this was to replace last winter's out-grown clothes, but I suspect that some other reason would have been found to justify that expensive journey had we not grown an inch. I didn't expect Mum to come up with the fare and had resigned myself to not seeing our new house and not celebrating Maureen's third birthday with her, so it was a marvelous surprise when a postal order for the fare arrived.

Mum's letters hadn't said much about the house, other than, "I think you'll like Ellen Street better than Upper Ground and its sunnier here than dirty old London." She was right about the south coast being sunnier, but the house itself was horribly disappointing. The notion that we'd moved to an area where housing was plentiful had raised hopes of modern plumbing, but 97 Ellen Street turned out to be yet another old, row house without such amenities. After the Aunts' modernized little house, I had to re-adjust to yet another unlit, outside toilet and a tin tub. However this kitchen did have a built-in old-style copper, so we didn't have to mess with kettles on bath night.

My two weeks in Hove went by so quickly. It seemed like I'd just arrived, and it was time to head back to Wales for the start of the new school year. There we learned, to our disappointment, that there was to be no Tredegar equivalent of Rosemead; we had to squeeze into the local Girls' High School, as in our early Reigate days. This time it wasn't such a crunch, probably because many Honor Oak girls switched back to the London school after the summer holidays—now that the Germans' preoccupation with the European front made London a less dangerous place to be.

Our teachers were happy to be in a proper school building again; Mrs. B had access to a science lab and, for Buzzer, there was a gym—without wall bars, I was glad to see—but we girls missed Rosemead. Black-topped netball courts, where we were now expected to amuse ourselves at lunchtime, were a poor substitute for Rosemead's green lawns, and games of Sticky Toffee became a thing of the past. Although this might have happened, anyway; for we were now the Upper Fifth, the most senior girls other than those august personages in the Sixth Forms from whom Prefects and Head Girls were selected. We might have felt it beneath our dignity to spend lunchtime running around, sweating and yelling, "Sticky Toffee!" Especially since this was an important year for us, preparing to sit our School Certificate exams [national school-leaving exams for grammar school students] in June. Given the war-related interruptions of the past five years, we had some major catching-up to do, we were told, sternly, and most of us were taking seven or eight subjects, so we really had to buckle down and take things seriously this year. Maybe it was as well that there was no sign of the St. Dunstans' boys in Tredegar—one of the first things we had noted on arrival, with considerable disappointment.

Both Bamber-Bowtells had come to Tredegar, to Kay's great disgust. But I was pleased; we had Mrs. B for physics, and Mr. B for history, and what an improvement Mr. B was over Frampie! No more dictated notes to be regurgitated on tests, and no more elaborate maps of military disbursements of cavalry and cannons in historic battles; no more upside-down cartoon moustaches, showing the location of marshes—which, all too often, were the downfall of one side or the other according to Frampie. I had only the vaguest idea of what a marsh really was, other than a place where it was difficult to move one's cannon; but I'd learned to dutifully reproduce those little upside-down moustaches and their consequences, in order to answer Frampie's test questions. Mr. B was a breath of fresh air in the classroom, even if he *was* an old goat out of it. Instead of dictating notes, he simply assumed that you'd done the reading assignment and made your own notes, so he launched straight into a discussion. Differences of opinion were encouraged as long as they were based on reasoning, and history became a subject I looked forward to, for the first time ever.

As winter set in, our time for roaming was sharply reduced, because the Aunts wouldn't let us go out after dark. "It's not as much fun during the day." said Peggy, and I agreed; though we were hard put to explain why, or how, the anonymity provided by the cloak of darkness had made the Merstham experience so satisfying. Early nightfall and winter weather also curtailed excursions up the mountain, and we grew quite restive over the paucity of Tredegar's offerings for our age group. There wasn't even a Youth Club. This gave rise to nostalgic memories of the one in Reigate, despite the fact that its most exciting offering had been the game in which, when the music stopped, the person in the clockwise-moving circle got to kiss the nearest person of the opposite gender in the counter-clockwise-moving circle. Of course, the boy-girl ratio was usually some small fraction, and even if there *was* a boy facing you when the music stopped, he was usually a spotty-faced, gangling creature; rarely the handsome fellow every girl in the room had her eye on. Our word for the Reigate Youth Club had been "b-o-r-i-n-g." But we now forgot its shortcomings and remembered only that it had provided a place where, for a penny or two, you could spend a Saturday evening hanging out with others your own age, sipping cheap lemonade (made from powder with a scented smell) and gnawing away at a stale rock bun.

It was quite a hike to the clock tower for our get-togethers with Peggy and

Kathleen, because the Aunt's house was about two-thirds of the way up one side of the valley, and the town square equally far up the opposite side. On the town side, the road was straight and steep, but on our side, it snaked down the mountain like a slalom course, every terrace connected to its nearest neighbors by tight U-bends. This made it about two miles by road from Albert Terrace to the bridge across the river at the bottom of the valley, but fortunately, each terrace was connected to its neighbors by flights of stone stairs, and clattering down these short cuts was a snap. Though, climbing back up entailed a lot of huffing and puffing, especially if we'd been on a shopping errand for the Aunts and had heavy bags to carry. Vehicles had to slalom along the entire length of this road, so we rarely saw anything on wheels, other than a few delivery vans and carts that brought coal, milk, bread and vegetables to the doorsteps of housewives willing and able to pay an extra penny or two.

The move to Tredegar brought about the demise of Plan B. Order Marks and Discipline Marks were left behind in Reigate, along with the prefects who introduced them. (That bunch of martinets was within a week or two of leaving school when we were re-evacuated and had simply gone home to their parents a little earlier than anticipated.) The teachers who'd seen the discipline system as petty nonsense, probably breathed a sigh of relief at being given a natural "out," but it was missed by those of us who had derived considerable amusement from the game that it had become.

However, I was probably alone in feeling positively dismayed by this turn of events. I didn't dare continue with Plan B now there was no measure of how close I was to serious trouble, and I was still groping around for Plan C when I became aware that I was doing just fine *without* a security blanket. And I felt like I had at age five, when I suddenly realized I couldn't hear my father's feet pounding along—he was no longer holding the seat of my bike and I was barreling along on my own! Again, as on that day, panic swiftly followed elation. Was this for keeps? Would I fall flat on my face when I next tried to go it alone—with no hovering hand as potential back up? But time, once again, proved that my newfound skill was indeed for keeps; only occasionally did I fall flat on my face. At the end of term, when I found that I could contemplate a good report card without dread, the sense of release was palpable. Finally ... about to celebrate my sixteenth birthday ... I was free of the problem that had dogged me so long. Gone was the need to devise all those silly plans!

In retrospect, I do wonder how valid my fears of grades-related ostracism were. Stemming, as they did, from experiences in Waterloo where I had stuck out like a sore thumb, had they been justified among the like-minded girls of a selective grammar school? I don't know. But, at the time, those fears had been powerful. The knots in my stomach were undeniably real; so was the euphoria that swept over me when I came up with a plan. Necessary or not, Plan A and Plan B had given me ways to fend off those knot-inducing fears; and whether the fears were real or imagined hardly matters for the purposes of this chronicle, in which my only concern is to tell it the way it was, in that place, at that time, as I remember it.

Just before I headed home for Christmas, I got a letter from my mother:

> I've left the old man, Gwen. Got tired of him and his nonsense and just walked out with Maureen and Derek without saying a dickybird [word]. I wish I couldve seen his face when he found us gone. No one to get dinner for him and hes got to take care of the dog too. That will please him, I dont think. But our landlady said no dogs so we couldnt bring Bobby which upset Maureen and Derek but weve only got two rooms here so theres no room for the dog anyway. It will be a squeeze with you too but anythings better than putting up with the old man who just wouldnt leave Derek alone. Poor kid he did his best and even took all his meals up to his bedroom just to keep out of his way but the old devil wasnt satisfied and hollered at him all the time up two flights of stairs. The neighbours must have heard him halfway down the street the racket he kicked up.

This was sobering stuff. The prospect of not having to endure Jack Weddinger over the holidays was not exactly unwelcome. But two rooms? For four of us? It did not sound promising.

When I found the shabby house at the address in Shoreham that I'd been given, the door was opened by a lumbering, wall-eyed creature with wild gray hair, great shaggy eyebrows and a spectacular hooked nose. "My God! A real live witch!" was my first thought, "And complete with cat," for a mangy black cat was cradled in a sort of hammock created by holding up the hem of a voluminous apron. This ancient animal, Old Tom, too fat and too decrepit to get around under his own propulsion, was, no doubt, responsible for the pervasive odor of cat pee that assailed my nostrils as I stood there under the scowling scrutiny of his mistress. She seemed surprised to learn that there was to be another occupant of her two ground floor rooms, and, because I was a little earlier than expected, there was no one home to vouch for me. But she let me in, and I sat awkwardly in her kitchen, listening to her extol the virtues of her other cat, Tiddles. *Tiddles?* Maybe I had maligned Old Tom. He may not be responsible for the smell in the house, after all, I thought.

When Derek came in, he said with a chuckle, "An' 'ow d'ya like our very own witch!" and I gathered that Mrs. Maplewood's bite was not as bad as her appearance. But neither was she exactly a ray of sunshine. A complex set of rules governed the sharing of the limited facilities offered by this small house, rules that she enforced with a fist of iron, and no deviations to allow for the fact that one of her tenants was only three years old. This meant that in the corner of the front room—the living-room-cum-female-sleeping quarters—a bucket resided for when Maureen couldn't wait until the prescribed hour to use the outdoor toilet. The bucket served all four of us after ten o'clock, the hour at which Mrs. Maplewood retired for the night. For she always locked the back door and took the key with her, muttering dementedly as she struggled up the stairs with Old Tom cradled in her apron and Tiddles weaving around her feet.

Sharing the kitchen with Mrs. Maplewood was difficult, but we "made the best of a bad job." At least Derek was no longer under constant attack and, he one day confided to me, was now spared the dread of walking in and finding our mother with a black eye or other telltale bruises. "I dunno 'ow I kept me 'ands off the ol' blighter! Knockin' 'er about like that," he added. And I realized that this tall, strong, soon-to-be-thirteen boy might not be able to keep his hands to himself much longer; our stepfather might get a well-deserved come-uppance, but my brother could be in deep trouble if a battered Jack Weddinger took himself to the police station and pressed charges. Far away, in the safety of my Tredegar "cocoon," I hadn't appreciated how rapidly the home scene had deteriorated, and I began to understand why we had exchanged Jack Weddinger's version of hell for Mrs. Maplewood's. "Out o' the bloomin' fryin' pan inta the fire!" as Mum put it one day, in a burst of frustration at the daily aggravations of our present situation.

I'd been home only a couple of days when Mum confessed, "It's not gonna be much of a Christmas, I'm afraid. Just one present fer Maureen … that's all I've got money fer." Derek and I stoutly declared that we didn't mind. Peace and quiet was better than presents, but Mum was upset on our behalf. Apparently, the money she earned cleaning houses wasn't enough to keep our escape hatch going *and* pay her bus fares to and from those jobs. "An' after the 'olidays, Derek'll need bus fares too, when school starts," she worried. It had been foolish to send the fare for me to come home for the holidays, I thought—but was selfish enough to be glad that she had—and it had made a big dent in her meager savings (the quarterly Co-op dividends on groceries). "There's not much left," she said. "So I'm lookin' round ta see if I c'n pick up another li'l job." Her prospects were not good—especially with a three-year-old in tow after Derek and I had to go back to school. It was unclear to me how long she could hold out, and abundantly clear that her flight from Ellen Street had been driven by desperation, not careful planning.

The dog then complicated matters. He spotted Mum one day as she was walking from the bus stop to Pansy's house (Pansy being one of the ladies she "did for"), and almost knocked her over in his frenzied joy. This was before the days of leash laws, and Bobby had a regular route that encompassed a number of houses where he knew he could count on a tidbit or two from householders susceptible to his doggy charms—Pansy being one of the more susceptible. Mum managed to elude Bobby that day by slipping out at the front, while Pansy distracted him at the back door, but next day he was waiting at Pansy's door when Mum arrived. The wily creature ignored Pansy's offerings when the time came for Mum's departure and caught a glimpse of her boarding the bus. He pursued the bus all the way to Shoreham, creating considerable mayhem in his wake, and gave her a deliriously happy greeting when she finally alighted. Derek took him back to Ellen Street and shut him in the house, but our stepfather must have let him out later, because Bobby reappeared, whimpering, on Mrs. Maplewood's front step. Understandably, she was *not* pleased and kicked up such a fuss that Mum knew the game was up. "It was touch an' go, anyway," she said, as we hurriedly packed our belongings to the accompaniment of Mrs. Maplewood's angry mutterings in the back room. "The money wasn't gonna last much longer. But Bobby really put the kibosh on it!"

Thus, Christmas Eve found us standing on the doorstep of 97 Ellen Street, a somber little group accompanied by an ecstatic dog; all was well with *his* world, at least, now that his family was back where it belonged. Jack Weddinger grudgingly let us in, though we had wondered whether he would, but there was little to eat in the house and certainly nothing of a festive nature. We'd resigned ourselves—quite happily—to an egg-and-chips Christmas dinner when the man of the house came rolling home from the pub with an enormous turkey that he'd "got from a Yank fer a few drinks." We'd none of us seen a turkey before; had never seen that amount of meat all in one piece, come to that. Not even the Odds' pre-war party hams had been *that* big!

The turkey was not a success. "What d'ya expect me ta do with that thing?" Mum asked in exasperation. "It won't even go in the bloomin' oven!" However, the turkey *did* fit—if put in the oven at just the right angle—but none of our roasting pans was large enough, and the hot fat and juices dripped on to the oven floor. Long before the bird was ready, the oven was a charred mess and the kitchen full of smoke. By the time we sat down to eat that under-cooked peace offering, Mum was exhausted and furious, Maureen was coughing from the smoke, and we all felt cheated of our egg and chips—

Derek especially, because he never ate meat, anyway. (Never had: he just didn't like it.) There was none of the usual Christmas fare, like stuffing and bread sauce, and Derek's dinner was particularly dismal: just Brussels sprouts and ungarnished mashed potatoes. There wasn't even any cheese—his usual source of protein—to grate over his potatoes. At intervals Mum muttered, "Bloomin' waste o' money if yew ask me!" And our stepfather kept saying, "Well ... this is a treat, ain't it?" and looked around the table for corroboration. In the interest of keeping the peace, I felt compelled to murmur assent—which earned me black looks from Mum. But she knew why I had to agree with him; she'd been in this position often enough, herself.

Returning to Ellen Street with her tail between her legs was probably one of the hardest things my mother ever had to do. But next day she had something to take her mind off her defeat: Maureen's cough turned into asthma, and we carried her over to the hospital, which was just across the road. She was admitted immediately, and it was hard to hand that limp little body over to the brisk, no-nonsense nurses in their starched caps and aprons. Rigid hospital rules did not allow for anyone to stay with Maureen, and we walked back to the house even more subdued than when we'd stood on the doorstep wondering whether we'd be refused admission.

My mother's worry and anxiety soon translated into rage at her husband, the person she saw as largely responsible. "All that smoke from yer rotten ol' turkey! On top of what the poor li'l blighter's just bin through ... all yer carryin' on, day after day ... then livin' in a couple o' miserable rooms 'cos we couldn't take n'more of yew. Yew ol' devil, yew!" she spat at him. "A bundle o'nerves, the poor kid is. An' they say nerves is what causes this asthma stuff. So no wonder she's lyin' over there in the 'ospital strugglin' fer ev'ry breath." Derek and I exchanged glances that said, "Oh, no! Why does she have to start another row?" But instead of flaring up, Jack Weddinger sat in his chair, staring into the fire, and said not a word. Was he as shaken by Maureen's illness as the rest of us? Shortly afterwards, the answer to this unspoken question seemed to be a resounding No, as we watched him go out for his usual before-dinner drinking session with a bunch of buddies down at the Green Man. He clearly wasn't upset enough to forgo that.

However, the question was reopened when he returned from the pub. We were waiting to start dinner, and as he came through the kitchen doorway, his face suddenly went chalk white, and he had to lean on the table for support. We assumed he'd had a drop too many, until he croaked, "What's *that*?" and pointed a shaking finger at a sheet that Mum had draped over two chairs pushed together so their backs formed a drying rack

"What's *that*? Just a sheet that wasn't quite dry, ya silly ol' bugger! What did ya think it was—a ghost? Ya'd bet'er take more wa'er with it!" Here, even my mother had to pause for breath. "Yew sh'd be ashamed of yerself, goin' boozin' with yer own baby ill in 'ospital."

This last statement, instead of making her husband hang his head—not that she had much hope of that—had the remarkable effect of restoring the color to his cheeks and the strength to his legs. For what Jack Weddinger had thought he was looking at was not a ghost, but the sheet-draped body of his dead child lying on a make-shift bed—two chairs pushed together in the time-honored fashion for sick children. So he *does* care about his little daughter, after all, I thought; she was probably the only person in the whole world that he felt affection for. Mum, however, would have none of this. "Don't be sa daft," she said scornfully, "'e just 'ad too much whisky in 'is belly. Yew know what whisky does to 'im. Always sends 'im awf the rails. I'm always glad when 'e runs out o' money an' 'as ta go back ta beer." She could be so hard, that mother of mine, so hard and unforgiving. My father certainly had it right when he said, after the "accidental" spilling of the slop bucket down old Ma Tanner's new stair carpet: "It don't pay t'get on the wrong side o' *yew*, May!"

Maureen was in hospital three long days and three long nights, and hospital rules decreed that we couldn't visit her, because "it is too upsetting for a child to have visitors." The house seemed so empty without her chatter, and Derek and I hardly knew what to do with ourselves. By the time she came home, it was almost time for me to go back to school, and I felt thoroughly cheated. I sat on the train to Tredegar, thinking about this and other Christmases, and came to the conclusion that our family clearly had no talent whatsoever for this particular holiday. Kay came back to Tredegar all bubbly about the wonderful Christmas she'd had, and it was a relief when, after hearing that my little sister had been in hospital, no one seemed to notice that I wasn't equally bubbly about mine. I made no mention of the disastrous Shoreham episode, even to Peggy; there was no way I wanted anyone in my Honor Oak life to know what a shambles the other part was.

◆　　◆　　◆

The setting for Tredegar must, at one time, have been quite lovely. It sits at the end of a valley, and a fast-flowing river follows every twist and turn of the valley, carving a path between what used to be unspoiled grass-covered mountains. Books like *How Green Was My Valley,* books about Wales that Kay and I devoured as fast as we could get to and from the library, all corroborated this picture of "what must have been." But as these volumes lamented at great length, the valleys of South Wales were now dotted with ugly pitheads and slagheaps, and fine coal dust permeated everything. Some slagheaps—great piles of gravel-sized coal-mining debris—had been there long enough for grass to have taken root. Indeed, the top of one had been leveled, and schoolgirls now played hockey on its grassy surface, and their school-mates jumped up and down and screamed and hollered in support when they were playing another school. Others, like the jet black "hill" that we passed every day on the way to school, were of more recent origin and emitted eerie wisps of what looked like smoke. Some of us held that the wisps were simply little clouds formed when moist warm air from inside the slag heap met cooler air; the no-smoke-without-fire school of thought pooh-poohed this, and added triumphantly that, even if it was right, what, other than fire, was heating up all that moist air? Most of us hurried past that "smoking" black mound that loomed high above us ... just in case it should burst into flames, like a smoldering heap of coal in the fireplace when given a nudge with a poker.

Mr. B, one day, took our history class down one of the local mines—a very different experience from the school outing in Dorset. There was no sun-dappled, muddy-bottomed river or brilliant blue kingfisher; instead, a terrifyingly rickety cage creaked its way down to the bottom of the main shaft, and we walked along a tunnel lit by a string of bare bulbs. The walls, roof, and floor of the tunnel, all were black, relieved only by occasional glints, reflections from smooth slabs of coal. There was the constant drip, drip, drip of water from the roof, and we had to pick our way carefully among puddles, all the while keeping clear of the rails, along which clanked metal hoppers heaped with coal. It was a far cry from the dry, well-lit sand tunnels we'd used as air raid shelters in Reigate, and, for all my consumption of books about the mines, I hadn't expected such unrelieved, dank darkness. Yet the miners that we saw trudging along a tunnel, hacking at the coal surface, or throwing great hunks of coal into the hoppers, all waved cheerily and asked jokingly if we were looking for jobs. How could they stand it, day after day, we asked ourselves on the way home—and for many days afterwards; which, I think, made Mr. B feel that his outing had achieved what he had hoped.

However, when we raised this question with the Aunts, Auntie Blodwen sniffed and said, "Miners today don't have any id-e-a-h how easy they have it. Shorrter days an' betterrr wages—an' they do nothing but complain! Always threatening to strrike, they arrr. Even in warrtime, look you ... when thairrr's a shortage of coal ferrr makin' tanks an' ships."

"Indeed t'goodness, mun! Tis a disgrrace." Auntie Megan muttered, shaking her head dolefully from side to side.

"But it's such a *dangerous* job!" said Kay.

"Diolch-yn-fawrrr! With all the safety rrrules they have now? T'is noth'n like the days when our poorrr Da was down the pits. Isn't that the gospel trruth Megan-bach?" Auntie Blodwen trilled angrily, and Auntie Megan nodded, making clucking noises in her throat. "No-one talked of strrikes then. Not till the unions and the likes of that Aneurrrin Bevan started stirrrin' them up. Led the minerrs in the Gen'rral Strrike, he did—an' what good did *that* do them? Just a lot of miserry ferr their poorr wives an' childrren, look yew!

"Nothing but a mischief-makerrr, that Nye Bevan, since he was a lad. Borrn in Tredegar, he was, and always inta trrouble … firrst in school, then when he went inta the mines. Lazy young devil, too—went t'sleep on the job, they say, but soon got t'be a big shot in the union. And the men coverred up for 'im! Always had his nose in a book, that one, and he didn't stay in the pit verry long. Memberrr o' Parrli'ment for Ebbw Vale he is now … an' still making trrouble, even in the House o' Commons. Arrgues with Churchill himself, he does, indeed to goodness! Always got his name in the paperrr, makin' a fuss overrr somethin' orrr otherrr. They should send him back down the mines … let him do somethin' useful, instead o' makin' a nuisance of 'imself."

Unwilling to provoke more rants from Auntie Blodwen, we never again raised the subject of a miner's lot, but endured many re-runs of her feelings about Nye Bevan whenever his name hit the headlines. However, intrigued by the memory of Auntie Blodwen's diatribes about Aneurin Bevan, I recently dipped into the life of this Tredegar-born miner's son, the sixth of ten children, who went down the mines at age thirteen. By the age of forty-eight he was a Cabinet Minister in the Labour government that swept into power immediately after the end of the war, and this irreverent, self-educated, widely read, brilliant orator did indeed often catch the headlines. He was sometimes referred to as a "one-man opposition party" to Churchill, and he trod on many toes. His enemies saw him as an arrogant troublemaker, but underneath that abrasive public persona there lurked a romantic fellow who loved poetry and music; like his father, who sang, and won prizes for poetry (written in Welsh).

It was impossible to live in a mining town without regular reminders of what was going on, literally, under your feet. Sometimes I'd be woken early, before daylight in wintertime, by miners making their way to work: the clomping of heavy boots, interspersed with clatter-clatter-clatter as they went down a stone-stepped short cut to the terrace below. This sequence would be repeated until the sounds faded to the point where I had to strain to be sure I could still hear them. After our trip down the mine, I would shudder at the memory of what these men faced every day: their descent into the dank bowels of the earth in that rickety cage, and the hours they'd spend, wresting coal from the walls of the tunnels, midst all the dust and the clanking of hoppers. Occasionally, one of the miners would start singing, usually a hymn, sometimes in Welsh, but always beautifully—as only the Welsh can. (Patty Morgan's Welsh uncle was right about this, too) Then another miner would join in, and another; and sometimes I'd even hear fainter voices from a more distant group. Once in full throat, the men sang non-stop, but eventually their voices grew too faint, and I would contentedly roll over and go back to sleep. This "dawn chorus" was a wondrous way to start the day, and I tried to will myself to wake early so as not to miss that moment when a miner might be moved to break into song. But my internal alarm clock was not reliable, so it remained a rare treat.

The clock tower, at the very heart of Tredegar, was the pride and joy of its citizens, and it was the tallest structure in town, other than the spire of the Anglican Church at the other end of the main street. Unlike English towns, with their liberal sprinkling of church spires, Tredegar had just the one; the other houses of worship—and they were numerous—were deliberately plain and squat and unadorned and weren't even *called* churches. Worshippers in Tredegar went "to Chapel, look you!" The Aunts had initially assumed that we would join them in their Chapel, but Kay protested vigorously, and we were allowed to attend the Anglican Church. To the Aunts, this High Anglican institution smacked of papism, and they clearly disapproved—they, and all but a handful of Tredegar's residents, judging by the almost non-existent congregation of St. Jude's. Canon Jones preached and declaimed loudly to row after row of empty pews in this huge and beautiful church, but his voice got lost in its shadowy vastness. Even the choir was too small to make itself heard over the thundering of the splendid organ, and the singing of the sparse congregation was … simply pathetic. I hardly dared do more than pretend to sing, for fear that I might lose my place and find myself singing alone, and I often thought back to the pleasure of belting out the hymns in the safety of the crowd that regularly filled Pulham's little church. I sorely missed the sense of belonging it had afforded me, but at least I could, once again, let the language of the King James Bible sweep over me; a luxury I hadn't enjoyed since I walked away from Margaret's church in Reigate.

The rest of Sunday was problematic. To the Aunts it was a no-work-and-no-pleasure day. Meals were cooked on Saturday to be eaten cold on the Sabbath. We were allowed to write a letter home—that was a *duty*, hence permissible—but everything else was forbidden: washing dishes, doing homework, darning socks, reading (other than the Bible), listening to the radio, even going out (other than to Church). The only exceptions were keeping the fire going, and washing the accumulated dirty dishes on Sunday evening—sometimes to the strains of Albert Sandler and his Palm Court Orchestra wafting from the radio, if Auntie Blodwen was in one of her "jolly" moods. The first time this happened, I saw Kay open her mouth to protest the inconsistency of this deviation from the Sunday protocol, but, wisely, she shut it quickly—thereby leaving open the possibility of Albert Sandler's violins to relieve the dreariness of countless silent Sunday evenings still to come. Another break came when we discovered a new way home from Church, a back way, over the mountain. But, very foolishly, we mentioned what fun it had been up there, on top of the world, with the wind—there was always wind—blowing through our hair, clearing our heads of the week's "cobwebs." *Fun*? On a *Sunday*? Frowns signaled disapproval. And from that day on, after the last hymn had been sung at St. Jude's, we had to wait outside the Aunts' Chapel and walk home through the town with them; and Sunday reverted to being the dreariest of days.

Our social life finally took a promising turn when we heard that there were Saturday Night dances in nearby Troed-y-Gwaer, and we begged the Aunts to let us go with a group of friends. "Trroed-y-Gwaerrr?" they hooted in unison. "Dog'n Tub Rrrow! Diolch-yn-fawrrr! Why would ye want to go thairrr, indeed t'goodness!" They refused to elucidate, beyond hinting darkly, "Look you ... you'll see ferrr yourrrselves!" For they had, in the end, agreed to let us go.

When we descended the stairs, bedecked out for this much-anticipated event, the Aunts were lying in wait to make sure we passed muster, I suppose, and after one look at Kay, their amusement knew no bounds. She had pulled out all the stops and was wearing her best dress, shoes with a bit of a heel, the silk stockings she'd been given for Christmas—fifteen minutes it had taken to get those blessed seams straight—and, the boldest stroke of all, bright red lipstick. She had contemplated going without her glasses but abandoned that idea after a few minutes spent bumping into things. At the sight of us, Auntie Megan laughed till she cried and had to cross her legs to prevent a leak of a different nature, and Auntie Blodwen spluttered, "Indeed t'goodness, gurrl! And just whairrr is it you think you'rrr goin'? Down Dog'n Tub Row they'll think t'is the Queen 'errself come ta visit!"

Poor Kay. Her cheeks burned scarlet, but she held back the tears until we'd shut the door behind us and could no longer hear their mocking laughter. "The old ... *cows!*" she finally burst out, and then the tears began to flow. I was secretly relieved that I'd escaped their derision by having no finery *and* by having refused Kay's offer to avail myself of her make-up. My refusal stemmed partly from pride—I never had enough pocket money for make-up—and partly from fear that I didn't know how to use the stuff and might end up looking like a clown. There was also guilt, based on Mum's scorn and disapproval of make-up; and, last but not least, it felt wrong to indulge in something she couldn't afford, no matter how much she might like to.

We repaired Kay's damaged make-up as best we could in the dim street lighting and continued on to meet our friends. Other host families had been equally scornful of Troed-y-Gwaer, which made us all the more determined to have a wonderful time at this, our first real dance. But on the way home, we reluctantly conceded that Dog'n Tub Row was an apt name for Troed-y-Gwaer, which consisted of a row of small ill-kept dwellings, with at least one mangy dog sprawled in front of each house and a tin tub on every back wall. (Not that there was any disgrace in being the victim of primitive plumbing, to my mind, as I thought of all the tin tubs in my life, but I lacked the courage to argue this point.)

The boys and girls inside the church hall had been equally disappointing. They, of course, had known one another for years and didn't exactly welcome our "invasion." Especially the girls. They looked daggers on the rare occasion when one of "their" boys danced with one of us. Even the boys that were bold enough to take this step were boringly tongue-tied and kept falling over their feet, according to the girls thus honored. It was more fun to dance with one another, they said, like we did on rainy lunch hours. We must have seemed such silly schoolgirls to the fifteen-sixteen year-olds of Troed-y-Gwaer, most of whom, we discovered, were already out at work. Indeed, some of the boys had traces of coal-dust embedded in their skin, a sure sign that they spent their days down a mine—perhaps, even, the one we had visited.

However, none of us was prepared to concede that our host families had been right about Troed-y-Gwaer. We told them that we'd had a great time and were stubborn enough to go back a number of times to make it seem like we really had. I don't know if we fooled anybody, but we certainly didn't fool ourselves, and when spring arrived, we found more pleasant ways to spend Saturday evenings. Even meandering around the park with your friends was more fun than a dance down Dog'n Tub Row, especially now that the flowerbeds boasted flowers and a band often graced the bandstand—though both flowers and music were too regimental for our taste.

That spring, the spring of 1945, good news started to pour in from the European front, and we listened eagerly every evening to the nine o'clock news (still preceded by the chimes of Big Ben, still bringing back memories of lying in bed as a child). I often thought about Uncle Reg's maps and wondered whether he was keeping up with "our" pins as the Allies raced across Europe, squeezing the enemy into an ever-smaller strip. But along with the good news and pictures of cheering crowds lining streets of newly liberated towns, there came grim talk of concentration camps with unspeakable horrors. Newsreels showing these horrors eventually reached Tredegar, and the Aunts tried to discourage us from going to see them. "T'is too terrible, indeed, ferrr young gurrls like you t'be seein'," they said. But we insisted. We were, after all, sixteen years old … surely old enough that we *should* know what was going on in the world.

Nothing prepared me for the images I saw on that movie screen: the match-stick limbs and skeletal bodies that looked scarcely human, yet were only too human; men, women and children, staring with huge, sunken eyes that were to haunt me for a long time afterwards. I shrank down in my seat, trying to stifle the cry that rose in my throat, only to hear it force its way out sounding hideously like a giggle. Tut-tutting heads turned toward me, and I wished for the earth to open up under that cinema seat. I was saved only by the darkness and the fact that I was surrounded by strangers—the cinema having been too full to find a seat next to my friends. No one could be sure who had "giggled," and eventually the turned heads went back to watching the screen, a screen that I could no longer bear to watch. I sat with closed eyes and tried to close my ears too, but couldn't silence the voice that was describing this indescribable scene.

I slowly realized that to stay for the film after those newsreel images would be even more obscene than the images themselves, and I was wondering how to escape without drawing attention to myself when I saw two familiar figures walking up the aisle—Kay and Kathleen. We went out together and found Peggy already outside. There was no giggling or grumbling that night; we walked home in silence, wrestling with the horror of what we had seen. I lay awake for a long time, waves of shame washing over me for the countless times we had roamed around whilst those horrors were unfolding, thoughtlessly giggling and grumbling about what now seemed such trivial difficulties. The Aunts held their tongues till the next morning but couldn't resist a gentle, "We told ye so, now, didn't we?" We agreed that it had been "too terrible," as they had said—but felt that we had done the right thing.

Then, suddenly, it was May 8th: the war was over! Though not completely unexpected, given the recent news from Europe, it was surprisingly hard to realize that it really was over, finished, done. No more air raid sirens, no more bombs, no more blackout, no more ration books, no more families getting dreaded telegrams from the War Office. We could finally throw away those pesky gas masks that had gone bump, bump, bump on our backsides going to and from school and on every journey of any length—except in Tredegar, where sirens never sounded, and our gas masks had sat gathering dust in cupboards. Last, but by no means least, *our days as evacuees would soon be over!* We'd be going home! After six years, almost: more than a third of our young lives.

By nightfall blackout curtains had been joyously ripped from every window, and the town was ablaze with light. After years of groping through the darkness with weak flashlights, the oft-talked-of pleasure of walking along well-lit streets was again a reality, and the entire town gathered at the clock tower—where else, in Tredegar! The square was a solid mass of people, all deliriously happy, smiling till their cheeks ached, and there were speeches and cheers and the band played. Then there was a lull, and suddenly a lone baritone voice started to sing, "Abide with me." In no time at all, everyone was singing this familiar hymn, and tears streamed down faces; tears that were not allowed to interfere with the singing or the rich descant that soared above the melody. To hear an entire town burst into song, spontaneously, was quite extraordinary, and as I write this more than sixty years later, my eyes are teary, and my arms crawl with goose bumps.

Once started, there was no stopping this Welsh crowd, and when Kay and I headed for home in the wee small hours of the morning, they were still going strong. We could hear them even as we lay in bed, too tired and too excited to fall asleep. Not till then had either of us paid attention to a little worm of anxiety that we'd pushed to the back of our heads all day: where would we two go when the school returned to London? Kay's family might still be evacuated (with her father's school), and mine was down in Hove. Had anybody thought about this?

Next morning, we discovered that somebody—Miss Ashley, the headmistress—had indeed thought about it. She informed us that Kay's parents had been contacted by phone, and she was to stay with a relative near the Peckham school until her family was de-evacuated. And a letter was already on its way to my phone-less household, informing my mother that a home would be found for me, and I would write as soon as I knew my new address. The important thing, in Miss Ashley's mind, though not in ours, was that we both finish out the school year with Honor Oak and sit our School Cert. exams in June. So, Miss Ashley added, wagging her large ungainly head in my direction and executing complicated maneuvers with her false teeth, she hoped that my mother would let me delay my return home for a few weeks for that purpose. My only other encounter with Miss Ashley had been at the time of the bus ticket scandal—when I had kept my gaze glued to the floor—and now I couldn't take my eyes off those ill-fitting dentures. I didn't dare look at Kay, but managed to murmur assent, and we escaped before disgracing ourselves by collapsing into giggles.

A couple of days later, we said goodbye to the Aunts and their snug little house and the "smoking" slag heaps and our mountain-top walks; goodbye to Wales and its singing miners, dreary Sundays, and everlasting rain; and, of course, goodbye to the war and everything that that meant. So many changes. At such whirlwind speed. On the train, as we sped back to London, I sat surrounded by the excited chatter of girls who would, within hours, be re-united with their families, for keeps this time. I nervously contemplated the fact that, for a few more weeks, I alone would still be an evacuee, sort of, the only one in the entire school; it was a daunting thought. Yet, said a little voice in my head, at least it puts off for a while the prospect of living in the same house as Jack Weddinger on a permanent basis.

◆   ◆   ◆

ADDENDUM

It is puzzling that I remember no joyous ringing of bells in Tredegar on VE Day [Victory in Europe Day]. I once heard a recording made in London that day, when, after six years of silence imposed by the war, what sounded like hundreds of church bells were rung at the same time; some played tunes, others rang complicated peals, most simply clanged out ding-dong-ding-dong-ding-dong. The result was a sound so stirring, so memorable, that it made my heart, quite literally, leap up in my chest—an effect that the "bells" section of Tchaikowsky's 1812 Overture comes close to achieving. I can't imagine a similar happening in Tredegar that left no traces in my memory. I suppose it's possible that Canon Jones's church possessed the only bell in that town of chapels; but I don't remember hearing even one bell pealing to celebrate the end of the war. Was St. Jude's simply too far away? Or was the wind, perhaps, in the wrong direction?

◆   ◆   ◆

I re-visited South Wales some sixty years after leaving it, and unlike Dorset where there'd been no significant changes, the Tredegar scene was almost unrecognizable. The valley had been largely restored to its earlier green-ness following the demise of the South Wales mining industry; gone were the ugly pit heads that had dotted the landscape, and the slag-heaps, having grown a carpet of grass, now melded in as small flat-topped hills. In part of the town, a major motorway was being constructed and many buildings had been demolished—but not the ugly old clock tower. It stood, as proudly as ever; surrounded by wreckage of the Tredegar we had known.

Chapter 26

Transitions

FITTINGLY, OUR EVACUEE LIFE officially came to a close as it had begun in September, 1939: on a big, noisy London train station, with much smoke and hissing steam and blowing of whistles. But gone now were the gas masks, and the tears shed were of a different nature as families were re-united and teachers could, at last, shed the burden of surrogate parent-hood.

From the faces in the crowd awaiting our arrival, I had picked out the Taylors, the family that had offered to house me for what was left of the school year, before Miss King introduced us; they, likewise, had picked me out. We were easily recognizable: the only people in that crowd scanning faces without knowing what we were looking for. Mrs. Taylor, short and ample of bosom, beamed and gave me a great, reassuring, welcoming hug, as did her older daughter, Laura, a grown-up young lady as different from her mother as it's possible to imagine. She was tall and gangly, with a long thin face and a nervous, jokey manner; and I liked Laura, immediately. But the younger daughter and I stared at one another in mutual dismay. We were about the same age and both knew, instantly, that the other was the exact type of girl we'd spent our lives trying to avoid. Mavis was one of those awesome creatures that I found so daunting: slim, clothes-conscious, good-looking and graceful, one who excelled at all sports and was bright enough to sail through as a B⁻ student, despite doing little or no work. The Mavises of this world were instantly and effortlessly popular; they had no need of Poor Grade Plans; indeed, it was their careless contempt that made such schemes necessary for the likes of me. And I knew that she saw me as one of those ungainly, despicable teachers' pets, who always did their homework, had no interest in clothes, and invariably ruined a game of netball or rounders [basketball and softball, more or less] because they couldn't run fast enough or catch a ball with any reliability.

All this flashed through my mind in a split second, and later, as we bounced and clanged along in a Peckham-bound tram, I desperately repeated a silent prayer: "Please God don't let us be in the same class!" Mavis sat at the front of the tram and stared stonily out the window, but Laura chattered happily alongside me, and before long I knew that my prayer had been answered: Mavis was a year younger than I was, praise be! (As always, relief mingled uncomfortably with a sense of hypocrisy about praying, when in need, to a God I had walked away from.) I'd also learned that, until last year, Laura too had been an Honor Oak girl and was now working. "She's a Technical Assistant in a *La-bor-a-tor-y*," interrupted Mrs. Taylor proudly, from the seat behind us, tapping me on the shoulder to make sure she had my attention for this important addition to my knowledge of the Taylor family. The two men in the family, Mr.T, as his wife called him, and Colin, had gone to a cricket match, but should be home when we arrived, I was told. And indeed they were. Colin said a curt "Hello," studied me briefly, and dismissed me from his ten-year-old world after ascertaining that I had no particular interest in cricket. Mr. T was of medium height and slender, polite but somewhat aloof, and seemed rather pre-occupied.

The Taylor family lived in a comfortable Council flat in the heart of Peckham, about a stone's throw from the store that sold Honor Oak school uniforms. The flat was a standard pre-war Council offering: six- or seven-story blocks of flats, with long brick balconies on each floor and asphalt-covered open spaces—which looked ugly, but made great traffic-free play areas for the children who lived in the flats. I now woke to the rumbling of trams and buses instead of the tramp of miners' boots, but I was glad of the modern plumbing and spaciousness of the Taylors' flat. As the tram had rattled its way towards Peckham the first night, the prospect of possibly sharing a room with Mavis had weighed heavily on my mind. Worse yet, might we have to share a bed, and would she, like Kay, try to establish her own "space" in the bed? But Mrs. Taylor had put me in Laura's room, "because she's out a lot in the evenings, so you'll have a nice quiet place to study for your exams. I remember how *she* used to shut herself away in this room before *her* School Cert! Mavis is closer to your age, I know, but she's not the studious type, so her room wouldn't be so good, unless you'd rather … " I hastily re-assured her that Laura's room was fine. And thanked my lucky stars that I also had a bed to myself.

My fears about the difficulties of co-existing with Mavis turned out to have been groundless. We took the same tram in the morning but, in school, followed paths that rarely crossed; when they did, we acknowledged one another only if our eyes accidentally met. Weekends were trickier, and by tacit agreement, neither of us wanting to distress Mrs. Taylor, Mavis and I allowed enough of a thaw in our frosty relationship that her kind-hearted mother never suspected the gulf between us. The lack of overlap in school was because no attempt had been made to integrate the two "schools" for the remaining two months of the term. We shared the building—just as we'd shared with local schools when evacuated—and as a result, we returnees were back in harness, with the same teachers and the same curriculum, without missing a beat. It was an impressive feat, given the turmoil of the past week, and the fact that returning teachers were also re-establishing their own living quarters.

As we explored our new school, it was the grounds that impressed us the most. For such a densely populated part of London, they were very extensive, much more extensive than the grounds of the schools we'd used in Reigate and Tredegar. Broad lawns sloped down to a stream edged with tall trees, beyond which there were a number of grassy playing fields, and, unexpectedly, there was a formal, stone-pathed rose garden, looking its beautiful best with the roses in full bloom when we first set eyes on it. It was a really lovely set-up, and the school building itself was unusual and interesting. A central grassy quadrangle with open-sided corridors gave access to the ground floor classrooms and other facilities, and the upstairs classrooms opened onto similar corridors overlooking the quadrangle; it was a cloister-like arrangement, that, with a few gothic arches, would have been positively monastic. Most classrooms had windows giving views of both quadrangle *and* grounds—a far cry from my old Hatfield Street School, with its windows placed so high that one could see only the sky! The overall result here, was a light, open, yet protected feeling. There was none of the shut-in atmosphere and echoing corridors of so many schools, though those open corridors were probably a bit chilly, come winter.

None of us had known what we were missing during the years of evacuation, but how our teachers must have yearned for all this as they struggled with the inadequacies of Rosemead: the poor lighting, the lack of heat, the blackboards perched precariously on easels. Interestingly, the headmistress of this domain had chosen the discomforts and uncertainties of evacuation for herself, leaving her second-in-command as acting head, here in Peckham. We had taken her presence for granted, and only now is it clear how much it meant to us at the time, how it helped us feel that we were the *real* Honor Oak School.

In what was left of that term, I unexpectedly got to know Miss Ashley quite well. She'd always been a remote, gowned figure that swept into Assembly each morning with great dignity—despite her strange, gangly gait—and, with equal dignity, swept out again at its completion. So I was dumbfounded when a letter from my mother arrived:

> Just a quick note Gwen to let you know that I'll be
> coming to your school on Thursday because theres
> something Miss Ashley wants to talk to me about. I

> got a letter asking me to come and see her if I could
> possibly manage it. She didnt say what it was about
> just that it was important so I'll be coming up on
> the 9 oclock train. I have to be back to get the old
> man his tea so dont know if I'll get a chance to see
> you. Love Mum.

My mother was coming to the school? *To see Miss Ashley?* I was appalled. Embarrassed at the very thought. Parents didn't talk to teachers, let alone to the headmistress! I hadn't known that Miss Ashley was even aware of my existence until she made arrangements for Kay and me when the school returned to London. I talked it over with Peggy, but we could neither of us think of anything important enough to bring my mother all the way from Brighton. So I swore Peggy to secrecy and nervously awaited my mother's visit. Not having seen Mum since the Easter holidays, I half hoped to see her—yet half hoped to be spared the embarrassment. On Thursday, in the middle of French, a prefect came to take me to Miss Ashley's room, and, scared stiff, I followed her—only to find my mother and Miss Ashley enjoying a cup of tea. This can't be about anything too awful, I thought. "Your mother and I have had a nice talk, and now she has to leave to catch her train, but I thought you'd like to just say hello before she went," said Miss Ashley. Mum and I dutifully said hello to one another, and then I was sent back to French, completely ignorant as to what was going on; until, a few days later, another letter arrived:

> Dear Gwen, I expect you are wondering what that
> was all about last Thursday but Miss Ashley thinks
> it would be best for you if you stayed at Honor Oak
> for two more years instead of going to Hove County
> School but shes not sure it can be arranged though
> I expect youd like that Gwen.

That was as close as anybody came to asking my opinion on this momentous proposal, but Mum was right. I didn't just *like* the idea of two more years at Honor Oak: I was ecstatic. Two more years of school, anywhere, would be welcome. But, at Honor Oak … what more could I wish for! I had started to worry about what would happen after I went home at the end of the school year, because many of my classmates were talking of leaving school and going to work. After all, we *were* about to sit our School Leaving Certificate exams … so would my stepfather finally get what he'd wanted for so long? Even if I went to Hove County School, would we—Mum and myself—be able to hold out for two long years against what I anticipated would be a daily barrage? I wasn't sure that we could. And, with grave doubts as to how I would fit in the unknown world of work, I'd been dreading the possibility of there being no more school in my future.

My mother's letter raised a number of questions, however. What made Miss Ashley come up with this idea? Was Hove County School notoriously undesirable? Unlikely: Hove was a model of respectability, I'd been told (certainly in comparison to racy, raucous Brighton, with all its "day-trippers" from London.) Or had Miss Ashley learned, somehow, of the problems on our home front? If so, how? I'd never breathed a *word* to anybody in the Honor Oak world. Had this been part of their mysterious talk? I cringed at the thought. Or had the talk centered on where I would live, who would pay the Honor Oak School fees (now that my family lived in Sussex), *and* the cost of the school uniform (for my miniscule Scholarship grant would be discontinued, too)?

No one ever discussed these matters with me, but, miraculously, by the time our School Cert. exams were finished, solutions had been found, Miss Ashley said, smiling broadly—and re-arranging her dentures—when she called me into her room, one day. She had unearthed a scholarship from a private philanthropist to cover tuition and books, and my mother had found distant relatives who lived not too far from the school. The relatives were Aunt Mary's parents, my cousin's wife's parents. How distant could you get! But it was the distance of their house from the school that mattered here. And so it was settled. I would indeed be spending my two Sixth Form years at Honor Oak! "Run along now, my dear," Miss Ashley went on. "There's that important meeting for the Upper Fifth. You mustn't miss that."

The meeting dealt with career options, and if my head was in a whirl on leaving Miss Ashley's room after hearing her wonderful news, it was spinning even faster when I left the meeting. By the time it had covered the options for School Certificate leavers—at best, secretarial/office work or nursing, it seemed—I was even happier about the news that Miss Ashley had just given me. She and my mother had miraculously engineered a two-year reprieve from a work world that held few attractions, though nursing still had a certain appeal, dating from the time of applying special oil to Maureen's eczema-covered head.

However, the options for girls staying on at school left me bewildered. I had somehow assumed that my two extra years would be more of the same, but, I now learned, I had to choose between Arts and Sciences. My best subjects were unquestionably Latin, French and Math, but I also learned that, if continuing with French, one should expect to spend summers in France, living with a French family, "possible again, thank goodness, now that the war is over!" beamed Miss Mapledorum, the teacher running this meeting. I didn't see the faintest hope of summers in France being on the cards for me. And there didn't seem to be many jobs that these Arts subjects led to, other than teaching. And I categorically rejected teaching at that point in my life. Much as I loved the world of school, I couldn't imagine spending my life immersed in it, pounding information into the heads of a bunch of girls and condemned to spinsterhood (a conclusion reached simply because only one of our Honor Oak teachers had been married ...)

Actually, the problem was that I *could* imagine it, only too clearly. The clincher was that I'd probably end up teaching Latin. It was my best, and favorite, subject but universally hated by students everywhere—based on my huge sampling of two schools, Honor Oak and St Dunstan's. How could there be any satisfaction in teaching something that no one wanted to learn? I knew at first hand how reluctant schoolgirl heads could be when it came to the acquisition of Latin. *Thank you, but no thank you,* I said to myself and began to consider the Science path: maths, physics and chemistry, perhaps? Chemistry was a complete unknown, but I liked the other two, was good in maths and could probably do reasonably well in physics if I put my mind to it. The job prospects seemed brighter with the Sciences: as I knew from Laura, they included working in laboratories—doing what, I knew not, beyond a vague idea of serious people in white coats measuring things. At least it wasn't teaching. But I hated the thought of dropping Latin and French and English. They were my favorite subjects!

I walked down the corridor afterwards, with all this rolling around in my head and my earlier elation considerably diminished. Why wasn't anything ever *easy*? It was going to be terribly difficult to make this choice. Then, suddenly, I had a clear image of Laura, so happy in her technician job, heading off every Monday morning with the white coat that Mrs. Taylor had washed and ironed with such care and pride. I somehow knew that Laura's wasn't a high-level job, but it sounded a lot more interesting than most first jobs. And she'd left school after only one year in the Sixth Form. That decided it. *I would go the Science route.* The decision was made, finally, in a flash. And, despite the regrets over dropping all my favorite subjects, I felt, immediately, that a huge burden had been lifted from my shoulders. It was, I now realize, the first time I'd made a decision for myself; everything had always been decided for me by teachers or parents or other adults. I also now realize that it was based on decidedly meager information: on ignorance of the world and what it had to offer; on all that white coat nonsense and the limitations I perceived for the Arts. But I didn't know that at the time. Neither did I know how to ask the questions that might have helped me choose which way to jump.

Laura and Mrs. Taylor were tickled pink by my decision, but the reaction in school was consternation. *"Dropping Latin?* What *will* Miss Ashley say?" said the teacher we called Rubby (short for Rubbermouth, on account of the way she pursed her lips into extraordinary contortions under stress of any kind). My announcement about pursuing the Science route had set that thin, flexible mouth going nineteen to the dozen, for she had been my Latin teacher for four years; she, understandably, expected me to continue with it—and I had serious regrets about walking away from Rubby's world. After all, it was she who had slipped a slim, well-thumbed volume of Ovid into my hand and shyly suggested that I'd probably enjoy translating it. We both derived much enjoyment from the ensuing "discussions" of her beloved Ovid, discussions entirely in the form of her lengthy written critiques of my translation efforts—handed back underneath my regular Latin assignments, because somehow Rubby knew that this had to be a secret between the two of us.

But Miss Ashley? Why would she care? I soon discovered why. Miss Ashley had, apparently, been a distinguished Latin scholar, the first woman to "take the Tripos" (or something) at Cambridge (or was it Oxford?). She always taught the Sixth Form Latin classes and, unbeknown to me, had her heart set on carving out a path along which I was to follow in her footsteps. Slumped in her favorite chair with a cup of tea balanced on her chest and tears in her eyes, Miss Ashley told me of these, now thwarted, plans that were to have included scholarships and prizes I'd never heard of. And I was suddenly ten years old again, standing in front of Mr. Pascoe, as tears welled in *his* eyes about the Preliminary Scholarship exam. Again I felt like an ungrateful worm. But more so, this time. Then, I'd been an innocent player; now, I was the one responsible for upsetting this well-wisher's plans on my behalf. For one who'd always striven not to do or say anything that would hurt anyone's feeling, I seemed to have quite a talent for bringing tears to the eyes of would-be benefactors … But, bad as I felt, I couldn't help thinking, "My, oh my! I would have been well and truly caught in the Latin-teacher trap." And this served to firm up my switch to the sciences. Guiltily, and probably unjustly, I wondered if Miss Ashley would have searched so diligently for a special scholarship to keep me on at Honor Oak, had she known that I was going to drop Latin—for physics, in which I had a less than stellar record. But she made no attempt to dissuade me, which only made me feel worse.

On the last day of school, there were teary good-byes for girls who weren't planning to return to school in September, unless they'd done poorly on their School Cert. exams and came back for a second bite at the apple. Beryl, one of our Rosemead foursome, was one such girl. But we knew that she wouldn't be back: fatalist that she was, Beryl would just shrug her sloping, athletic shoulders and get on with the rest of her life. With Maggie long since gone, Peggy and I would be all that was left of our tight-knit little group … yet, so permanent it had seemed! We none of us would have believed that it would prove to be so short-lived. Peggy and I said sad good-byes to Beryl, and a cheery "See ya in September!" to one another at the point where our paths separated on our last walk home together. Then I packed my suitcase, again, said fond good-byes to Mrs. Taylor and Laura and headed for Hove for the summer holidays.

◆　　◆　　◆

A wonderful summer it turned out to be, that first summer of peace. Peace reigned even on our home front. Well, not exactly peace, but a kind of cease-fire. A product, perhaps, of the general euphoria that the war was a thing of the past.

To my astonishment, Mum's hair-training zeal (as applied to my little sister) was also a thing of the past. Maureen was allowed all the hair-dos I had longed for—ribbons, headbands, long hair, and bangs—and was never subjected to the hated giant hair slides. The zeal had been there to begin with. Maureen's first few wisps of hair had been moistened lovingly with spit and shaped into a spike that, in the fullness of time, came to resemble first a cresting ocean wave, then a "sausage roll." But any attempt to encourage curls had now lapsed, though Maureen's hair looked a lot more promising than mine ever had, and new wisps curled prettily on her neck without any encouragement. Part of me was happy that my little sister was to be spared the embarrassment of having her hair "trained"; but another part was sad, because my mother seemed, quite suddenly, older. Older and tireder. She'd found the energy to fight poverty throughout the thirties and survive the London Blitz, but something in her died, I think, when she had to crawl back to Jack Weddinger with her tail between her legs after the Maplewood fiasco.

However, the cease-fire on our domestic front was a welcome change, and Derek was more at ease than I'd seen him for some time. Moreover, he had yet another reason to be feeling better about himself: on his second shot at the Scholarship Exam, he'd qualified for entry into Brighton Technical College and was planning to study Architecture. He'd always felt bad, I think, about not passing the Scholarship Exam first time; though it was probably a near miss because he was accepted by Archbishop Temple, a really good school, and did well there. Unfortunately, when we moved to Hove there was no equivalent school, and he'd been bored out of his mind at the local secondary school, so he was quite chuffed about the prospect of the Technical College.

"I dunno what the ol' man will say when 'e finds out Derek won't be leavin' school at Christmas when 'e's fourteen," Mum said to me, with a proud chuckle. "We'd best keep quiet about it as long as we can. 'Cos 'is nibs carried on alarmin' when I told 'im yew was stayin' on at Honor Oak. I shut 'im up by tellin' 'im it was all arranged by yer 'eadmistress, so there was nothin' we could do about it. Then 'e wanted ta know, 'Is the bloody 'eadmistress gonna feed an' clothe 'er till she's bloody eighteen?' So I said that was all tak'n care of an' it wasn't gonna come out of 'is pocket, so 'e might as well shuddup about it!"

"How *is* all that going to be paid for?" I asked. This had been worrying me; as had the question of who had paid Mrs. Taylor for my room and board and miscellaneous expenses. The tram fares to school had given rise to an awkward moment when I realized that my pocket money wouldn't cover them and had to ask her for money. There was just a hint of hesitation before she gave it to me, enough that I wondered whether this was something she hadn't bargained on. Never before had this issue cropped up; as an evacuee, all such expenses had been covered by the government, and I doubt whether anybody had given it a moment's thought in my quasi-evacuee Peckham situation. Was I supposed to get the fare money from my mother? I didn't like to do that either and had salved my conscience by walking home from school every day to spare Mrs. Taylor as much as I could—letting her think that I was staying for after-school activities. Now I wanted some clarification, so that I wouldn't run into similar problems with Aunt Mary's parents. But all I ever got out of Mum was, "Oh-h, don't yew worry about it. That's all tak'n care of." From which I concluded that these expenses would probably come out of her Co-op Savings Bank, as had the cost of my room and board in Peckham, no doubt.

My brother and I had a marvelous summer together. The beaches were open again, and the barbed wire had been removed, so we made the most of our first summer-long seaside holiday. We also took the dog for long walks and explored the area in which we now lived—a much less industrial area than Waterloo, and with few gaping bombsites. Most houses had a cream-colored stucco finish, which made everything looked brighter and cleaner than the sooty unadorned brick of London, and persistent sea breezes kept the air fresher, made it smell good. There seemed to be more sunshine, too; this was, after all, a resort area, and there was a reason people chose to spend their holidays here!

We particularly loved to roam around Brighton, with its Regency architecture: street after street of bow-fronted row houses, stemming from the time when King George III chose to build himself a summer residence in a small fishing village that rapidly caught on as *the* fashionable watering place. George's "summer cottage," an exotic, onion-domed palace known as The Pavilion, is now Brighton's museum show piece, and to give some idea of the scale of the place, its stables were at some point converted into a concert hall! George's folly left Brighton with a unique architectural legacy that gives the town its character, and gave two roaming teenagers a great deal of pleasure in the summer of 1945. It was vague and unfocussed, that pleasure, but something that London's rows of flat-fronted brick houses had never evoked—in me, at least, though I can't speak for my brother. We never actually discussed it, but I can't help feeling that Derek's decision to study Architecture may have reflected the influence of King George's legacy. It certainly left me with an abiding fondness for Regency architecture, though I have but one specific memory of its impact at the time: a sudden recognition, that a front door could be an object of beauty and interest, given an elegant transom, impressive pillars, or simply a handsome knocker.

Brighton's pebbly beaches had always been hard on the feet, and now there was the additional hazard of rusty old barbs from the recently removed barbed wire—especially tricky when you were in the water, jumping the waves. None of this put us off, and Derek and I swam almost every day; but Maureen, who turned four that summer, was too little for the big waves and much too young to reliably watch out for barbs, so we had to go without her. To compensate, we sometimes took her to a swimming pool, but it wasn't really a fair substitute, and we all knew it—especially Maureen.

Rightly or wrongly, I remember that summer as one of endless sunshine. Though there was at least one memorable rainy day—a day on which Derek and I got caught on the beach in a downpour. We happily swam in the rain, assuming it would soon stop, but the rain kept falling harder and harder, and the clothes that we'd left on the beach were getting wetter and wetter. We finally decided to cut our losses, rushed up the beach to the two sodden piles and faced in opposite directions as we hurriedly changed—with no attempt at modesty, since not a soul was in sight. We ran off the beach, up the steps to the promenade, wet clothes clinging crookedly to damp skins, and to our astonishment, a great cheer went up. Only then did we see the sea of heads, at least one in each window of the tall building that overlooked "our" beach—a block of flats that had stood empty for a long time, but had recently, unbeknownst to us, been commandeered as quarters for sailors on shore leave! It was a while before I swam off that beach again, long enough for that batch of sailors to be back on their ships.

We often went walking with the dog on the South Downs—the chalk ridge that meanders along the Sussex Coast. Those walks with Derek and Bobby re-kindled my love affair with chalk hills and their soft-but-sharp, green-against-blue silhouette against the sky, their quiet timelessness emphasized by the scattering of neglected tumuli—all that remains of the Romans who used these hills as lookout points. Toward the end of the summer Mum and Maureen came too, and we picked blackberries, filling as many bags and jars as our stained and sticky fingers could carry home on the bus. Next day the kitchen was filled with the aroma of boiling jam—until we ran out of sugar. With this in mind, we had hoarded sugar for weeks, eking it out of our rations; for ration books had not been thrown away along with our gas masks, and nor would they be, for several years to come. But by late afternoon, jar after gleaming jar of yummy blackberry jam sat on the kitchen table, waiting to be labeled when cool. A very satisfying conclusion to our labors of the day before. We ate as many of the remaining blackberries as we could, and as quickly as we could before the fruit spoiled—refrigerators being an unknown luxury on Ellen Street. The rest we gave to a family with half a dozen children, and they made short work of them, down to the very last blackberry.

It was a summer that left memories of lots of good times. In particular, it stands out as a time of rare closeness with my brother. Although I have an uncomfortable memory of a thought that occasionally popped into my head when he and I were off on some excursion together, just the two of us: "This is only happening because Bertie's no longer with us … " And then came the guilt that always followed this ungenerous thought.

The news of the end of the war with Japan we celebrated quietly at home. There was no spontaneous hymn singing, perhaps because of a dearth of Welsh singers on the South Coast. Or perhaps, because the war in the Pacific did not touch the people of Britain as the war in Europe had; though many families had a son or a husband or a father who was a prisoner of war in Japanese hands. But another factor was the mushroom cloud that hung over this peace agreement. The devastation wrought by one atomic bomb would have been unbelievable were it not for the photographs we stared at in the papers, and so many disturbing questions were raised by this new weapon that it was hard to know whether to be glad or sad about the end of the Pacific war. Like many who were bewildered by talk of atom-splitting, radioactivity, and the consequences thereof, my mother's take on it was a simple, "All I c'n say is, thank Gawd the Germans didn't 'ave one!"

As the start of school drew near, I began to get cold feet about my plunge into the sciences, and the books I'd brought home from the school library for a bit of background reading to give myself a head start, did not quiet my fears. The history of electricity and magnetism quickly revealed how much I didn't know, and the mathematics book left me mystified before the end of the first chapter by lots of exclamation marks scattered throughout. When the author pronounced, "it is left to the student to prove that the solution is 5!" I thought it was a joke whose point I'd missed—and I closed the book in a hurry. (A few weeks later, I learned in maths that 5! is simply shorthand for 5 x 4 x 3 x 2 x 1, so I need not have panicked.) Derek, quite unknowingly, further undermined my confidence one stormy day as we stood on Hove pier looking down at the churning waters of the English Channel, and he asked why the foam on a wave was white whilst the wave itself was green. I realized that I had absolutely no idea. *What had I let myself in for?* Had I made a wise decision that day, as I walked down the corridor with my head in a whirl? However, I assumed it was too late to switch back to Latin and French, even if I wanted to, so I'd just have to live with it. But I felt decidedly nervous.

All hell broke loose the day our stepfather picked up the letters that the postman had just put through the letterbox and saw a big, fat, official-looking letter for Derek, from the Technical College. "The *two* of 'em not earnin' a penny fer their keep!" he roared; and the domestic cease-fire was over. Mum quickly leapt into full battle mode, and by nightfall things were so bad that we four moved upstairs. We came in and out by the upper front door and only went downstairs to use the kitchen and the lavatory. It was madly inconvenient and entailed a lot of carrying of dishes up or down stairs, but it minimized the face-to-face confrontations and allowed for the rage to die down somewhat.

A week later I headed back to London, where I was to spend the next two years with Aunt Mary's parents, and as usual, I left with mixed feelings. Saying goodbye to Maureen got harder and harder as she got older and more fun to play with, and reading books to her had figured largely over that summer, something that would be horribly missed by both of us. In addition, I felt terrible about leaving Derek to deal with Jack Weddinger's renewed hostility. Just when my brother needed me most, I was deserting him, and I could only hope that our newfound "togetherness" would survive. My poor mother, too. I knew that she'd move out of the house—not just up a flight of stairs—if she had the money. But she'd be getting steadily farther from that goal, if, as I suspected, her savings were being depleted to keep me in school. A couple of days before I left, Mum pulled a pound note out of her purse, saying, "Fer yer train fare an' pocket money fer the month. An' it ain't out of 'is lordship's 'ousekeepin' money, so yew don't 'ave ta worry about that!" Now I *knew* who was paying for "all the other stuff" connected with my two extra years at Honor Oak; and, for the first time, I wondered whether I should have left school and gone to work.

◆   ◆   ◆

ADDENDUM

With the benefit of hindsight, I have no regrets about my decision to switch to the Sciences. However, I am astonished to think how casually that choice was made: no guidance counselors, and no advice from the teachers who knew me. Indeed, it never occurred to me to talk to any of those teachers, and I would have been too shy to do so, even if it had. I won't pretend that there weren't occasions during my student days when I wondered why the heck I had made the switch. There *were* moments when I envied friends who could spend all the time they wished, often into the wee small hours, reading and discussing literature and poetry without feeling guilty about their neglected studies—the price we science types paid when we dabbled in these waters. Once, a few of us, dissatisfied with dabbling, decided to take a little dip, and we persuaded a professor to let us audit his course on sixteenth century poetry. He was amazed by our request and we by *his* invitation to do one of the assignments—which he actually read and commented on. I wish I could report that it led to a lifelong interest in sixteenth century poetry. But it was a wonderful change of pace, and I'll always be grateful to that gentle man who allowed us a glimpse into *his* passion for the *Silver Poets of the Sixteenth Century*—the anthology we used. In marked contrast, I never met an Arts student auditing a science course; indeed, many boasted of their ignorance of, and lack of interest in science, an attitude that has always struck me as irritating. And pathetic.

Once my student days were over, that science switch served me well. It got me my first job in what Mrs. Taylor so painstakingly pronounced "a La-bor-a-tor-y," a job that was, indeed, a lot more interesting than most first jobs. Furthermore, I did wear a white coat and measure things, so my rationale for the switch was not completely ridiculous! Much later, all that science background provided the basis for a second career: as a physics teacher. Yes, I did eventually end up in the classroom. But I was, by then, married, and the specter of spinsterhood, at least, was no longer a threat! I was pleasantly surprised to discover that teaching could be very rewarding: notably, there was the satisfaction of seeing the occasional "light bulb" go on in the head of a youngster. Even the student "reluctance" factor was manageable; perhaps because, in American high schools, physics is an elective course, so physics teachers have the luxury of teaching those who want to be taught and the privilege of dealing with some very bright young people.

In my adult life, I've been able to do a lot of reading and have enjoyed the good fortune of having books readily available, all those books for which there was no time when I was a student. So, at the end of the day, I feel that the switch to science enriched my life, and I've been able to swim in two intellectual pools! Had I stuck with Latin and French, I might now know only the world of the Arts. Of course, maybe I would have put pen to paper a wee bit earlier … would not have waited till I was in my sixties to embark on this Chronicle. Maybe.

Chapter 27

Last Stop, All Change

MY LAST PORT OF call as a schoolgirl was Forest Hill, where Aunt Mary's parents lived. Life there was, at first, a strange neither-fish-nor-fowl experience. Droves of service men and women were returning home to pick up the threads of pre-war lives, and for months, everyone I bumped into had a husband, a father, a son, a brother, some relative or neighbor, who, midst much rejoicing, had just been de-mobbed [released from the armed services]. I, however, was still dealing with a war—our own family war—that kept me away from home after all my evacuee classmates had been reunited with their families. But the flow of returnees eventually slowed to a trickle, and I settled into my quasi-evacuee status. After all, I was an old hand at this, and with no bombs or battlefields to worry about, it was certainly easier than the real thing.

Mr. and Mrs. Grendell did everything they could to make a shy, awkward sixteen-year-old feel welcome, though it was many years since they'd had dealings with a teenager—their youngest child being now in her late twenties. I had met the Grendells when I was living in Merstham, but hadn't paid them close attention, and I doubt that they'd done more than register my existence; they'd come to visit their daughter and granddaughters, not some cousin of their son-in-law. However, as I stood on their doorstep in early September with my much-traveled suitcase, it was comforting to know that they were family—sort of—and I was not a complete stranger to them, or they to me.

Even before the door opened, I recognized Mrs. Grendell's smoker's cough. She wasn't in Aunt-mum's class: she could smoke and cough, smoke and talk, or cough and talk, but had not mastered the art of doing all three at the same time. Neither could she be accused of "talkin' the 'ind leg awf a donkey," like Aunt-mum, for her conversational contributions were usually terse and monosyllabic. She did occasionally indulge in lengthy grumbles about things such as the still skimpy meat ration and the price of coal, but never seemed to mind if her audience drifted away, leaving her talking to herself. "The first sign o' madness, they do say, Mother!" her husband, Arthur, would tease, when he found her declaiming to an empty room. He was a lovely, jocular man, and I grew very fond of him. Though his dictatorial attitude concerning the control knob of the radio was disconcertingly at odds with his otherwise benevolent nature: he *hated* to come home and find that the radio had been tuned to a different station.

A tall, heavy man, with a mane of white hair, bright blue eyes and a splendid beak of a nose, Mr. Grendell cut a striking figure, in spite of his comical rolling gait—due to a gammy leg, not to years at sea. He was a guard on passenger trains, and his life had been spent riding the rails, not the waves, so that leg must have been a serious handicap. Dozens of times a day he had to walk the length of a train checking that all doors were shut, then wave a flag and blow the whistle that the engine driver was waiting for, and leap into the guard's compartment at the end of the now moving train. Mrs. Grendell worried about the dangers this posed for her husband, but I never heard him complain. Indeed, no matter how exhausted he looked when he came through the door, he always had a kiss and a joke for his wife. And we could tell at a glance if he'd had a "red letter day," a day on which an unaccompanied child had ridden in his guard's van for safe keeping, and he'd had the pleasure of chatting and sharing Knock-Knock jokes before delivering his young passenger to some relative standing anxiously on a platform somewhere.

Forest Hill, a convenient bike ride from Honor Oak School, was a dreary corner of Southeast London and did not live up to the promise of its name. There was a discernible hill, but no trace of a Forest, apart from a few sad trees that bravely put out new leaves each year, doing their best to provide relief to an otherwise unbroken landscape of dismal, turn-of-the-century, two-story brick houses. Once again I found myself living in a small Victorian row house, with two rooms down and two up, an add-on kitchen at the back and the usual limited plumbing. There was also the familiar smell of boiling vegetable scraps, for the Grendells, like their daughter in Merstham, kept chickens at the end of the garden. That horrible smell! It seemed to follow me wherever I went.

The smell and inadequate plumbing turned out to be the least of my worries. There was a larger fly in this ointment, in the shape of Hope, the Grendell's youngest, and unmarried, daughter. Everything about this lean, angular, gangly young woman was on a large scale—nose, chin, and even the pores of her skin—and her stooped frame seemed uncertain what to do with the long limbs and the large appendages at their extremities. Worse yet, she had an unwashed odor that was especially strong when she "had the curse." Yet she did wash, daily and thoroughly, in the dark little kitchen. I know, because I often witnessed her ablutions in the morning, as I waited my turn at the sink. So it's not clear why she smelled, but it made her totally repellent at close quarters; and she and I had to sleep in the same bed; very close quarters indeed. I couldn't bear for any part of Hope to touch any part of me and suffered agonies every night as I wrestled with the urge to carve out a "space" for myself in that bed—in emulation of Kay's efforts in the feather bed we'd shared in Wales. I had to keep telling myself that I was the invader here, that this, after all, was Hope's bedroom and Hope's bed. And that, considering the options, she was possibly less to put up with than Jack Weddinger was. So I kept my shudders to myself and always assured the Grendells, and my mother, that everything was fine.

Had the Hope-problem been limited to her unfortunate physical attributes, there would have been room for pity (I like to think), but it didn't take long to discover that she was also "a born trouble-maker," as old Aunt Lil had told me back in my Merstham days. Hope went about meddling and stirring up mischief—always in the guise of doing good—as when she'd emptied out Aunt Lil's flat while she was in hospital. I was now inclined to take the old lady's version of that incident with a smaller pinch of salt. Especially after hearing Mrs. Grendell beg her daughter, "keep yer nose out of other people's business, won'cha … yew on'y make things worse," when Hope was prattling on about some friend she was helping out. Hope invariably responded to her mother's plea with a laugh, and that throaty laugh—insincere, at best, calculating and malicious, at worst—used to make my skin creep. I have never loathed anyone as I loathed Hope.

Needless to say, in the Grendells' little Victorian house, there were the familiar difficulties associated with limited plumbing. In particular, the indignities of bath night loomed large again, in yet another kitchen that was the main thoroughfare to the back door. But I was rescued from all this when Louie had a bathroom installed in her Aquinas Street flat and insisted that I come and use it. I didn't have to be asked twice and gladly cycled seven miles each way every Sunday to soak in blissful privacy in a deep bathtub full of hot water that could be topped up by the turn of a tap should it get a little cool. What luxury! After all the tin tubs I'd ladled water into and out of, and after the Welsh Aunts, who regarded warm water in excess of two inches as positively sinful "indeed t'goodness, gurrl!" When I emerged, toastie-warm and pink from this unaccustomed, sinful wallowing, Louie always had a great spread awaiting me on the table: Sunday tea. And after Harry was de-mobbed, there we were again, the three of us, sitting down to winkles and celery for tea, as on pre-war Sundays.

Yet, there were differences. Butter, still rationed, was spread more thinly than of yore, and there were no goldfinches and canaries singing their hearts out, but the biggest change was in Louie and Harry, themselves. Gone was their old lovey-dovey playfulness; they were both subdued and tight-lipped and carefully avoided eye contact. I was puzzled, because in many ways their lives had improved.

Harry had finally "got 'is cards" from the printers' union (something he'd been waiting for since he started work at fourteen). So he now had a real job, no longer suffered the indignity of being a grown man employed as a messenger boy, and this must have helped his ego, not to mention his pocketbook. Louie's job had improved, too. She still worked "over the river" at Hoare's Bank, but now spent less time on her knees, scrubbing floors, and more on her feet, dusting and sweeping and serving afternoon tea in fine china on an elegant tray to the "Big Boss," Sir Peter himself.

Despite all this, Louie and Harry were not the happy couple they'd been before the war, and not until Mum told me, many years later, about Harry's wartime affair, did I understand why. "When 'Arry was de-mobbed at the end o' the war an' 'ad ta make a choice b'tween 'is lady loves, 'e begged Louie ta take 'im back—but the other woman kicked up quite a stink," Mum said. "It fair broke Louie's 'eart, it did … , she'd always worshipped the ground 'Arry walked on." And I suddenly had a poignant wartime memory of Louie, with unquestioning devotion, refusing to let anyone sit in Harry's empty chair, because she was, "savin' it fer 'im', when 'e comes 'ome at the end o' this blessed ol' war."

Despite the tension in their flat, I looked forward to spending Sundays with them and popping round to see Aunt-mum, though her Coin Street house was no longer the rambunctious place of my early memories. Uncle Ernie was now dead, all the 'Odds an' 'Arrises were married with homes of their own, and Aunt-mum was always glad of someone to talk to other than herself. Though I suspect that she didn't let that inhibit her monologues. Occasionally, George and Kitty would stop by, or Rosie and Perce, and the house would then sound more like its old self. But, Aunt-mum lamented, "Viley and 'er Tom, they live on some ol' army base up norf', so I sometimes go fer mumfs wivout seein' li'l Leonard, me on'y gran'son." She seemed to blame this on Tom, "fer bein' sich a lazy bligh'er. Too bone idle ta git out'a the army an' git 'isself a real job, that one is." However, she wouldn't be the Aunt-mum I'd known for as long as I could remember, if she didn't have *something* to complain about; in fact, it was good to find her grumbling with her familiar zest: still coughing-smoking-and-talking, as only she could.

One weekend, I accepted an invitation from Betty Marsh—we still corresponded regularly—to visit her in Dorking, just south of London. The visit was not exactly a success, although Betty and Esme (her landlady, a young mother whose husband was still overseas) did their best to make me welcome. Long tree-lined walks with them were a refreshing change from the built-up streets of Forest Hill, but I was ill at ease in their well-heeled, well-upholstered world of detached houses, large gardens, matching furniture, and everything in its place. As in the restaurant with Betty and her mother many years earlier, I was acutely aware of how well dressed these folks were and how much they took all their creature comforts for granted. And once again, I didn't know where to hide my badly bitten nails and shabby shoes.

I did enjoy the level of conversation in Dorking and was beginning to feel less of a misfit when an unexpected incident drove my level of discomfort sky high again. After brushing my teeth (in a de luxe, floor-to-ceiling-tiled-bathroom), I realized that I hadn't said goodnight, and not wanting to appear rude, went back downstairs. I could hear the murmur of voices coming from the sitting room, so I knocked on the door before pushing it open—and gazed, open-mouthed, at the sight of Betty and Esme, sitting in the dark in front of a glowing fire, naked from the waist up, with a bowl of water on a small table and wash cloths in their hands. Their backs were toward me, but they both turned and, completely unabashed, presented me with a full view of their bobbing breasts, sharply shadowed and outlined by the light of the fire. I murmured an embarrassed "Goodnight" and fled, astounded by the carefree cheeriness of the Goodnights that followed me up the stairs. I lay awake for a long time, wondering how I could face these two ladies in the morning. The most brazen of my schoolmates would modestly turn so as to present a bare back in a door-less booth after swimming, so I had been unprepared for such an encounter in that respectable Dorking sitting room. I have since wondered whether Betty and Esme went to boarding schools and there became inured to lack of privacy in communal washrooms. Certainly, the next morning they acted as if nothing untoward had happened, but I, steeped in working class prudery, could not look at their now-covered chests without seeing them as I had the night before, and I was relieved when the time came to take the train back to London.

Time and time again I mulled over this incident, much as one's tongue cannot let a sore tooth alone. Sometimes shock prevailed—at age sixteen, those bare breasts had been my first exposure to an open display of nudity—but more often, puzzlement dominated. Why, oh why, with that superb bathroom at their disposal, did those two ladies choose to share a bowl of water in front of the fire? It was a situation not unlike the one that I rode miles to avoid every Sunday! In the world that I knew, the hard-earned comfort and ease of the bathroom would have won out, every time.

A few years later, D.H Lawrence opened up new vistas of sensual pleasure and gave me a glimmer of a clue as to what I had witnessed that night: two young women, close friends, choosing the pleasure of bathing together in front of a fire over the convenience of a magnificent but joy-less bathroom. It was an astonishing, alien idea. Had such pleasures always existed, un-noticed, all around me? If so, like nudity, they were kept behind closed doors, carefully hidden from young eyes. In the working class world, was all this prudery a necessary defense against lack of privacy? I don't know. I do know that I was well into my sixties before I was comfortable enough "in my skin" to walk around naked—even when alone, and in my own bedroom. But maybe that was just my own personal hang-ups. However, the general absence of pleasure for pleasure's sake that I had observed, day in and day out—that, surely, was too widespread to be just me; more likely, the continuous striving against privation simply enmeshed the folks of my world in a tangled net of limitations.

To my relief, there were no more invitations to Dorking, and Betty started taking me to matinees, instead. "Something I've wanted to do with you, Gwynneth, for a *long* time, but there was always the worry about air raids. So now we'll just have to make up for lost time, won't we!" she chuckled happily, as we settled into our seats in a posh West End theater for the first of these treats. We saw a stirring drama, *Edward My Son*, and in the intermission we had tea and biscuits served to us, in our seats, on little trays; another time it was *Swan Lake* at Covent Garden, where I loved everything I saw and heard—including the grandeur of the Opera House itself. The musical, *No! No! Nanette* was silly and tedious, I thought, but Betty raved about it, and for fear of hurting her feelings, I pretended to have enjoyed it. That age-old dilemma! How to tell a white lie, without setting myself up for more of something I hadn't enjoyed? Memories sprang to mind of watching boys pummeling one another in boxing matches at The Ring with the Hodds, and morning after morning of Gran's cold porridge. I feared that I had let myself in for hours of boring musicals for which I'd have to keep faking enjoyment, but apparently I was not a good enough faker for Betty. Thereafter, she stuck to plays and ballets, adding enormously to my education and whetting my appetite for more of this good stuff.

◆   ◆   ◆

Only a handful of my evacuee classmates had decided to stay on for the Sixth Form, but I was shattered to find that Peggy was not among them. I felt truly bereft without her broad, mischievous grin to greet me. Apparently, her family had moved over the summer, so presumably she was in some other Sixth Form, feeling equally bereft. And I was now the only survivor of our Rosemead foursome! At the end of last term Peggy and I had said our usual casual goodbye and didn't exchange addresses, so neither of us now knew where the other lived. I was suddenly furious about our train agreement: if only we'd known that the year in Tredegar was to mark the end of our friendship ... in retrospect, what idiots we had been.

Kay had decided to stay on at school, but by unspoken agreement, she and I went our separate ways. She did once invite me to her home for dinner—"Daddy wants to meet you," she said. And he really did. He was eager to know about me, my family, what subjects I liked, and he was curious about my continued enrolment at Honor Oak. But I made no mention of my philanthropist; I wasn't sure whether that was a secret between Miss Ashley and me. Knowing Kay's difficulties with her father, it was an uncomfortable evening, and I was glad that I was never invited again.

Also missing from the school scene was Mrs. Bamber-Bowtell and most of our old teachers. They had probably sunk back gratefully into their interrupted retirements now the younger teachers were returning from the armed services—many of whom were married, which was quite an eye-opener. However, the biggest shock that Honor Oak had in stock for me on the first day of school, was hearing my name called during Assembly and having to force my fat, awkward, embarrassed self across the stage in front of the whole school to have a prefect badge pinned onto my blouse. Me? A prefect? This was a development I'd never anticipated. I had always assumed that there was a permanent black mark against me, as a result of Plan B and my record-breaking accumulation of Order Marks. It was bizarre to think that, if the martinets' discipline scheme had remained in effect, I would now be doling out Order Marks instead of collecting them. I'm afraid I wasn't much of a disciplinarian. This role reversal seemed distinctly hypocritical, and I often "looked the other way." But I did diligently supervise the after-school-detention room, collect the milk money from the Third Form—my allotted form—and assume various other responsibilities that were expected of prefects.

As I'd feared, the sciences did not come as easily as Latin and French. Chemistry, in particular, was difficult: a morass of seemingly disconnected facts to be memorized. I floundered, completely overwhelmed, until, flipping through our massive textbook during one of many panic attacks, I happened upon the Periodic Table and ... Open Sesame! There *was* a "pattern," a logical ordering, to all those facts! Curiously, in that same year, 1945, a few miles from Forest Hill on the other side of the Thames, a young boy named Oliver Sacks had a similar experience, which he describes in his book, *Uncle Tungsten*. As he tells it, when he climbed for the first time up a flight of stairs in London's Science Museum, there, on the wall, was a huge Periodic Table. It provided "a key to the universe" for this boy, and the vast collection of facts about the elements that he'd already amassed began to fall into place. My knowledge of chemical behavior was pitiful in comparison, but it, too, began to make sense after I chanced upon the Periodic Table.

Nevertheless I had to work hard to do well in my two Sixth Form years and prove that my switch to science had not been entirely foolish, so spare time was in short supply and my social life correspondingly meager. It didn't help that I had to repair dozens of punctures in my bicycle tires, caused by zillions of tiny glass shards lurking along the roads, the last remains of windows blown out in air raids. Before long, my pre-war vintage inner tube (new ones were hard to come by) was essentially all patches and difficult to squeeze back into the tire without pinching it and creating a new puncture. This led to a sense of constant crisis, because the bike was a crucial factor in my new living arrangement: the journey to school by bus or tram "went all round the bloomin' mulberry bush"—Mum said, after doing it one day—but, by bike, there was a short cut across a pedestrian bridge. With the passage of time, my skill in puncture-repair grew, the glass fragments gradually disappeared (all embedded in tires of long-suffering cyclists, no doubt), and I got a new inner tube—so, eventually, I was able to take the occasional deep breath and do something just for fun.

In the course of that daily bike ride, I often met up with a girl who was in all my classes. She was also a newly minted prefect, so we had much to talk about and became good friends. Monica was my first friend from the "Peckham school," the part that had remained in London throughout the war. They called us the "evacuee school," and the gulf between the two persisted for a couple of years, particularly among the senior girls. Certainly, in the Sixth Form Common Room, we all, at first, trod carefully with the strangers we were meeting for the first time and gravitated towards the faces we'd known for five years. This is how Joyce Butler and I struck up an unexpected friendship. It was unexpected because, until now, each in our own tight cluster of friends, we had more or less ignored one another. But now, both of us were lone survivors of those clusters. At first I was leery of this girl, whose group I'd thought of as rather "fast," into clothes and lipstick and boys, forever trying to push the envelope when it came to the rules governing school uniform. The sock rule seemed particularly irksome to them, and they were frequently sent home to remedy an infringement of this requirement. The most notable instance was on the day of a choir concert when Joyce was sent home to cover her bare ankles before being allowed to sing her solo—which happened to be Handel's "How Beautiful Are The Feet." With remarkable self-control, Joyce did not, like half her audience, collapse into giggles during her solo.

It was Joyce's beautiful, effortless voice, rich and full for one so young, that opened up the world of music for me one day, when I was sitting on the floor, doing homework while she rehearsed "The Shepherd on the Rock." I was taken unawares and captivated—seduced even—by Schubert's lovely, liquid melodies, by the delicate interweaving of the two voices, clarinet and singer (scarcely aware of the piano on that first hearing, I fear). I'd never paid much attention to music, but suddenly I "saw" the melodies, climbing, tumbling, twisting and twining vine-like, then miraculously disengaging in readiness for a fresh "dance," whilst subtle, shifting emotions unexpectedly swelled and faded somewhere under my rib cage. Later that evening, gazing at Joyce's score, I marveled that such a fantastic complex of experiences had been somehow "contained" within those little black marks marching across a piece of paper.

I promptly signed up for Choir and a class on Music Theory, and Miss Attridge, the music teacher, generously forgave me all the years when I'd been nothing but a thorn in her side, the years when Music had been classified as "unimportant," according to Plan A. She even included me in Saturday morning excursions to the Albert Hall to hear rehearsals of orchestral concerts, concerts that we then heard, uninterrupted, in the evening. For me, a blank slate as regards music, a better initiation into classical music could not have been devised. And, for "Atty's girls" as we came to be known, everything was free, because she was an old friend of the conductor, Charles Hambourg. He rented the Albert Hall for these concerts and assembled a group of musicians for the pleasure of conducting them himself. What an eye-opener it was for us girls to learn that the world contained people who could do this kind of thing; and to discover that this particular example was a friendly teddy bear of a man, with great, shaggy eyebrows, a booming laugh, and an expansive belly encased in a favorite, shabby, old cardigan.

Joyce and I made an improbable pair: awkward, shy, overweight me, and this lithe, graceful girl, easy-going and sociable, with her laughing gray eyes and myriad tiny dimples that came and went like "cat's paws" on water ruffled by a breeze. Another marked difference was in the realm of clothes and lipstick and boys. I had no money for anything other than my school uniform and other essentials, though I did once purchase some powder and a lipstick, feeling horribly guilty about wasting my mother's hard earned pennies. When alone in the house, I nervously tried it out. One glance in the mirror told me that the painted face staring back was not "me". I could not appear in public wearing it, and I was horrified to find how hard it was to scrub off all traces of the lipstick. Afterwards, I couldn't bring myself to throw the stuff away; that seemed only to compound the original waste, so it lay buried among my undies for a very long time, flooding me with guilt whenever I accidentally came across it.

As for boys, there was the undeniable fact that when our peers from our "brother" school, St. Dunstan's, joined forces with us for a dance in the gym, they seemed totally unaware of my existence. I always hoped that one of our Merstham boys, the quarry trio, would show up, but was always disappointed and invariably spent a miserable evening—in an ill-fitting frock, borrowed from Louie or Hope—dancing with other girls or hugging the wall, pretending to have a good time. Based largely on the lack of any discernible male response to my charms during those Sixth Form years, I grew resigned to the idea of spinster-hood, after all. Sadly resigned, though I couldn't have said exactly why it left me sad. And, of course, it did demolish one of my reasons for having rejected the Arts ...

Despite all our differences, Joyce and I became firm friends. Before long I was a regular visitor to her home, where her parents, good-hearted working class folks, welcomed me with open arms as the second daughter they'd never had. For Joyce was an only child, (the only only child I'd ever known, other than lonely little Gloria, of Gloucestershire). Joyce, too, welcomed me as a "some-time sister." If nothing else, I provided relief from the undivided adult attention that was normally focussed exclusively on her—in spades, since the upper floor of the Butler house was occupied by her childless Aunt Dot and Uncle Jack, who also doted on Joyce. These four adoring adults were, no doubt, making up for the past six years, when the object of their adoration had been evacuated, and at times I felt quite sorry for Joyce. Away from home, she had enjoyed a lot more independence than these loving folks now wanted her to have.

On one of my weekly trips to Waterloo, I was maneuvering my bike across the tramlines at The Elephant and Castle, the maze I'd first mastered as a ten-year-old with Viley, when I became aware of changing "hats," switching from my Forest Hill persona to my Waterloo persona. I also realized that the Elephant and Castle was the point at which I always changed those hats. Further reflection revealed how many other hats I wore in the course of an average week: my in-school hat, my out-of-school-with-Joyce hat, and the one I assumed when out-of-school-with-Joyce-and-her-family. Then there was my Betty-Marsh hat and the at-home-in-Hove hat. Seven hats and seven persona. Which was the real me? *Was* there a real me? Perhaps I was some mix, a chameleon-like creature, adapted to fitting into my surroundings—a useful attribute for an evacuee, no doubt. Maybe that was how I had survived six different households in six years—seven in seven years, counting my present quasi-evacuee situation. These were perturbing questions, and they were to haunt me for a long, long, time, especially when I found myself in yet another new situation, assuming yet another new hat.

The second of my Sixth Form years, my last year of school, was for Maureen, her first. It was hard to believe that her little head was about to start wrestling with arithmetic, with things like carrying and borrowing tens. And it was troubling to think that she'd be at the mercy of whatever teachers fate had in store for her, in an old school building that backed on to the gas works and one of those huge gas holders with a dome that kept rising and falling. It did not look promising. None of this would matter if her first teacher were as nice as mine, my adored Miss Johnson, but what were the chances, I wondered, of there being another Miss Johnson lurking in the wings for Maureen? However there was nothing, absolutely nothing, that I could do to protect my little sister in the world she was about to enter, and I was soon preoccupied with lots of changes in my own school world.

A number of my fellow Sixth Formers had left, some, including Joyce and Kay, to attend teacher training colleges, but the biggest surprise was the choice of Monica and me as joint Head Girls, one Peckham girl and one evacuee girl, to help meld the two schools. *Head Girl?* This was more astonishing than being a prefect. For a while I'd wake in the morning thinking I must have dreamed it, and then, as reality asserted itself, how proud Mr. Pascoe would be, if he could have known. My father, too. Although perhaps Dad, like Mum, would never have actually *told* me that he was proud. Praise was a rare commodity then. Unlike today, when every accomplishment, however minor, seems to be acknowledged with, "Good job! Give me a high five!" Many years later I learned that my mother did actually sing my praises, long and loud, to Derek and Maureen when I wasn't there. Too long and too loud, apparently, for it led my brother to coin a new adjective for being "all Gwenned out." (Maureen is convinced that frequent bouts of being Gwenned out were a factor in Derek's coolness, his reluctance to talk to me, which caused me such distress. And, she confessed, "I *hated* you for a while when I was in my teens. When Mother was all "Gwen this" and "Gwen that," and I could do nothing right!") I can only feel thankful that my brother and sister were able, eventually, to forgive me for having been unknowingly held up as a sort of "gold standard" by our mother.

I never became comfortable with the public exposure that came with the role of Head Girl. Every morning, one of us had to escort Miss Ashley on stage for Assembly, and I was always afraid that I would drop the sheaf of announcements, or the Bible with its page marker at the chosen passage, and would have to sort everything out up there on the stage. I had to steel myself to walk across that stage in front of the whole school and would gladly have let Monica do the honors every day. But the Assistant Head scotched that idea in no uncertain terms when I timidly raised it. Occasionally Miss Ashley, all gowned and ready to sweep across the quadrangle, would say, "Oh, … just give me my teeth, dear, please." And whichever of us was on duty had to pass her the glass in which her dentures resided when not in her mouth. This came to be known as The Trial by Teeth, but fortunately, it was not a daily occurrence. However, one day Miss Ashley asked me to hand her the dentures themselves ... She did have the grace to give me a clean hankie with which to dry them, and—perhaps because of the look on my face as I complied—this request was never repeated.

But for me, by far the worst of the Head Girl ordeals entailed selecting a passage from the Bible and reading it aloud at Assembly, and I slept badly for several nights when faced with "doing a reading." I was deathly afraid that nothing but a silly croak would emerge when I opened my mouth, that I would stand, helpless and hopeless, in front of the entire student body, waiting for the first giggle to set the whole school rocking with laughter. Of course it never happened, and I somehow survived these readings, but I couldn't wait for the day when they would no longer be part of my job description.

Monica and I left no memorable legacies for future generations of Honor Oak girls—certainly no draconian disciplinary measures—so I suppose we must be judged as having failed to make the most of that opportunity to try our wings as leaders: the opportunity that British schools give their Head Girls just before they venture out into the real world. However we may have inadvertently, by example, helped to unite

the two branches of the school. For unlike the previous year's Head Girls—like us, one from each branch—there was no rivalry between Monica and me. There was every opportunity for it, since we shared all the same classes and were neck and neck in every subject, but we both accepted that sometimes Monica did better than me, and sometimes I did better than her. And we remain good friends to this day.

Soon teachers were talking about applications to universities and our "Highers" [roughly equivalent to four AP exams]. It suddenly became clear that three more years of "school" were being dangled in front of me, three more years before I'd go to work in the sense that Jack Weddinger and my non-school world understood the word. I was delighted at the prospect, but what about those I'd be sentencing to three more years of dealing with the Ellen Street scene? Because there, things had gone down hill rapidly—aggravated by the fact that I was still not earning my keep. As always, I kept these thoughts to myself and promised my teachers to discuss the idea of university with my mother when I went home for Christmas.

Which I did, but fully expected her to sigh and say something like, "Three more years of 'is lordship's nonsense? I'm afraid not, Gwen. Yew've 'ad a good run fer yer money, but enuff's enuff, as the poor gel said!" Instead, without a moment's hesitation—and with no idea what a university was—she declared, "If they think yew can do it, then yew should 'ave a try. That's what yer father would've wanted."

Then, to my surprise, my mother launched into a story, one I'd never heard. It was about a promise my Dad had asked of her way back, when I was about six years old:

"We was sittin' in front of the fire one evenin' after yew' children 'ad gone ta bed, an' yer Dad was readin' aloud ta me while I did some mendin', like we of'en did. I suddenly realized that 'is voice 'ad stopped, an' 'e was starin' inta the fire with the open book just layin' there, on 'is lap.

"'Whas'sa mat'er, Joe?' I asked.

"'I wan'cha ta promise me somethin', May,' 'e said. 'Becos' I some'ow don't think I'm gonna live ta see my children grow up … '

"'Go on, ya daft thing,' I said. 'Whatever makes ya say a thing like that? Ain'cha feelin' well?'

"'No, no … it's not that, not exac'ly. It's just a feelin' I've 'ad … fer a while now. An' if I'm not 'ere ta see 'em grow up, I wan'cha ta promise me, May, that they'll get as much schoolin' as they can. As much as they c'n benefit from.'

"Somethin' in 'is voice made me realize that 'e meant ev'ry word 'e said. An' that it was real important to 'im. I s'pose 'cos, like me, 'e 'ad ta leave school an' go ta work when 'e was thirteen. So I give 'im me promise, an' that seemed to put 'is mind at rest."

So my Dad *would* have been proud of me for having made it this far; and prouder still, if the university notion should come to fruition. I no longer remembered the sound of his voice, though I tried hard to keep memories of him alive and vivid; but although she hadn't given me *that* back … nobody could … , my mother *had* just given me something equally precious: a glimpse of the kind of man he was. Blissfully unaware of how much this meant to me, she went on in her no-nonsense way, "We never talked about it agin, not till just before 'e died … a couple'a years later, so 'e was right about not livin' t'see yew grow up. 'E asked me then, as 'e was dyin', if I remembered the promise about yer schoolin'. I told 'im, o' course I did. An' not ta worry, I meant ta stick by it."

"O' course," she added, "I didn't realize what I was lettin' meself in for!"

We were in the middle of doing the dishes, and I stood staring at her, with the dishtowel in my hands forgotten, as the implications of this story sank in. All those battles with Jack Weddinger over keeping us in school, all driven by a promise to our Dad twelve years ago? A promise that no one but she had known about until a few moments ago when she shared it with me! I'd always assumed some inner vision of her own that gave her so much courage and determination; and for so long—my entire time at Honor Oak. And now she was willing to tackle an even bigger fight. *For three more years.* What an amazing woman! More amazing than I had ever realized. And she was right: when she made that promise back in 1935, she really didn't have any idea what she was letting herself in for. She had no way to anticipate an uncooperative second husband; or six years of war lurking over the horizon; or how our school needs would play out. In particular, I don't suppose that she, or my Dad, ever dreamed that we might go on "benefittin' from our schoolin'" until we were in our twenties!

This newfound admiration for my mother mingled uncomfortably with the old anger that had grown steadily over the years as the disastrous consequences of her second marriage unfolded. It had always been hard to live with, that anger, and now it would be harder still. Futhermore, the promise she'd given my Dad—and how seriously she'd taken it—made it even more difficult to understand why she had allowed me to miss that all-important Preliminary Exam. However, given how strenuously she'd fought since then, and the personal sacrifices she'd cheerfully made, I never had the heart to raise that question. I was, I think, afraid at some level that her answer might be indefensible.

The remainder of the school year was one long round of applications, interviews and exams. There were class exams, entrance exams, scholarship exams, and, finally, the Highers. The Oxford and Cambridge Scholarship exams were a ridiculous exercise in futility, and I don't know who insisted on Monica and me having a shot at them—someone with delusions of grandeur, that's for sure. The timing could hardly have been more unfortunate, coming as it did in the middle of the winter of 1947, the coldest winter since Samuel Pepys' day; goldfish froze solid in living room aquariums, and the whole country shivered through week after week of bitter cold and brown-outs. Many businesses and schools were closed, including Honor Oak School, but for two weeks Monica and I rode our bikes every day to the otherwise empty school. We studied with a teacher in the nurse's room, the only room small enough to heat with a one-bar electric fire that glowed dull red during brown outs and gave off *just* enough heat—provided we wore our coats, scarves and gloves.

Then, for four days in a row, we had to get ourselves across London and sit in an equally frigid huge Examination Hall, staring at questions for which we were woefully ill prepared. One Math paper was full of typing errors, I thought, looking at the superfluous *h*'s after each trig function (sinh x, instead of sin x, for example), until it dawned on me that there were too many to be accidental. Not long after, we got to the chapter in our textbook that explained all those *h*'s—too late for Monica and me to have any hope of going to Cambridge or Oxford.

The severe cold spell added another farcical aspect to this venture, because in order to reach the Examination Hall in time, we had to catch the first tram of the day, and tram lines were still frozen solid at 'points'—where one tram line meets another. The tram would come to a jolting, screeching halt at each junction, and the driver then used it as an icebreaker, backing up and taking several runs at the frozen rail switches until the tram could make it onto the next section. Whereupon the shivering, and by now wide-awake, passengers gave a rousing cheer for these heroic efforts. All this jolting back and forth was hardly an auspicious start to the day, and by the time we reached the Examination Hall it was a wonder that Monica and I could remember that 2+2 = 4, let alone what we'd been cramming for the past two weeks.

I don't think I've ever worked as hard as I did that last year at Honor Oak. But it was a good year. I felt focussed and, for the first time ever, had a clear-cut goal: acceptance at a university. Unfortunately, for eighteen-year-olds like us in that year, 1947, universities and colleges were swamped with returning service men and women who had to be given priority, and places could not be allotted to us until after the end of July. I had provisional acceptances at two universities—if the results of my Highers met their standards—but there might not be a place left by August ... and there was still the question of money. Would I get a County scholarship? Enough to provide the complete wherewithal? Anything less meant that I'd have to drop the whole idea. At the end of the school year, the outcome still depended on three things: my exam results, the availability of a provisional acceptance, *and* the generosity of the County of East Sussex. But there was nothing more to be done; I simply had to wait till sometime in August for the rest to unfold.

Just before term ended I heard from my benefactor, the philanthropist who had paid for my tuition and books for the past two years. I'd often wondered what this person was like. In truth, I'd even wondered whether there *was* such a person. Perhaps it was Miss Ashley herself? She had been so vague about "having found someone," and in two years, there'd been no further mention of this mysterious someone. But there was, indeed, a real live person, and I was invited to join him for tea.

I assumed that there would be a number of beneficiaries like myself at this tea. But when I entered the elegant, book-lined room overlooking an equally elegant walled garden, there was no one other than a pink-skinned, blue-eyed, elderly gentleman with a mop of silver hair—a healthy, vigorous version of poor Mr. Wilson of Aquinas Street. To my further dismay, this personage was ensconced in a winged armchair beside a small, highly polished table set for two. Alarm must have been written all over my face, because my host skillfully put me at ease by introducing himself and adding, "I'm *so* pleased to meet you at last, Miss Redfern." He immediately launched into questions about me and my plans and my family (needless to say, I glossed over the family stuff), as we ate the thinnest of cucumber sandwiches and drank delicately-flavored tea out of the thinnest of china cups. The only awkward moment was when his shaggy white eyebrows shot up on hearing that I was not going to study

Classics at Oxford or Cambridge. I suppose Miss Ashley still harbored those dreams at the time she'd enlisted his help on my behalf, and had no occasion to tell him of my switch to physics. He did not press me on the reason for the switch, but I sensed that he was disappointed and felt guilty to be the agent of disappointment for this benevolent, generous man, whose timely help had made such a difference.

◆　　◆　　◆

In July, after I bid final fond farewells to Honor Oak, the remaining uncertainties about the future left me in a kind of limbo, and I couldn't start looking for a real job. This didn't improve matters on the home front; things there had seriously deteriorated, as I discovered the moment I walked in the door. My mother had a terrible black eye and my brother a chipped front tooth, the result of his intervention in the fight that had produced the black eye. This domestic situation, I soon discovered, was taking a heavy toll of Derek. He had again retreated into a shell of silence, and my first reaction was to abandon the idea of university. But Mum said, "Don't be sa daft! We're not gonna give in ta the ol' devil, now. Not when we've got this far. If yew git in, then yew should go!" And she persuaded me to at least wait for all the "ifs" to be settled, before I turned down my university place.

I marked time that summer by working two jobs, plus two weeks as a dishwasher-waitress at a Chamber Music Summer School, an event organized every summer by Charlie Hambourg, he of the Albert Hall concerts. The Summer School, housed in a swanky boarding school near Winchester, provided professional coaching for amateur musicians, and we girls, when through with our chores, were free to mix with the paying /playing guests and enjoy all the facilities. These included a pool, tennis courts, and almost non-stop musical happenings, so it was a kind of paid holiday. The idea of chamber music had caused considerable sniggering at home, when I had first broached the idea the previous summer.

"Sounds comical, that do!" said my mother.

"Makes yer think o' bangin' on a jerry [chamber pot] with a spoon!" said Derek.

"Or "tinkle tinkle tinkle" when yer usin' one!" chortled Mum, and we all fell about, laughing. I knew nothing about chamber music at the time, so I couldn't disabuse them of these images until after my first two-week stint. Even then it was hard to convey the extra-ordinary atmosphere that pervades a gathering of enthusiastic amateur players, and impossible to describe the experience of being surrounded from early morning till late at night with the strains of string quartets. Some renditions were exquisite, others decidedly less than exquisite, and what an education *that* was for my untrained seventeen-year-old ears. It allowed me to start discriminating between the good and the not-so-good: a truly priceless experience.

The rest of the summer, I worked in a shoe shop and wheeled an invalid along the sea front on weekends and evenings. The wheelchair job did not pay well, but was interesting because the invalid herself was interesting. Her name was Doris, and she gave me a copy of a slim volume of poetry she'd written, so that we could discuss her poems while we sat on the sea front. Poetry had never been my strong point, and I felt very inadequate for this unanticipated aspect of my Doris-wheeling job. But these discussions were the highlight of Doris's otherwise empty days, according to her sister, Violet, with whom Doris stayed every summer to give her a break from the Royal Hospital for Incurables where she spent the rest of the year. I shuddered to think how it must feel to return to a place with this doom-laden name (happily, it was later changed to the Hospital for Neurological Diseases), yet Doris, somehow, found the drive to write poetry. Not publishable, except by a vanity press—Doris's birthday surprise for her sister—but it *was* poetry. I had never been able to produce a single line of poetry (indeed, had to make a deal with a friend to write it on my behalf ...), so I was very impressed. Violet told me that Doris had been athletic, and a powerful swimmer, before she was smitten at the age of eighteen by the 1918 influenza and never walked again. Now, in speech so slurred that I had to concentrate hard to understand it, Doris told me that one of her few remaining pleasures was the feel of the wind on her face, as she watched the waves curl and break and listened to the protesting hiss of pebbles being dragged into the water by the backwash. It brought back memories, she said, of when she could run into the waves and swim far out, farther out and faster than anyone else. Poor Doris. Still quick of mind, still able to laugh and joke, but trapped in this drooling, distorted, helpless body: a steadily deteriorating body, Violet told me, tearfully.

Afternoons with Doris put our domestic troubles in a different perspective, but the Ellen Street scene was pretty bad. My mother often had bruises, and we now lived, more or less permanently, in the upper part of the house. Unfortunately, this put three grown people and one active five-year-old in the room over Jack Weddinger's head, and he was always yelling up the stairs to complain about the noise. Mum's standard response was to ignore him, or to yell back, with various suggestions as to where he could go if he didn't like it.

Toward the end of the summer, I walked away from the shoe shop job in disgust at some of the dubious practices I'd witnessed. The final straw was the owner's expectation that I would pair up mismatched shoes (one from the window display, the other from a box containing what should have been its partner, but was sometimes a different size), then put them on the

Special Sale table and knowingly sell them to some unsuspecting customer. The mismatched pairs happened to be children's shoes, which made this even more unpalatable. The existence of the mismatch meant that some youngster was walking around with a size three shoe on one foot and a three-and-a-half on the other, and I just couldn't bring myself to send some other child out of the shop with the opposite mismatch. So I simply refused, then walked out and never went back.

I expected my mother to be furious. The shop happened to be owned by the family she cleaned house for, and I'd probably put her job in jeopardy, too. But she was delighted, I think, that I'd finally shown evidence of having inherited a few of her genes, and all she said was "Good fer yew! It's time someone told that Mrs. Frank where ta get off." I tried to clarify that I hadn't actually told anybody where to get off, but she had already embarked on a rant about Mrs. Frank: "Typical ol' Jewess! Rollin' in money they are, but she goes out of 'er way ta cheat me of ten minutes ev'ry day! Turns 'er clock back after I get there, she does. Yet she knows I 'ave t'pick Maureen up from school a' twelve o'clock sharp, an' it makes me late always. It's just not right fer a li'l five-year-old ta wait around, standin' outside the school in all weathers, just so Mrs. Frank c'n squeeze a few mis'rable minutes out o' me."

For as long as I could remember Jews had been on my mother's Do-Not-Like list, right up there with Winston Churchill and the Royal family. Back when we'd trudged along The Cut, she was forever on about their cheating ways (most of the shops there were owned by Jews, according to her), and Mrs. Frank had only reinforced these notions, I fear. For all her bravado, I think my mother *was* afraid that she would lose her job because of what I'd done—a job that she could ill afford to lose. But Mrs. Frank never said anything about me walking out of the shop, and I like to think that her conscience *did* experience a little tweak.

I always made sure that Jack Weddinger witnessed me handing over my earnings to Mum, but it didn't seem to sweeten his temper, and on one occasion, when old Aunt Lil was visiting for a few days, he got really aggravated about the noise over his head. "Stop that bloody racket! Sounds like a troop of elephants, up there!" he yelled, and then banged on his ceiling with a broom handle. Well ... that did it.

"*Noise*, 'e says? I'll show the ol' bugger what noise *really* is!" said Mum, as she clambered up on the table and jumped off (all 170 pounds of her), landing with a colossal thump right over his head. The floor shook alarmingly but did withstand this onslaught, and after the third jump he was begging her to stop. Triumphantly, she yelled down, "Just thought I'd give ya somethin' ta *really* complain about, yew ol' misery, yew!" and then she turned to us with a grim smile, "That'll teach 'im ta show me up in front o' me company!"

Throughout these shenanigans, Aunt Lil had sat in the pose that I knew so well: one hand covering her mouth and muttering, "Oh, me Gawd! Oh, me Gawd!" When the storm had subsided, the hand was transferred to her chest, and she said, "Lor' love a duck, May! Yew 'ad me 'eart in me mouf. I fought yew was gonna go straight frew this floor an' land right on 'is bloomin' 'ead!" I'd had the exact same fear, but my mother, apparently, had been through this scenario before. Once, when a school friend of Maureen's came over to play, the complaints had culminated in ceiling-banging "in front o' company." So she knew that the floor in this turn-of-the-century house was sturdier than one might think. And Jack Weddinger should have known that, in his wife's book, it was one thing to deal with a domestic crisis in private, but to be shamed in front of company was a different matter.

This episode shook Aunt Lil up more than I would have expected, given her own turbulent life with *her* "ol' man" in her younger days. As she was leaving, she took my face in both hands to give me one of her big smacking kisses, and said huskily, "Wha' yaw poor muvver 'as ta pu' up wiv', Gwen, wiv' that ol' devil. An' Derek an' li'l Maureen, too. It ain't right … it jus' ain't right, is it, nah?" To which I could only answer, "No. It isn't," feeling unbearably guilty, because I was the lucky one who was almost certainly about to escape from this battlefront. For I had by then received the results of my Highers, and both provisional acceptances had been confirmed. I'd decided on Bedford College, part of London University, and the only question remaining was how all this would be paid for. My exam scores *had* made me eligible for a scholarship, but until I'd jumped through one more hoop, an interview with the County Committee, I had no idea whether the grant would be adequate.

At that County interview I struck up an immediate friendship with another interviewee, a striking, statuesque blond called Isabel. Such an exotic name, I thought; I'd encountered Isabels only in fiction. She invited me to spend a day cycling with her, adding nonchalantly, "Here's our number," and handed me a scrap of paper with POY 3 scribbled on it. "Just give a ring, and we'll sort out a date." It took a moment for it to register that I was looking at a telephone number, never having known any one with a phone, and I hoped that my surprise wasn't too obvious to this sophisticated creature, who clearly took such things for granted.

After a couple of false starts, I successfully wrestled with the pay phone on the corner of Ellen Street, and Isabel and I spent a wonderful day cycling along narrow roads and leafy lanes at the foot of the South Downs before going back to her house for tea. I was over-awed by Isabel's house, the most charming, elegant house I'd ever seen. Covered with roses, and with fabulous views of the Downs, it was the "big house" in the village of Poynings where her father was "the doctor," and both her parents were as charming and elegant as their house. And they made me so welcome that I was sorry when the time came for me to catch the train back to Ellen Street.

In the course of that day I was surprised to find that, for all her privileges, Isabel was curiously unhappy and lacking in self-confidence; she was even more nervous than I was about the university world we were hoping to enter. Part of the problem was that her only brother had been killed during the war, and her parents' hopes for the future were now vested entirely in Isabel, who felt doomed to disappoint them. "Alistair was the clever one," she'd told me, rather bitterly. "He was going into medicine, too, which was lovely for Daddy. But me ... I'm just reading English ... and not sure I can do even that very well. Poor Daddy. He pretends to be pleased, but I know how disappointed he is."

At least high parental expectations were not among my worries, I thought, as I listened to her troubled voice. Anything I accomplished was a minor miracle to the folks in my world, as I'd learned on a regular basis ever since I was fourteen—the age at which kids of that world were expected to go out to work. Whenever Mum and I bumped into a neighbor on the way to the shops, the astonished reaction was, "*She's still in school? At 'er age!*" And I'd stand, creased with embarrassment, while my mother, in self-defense, related some recent achievement of mine. To which these ladies would invariably shake their heads in amazement. Nevertheless, their response was usually, "I still 'fink yer a fool ta keep 'er in school s'long. 'Specially bein' a girl, an' all. Soon as she's done, she'll be awf an' married, an' yew won't see a penny from 'er fer all this education, yew mark my words!"

I should not have been surprised at Isabel's angst: it was actually in keeping with my recent recognition that every girl I knew seemed to have "home" problems. As evacuees, I'd heard girls grumble and complain about their host families, but rarely about their own. Kay's difficulty with her father was the only instance I'd encountered then, but now, with everyone back in their home setting, there were just as many complaints and grumbles. Hard as it was for me to believe, enjoying an uninterrupted childhood in an intact family, having a father with a respected white collar job and parents who were pillars of their church, living in a modern house—even one that you owned—none of these things guaranteed a family life devoid of tensions, apparently. The problems were usually more subtle than those in our household, but, for that reason, were perhaps more difficult to live with; they didn't, of necessity, unite family members, as ours had united us against Jack Weddinger

It didn't take much reflection to conclude that, regrettably, there was no way I could ever invite Isabel to Ellen Street. This conclusion was sharply reinforced by Mum's response as I answered the questions she peppered me with, questions about my day with Isabel. At the end of my recital, she turned abruptly and bent over the sink, giving our little milk saucepan a scouring, the like of which it had never before been subjected to. Intent on that blackened old pan, she finally said, "A doctor's daugh'er, eh? Goin' up in the world, ain't we! Soon be tuppence ta talk ta yew, I s'pose."

I'd heard sentiments like this many, many, times from Louie and sundry others, but *never* from my mother; the mix of pride and loss that I heard in her voice that day made me wish I could turn the clock back and close the gulf that suddenly yawned between us. Until I realized that she wouldn't want me to do that, either. "Oh, c'mon, Mum ... you know it won't be like that ... " was all I could manage by way of comfort, as she continued to scrub away, bent over at the sink. She gave no answer, and a long painful silence filled the kitchen—until Maureen came bursting in with some urgent need.

Finally, came the day when the postman brought a letter from the County. I happened to be alone in the house, apart from Jack Weddinger, and I stood staring at the envelope, afraid to open it. There had been other official letters like this, exam results and college acceptances and rejections, but this was the letter that would settle the final "if." There *had* to be a grant that covered everything ... or all the hoops I'd jumped through would have been in vain, and the thought of failing at this, the very last hoop, was more than I could bear. Eventually I tore open the envelope with trembling fingers and forced myself to read the letter: " ... pleased to announce ... a three-year grant of two hundred and fifty pounds per year ... subject to satisfactory progress ... " I stood, dazed, not paying attention to all the fine print that followed. Two hundred and fifty pounds? Every year? *Twice* what my poor father had ever brought home? Then the full implications sank in. I would indeed be going to university!

I wanted to run and jump for joy, to shout this wondrous news at the top of my lungs from very highest point on the Downs for the entire world to hear. But I couldn't delay, for even one minute, breaking the news to Mum when she came in ... so I couldn't leave the house ... and dared not shriek or jump where I was ... not with my stepfather in the room below. By default, the dog was the sole recipient of my delight, and I buried my face in his fur, laughing and crying and hugging him tight, so tight that he yelped. In doggy fashion, Bobby immediately forgave me and licked my face, wagging his tail and seeming to share my joy. Which was the scene that greeted Mum when she walked into the room.

Her way of celebrating was to rush downstairs and wave the letter triumphantly under her husband's nose. "See! Look at this! More than she'd be gettin' if she'd gone out ta work when yew wanted 'er to! More than any of yore precious daughters ever earned at 'er age, I bet!" Strangely, this development, which meant that for three years I wouldn't cost him or my mother a penny, only fed my stepfather's fury (perhaps because I still would not actually contribute to the housekeeping every week), and the next couple of weeks were sheer hell. I learned, as Derek had much earlier, what it was like to walk into the house and, on an almost daily basis, find our mother with a fresh batch of bruises.

Things came to a head the Sunday before I was to leave for college. Jack Weddinger came back from the pub, hungry, and he flew into a rage when Mum wouldn't give him any of the roast lamb and mint sauce that we were enjoying upstairs in our separate living quarters. He ranted and raved and screamed and hollered and, though we did our best to ignore him, ruined our enjoyment of this special meal that Mum had cooked for my last weekend at home. Trust him, I thought, as we ate our way grimly though my mother's offering, trust him to spoil one of the few remaining pleasures of her life. For she no longer seemed to do anything just for the joy of it—other than to surprise us with favorite meals, such as pancakes on a day that wasn't even a Tuesday, let alone Shrove Tuesday. How long could she go on like this, I wondered fearfully.

Afterwards, I was carrying the now-empty roasting pan down to the kitchen when my stepfather came out of his room, punching the air with his fists and bellowing about what he'd do to Mum when he got hold of her. Something in me snapped. The next thing I remember is standing on the stairs—a couple of stairs from the bottom it must have been, because I was staring down on the domed ridge of his bald pate—in the act of whacking him on the head with the roasting pan. Time after time after time. I had absolutely no memory of starting to hit him. And no idea how many whacks I had rained on his head ... though the dents in the pan and the bumps on his bony head suggested double digits ... He staggered back to his room, looking dazed, and my knees suddenly turned to jelly, so I dared not move. I sat on the stairs shaking like a leaf, still holding the baking tin, until Mum came and took it out of my hands.

I was horrified at what I had done. And afraid. Deeply afraid. *For I had no memory of raising my arms and bringing them down for the first blow.* Suppose I'd been holding the carving knife instead of the roasting pan ... I could have killed the man ... I had not known that I was capable of such an act ... that I could be so completely out of control ... and I did not like this new knowledge. It scared me. I hated the self that had suddenly been revealed. Renewed hatred for my mother welled up, too ... for having married the man. This incident showed so clearly the effect of that choice on our family—even on me, the one who'd been allowed to flee the home front for so much of the time. I didn't know how to deal with this new hatred, let alone reconcile it with my recently augmented admiration for her. Never, before or since, have I felt so conflicted about anyone as I felt then about my mother.

Jack Weddinger was astonishingly subdued for the next few days. "Yew seem to 'ave knocked some sense into 'im!" said Mum, tickled pink at this unlikely turn of events. But I, too, felt subdued, as I thought about the repercussions of what-could-have-been. Visions of newspaper headlines, "LOCAL GIRL KILLS STEPFATHER WITH CARVING KNIFE," flashed through my mind. Thank God I *hadn't* killed him, but he could still go to the police station with all those bumps on his head, and I'd be charged with something. Assault and battery, was that what I was guilty of? "I didn't mean to do it! Something in me snapped," would *not* be an adequate defense, I felt sure. So there remained the nightmarish possibility of newspaper placards at street corners blazoning out in crude lettering: "PRISON INSTEAD OF UNIVERSITY FOR SCHOLARSHIP GIRL!" And everything that had been done on my behalf would have been in vain. So much help, by so many people: by the Hodds, Mr. Pascoe, Betty Marsh, Miss Brophy, Miss Ashley, my benefactor, my mother (especially my mother), all their efforts wasted. My father's vision, too—the vision that had made Mum fight so hard to keep us in school. I was to torture myself with thoughts like these for weeks and months to come. They did gradually fade, but not as quickly as the bumps on Jack Weddinger's head ... However, the dents in the roasting pan turned out to be permanent, and I still occasionally have a flashback to that moment of horror, the moment I realized that I'd been hitting a man on the head without knowing that I was doing it.

A few days later, I got off a bus at Coin Street, carrying a brand new suitcase in place of the one that had accompanied me for the last eight years in my journeying around England and Wales. There was a crisp new pound note in my pocket, thrust there by my mother when she saw me off at Brighton Station: "Just to 'elp till yer grant comes through, Gwen. I c'n send a bit more if ya really need it. An' Louie says yew c'n borrer from 'er, too. A good ol' stick, she is, that Louie."

Thus, I started my new life, walking along Stamford Street only a stone's throw from Number Nine Coin Street where it had all begun. I was heading for Aquinas Street and Louie's flat, where I would be living, at least until things got sorted out. For there was no college dormitory accommodation available—one of the Halls of Residence, demolished by a bomb, was still being re-built—and I had no money for lodgings, since I had yet to see a penny of that wondrously generous grant the County had written to tell me about. The sum total of my worldly wealth was twenty pounds in a Post Office savings account plus the pound Mum had just stuffed into my pocket. I had no idea how long twenty-one pounds would last, given the unfamiliar expenses I would probably incur in my first few days and weeks as a university student. What would I have done without Louie to fall back on, I wondered? Once again, she'd come up trumps for me: no other landlady would wait to be paid till the County bureaucracy started grinding out checks with my name on them. I was very nervous about getting into debt, even to Louie, fearful lest there should be some glitch about the grant, after all, but I tried to stifle my unease.

There was something very fitting about the fact that I had returned, boomerang-like, to the point from which I had been "launched." No longer a child nor a schoolgirl, I marveled for the millionth time about the near-miraculous change in my fortunes: from that inauspicious beginning as the unwelcome third occupant of Old Ma Tanner's "second floor front," to an eighteen-year-old on the brink of university. I couldn't help but wonder to what extent I had been a deliberate player in that process, not simply a compliant vehicle for the visions of others. I could count on one hand the situations where I had struck out on my own: the failed attempt to run away, the switch to the sciences, the refusal to sell mismatched shoes, and, of course, quite literally, the pounding of the roasting pan on my stepfather's head. Mostly, I'd just gone along with whatever the adult world decreed, even big decisions, like staying on at Honor Oak after the war.

I realized, for the first time, that I had always embraced arrangements that separated me from home and family: the three years I was now embarking upon; the two extra years at Honor Oak; and, way back, when I'd sort-of-consciously decided to remain an evacuee and didn't ask if I, too, could go home when Derek did. How had my mother felt about all this? Had she felt rejected and hurt by my eagerness to put space between us? I'd only paid attention to her willingness to do whatever she saw as a way for me to make something of myself. And I was ashamed, now, when I thought about how thoughtless I had been.

I also wondered to what extent World War II itself had contributed to my "miracle." Evacuation had taken me to parts of the country that I would never have seen and made me a player in ways of life that I could not otherwise have known: on a remote farm, in villages and small towns, and in a Welsh mining town. It had also made school a more dominant player in my life. Teachers—people who had a broader vision than anyone I knew in Waterloo, people who thought beyond the Co-op token kiosk—had taken the role of surrogate parents for us evacuees. On a more mundane level, evacuation had also rescued me from the day-to-day challenges of Waterloo: from the battlefield that our family life had become; from my Aquinas Street tormentors; from the taunts that walking these city streets in a posh school uniform would have provoked; from remarks in response to my new lah-dedah way of talking. Hurt-but-angry comments such as, "Too good fer us nah, ain'cha?" had always stirred up a host of guilt feelings when I was home during school holidays. Then, I'd always known that I would soon be taking a train and leaving Waterloo behind; having to deal with them on a daily basis all those years was hard to imagine.

Would I have been able to withstand the pressures of daily life in Waterloo, as I carved out a place for myself in Honor Oak School? I wasn't sure. Those doubts were reinforced when, as I turned the corner into Aquinas Street, my stomach lurched—even now—at the thought that I might bump into Hazel Henderson! Other memories came flooding back, and I wondered if Jean Sunnebank, Margery Strutt, and Phyllis Turner were still around. I felt distinctly nervous at the prospect that we might meet. What would I say to them? Or they, to me? Come to that, would we even recognize one another? Maybe they'd gone through as many changes, and worn as many new hats, as I had. This led me to think about the new hats that I'd probably be donning tomorrow, and throughout the next three years. That thought took me back swiftly to the scene in the kitchen after the day with Isabel; and I hoped, as hard as I knew how to hope, that my mother had been wrong; that the gulf between us would not grow impossibly wide, as I had tried that day, rather feebly, to reassure her.

At that point in time there was no way I could know that Mum and I would both be proven right. I *would* find it impossible to bring any of my university friends to Ellen Street; they were all doctors' daughters or the equivalent thereof; indeed, one had a father who was an editor of the paper that offered Dad a motor car ride as a prize. The gulf *was* too wide; it would not have worked. But in my first job I met someone, another physics graduate, whom I did introduce to the world of Ellen Street—albeit with great trepidation. On his first visit, he took one look around and suggested that the place could do with a fresh coat of paint, and before my mother knew what was happening, she'd chosen a color, and he'd purchased the paint and was happily slapping it on the walls, wearing a large knotted handkerchief to protect his hair from splashes and singing bawdy songs at the top of his lungs. To my mother's astonished delight. And mine.

Throughout this performance, when not singing along, Mum was protesting, "It's the lan'lord's job ta take care o' that, ya know ... an' ta pay fer the paint." Despite her protests, David had sung and painted his way into my mother's heart. And a year or so later, David was the man I married, the man who surprised me by wanting me as a woman and gave me four wonderful children, who, in their turn gave us an abundance of equally wonderful grandchildren. And we all lived happily ever after ... give or take a few bumps in the road.

Epilogue

Derek

Sadly, my brother's life did not work out well. At age seventeen, unable to deal with the home front any more, Derek told a recruiter he was eighteen and joined the marines—which spelled the end of his dreams of a career as an architect.

He liked marine life, enjoyed dangerous stuff like parachuting into guerilla-infested jungles. However, at the insistence of a neurotic wife, mother of his four children, he left the service early, too soon for a pension; and he never found a job commensurate with his talents.

Derek essentially smoked his way into an early grave, but in his final years drew comfort from a quiet life with a loving second wife. He became a passionate gardener, enjoyed long walks with his beloved dog, solving crossword puzzles, and reading every book he could lay his hands on. Like father, like son, I realize, rather belatedly.

Bertie

Bertie, upon whom I never set eyes after that visit with Derek to the Home for Problem Boys, did surprisingly well considering his always-abysmal performance in school. He too donned a uniform, that of the navy, and became a gunner.

Later, with a nice pension to cushion his needs, he was found to be good with his hands and became an accomplished and valued mechanic, and worked on a large farm, keeping all the machinery in good order.

He married and fathered two sons, both of whom went to University and became engineers. And, I learned much later, his wife earned a science degree from the Open University after their boys were grown. All of which makes one wonder about thinking Bertie "slow" and "stupid" when he was a child—when dyslexia was not exactly a household word.

Sadly, Bertie died young; in his forties or fifties—from a brain tumor, I believe.

Maureen

My little sister *did* get a nice teacher for her first term in school, but later had more mixed results and ended up with little interest in scholastic matters. Until suddenly, at age thirteen, she wanted a second stab at the Scholarship Exam, but her Headmistress said, "No! She doesn't stand a chance."

This was akin to waving a red flag in front of a charging bull, and Mum sprang into battle mode, still true to the promise she'd given my Dad so long ago—though this child was not as much as a twinkle in anyone's eye when that promise was made.

"Maureen has the right to try if she wants to," insisted Mum, "the right to risk failure, should that be the outcome." To the chagrin of the Headmistress, Mum prevailed. And so did Maureen: she passed the Exam, went to the Technical College, became a successful executive-style secretary, and was known fondly in the work place as "Chuckles" for her wonderful, bubbly, throaty laugh.

In due course, Maureen followed in our mother's footsteps and launched three well-educated children into the world, against considerable odds. And, like her brother, she found great happiness in a second marriage.

As for my mother ...

Mum died at the age of 88, having outlived two more husbands, she said, with considerable satisfaction.

Jack Weddinger, ornery to the last, died the week before David and I set off for America with our two little ones. Which made a difficult week even more so.

Then there was Fred Gardner: frail, gentle Fred, who was 82 when they married. Short and sweet was this marriage, with my mother nursing Fred through what time he had left. Which was precisely her intent, the day she rented a wheelchair and trundled him to the Registrar's Office to get hitched.

She lived alone, still on Ellen Street, for more than twenty years in a small Council flat that she loved. Legally blind for much of that time, she was defiantly self-sufficient, though we, her offspring, did eventually bully her into installing a phone.

She came on several visits to America, once with Auntie Ada. Two eighty-year-olds who had themselves a ball, as they left shop assistants and bus drivers chortling in their wake. They swung on swings and wandered around Princeton, invariably getting lost and being brought back to our house by kind strangers until they learned to tie ribbons to trees to find their way back. Every night they lay awake, giggling like a couple of kids, and the house was strangely quiet and empty after they left.

My mother had her ears pierced in her late seventies. Then fell in love, head-over-heels in love, at the age of 81 with a fella she met on the platform of Victoria Station while waiting for a train. A very nice fella, was Harry, and Mum blushed and giggled like a young girl whenever he phoned. They came close to marrying, but this marriage was not to be, and she nursed her new love through his final illness. Devastated by Harry's death, she was never again her feisty old self.

Finally felled by a series of strokes, my mother died in her sleep we were told, after a year or so of not recognizing anybody, not even us, her children. A sad sort of end, especially for one who did so love to have the last word. It was certainly not an end she would have wished for herself, "or fer me worst enemy!" she always declared.

Afterword

Recently some further family history about my cousin-brother, Bertie, has come my way, history that I would like to share with any reader who has stuck with the story thus far.

While on a visit to London, I had the great pleasure of meeting with one of Bertie's two sons, the wife of that son, and one of their two sons. Subsequently, they have provided me with a great collection of photos, lots of insights into Bertie's life after he disappeared from mine, and, perhaps most precious of all, a copy of his account of his early memories.

Although brief, that account is too long to include here in its entirety, but below is a short excerpt so that you, too, will hear Bertie's 'voice'—through his wife, who wrote it all down for him—telling of a momentous day in his young life:

> "Really, nothing happened until Bertie was 7 years old, and then his life fell apart—he remembered that very well! Sometime in 1938 Joe Redfern died, and it was only then that Bertie found out that the man who walked out of the room whenever he walked into it was his real father.
> … Bertie ran screaming out of the room, up 3 flights of stairs to his grandfather. He felt sure his grandfather would tell him it wasn't true, but of course he didn't."

Bertie's memory was a wee bit wobbly—he was, in fact only five-and-a-half when my father died in January 1937—and I don't recall him running screaming up to Grampa Benson (but that may well be my memory at fault). However, on the emotional level, Bertie's moving account certainly matches my memory of that awful scene in the kitchen when his real father broke the news of his true parentage to him.

On a lighter note, Bertie also mentions that he and Derek "were called 'The Black & White Twins' because Derek was as dark as Bertie was white-blonde." This detail I had completely forgotten until Bertie's mention of it jogged my memory.

I also learned from my newfound family members that Bertie and Derek did, in fact, get together a few times as grown men—already married and with young families. I was happy to hear this, but sad that it did not, apparently, lead to a revival of the close brotherly relationship they'd enjoyed as boys.

Gwen Southgate
July, 2011

2108236R00169

Printed in Great Britain
by Amazon.co.uk, Ltd.,
Marston Gate.